P9-APG-562

BIBLICA ET ORIENTALIA

(SACRA SCRIPTURA ANTIQUITATIBUS ORIENTALIBUS ILLUSTRATA)

19/A

biblica et orientalia - 19/A

JOSEPH A. FITZMYER, S.J.

THE ARAMAIC INSCRIPTIONS OF SEFIRE

REVISED EDITION

EDITRICE PONTIFICIO ISTITUTO BIBLICO — ROMA 1995

1967, First Edition
1995, Second revised Edition

ISBN 88-7653-347-8

Editrice Pontificio Istituto Biblico
Piazza della Pilotta 35 – 00187 Roma, Italia

To the Memory of

Professor William F. Albright,

My Revered Teacher:

In Gratitude

CONTENTS

PLATES

PREFACE

The first edition of this commentary on the Aramaic Inscriptions of Sefire appeared more than twenty-five years ago. Since the first publication of these texts in 1931 and 1958 they have been the subject of much scholarly discussion and interpretation. The last quarter of a century has also witnessed considerable study of them. Since the first edition of this book has gone out of print, I have been encouraged by the publisher to prepare a revision of it, which I have been glad to undertake. Over the years since 1967, when the first edition appeared, I have had an interleaved copy of the book, into which I have entered references to articles and books that have treated the Sefire inscriptions. In it I recorded reactions to my interpretation and criticisms of it, with my own personal reactions to them. These jottings over the years have enabled me to prepare this revision. I have tried to cope with all the subsequent suggestions for the understanding of these important Aramaic texts.

The only part of the book that remains unchanged are the photographs and the plates. These I obtained from Jean Starcky during the year 1957-58, when I worked with him in the Scrollery of the Palestine Archaeological Museum, and he graciously allowed me to publish them as part of my commentary on the texts. I have not tried to alter his work, because I consider it important that one can see the readings and drawings that were made at that time. I have often interpreted certain letters differently from the readings of A. Dupont-Sommer and J. Starcky, but I record them in my transcription of the text in modern type, and the student of these inscriptions can easily judge my readings against what is recorded in such photographs and facsimiles. These plates will also enable one to judge readings proposed by other scholars as well. One important addition has been made, a new set of photographs of Sf I A 24, which B. Zuckerman had made available to A. Lemaire (published in *Syria* 62 [1985] opposite p. 35) and which he has allowed me to reproduce here.

I am indebted to all those who reviewed the first edition of this study, and I only hope that I have understood all the criticism, positive and negative, that they have expressed. I am likewise indebted to a number of persons who have helped me in the production of this volume: to Alan C. Mitchell, S.J., who has helped me in various ways to get this revision into a camera-ready format; to Eugene Rooney, S.J., the director of the Woodstock Theological Center Library, housed at Georgetown University, and to his staff for their help in getting needed publications. Likewise to W. Pitard and B. Zuckerman for a new photograph of line 24 of Sefire I, and to A. Gianto, S.J., of the Biblical Institute in Rome, the editor of the series in which this revision appears.

Joseph A. Fitzmyer, S.J.
Professor Emeritus, Biblical Studies
The Catholic University of America
Resident at:
Jesuit Community, Georgetown University
Washington, DC 20057-1735

LIST OF ABBREVIATIONS

(for incomplete entries with an author's name, see the bibliography)

A — *Aḥiqar* (= *AP*, 204-48)
AA — G. Garbini, "L'Aramaico antico"
AAASH — *Acta antiqua academiae scientiarum hungaricae*
AAG — S. Segert, *Altaramäische Grammatik*
AANL Rendic — *Atti della Accademia Nazionale dei Lincei, Rendiconti* (Rome: Accademia dei Lincei)
AC — J. J. Koopmans, *Aramäische Chrestomathie*
AcOr — *Acta orientalia* (Batava)
AD — G. R. Driver, *Aramaic Documents of the Fifth Century B.C.* (2d ed.; Oxford: Clarendon, 1957)
AfO — *Archiv für Orientforschung*
AG — R. Degen, *Altaramäische Grammatik der Inschriften des 10.-8. Jh. v. Chr.* (Abhandlungen für die Kunde des Morgenlandes 38/3; Wiesbaden: Steiner, 1969)
AGJU — Arbeiten zur Geschichte des antiken Judentums und des Urchristentums
AH — F. Rosenthal (ed.), *Aramaic Handbook* (Porta linguarum orientalium ns 10; 2 double vols.; Wiesbaden: Harrassowitz, 1967)
AHW — W. von Soden, *Akkadisches Handwörterbuch* (3 vols.; Wiesbaden: Harrassowitz, 1965-81)
AION — *Annali dell'Istituto Orientale di Napoli*
AIPHOS — Annuaire de l'institut de philologie et d'histoire orientales et slaves (Brussels)
AJSL — *American Journal of Semitic Languages and Literatures*
AMI — *Archäologische Mitteilungen aus Iran*
AnArchSyr — *Les annales archéologiques de Syrie*
AnBib — Analecta biblica
ANESPT — J. B. Pritchard, *Ancient Near East Supplementary Pictures and Texts* (Princeton, NJ: Princeton, University, 1969)
ANET — J. B. Pritchard, *Ancient Near Eastern Texts Relating to the Old Testament* (2d ed.; Princeton, NJ: Princeton University, 1955)
ANHW — G. Dalman, *Aramäisch-Neuhebräisches Handwörterbuch zu Targum, Talmud und Midrasch* (Göttingen:

	Pfeiffer, 1938)
AnOr	Analecta Orientalia
AnStud	*Anatolian Studies*
Anton	*Antonianum*
AOS	American Oriental Society
AP	A. Cowley, *Aramaic Papyri of the Fifth Century B.C.* (Oxford: Clarendon, 1023)
ARAB	D. D. Luckenbill, *Ancient Records of Assyria and Babylonia*
ARM	A. Parrot and G. Dossin (eds.), *Archives royales de Mari: Transcriptions et traductions* (Paris: Imprimerie Nationale, 1950--)
ArOr	*Archiv Orientální*
ARW	*Archiv für Religionswissenschaft*
AšOstr	*Aššur Ostracon* (M. Lidzbarski, *Altaramäische Urkunden aus Assur* [Leipzig: Hinrichs, 1921] 5-15)
Aug	*Augustinianum*
BA	*Biblical Archaeologist*
BAG	C. Bezold and A. Goetze, *Babylonisch-Assyrisches Glossar* (Heidelberg: Winter, 1926)
BASOR	*Bulletin of the American Schools of Oriental Research*
BBVO	Berliner Beiträge zum Vorderen Orient
BeO	*Bibbia e oriente*
BHT	Beiträge zur historischen Theologie
Bib	*Biblica*
BibOr	Biblica et orientalia
BLA	H. Bauer and P. Leander, *Grammatik des Biblisch-Aramäischen* (Halle a. d. S.: Niemeyer, 1927)
B-M	*Bauer-Meissner Papyrus* (Bauer-Meissner, *Sitzungsberichte der preussischen Akademie der Wissenschaften* 72 [1936] 414-24)
BMAP	E. G. Kraeling, *The Brooklyn Museum Aramaic Papyri* (New Haven, CT: Yale University, 1953)
BMB	*Bulletin du Musée de Beyrouth*
BO	*Bibliotheca orientalis*
BZ	*Biblische Zeitschrift*
BZAW	Beiheft zur *ZAW*
CAD	I. Gelb et al. (eds.), *The Assyrian Dictionary of the Oriental Institute of the University of Chicago*

	(Chicago, IL: University of Chicago, 1956--)
CBQ	*Catholic Biblical Quarterly*
CH	*Code of Hammurabi*
CIS	*Corpus inscriptionum semiticarum*
CML	G. R. Driver, *Canaanite Myths and Legends* (Old Testament Studies 3; Edinburgh: Clark, 1956)
CRAIBL	*Comptes rendus de l'Académie des inscriptions et belles-lettres*
CT	*Cuneiform Texts from Babylonian Tablets, etc., in the British Museum* (London: British Museum, 1896--)
DBSup	*Dictionnaire de la Bible, Supplément* (Paris: Letouzey et Ané, 1928--)
DISO	C.-F. Jean and J. Hoftijzer, *Dictionnaire des inscriptions sémitiques de l'ouest* (Leiden: Brill, 1965)
EA	J. A. Knudtzon, *Die El-Armarna Tafeln* (Vorderasiatische Bibliothek 2; repr., Aalen: Zeller, 1964)
EHO	F. M. Cross, Jr. and D. N. Freedman, *Early Hebrew Orthography*
Ephem	M. Lidzbarski, *Ephemeris für semitische Epigraphik* (3 vols.; Giessen: Töpelmann, 1902-15)
ErIsr	Eretz Israel
ESBNT	J. A. Fitzmyer, *Essays on the Semitic Background of the New Testament* (London: Chapman, 1971; repr., Missoula, MT: Scholars, 1974)
EstBíb	*Estudios bíblicos*
GB	W. Gesenius and F. Buhl, *Hebräisches und aramäisches Handwörterbuch über das Alte Testament* (17th ed.; Berlin: Springer, 1949)
GBH	P. Joüon, *Grammaire de l'hébreu biblique* (2d ed.; Rome: Biblical Institute, 1947)
GCS	Griechische christliche Schriftsteller
GPL	Z. S. Harris, *Grammar of the Phoenician Language* (AOS 8; New Haven, CT: American Oriental Society, 1936)
Grundr	C. Brockelmann, *Grundriss der vergleichenden Grammatik der semitischen Sprachen* (2 vols.; Berlin: Reuther und Reichard, 1908-13)
HALAT	W. Baumgartner et al. (eds.), *Hebräisches und*

	aramäisches Lexikon zum Alten Testament (5 vols.; Leiden: Brill, 1967--)
HSS	Harvard Semitic Studies
HTR	*Harvard Theological Review*
HTS	Harvard Theological Studies
HUCA	*Hebrew Union College Annual*
IAS	A. Lemaire and J.-M. Durand, *Les inscriptions araméennes de Sfiré*
IEJ	*Israel Exploration Journal*
JA	*Journal asiatique*
JAOS	*Journal of the American Oriental Society*
JANES	*Journal of the Ancient Near Eastern Society*
JBL	*Journal of Biblical Literature*
JCS	*Journal of Cuneiform Studies*
JEOL	*Jaarbericht 'Ex oriente lux'*
JJS	*Journal of Jewish Studies*
JNES	*Journal of Near Eastern Studies*
JNSL	*Journal of Northwest Semitic Languages*
JPOS	*Journal of the Palestine Oriental Society*
JRAS	*Journal of the Royal Asiatic Society*
JSem	*Journal for Semitics*
JSOT	*Journal for the Study of the Old Testament*
JSOTSup	Supplements to *JSOT*
JSS	*Journal of Semitic Studies*
KAI	H. Donner and W. Röllig, *Kanaanäische und aramäische Inschriften*
KB	L. Koehler and W. Baumgartner, *Lexicon in Veteris Testamenti libros* (Leiden: Brill, 1958)
LFLAA	P. Leander, *Laut- und Formenlehre des Ägyptisch-Aramäischen* (Göteborg: Elander, 1928 [= *Göteborgs Högskolas Årskrift* 34/4])
MAOG	*Mitteilungen der altorientalischen Gesellschaft*
MIO	*Mitteilungen des Institus für Orientforschung*
MPAIBL	*Mémoires présentés à l'Académie des Inscriptions et Belles-Lettres*
MUSJ	*Mélanges de l'Université Saint-Joseph*
MVAG	*Mitteilungen der vorderasiatisch-aegyptischen Gesell-*

schaft

NSI	G. A. Cooke, *A Text-Book of North Semitic Inscriptions* (Oxford: Clarendon, 1903)
OBO	Orbis biblicus et orientalis
OLP	Orientalia lovaniensia periodica
OLZ	*Orientalistische Literaturzeitung*
Or	*Orientalia*
OrLovAn	Orientalia lovaniensia analecta
OrSuec	*Orientalia suecana*
OTS	*Oudtestamentische Studiën*
Pad	Padua Aramaic Papyrus Letters (*RSO* 35 [1960] 11-24)
PEQ	*Palestine Exploration Quarterly*
PPG	J. Friedrich, *Phönizisch-Punische Grammatik* (AnOr 32; Rome: Biblical Institute, 1951)
PRU	C. F. A. Schaeffer, *Le Palais Royale d'Ugarit* (Paris: Imprimerie Nationale, 1955--)
PS	*Palestinskij Sbornik*
RA	*Revue d'assyriologie et d'archéologie orientale*
RArch	*Revue archéologique*
RB	*Revue biblique*
RE	Paulys *Real-Encyclopädie der classischen Altertumswissenschaft* (ed. G. Wissowa et al.; Stuttgart: Metzler -- Druckenmueller, 1905-1978)
RES	*Répertoire d'épigraphie sémitique*
RevQ	*Revue de Qumran*
RHR	*Revue de l'histoire des religions*
RivB	*Rivista biblica*
RLA	*Reallexikon der Assyriologie*
RSO	*Rivista degli studi orientali*
SBLMS	Society of Biblical Literature Monograph Series
ScrHier	*Scripta hierosolymitana*
SEL	*Studi epigrafici e linguistici sul vicino oriente antico*
TSSI	J. C. L. Gibson, *Textbook of Syrian Semitic Inscriptions: Volume II* (Oxford: Clarendon, 1975)
TUAT	*Texte aus der Umwelt des Alten Testaments* (2 vols.; ed. O. Kaiser; Gütersloh: Mohn, 1982-91)
TZ	*Theologische Zeitschrift*

UF *Ugarit-Forschungen*
UT C. H. Gordon, *Ugaritic Textbook* (AnOr 38; Rome: Biblical Institute, 1965)

VAB *Vorderasiatische Bibliothek*
VD *Verbum Domini*
VT *Vetus Testamentum*
VTSup Supplements to *VT*

WA J. A. Fitzmyer, *A Wandering Aramean: Collected Aramaic Essays* (SBLMS 25; Missoula, MT: Scholars, 1979)
WMANT Wissenschaftliche Monographien zum Alten und Neuen Testament
WO *Die Welt des Orients*
WZKM *Wiener Zeitschrift für die Kunde des Morgenlandes*

ZA *Zeitschrift für Assyriologie*
ZAH *Zeitschrift für Althebraistik*
ZAW *Zeitschrift für die alttestamentliche Wissenschaft*
ZDMG *Zeitschrift der deutschen morgenländischen Gesellschaft*
ZDPV *Zeitschrift des deutschen Palästina-Vereins*

CD Damascus Document of the Cairo Genizah
1QapGen Genesis Apocryphon from Qumran Cave 1
1QIsa[a] Isaiah Scroll A from Qumran Cave 1
4QEn Enoch texts from Qumran Cave 4
4QpNah Pesher on Nahum from Qumran Cave 4
4QTob ar Tobit texts from Qumran Cave 4 in Aramaic
11QtgJob Targum of Job from Qumran Cave 11

INTRODUCTION

In 1931 Sebastien Ronzevalle, S.J. first published the text of the so-called Sujin stele.[1] Subsequently scholars pointed out the need of a fresh study of this inscription, based on the stele itself and on new and adequate photographs. This need was met by the publication of André Dupont-Sommer and Jean Starcky, "Les inscriptions araméennes de Sfiré (Stèles I et II)."[2] This publication is obviously the fruit of many long hours of concentration on the stone itself and must now be considered the *editio princeps* of this inscription. It consists of an important introduction about the finding of the steles, a transcription, translation, commentary, glossary and, what is most important of all, twenty plates of hand-copies and excellent photographs.

Since there is good reason to believe that Ronzevalle was misled by the natives concerning the place where the steles were found and his own efforts at excavating Sujin in 1930 brought to light nothing new in the way of additional fragments, the new editors have abandoned the title "Sujin stele" for the more accurate designation, Sefire stele I. As far as can be ascertained today, almost seventy-five years later than the time of the first discovery, they were found at Sefire, a small village about 22 km. southeast of Aleppo in Syria.[3] The village of Sujin is about 1.3 km. northeast of Sefire. In addition to the fresh study of Sefire stele I the article of Dupont-Sommer and Starcky contains the first publication of another very fragmentary inscription from the same place, Sefire stele II. Both of these inscriptions were acquired by the Damascus Museum in 1948. A third stele from the same place was acquired by the Beirut Museum in 1956 and was published by Dupont-Sommer with the collaboration of Starcky in 1958.[4] All three inscriptions are related not only by their provenience but also by their contents, script, and lan-

1 "Fragments d'inscriptions araméennes des environs d'Alep," *MUSJ* 15 (1930-31) 237-60. Dupont-Sommer and Starcky say of this publication: "Cette édition n'est pas sans mérite, mais elle a été faite dans des conditions peu favorables: bien des lectures y apparaissent extrêmement incertaines, et les photographies publiées sont généralement insuffisantes."

2 *MPAIBL* 15 (1960, appeared 1958) 197-351, plus 29 plates.

3 R. Dussaud (*Syria* 9 [1028] 171) identified Sefire with Šipri, mentioned in the treaty of Šupiluliumma and Mattiwaza (14th cent. B.C.); but this identification is questionable.

4 "Une inscription araméenne inédite de Sfiré," *BMB* 13 (1956, appeared in 1958) 23-41. I shall refer to the three steles of Sefire as Sf I, Sf II, Sf III.

guage. A comparative study of them was called for, and this was attempted by me in the first edition of this book.

The reader is referred to the articles of Dupont-Sommer and Starcky for the details about the acquisition of the inscriptions, their physical description, and the discussion of their script. It is sufficient to note here that the editors are of the opinion that the same stone-cutter engraved not only both sides of stele I (against the suggestion of Ronzevalle), but also steles II and III. The type of writing points to a date "vers le milieu du VIIIe siècle avant J.-C., après celles de Kilamou, du Zakir et de Panamou et avant celles de Bar-Rekoub et d'Azitawadda,"[5] the same date as that given by Ronzevalle.[6] Starcky has contributed a very useful discussion of the comparative epigraphic material in Appendix II, "Remarques épigraphiques."[7]

The three steles preserve the text of a treaty or treaties made by a north Syrian ruler. In the first two of them he is named as Mati'el (*Matī''el*), the son of 'Attarsamak, the king of Arpad. Apparently in the position of a vassal, he concluded a pact with Bar-Ga'yah, the king of KTK, a powerful neighboring overlord. It is not easy to determine the relation of the three steles to each other or to establish their relative dating or sequence. Even the form of them is puzzling, for the first two, engraved on several sides of the stone employed, suggest a shape that was roughly a truncated pyramid, whereas the third one was simply a flat slab, engraved on only one side. They may all be part of one text, as J. C. Greenfield has maintained.[8] Lemaire-Durand (*IAS*, 56-58) have, however, proposed that the three texts represent different forms of the treaty that was renewed at different intervals; that would account better for the slight differences in stipulations, curses, etc. The three, together with the Akkadian text of the *adē* of Mati'ilu would then constitute four texts in which the oaths of the king were recorded.

But the question may be asked whether what we call Sefire I, Sefire II, and Sefire III today are in the correct order, an issue that has been raised recently and will be discussed in due course.

---

5 "Les inscriptions," 202.

6 "Fragments," 240. Cf. now J. Naveh, *The Development of the Aramaic Script* (Proceedings of the Israel Academy of Sciences and Humanities 5/1; Jerusalem: Israel Academy, 1970); also his "The Scripts in Palestine and Transjordan in the Iron Age," *Near Eastern Archaeology in the Twentieth Century: Essays in Honor of Nelson Glueck* (ed. J. A. Sanders; Garden City, NY: Doubleday, 1970) 277-83.

7 "Les inscriptions," 329-34.

8 See his review of the first edition of this book in *JBL* 87 (1968) 241; cf. *AcOr* 29 (1965) 1 n. 2.

The *terminus ante quem* for the three inscriptions is 740 BC, the year in which the Assyrian king Tiglathpileser III conquered Arpad and made it part of the Assyrian Empire. The Sefire inscriptions presuppose the autonomy and political independence of Arpad. Mati'el was already the king of Arpad in 754 BC, for in the spring of 754-53 he concluded a treaty with the Assyrian Aššurnirari V, appearing in the Akkadian text as Mati'ilu. It is not possible to say how long Mati'el was king before this time or whether the treaty with Bar-Ga'yah recorded in Sf I and Sf II preceded or followed that with Aššurnirari V. M. Noth was of the opinion that Sf I B was an early form of a treaty between Mati'el and Bar-Ga'yah, possibly dating before 754 BC, and that Sf I A represented a newly-composed renewal of Sf I B, from sometime after 754, being occasioned precisely by the new relationship with Aššurnirari.[9] H. Donner and W. Röllig have rather been inclined to date Sf I in the period before 754, and Sf II and Sf III after 754.[10]

The question of the relative date of the Sefire inscriptions is involved in the relationship of the three inscriptions, one to the other. Mati'el and Bar-Ga'yah are indicated as the contracting parties in Sf I A 1; B [1]; Sf II A 3; B [2], [5]; C 14. But Mati'el's name does not appear in fragmentary Sf III, even though the kings of Arpad are mentioned (lines 1, 3, 16, 27). The name of Bar-Ga'yah is restored in Sf III 25, with hesitation. Noth thought that certain features in Sf III presupposed a different historical situation, so that Sf III possibly represented a treaty of Bar-Ga'yah with some other (later?) ruler(s) of Arpad.[11] And yet the external similarity of the three steles is such that it is hard to separate even Sf III from Mati'el. The data, however, are so meager that no definitive judgment seems possible in this matter.

The question raised by H. F. van Rooy is more important. That concerns the structure and the order of items in the inscriptions. As it stands today, Sf I has the following order: A 1-7, Introduction; A 7-14, List of gods; A 14-42, Treaty curses; B 1-6, Introduction; B 7-45, Treaty-stipulations; C 1, Document of Mati'el and Bar-Ga'yah; C 2-25, Added document of Mati'el alone. What remains of Sf II reveals that A contains treaty-curses (corresponding to Sf I A 21-31); Sf II B contains stipulations (corresponding to Sf I B 21-28); Sf II C details regulations for the protection of the treaty (corresponding to Sf I C, without the addendum written by Mati'el alone). Sf III contains only stipulations. When studied together, the steles reveal that the order of Sf I must have

9 *ZDPV* 77 (1961) 122-23.

10 *KAI* 2. 274.

11 *ZDPV* 77 (1961) 128-38.

been A, D, B, C (side D, now missing, would have been a continuation of side A); the order of Sf II must have been A, C, B, D. The structure of the treaties would have been: Introduction, List of gods, Curses, Document clause, Stipulations (to which Sf I had an Addendum, composed by Mati'el). This structure, then, would agree with the structure of Assyrian treaties of the first millennium. In this regard Van Rooy disagrees with the analysis of both McCarthy (1978) and Noth (1961), who sought to claim that Sf I B was the real beginning of the treaty-text.

The several inscriptions from Sefire, as well as the Akkadian treaty of Mati'el with Aššurnirari V in 754 BC and the alliance of Mati'el with Sardur III of Urartu, which Tiglathpileser III eventually brought to an end, give us an inkling of the complicated political situation that existed in northern Syria in the middle of the eighth century BC. All such ententes must have come to an end when Tiglathpileser III began his reign with a series of campaigns that defeated the Arameans in Mesopotamia, Sardur III in Urartu, and Mati'el in Arpad. Neo-Assyrian might was thus reasserted. All these details provide an interesting historical background for the reigns of Jeroboam II in Israel (786-747) and of Uzziah in Judah (783-742), as well as for the career of the prophet Amos, in whose oracles Asshur significantly does not appear.

BIBLIOGRAPHY

A. Sefire I: Older Discussions (before 1958)

Alt, A. 1934. "Die syrische Staatenwelt vor dem Einbruch der Assyrer," *ZDMG* ns 13 (= 88): 233-58; repr. in *Kleine Schriften zur Geschichte des Volkes Israel* (3 vols.; Munich: Beck, 1953-59) 3. 214-32.

Aro, J. 1959. "Die semitischen Zischlaute *(ṯ), š, ś* und *s* und ihre Vertretung im Akkadischen," *Or* 28: 321-35.

Bauer, H. 1932-33. "Ein aramäischer Staatsvertrag aus dem 8. Jahrhundert v. Chr.: Die Inschrift der Stele von Sudschīn," *AfO* 8: 1-16; cf. *Revue archéologique syrienne* 2 (1932) 100-107.

Ben-Hayyim, Z. 1951. הנסתרות בארמית הקדמונית ("The Third Person Plural Feminine in Old Aramaic)," *M. Schwabe Volume* (ErIsr 1; Jerusalem: Israel Exploration Society): 135-39.

Borger, R. 1956. *Die Inschriften Asarhaddons Königs von Assyrien* (AfO Beiheft 9; Graz: Weidner): 107-9 (§69: Der Vertrag mit Baal von Tyrus).

Bottéro, J. 1958. "Les divinités sémitiques anciennes en Mésopotamie," *Le antiche divinità semitiche* (Studi semitici 1; ed. S. Moscati; Rome: Università di Roma): 17-63.

Cantineau, J. 1931. "Remarques sur la stèle araméenne de Sefiré-Soudjin," *RA* 28: 167-78.

Contenau, G. 1957. "La cryptographie chez les Mésopotamiens," *Mélanges bibliques rédigés en l'honneur de André Robert* (Travaux de l'Institut Catholique de Paris 4; Paris: Bloud et Gay): 17-21.

Cross, F. M., Jr. and D. N. Freedman. 1952. *Early Hebrew Orthography: A Study of the Epigraphic Evidence* (AOS 36; New Haven, CT: American Oriental Society): 27-29.

Dhorme, E. 1937. *L'Evolution religieuse d'Israël: Tome I, La religion des Hébreux nomades* (Brussels: Nouvelle Société d'Editions): 217-19.

Donner, H. 1957. "Neue Quellen zur Geschichte des Staates Moab in der zweiten Hälfte des 8. Jahrh. v. Chr.," *MIO* 5: 155-84, esp. 161-62.

------. 1957-58. "Zur Inschrift von Sūdschīn Aa 9," *AfO* 18: 390-92.

Dossin, G. 1944. "BRG'YH, roi de KTK," *Muséon* 57: 147-55.

Driver, G. R. 1932. "Notes on the Aramaic Inscription from Soudschin," *AfO* 8: 203-6.

------. 1948. *Semitic Writing* (Schweich Lectures, 1944; London: Oxford University): 121, 127.

Dupont-Sommer, A. 1949. *Les Araméens* (L'Orient ancien illustré; Paris: Maisonneuve): 55-60, 70-71

Dussaud, R. 1930. "Séance du 20 juin," *CRAIBL*: 155-58, esp. 155-56.

------. 1931. "Nouvelles inscriptions araméennes de Séfiré, près d'Alep," *CRAIBL*: 312-21.

------. 1932. "Inscriptions araméennes de Sefiré (Soudjin)," *Syria* 13: 401-2.

Eissfeldt, O. 1956. "El und Jahwe," *JSS* 1: 25-37; abstracted in D. Sinor, *Proceedings of the Twenty-Third International Congress of Orientalists, Cambridge 21st-28th August 1954* (London: Royal Asiatic Society, [1954?]) 94-95.

------. 1954-59. "Jahwe's Verhältnis zu 'Eljon und Schaddaj nach Psalm 91," *WO* 2: 343-48.

Elliger, K. 1947. "Sam'al und Hamat in ihrem Verhältnis zu Ḫattina, Unqi und Arpad: Ein Beitrag zur Territorialgeschichte der nordsyrischen Staaten im 9. und 8. Jahrhundert v. Chr.," *Festschrift Otto Eissfeldt zum 60. Geburtstage* ... (ed. J. Fück; Halle a. d. S.: Niemeyer): 69-108, esp. 89-90, 93-94, 107.

Epstein, J. N. 1942. "Notes on the Sujin Pact," *Kedem* 1: 37-43 [Hebrew].

Euler, K. F. 1937. "Die Bedeutung von *spr* in der Sudschin-Inschrift im Lichte des ATlichen Gebrauchs von *sepaer*," *ZAW* 55: 281-91.

Forrer, E. 1921. *Die Provinzeinteilung des assyrischen Reiches* (Leipzig: Hinrichs) 108.

Friedrich, J. 1924. "Der hethitische Soldateneid," *ZA* 35: 161-91.

------. 1926. *Staatsverträge des Ḫatti-Reiches in hethitischer Sprache* (MVAG 31/2; Leipzig: Hinrichs): 1-48.

------. 1936. "Kein König פלמה in der Stele von Sudschin," *ZA* ns 9: 327-28.

Friedrich, J. and B. Landsberger. 1933. "Zu der altaramäischen Stele von Sudschin," *ZA* ns 7 (= 41): 313-18.

Garbini, G. 1956. "L'Aramaico antico," *Atti della Accademia Nazionale dei Lincei, Memorie,* Classe di scienze morali, storiche e filologiche 8/7/5 (Roma: Accademia Nazionale dei Lincei): 235-83, esp. 264-70.

------. 1956a. "Sul nome *Y'dy,*" *RSO* 31: 31-35.

------. 1956b. "Note aramaiche: 1. *p* > *b* in ya'udico," *Anton* 31: 310-11.

------. 1958. "Considerazioni sulla parola ebraica *peten,*" *RivB* 6: 263-65.

Gehman, H. S. 1944. "ספר, an Inscription, in the Book of Job," *JBL* 63: 303-7.

Greenfield, J. C. 1956. "Lexicographical Notes I," *HUCA* 29: 203-28.

Hempel, J. and H. Bauer. 1932. Review of Ronzevalle's article, *ZAW* 50: 178-83.

Henninger, J. 1953. "Was bedeutet die rituelle Teilung eines Tieres in zwei Hälften? Zur Deutung von Gen. 15,9ff." *Bib* 34: 344-53.

Herzfeld, E. 1933. "Summa imis confundere," *AMI* 5: 143-48.

Janssen, J. M. A. 1955-56. "Egyptological Remarks on *The Story of Joseph in Genesis*," *JEOL* 14: 63-72.

Korošec, V. 1931. *Hethitische Staatsverträge: Ein Beitrag zu ihrer juristischen Wertung* (Leipziger rechtswissenschaftliche Studien 60; Leipzig: Weicher).

Landsberger, B. 1948. *Sam'al: Studien zur Entdeckung der Ruinenstätte Karatepe* (Erste Lief.; Ankara: Veröffentlichungen der türkischen historischen Gesellschaft): 58-59 n. 147.

Langdon, S. 1933. "Note on the Aramaic Treaty of Bar-ga'aya and Mati'el," *JRAS*: 23-24.

Littmann, E. 1935. "Notes et études d'archéologie orientale," *OLZ* 38: 166-68.

Luckenbill, D. D. 1926-27. *Ancient Records of Assyria and Babylonia* (2 vols.; Chicago, IL: University of Chicago).

Mendenhall, G. E. 1954. "Covenant Forms in Israelite Tradition," *BA* 17: 50-76.

Montgomery, J. A. 1934. "Notes on Early Aramaic Inscriptions," *JAOS* 54: 421-25, esp. 424-25.

Parrot, A. 1939. *Malédictions et violations de tombes* (Paris: Geuthner): 33-34.

Pohl, A. 1956. "Personalnachrichten," *Or* 25: 153-61, esp. 159.

------. 1958. "Personalnachrichten," *Or* 27: 288-91, esp. 290-91.

Ronzevalle, S. 1930-31. "Fragments d'inscriptions araméennes des environs d'Alep," *MUSJ* 15: 237-60.

Rosenthal, F. 1939. *Die aramaistische Forschung seit Th. Nöldeke's Veröffentlichungen* (Leiden: Brill; repr. 1964): 13.

------. 1955. "The Treaty Between *KTK* and Arpad," *ANET* : 503-504b.

Rost, P. 1893. *Die Keilschrifttexte Tiglat-Pilesers III.* (Leipzig: Pfeiffer).

Schiffer, S. 1911. *Die Aramäer: Historisch-geographische Untersuchungen* (Leipzig: Hinrichs).

Tallqvist, K. 1938. *Akkadische Götterepitheta* (Helsinki: Societas Orientalis Fennica).

Thureau-Dangin, F. and M. Dunand. 1936. *Til-Barsib* (Bibliothèque archéologique et historique 23; 2 vols.; Paris: Geuthner): 1. 141-60, esp. 141-51.

Torczyner, H. et al. (eds.). 1938. *Lachish I: The Lachish Letters* (The Wellcome Archaeological Research Expedition to the Near East: Publications 1; London: Oxford University): 60-61.
Tsevat, M. 1959. "The Neo-Assyrian and Neo-Babylonian Vassal Oaths and the Prophet Ezekiel," *JBL* 78: 199-204.
Unger, M. F. 1957. *Israel and the Aramaeans of Damascus: A Study in Archaeological Illumination of Bible History* (London: J. Clarke).
Weidner, E. F. 1932-33. "Der Staatsvertrag Aššurnirâris VI [= V] von Assyrien mit Mati'ilu von Bīt-Agusi," *AfO* 8: 17-34.

B. Sefire I: More Recent Discussions (from late 1958 on) and Sefire II and III

Abou-Assaf, A., P. Bordreuil, and A. R. Millard. 1982. *La statue de Tell Fekherye et son inscription bilingue assyro-araméenne* (Etudes assyriologiques, Cahier 7; Paris: Editions Recherche sur les civilisations).
Astour, M. C. 1979. "The Arena of Tiglath-Pileser III's Campaign against Sarduri II (743 B.C.)," *Assur* 2/3: 1-23, esp. 6 n. 36.
Aristar, A. M. R. 1987. "The Semitic Jussive and the Implications for Aramaic," *Maarav* 4: 157-89.
Aufrecht, W. E. and J. C. Hurd. 1975. *A Synoptic Concordance of Aramaic Inscriptions (According to H. Donner & W. Roellig)* (The International Concordance Library 1; Missoula, MT: Scholars).
Bange, L. A. 1971. *A Study of the Use of Vowel-Letters in Alphabetic Consonantal Writing* (Inauguraldissertation 1961-62 an der Universität Oxford; Munich: Verlag Uni-Druck).
Barnett, R. D. 1967. "Layard's Nimrud Bronzes and Their Inscriptions," *E. L. Sukenik Memorial Volume (1889-1953)* (ErIsr 8; Jerusalem: Israel Exploration Society): 1*-7* (+ pls. I-VIII).
Barré, M. L. 1983. *The God-List in the Treaty between Hannibal and Philip V of Macedonia: A Study in Light of the Ancient Near Eastern Treaty Tradition* (Johns Hopkins Near Eastern Studies; Baltimore/London: The Johns Hopkins University).
------. 1985. "The First Pair of Deities in the Sefîre I God-List," *JNES* 44: 205-10.
Ben-Ḥayyim, Z. 1970-71. "עם העיון בכבותות ספירה (Comments on the Inscriptions of Sfiré)," *Lešonenu* 35: 243-53.
Bickerman, E. 1976. "Couper une alliance," *Studies in Jewish and Christian History* (AGJU 9/1-3; Leiden: Brill, 1976-86) 1. 1-32.
Borger, R. 1961. "Zu den Asarhaddon-Verträgen aus Nimrud," *ZA* 54:

173-96.

------. 1983. "Assyrische Staatsverträge," *TUAT* 1: 155-77.

Brauner, R. A. 1977. "Old Aramaic and Comparative Semitic Lexicography," *Gratz College Annual of Jewish Studies* 6: 15-33.

Brekelmans, C. 1963. "Sefire I A 29-30," *VT* 13: 225-28.

Caquot, A. 1962. "L'Alliance avec Abram (Genèse 15)," *Sem* 12: 51-66.

Cardascia, G. 1975. "La malédiction par le sel dans les droits du Proche-Orient ancien," *Festschrift für Erwin Seidl* ... (ed. H. Hübner et al.; Cologne: Hanstein): 27-34, esp. 28.

Cazelles, H. 1971. "Tal'ayim, Tala et Muṣur," *Hommages à André Dupont-Sommer* (Paris: Maisonneuve): 17-26.

------. 1982. "La rupture de la berît selon les Prophètes," *JJS* 33: 133-44, esp. 133-37.

Cogan, M. 1974. *Imperialism and Religion: Assyria, Judah and Israel in the Eighth and Seventh Centuries B.C.E.* (SBLMS 19; Missoula, MT: Scholars): 42-64.

Couroyer, B. 1988. "*'Edût:* Stipulation de traité ou enseignement?" *RB* 95: 321-31.

Crawford, T. G. 1992. *Blessing and Curse in Syro-Palestinian Inscriptions of the Iron Age* (American University Studies 7/120; New York: P. Lang).

Croatto, S. 1968. "Ṭobā como 'amistad (de alianza)' en el Antiguo Testamento," *AION* 18: 385-89.

Dahood, M. 1975. "Isaiah 51,19 and Sefîre III 22," *Bib* 56: 94-95.

Dalley, S. 1979. "dNIN-LÍL = Mul(l)is(s)u, the Treaty of Barga'yah and Herodotus' Mylitta," *RA* 73: 177-78.

Degen, R. 1967. "Zur Schreibung des Kaška-Namens in ägyptischen, ugaritischen und altaramäischen Quellen: Kritische Anmerkungen zu einer Monographie über die Kaškäer," *WO* 4: 48-60.

------. 1969. *Altaramäische Grammatik der Inschriften des 10.-8. Jh. v. Chr.* (Abhandlungen für die Kunde des Morgenlandes 38/3; Wiesbaden: Steiner): 9-17 et passim, esp. 139-44; Sf II: 17-19 et passim; Sf III: 19-23 et passim.

Deist, F. E. 1971. "The Punishment of the Disobedient Zedekiah," *JNSL* 1: 71-72.

Delcor, M. 1966. "Les attaches littéraires, l'origine et la signification de l'expression biblique 'Prendre à témoin le ciel et la terre," *VT* 16: 8-25, esp. 12-13.

Dion, P.-E. 1974. *La langue de Ya'udi: Description et classement de l'ancien parler de Zencirli dans le cadre des langues sémitiques du nord-ouest* (Editions SR 1; Waterloo, Ont.: Corporation pour le

publication des études académiques en religion au Canada).
Donner, H. 1962. "Zu Gen 28,22," *ZAW* 74: 68-70.
------. 1970. "Adadnirari III. und die Vasallen des Westens," *Archäologie und Altes Testament: Festschrift für K. Galling ...* (ed. A. Kuschke and E. Kutsch; Tübingen: Mohr [Siebeck]): 49-59.
Donner, H. and W. Röllig. 1962-64. *Kanaanäische und aramäische Inschriften* (3 vols.; Wiesbaden: Harrassowitz): 2. 238-58 (§222); Sf II: 2. 258-64 (§223); Sf III: 2. 264-74 (§224).
Dupont-Sommer, A. 1957. "Une stèle araméenne inédite de Sfiré (Syrie) du VIIIe siècle av. J.-C.," *CRAIBL*: 245-48.
------. 1958. "Un traité araméen du VIIIe siècle av. J.-C.," *CRAIBL*: 177-82.
------. 1959. "Une stèle araméenne inédite de Sfiré (Syrie), du VIIIe siècle avant J.-C." *Akten des vierundzwanzigsten internationalen Orientalisten-Kongresses, München, 28. August bis 4. September 1957* (ed. H. Franke; Wiesbaden: Deutsche Morgenländische Gesellschaft, 1959) 238-41.
------. 1960. "Trois stèles araméennes provenant de Sfiré: Un traité de vassalité du VIIIe siècle avant J.-C.," *AnArchSyr* 10: 21-54 (+ 10 pls.).
------. 1967. "Ancient Aramaic Monumental Inscriptions," *AH* 1/1. 1-9 (§2); 1/2. 1-7.
Dupont-Sommer, A. and J. Starcky. 1956 (appeared 1958). "Une inscription araméenne inédite de Sfiré," *BMB* 13: 23-41 (+ pls. I-VI) [= Sf III].
------. 1960 (appeared in 1958). "Les inscriptions araméennes de Sfiré (stèles I et II)," *MPAIBL* 15: 1-95 (+ pls. I-XX); Sf II: 97-125 (+ pls. XXI-XXVIII).
Eph'al, I. 1982. *The Ancient Arabs: Nomads on the Borders of the Fertile Crescent, 9th-5th Centuries B.C.* (Jerusalem: Magnes; Leiden: Brill).
Fales, F. M. 1982 (appeared 1984). "Massimo sforzo, minima resa: Maledizioni divine da Tell Fekherye all'Antico Testamento," *Annali della Facoltà di Lingue et Letterature straniere di Ca' Foscari* 21/3: 1-12.
------. 1986. Review of Lemaire-Durand, *IAS*, *RA* 80: 88-93.
------. 1990. "Istituzioni a confronto tra mondo semitico occidentale e Assiria nel I millennio a.C.: Il trattato di Sefire," *I trattati nel mondo antico: Forma, ideologia, funzione* (Istituto Gramsci, Seminario di Antichistica; Roma: L'Erma di Bretschneider): 149-73.
Farzat, H. 1972. *Le royaume araméen d'Arpad* (Paris: dissertation, University).

Fensham, F. C. 1962. "Malediction and Benediction in Ancient Near Eastern Vassal-Treaties and the Old Testament," *ZAW* 74: 1-9.

------. 1962a. "Salt as Curse in the Old Testament and the Ancient Near East," *BA* 25: 48-50.

------. 1963. "Clauses of Protection in Hittite Vassal-Treaties and the Old Testament," *VT* 13: 133-43, esp. 137-38.

------ 1963a. "Common Trends in Curses of the Near Eastern Treaties and *Kudurru*-Inscriptions Compared with Maledictions of Amos and Isaiah," *ZAW* 75: 155-75.

------ 1963b. "The Wild Ass in the Aramean Treaty between Bar-Ga'ayah and Mati'el," *JNES* 22: 185-86.

------. 1964. "The Treaty Between Israel and the Gibeonites," *BA* 27: 96-100.

------. 1967. "Covenant, Promise and Expectation in the Bible," *TZ* 23: 305-22.

Fitzmyer, J. A. 1958. "The Aramaic Suzerainty Treaty from Sefîre in the Museum of Beirut," *CBQ* 20: 444-76.

------. 1961 (appeared March 1962). "The Aramaic Inscriptions of Sefire I and II," *JAOS* 81: 178-222; Sf II: 208-15.

------. 1967. *The Aramaic Inscriptions of Sefîre* (BibOr 19; Rome: Biblical Institute) Sf I: 9-77; Sf II: 79-93; Sf III: 94-120.

------. 1969. "A Further Note on the Aramaic Inscription Sefire III. 22," *JSS* 14: 197-200.

Fox, M. 1973. "*Tôb* as Covenant Terminology," *BASOR* 209: 41-42.

Frankena, R. 1965. "The Vassal-Treaties of Esarhaddon and the Dating of Deuteronomy," *OTS* 14: 122-54, esp. 134-36.

Freedman, D. N., A. D. Forbes, and F. J. Andersen. 1992. *Studies in Hebrew and Aramaic Orthography* (Biblical and Judaic Studies from the University of California, San Diego 2; Winona Lake, IN: Eisenbrauns).

Galling, K. 1967. "Miscellanea archaeologica 4: Das Salben der Mutterbrust (Sfire I A 21f)," *ZDPV* 83: 134-35.

Galter, H. D. 1986. Review of Lemaire-Durand, *IAS*, *BO* 43: 445-47.

Garbini, G. 1959. "Nuovo materiale per la grammatica dell'aramaico antico," *RSO* 34: 41-54.

------. 1961. "Sefîre I A, 28," *RSO* 36: 9-11.

------. 1967. "Appunti di epigrafia aramaica," *AION* 17: 89-96, esp. 89-92.

------. 1969. "Studi aramaici -- 1-2," *AION* 29: 1-15.

------. 1971. "The Phonetic Shift of Sibilants in Northwestern Semitic in the First Millennium B.C.," *JNSL* 1: 32-38.

------. 1974. "Sul nome 'Athtar/'Ashtar," *AION* 34: 409-10.

Garcia-Treto, F. O. 1967. "Genesis 31,44 and 'Gilead,'" *ZAW* 79: 13-17.

Garelli, P. 1971. "Nouveau coup d'oeil sur Muṣur, *Hommages à André Dupont-Sommer* (Paris: Maisonneuve): 37-48.

------. 1982. "Importance et rôle des Araméens dans l'administration de l'empire assyrien," *Mesopotamien und seine Nachbarn: Politische und kulturelle Wechselbeziehungen im alten Vorderasien vom 4. bis. 1. Jahrtausend v. Chr.* (BBVO 1; Berlin: Reimer): 437-47.

Garelli, P. and V. Nikiprowetsky. 1974. *Le Proche-Orient asiatique: Les empires mésopotamiens, Israël* (Paris: Presses Universitaires de France): 96-116, 231-34.

Garr, W. R. 1985. *Dialect Geography of Syria-Palestine, 1000-586 B.C.E.* (Philadelphia, PA: University of Pennsylvania).

Gelb, I. 1962. Review of D. J. Wiseman, *Vassal-Treaties of Esarhaddon*, *BO* 19: 159-62.

Gerstenberger, E. 1965. "Covenant and Commandment," *JBL* 84: 38 51.

Gevirtz, S. 1961. "West-Semitic Curses and the Problem of the Origins of Hebrew Law," *VT* 11: 137-58.

Gibson, J. C. L. 1975. *Textbook of Syrian Semitic Inscriptions, Volume II: Aramaic Inscriptions, Including Inscriptions in the Dialect of Zenjirli* (Oxford: Clarendon): 18-43 (§7); Sf II: 44-46 (§8); Sf III: 2. 46-56 (§9).

González Lamadrid, A. 1969. "Pax et bonum: 'Shalôm' y 'tôb' en relación con berit," *EstBíb* 28: 61-77.

González Nuñez, A. 1965. "El rito de la alianza," *EstBíb* 24: 217-38.

Grayson, A. K. 1987. "Akkadian Treaties of the Seventh Century B.C.," *JCS* 39: 127-60.

------. 1987a. *Assyrian Rulers of the Third and Second Millennia BC (to 1115 BC)* (The Royal Inscriptions of Mesopotamia: The Assyrian Periods; 2 vols.; Toronto: University of Toronto, 1987, 1990)

Graziani, S. 1979. "Note sui Sibitti," *AION* 39: 673-90.

Greenfield, J. C. 1964. "בחינות לשוניות בכתובת ספירה," *Lešonenu* 27-28 (1964) 303-13.

------. 1965. "Studies in West Semitic Inscriptions, I: Stylistic Aspects of the Sefîre Treaty Inscriptions," *AcOr* 29: 1-18.

------. 1966. "Three Notes on the Sefire Inscription," *JSS* 11: 98-105.

------. 1967. "Some Aspects of Treaty Terminology in the Bible," *Fourth World Congress of Jewish Studies, Papers* (Jerusalem: World Union of Jewish Studies): 1. 117-19.

------. 1967-68. "קווים דיאלקטיים בארמית הקדומה (Dialectal Traits in Early Aramaic)," *Lešonenu* 32: 359-68.

------. 1968. Review of J. A. Fitzmyer, *Aramaic Inscriptions*, *JBL* 87: 240-41.

------. 1969. "The 'Periphrastic Imperative' in Aramaic and Hebrew," *IEJ* 19: 199-210.

------. 1974. "Standard Literary Aramaic," *Actes du premier congrès international de linguistique sémitique et chamito-sémitique* (Janua linguarum, ser. practica 159; ed. A. Caquot et D. Cohen; The Hague: Mouton): 280-89.

------. 1978. "The Dialects of Early Aramaic," *JNES* 37: 93-99, esp. 94-95.

------. 1978a. "Some Reflections on the Vocabulary of Aramaic in Relationship to the Other Semitic Languages," *Atti del secondo congresso internazionale di linguistica camito-semitica, Firenze 16-19 aprile 1974* (Quaderni di semitistica 5; ed. P. Fronzaroli; Florence: Istituto di Linguistica e di Lingue Orientali, Università di Firenze): 151-56.

------. 1978b. Review of J. C. L. Gibson, *Textbook, IEJ* 28 (1978) 287-89.

------. 1979. "Early Aramaic Poetry," *JANES* 11: 45-51.

------. 1981. "Aramaic Studies and the Bible," *Congress Volume Vienna 1980* (VTSup 32; Leiden: Brill): 110-30.

------. 1986. "An Ancient Treaty Ritual and Its Targumic Echo," *Salvación en la palabra: Targum--Derash--Berith en memoria del profesor Alejandro Díez Macho* (ed. D. Muñoz León; Madrid: Cristiandad): 391-97.

------. 1991. "Some Glosses on the Sfire Inscriptions," *Maarav* 7: 141 47.

------. 1991a. "Asylum at Aleppo: A Note on Sfire III, 4-7," *Ah, Assyria ...: Studies in Assyrian History and Ancient Near Eastern Historiography Presented to Hayim Tadmor* (ScrHier 33; Jerusalem: Magnes): 272-78.

Grelot, P. 1968. Review of J. A. Fitzmyer, *Aramaic Inscriptions, RB* 75: 280-86.

Grintz, J.. M. 1966. "The Treaty of Joshua with the Gibeonites," *JAOS* 86: 113-26, esp. 119, 123.

Habel, N. 1972. "'Yahweh, Maker of Heaven and Earth': A Study in Tradition Criticism," *JBL* 91: 321-37, esp. 321-23.

Haines, B. L. 1967. *A Palaeographical Study of Aramaic Inscriptions Antedating 500 B.C.* (Cambridge, MA: Dissertation, Harvard Divinity School [noted in *HTR* 60 (1967) 489]).

Hawkins, J. D. 1972-75. "Hamath," *RLA* 4: 67-70.

------. 1976-80. "Jaḫan," *RLA* 5: 238-39.

------. 1981. "KTK," *RLA* 6: 254-56.

------. 1982. "The Neo-Hittite States in Syria and Anatolia," *Cambridge Ancient History* (rev. 2d ed.; ed. J. Boardman; Cambridge, UK: Cambridge University): 3/1. 372-441.

------. 1983. "The Hittite Name of Til-Barsip: Evidence from a New Hieroglyphic Fragment from Tell Ahmar," *AnStud* 33: 131-36.

Herrmann, W. 1969. "Aštart," *MIO* 15: 6-55.

Hillers, D. R. 1964. *Treaty-Curses and the Old Testament Prophets* (BibOr 16; Rome: Biblical Institute).

------. 1964a. "A Note on Some Treaty Terminology in the Old Testament," *BASOR* 176: 46-47.

Huehnergard, J. 1987. "The Feminine Plural Jussive in Old Aramaic," *ZDMG* 137: 266-77.

------. 1987a. Review of W. R. Garr, *Dialect Geography, JBL* 106: 529-33.

Huffmon, H. B. 1966. "The Treaty Background of Hebrew *yāda'*," *BASOR* 181: 31-37.

Hurvitz, A. 1982. "The History of a Legal Formula, *kōl 'ăšer ḥāpēṣ 'āśāh* (Ps cxv 3; cxxxv 6)," *VT* 32: 257-67, esp. 265.

Hutter, M. 1993. "Kultstelen und Baityloi: Die Ausstrahlung eines syrischen religiösen Phänomens nach Kleinasien und Israel," *Religionsgeschichtliche Beziehungen zwischen Kleinasien, Nordsyrien und dem Alten Testament* (OBO 129; ed. B. Janowski et al.; Fribourg: Universitätsverlag; Göttingen: Vandenhoeck & Ruprecht): 86-108.

Ikeda, Y. 1979. "Royal Cities and Fortified Cities," *Iraq* 41: 75-87, esp. 79 n. 31.

------. 1993. "Once Again *KTK* in the Sefire Inscriptions," *Avraham Malamat Volume* (ErIsr 24; ed. S. Aḥituv et al.; Jerusalem: Israel Exploration Society): 104*-108*.

Kaufman, S. A. 1974. *The Akkadian Influences on Aramaic* (Assyriological Studies 19; Chicago, IL: University of Chicago).

------. 1982. "Reflections on the Assyrian-Aramaic Bilingual from Tell Fakhariyeh," *Maarav* 3 (1982) 137-75.

Kitchen, K. A. 1979. "Egypt, Ugarit, Qatna and Covenant," *UF* 11: 453-64.

Klengel, H. 1965. "Der Wettergott von Ḫalab," *JCS* 19: 87-93.

Koopmans, J. J. 1960. Review of Dupont-Sommer and Starcky, *BO* 17: 51-52.

------. 1962. *Aramäische Chrestomathie* (Leiden: Nederlands Instituut voor het Nabije Oosten): 1. 41-59 (§10); Sf II: 1. 59-62 (§10); Sf III: 1. 62-69 (§10).

Korošec, V. 1961. "Quelques traités de l'époque néo-assyrienne," *In honorem Henrici Levy-Bruhl* (Romanitas 3-4; Rio de Janeiro: Romanitas Livraria): 261-77.

------. 1976. "Die Götteranrufungen der keilschriftlichen Staatsverträgen," *Or* 45: 120-29, esp. 128-29.

Krebernik, M. 1984. Review of Lemaire-Durand, *IAS*, *ZA* 74: 156-60.

Kutsch, E. 1970. "Sehen und bestimmen: Die Etymologie von ברית," *Archäologie und Altes Testament: Festschrift für Kurt Galling* (ed. A. Kuschke and E. Kutsch; Tübingen: Mohr [Siebeck]): 165-78.

Kutscher, E. Y. 1971. "Aramaic," *Linguistics in South West Asia and North Africa* (Current Trends in Linguistics 6; The Hague: Mouton): 347-412.

L'Hour, J. 1962. "L'Alliance de Sichem," *RB* 69: 5-36, 161-84, 350-68.

Lack, R. 1962. "Les origines de *'Elyôn*, le Très-Haut, dans la tradition cultuelle d'Israël," *CBQ* 24: 44-64.

Layton, S. C. 1988. "Old Aramaic Inscriptions: Literary Sources for the History of Palestine and Syria," *BA* 51: 172-89.

Lemaire, A. 1981. "Sfiré I A 24 et l'araméen *št*," *Henoch* 3: 161-70.

------. 1984. "Qui est Bar Ga'yah roi de KTK? Vers la solution d'une énigme historique," *JA* 272: 473-74.

------. 1985. "Notes d'épigraphie nord-ouest sémitique," *Syria* 62: 31-47, esp. 33-35.

------. 1986. "Les écrits araméens," *Ecrits de l'orient ancien et sources bibliques* (Ancien Testament 2; ed. A. Barucq et al.; Paris: Desclée): 241-69, esp. 251-52.

Lemaire, A. and J.-M. Durand. 1984. *Les inscriptions araméennes de Sfiré et l'Assyrie de Shamshi-Ilu* (Ecole Pratique des Hautes Etudes 2 / Hautes Etudes Orientales 20; Geneva/Paris: Librairie Droz).

Limburg, J. 1969. "The Root ריב and the Prophetic Lawsuit Speeches," *JBL* 88: 291-304, esp. 299-301.

Lipiński, E. 1975. *Studies in Aramaic Inscriptions and Onomastics I* (OrLovAn 1; Louvain: Leuven University): 27-76.

------. 1975a. "Staatsverträge zwischen Katk und Arpad, *Religionsgeschichtliches Textbuch zum A. T.* (ed. W. Beyerlin; Göttingen: Vandenhoeck & Ruprecht): 272-82.

------. 1977. "North-west Semitic Inscriptions," *OLP* 8: 81-117.

------. 1978. "State Treaties between Katk and Arpad," *Near Eastern Religious Texts Relating to the Old Testament* (ed. W. Beyerlin; London: SCM): 256-66.

------. 1978a. "La correspondence des sibilantes dans les textes araméens et les textes cunéiformes néo-assyriens," *Atti del secondo congresso internazionale di linguistica camito-semitica, Firenze, 16-19 aprile 1974* (ed. P. Fronzaroli; Quaderni di semitistica 5; Florence: Istituto di linguistica e di lingue orientali, Università di Firenze): 201-10, esp. 205, 208.

------. 1979. "Aram et Israël du Xe au VIIIe siècle av. n. è.," *AAASH* 27: 49-102, esp. 75 n. 79.

------. 1986. Review of Lemaire-Durand, *IAS*, *OLZ* 81: 351-54.

------. 1989-90. Review of H. S. Sader, *Les états araméeens, WO* 20-21: 301-3.

------. 1986. Review of Lemaire-Durand, *IAS*, *BASOR* 264: 85-86.

Liverani, M. 1961. "Bar-Guš e Bar-Rakib," *RSO* 36: 185-87.

Lohfink, N. 1991. "*'d(w)t* im Deuteronomium und in den Königsbüchern," *BZ* 35: 86-93.

Loretz, O. 1966. "*B^{e}rît* -- 'Band--Bund,'" *VT* 16: 239-41.

Loza, J. 1971. "Les catéchèses étiologiques dans l'Ancien Testament," *RB* 78: 481-500, esp. 493-94.

Malamat, A. 1973. "The Arameans," *Peoples of Old Testament Times* (ed. D. J. Wiseman; Oxford: Clarendon): 134-55.

------. 1976. "הצעה חדשה לזיהויה של 'כתך' בכתובות ספירה (A New Proposal for the Identification of KTK in the Sefire Inscriptions)," מפקדים ומגילות־יחס ומשמעותם ההיסטורית לימי שאול ודוד (*Census Lists and Genealogies and Their Historical Implications* (ed. M. Razin and S. Bendor; Haifa: University of Haifa) vii-xi.

Malbran-Labat, F. 1987. Review of Lemaire-Durand, *IAS*, *RHR* 204: 84-86.

Martínez Borobio, E. 1991. "*Dmwt', ṣlm, nṣb*: Estatua en la epigrafía aramea," *Sefarad* 51: 85-97.

------. 1992. "'Erigir una estatua' en las antiquas dedicaciones arameas," *Sefarad* 52: 173-80.

Mazar, B. 1962. "The Aramean Empire and Its Relations with Israel," *BA* 25: 98-120, esp. 116-20; repr. *BAR* 2 (1964) 127-51, esp. 146-51.

------. 1986. "The Aramean Empire and Its Relations with Israel," *The Early Biblical Period: Historical Studies* (ed. S. Aḥituv and B. A. Levine; Jerusalem: Israel Exploration Society): 151-72 (revised version of *BA* 25 [1962] 98-120).

McCarthy, D. J. 1963. *Treaty and Covenant: A Study in Form in the Ancient Oriental Documents and in the Old Testament* (AnBib 21; Rome: Biblical Institute) 51-67, 189-94; *New Edition Completely Rewritten* (AnBib 21A; Rome: Biblical Institute, 1978).

------. 1972. *Old Testament Covenant: A Survey of Current Opinions* (Growing Points in Theology; Richmond: John Knox; Oxford:

Blackwell).
------. 1979. "Ebla, *ὅρκια τέμνειν*, *ṭb*, *šlm*: Addenda to *Treaty and Covenant*," *Bib* 60: 247-53.
------. 1982. "Covenant 'Good' and an Egyptian Text," *BASOR* 245: 63-64.
Menzel, B. 1981. *Assyrische Tempel* (Studia Pohl, ser. maj. 10/I-II; Rome: Biblical Institute): 117, 115*.
Millard, A. R. 1970. "'Scriptio continua' in Early Hebrew: Ancient Practice or Modern Surmise?" *JSS* 15: 2-15.
------. 1973. "Adad-nirari III, Aram, and Arpad," *PEQ* 105: 161-64.
Millard, A. R. and H. H. Tadmor. 1973. "Adad-nirari III in Syria: Another Stele Fragment and the Dates of His Campaigns," *Iraq* 35: 57-64.
Moran, W. L. 1963. "The Ancient Near Eastern Background of the Love of God in Deuteronomy," *CBQ* 25: 77-87.
------. 1963a. "A Note on the Treaty Terminology of the Sefîre Stelas," *JNES* 22: 173-76.
Moriya, A. 1980. "'dy kō," *Kyūshū-Kyōritsu-Daigaku Kiyō* 15: 165-76.
------. 1985. "The Functions of the Gods in the Aramaic Inscriptions of Sefire," *Oriento* 25: 38-54.
Mouterde, P. 1958. Notice of Dupont-Sommer's article and mine (on Sf III), *MUSJ* 35: 242-45.
Muffs, Y. 1982. "Abraham the Noble Warrior: Patriarchal Politics and Laws of War in Ancient Israel," *JJS* 33: 81-107, esp. 91-92.
Na'aman, N. 1978. "Looking for KTK," *WO* 9: 220-39.
Nober, P. 1959. "Ad inscriptionem aramaicam Arpadensem (adnotationes criticae)," *VD* 37: 171-75.
Noth, M. 1961. "Der historische Hintergrund der Inschriften von sefîre," *ZDPV* 77: 118-72; repr. in *Aufsätze zur biblischen Landes- und Altertumskunde* (ed. H. W. Wolff; Neukirchen-Vluyn: Neukirchener-V. 1971) 2. 161-210.
Oden, R. A. Jr. 1977. "*Ba'al Šamēn* and *'El*," *CBQ* 39: 457-73.
Pardee, D. 1978. Review of J. C. L. Gibson, *TSSInscriptions, Volume 2*, *JNES* 37: 195-97.
Parnas, M. 1975. "עֵדוּת‘, ’עֵדֹות‘, ’עֵדְוֹת‘ במקרא על רקע תעודות חיצוניות (‘Edūt, ‘Edōt, ‘Edwōt in the Bible, against the Background of Ancient Near Eastern Documents)," *Shnaton* 1: 235-46.
Parpola, S. 1974. "The Alleged Middle/Neo-Assyrian Irregular Verb **naṣṣ* and the Assyrian Sound Change, *š* > *s*," *Assur* 1/1: 1-10, esp. 4 n. 13.
------. 1987. "Neo-Assyrian Treaties from the Royal Archives of Nineveh," *JCS* 39: 161-89.

Parpola, S. and K. Watanabe. 1988. *Neo-Assyrian Treaties and Loyalty Oaths* (State Archives of Assyria 2; Helsinki: University Press): 8-15.

Picard, C. 1961. "Le rite magique des εἴδωλα de cire brûlés, attesté sur trois stèles araméennes de Sfiré (vers le milieu du VIIIe s. av. notre ère)," *RArch* 2: 85-88.

Polzin, R. 1969. "HWQY' and Covenantal Institutions in Early Israel," *HTR* 62: 227-40, esp. 235.

Pomponio, F. 1990. *Formule di maledizione della Mesopotamia preclassica* (Testi del Vicino Oriente antico 2: Letterature mesopotamiche; Brescia: Paideia).

Priest, J. F. 1964. "Ὅρκια in the *Iliad* and Consideration of Recent Theory," *JNES* 23: 48-56.

Puech, E. 1982. "Les inscriptions araméennes I et III de Sfiré: Nouvelles lectures," *RB* 89: 576-87.

------. 1982-84. "La racine *śyt* -- *š'ṭ* en araméen et en hébreu: A propos de Sfiré I A 24, 1 Q H[a] III, 30 et 36 (= XI, 31 et 37) et Ezéchiel," *RevQ* 11: 367-78.

------. 1992. "Les traités araméens de Sfiré," *Traités et serments dans le Proche-Orient ancien* (Supplément au Cahier Evangile 81; Paris: Editions du Cerf): 88-107.

Rabinowitz, J. J. 1958. "Ad inscriptionem aramaicam," *Bib* 39: 401.

Reiner, E. 1969. "Akkadian Treaties from Syria and Assyria," *ANESTP*, 531-41.

Rendtorff, R. 1994. "*'El* als israelitische Gottesbezeichnung: Mit einem Appendix: Beobachtungen zum Gebrauch von הָאֱלֹהִים," *ZAW* 106: 4-21.

Renger, J. 1971. "Notes on the Goldsmiths, Jewelers and Carpenters of Neobabylonian Eanna," *JAOS* 91: 494-503.

Richter, W. 1965. "Die *nāgīd*-Formel: Ein Beitrag zur Erhellung des nāgīd-Problems," *BZ* 9: 71-84.

Rimbach, J. A. 1978. "Bears or Bees? Sefire I A 31 and Daniel 7," *JBL* 97: 565-66.

Rössler, O. 1982. "Die Verträge des Königs Bar-Ga'yah von Ktk mit König Mati'-Il von Arpad (Stelen von Sefire)," *TUAT*: 1. 178-89.

Rooy, H. F. van. 1989. "The Structure of the Aramaic Treaties of Sefire," *JSem* 1: 133-39.

------. 1991. "A Few Remarks on the Aramaic Treaties from Sefire," *JNSL* 17: 145-49.

Rosenthal, F. 1960. "Notes on the Third Inscription from Sefîre-Sûjîn," *BASOR* 158: 28-31.

------. 1969. "The Treaty between *KTK* and Arpad," *ANET* (3d ed. with supplement, 1969): 659-61; also in *ANESTP*, 659-61.

Sacchi, P. 1960-61. "Osservazioni sul problema degli Aramei," *Atti dell'Accademia toscana di scienze e lettere: La Colombaria* 25: 85-142, esp. 127-31.

------. 1961. "Osservazioni storiche alla prima iscrizione aramaica di Sfire," *AANL Rendic* 8/16/5-6: 175-91.

Sader, H. S. 1987. *Les états araméens de Syrie depuis leur fondation jusqu'à leur transformation en provinces assyriennes* (Beiruter Texte und Studien 26; Wiesbaden: Steiner): 120-36.

Schuler, E. von. 1965. *Die Kaškäer: Ein Beitrag zur Ethnographie des alten Kleinasiens* (Untersuchungen zur Assyriologie und vorderasiatischen Archäologie 3; Berlin: de Gruyter): 67-88.

Schuttermayr, G. 1970. "*RḤM* -- Eine lexikalische Studie," *Bib* 51: 499-525, esp. 516.

Segert, S. 1964. "Zur Schrift und Orthographie der altaramäischen Stelen von Sfire," *ArOr* 32: 110-26.

------. 1975. *Altaramäische Grammatik mit Bibliographie, Chrestomathie und Glossar* (Leipzig: VEB Verlag Enzyklopädie): 38-39, 493-94 et passim; Sf III: 494 et passim..

------. 1978. "Vowel Letters in Early Aramaic," *JNES* 37: 111-14.

Seton Williams, M. V. 1961. "Preliminary Report on the Excavations at Tell Rifa'at," *Iraq* 23: 68-87.

Sherman, M. E. 1966. *Systems of Hebrew and Aramaic Orthography: An Epigraphic History of the Use of Matres Lectionis in Non-biblical Texts to ca. A.D. 135* (Cambridge, MA: Dissertation, Harvard Divinity School [noted in *HTR* 59 (1966) 455-56]).

Soden, W. von, 1961. "Azitawadda = Mattî von Atunna: KTK und Kasku," *OLZ* 56: 576-79, esp. 578-79.

------ 1966, 1968. "Aramäische Wörter in neuassyrischen und in neu- und spätbabylonischen Texten: Ein Vorbericht. I (*agâ-mūš*)," *Or* 35: 1-20; "II (*n-z* und Nachträge)," 37: 261-71.

------. 1985. "Das nordsyrische *KTK/Kiski* und der Turtan Šamši-ilu: Erwägungen zu einem neuen Buch," *SEL* 2: 133-41.

Soggin, J. A. 1968. "Akkadisch TAR *berîti* und hebräisch כרת ברית," *VT* 18: 210-15.

Soyez, B. 1972. "Le bétyle dans le culte de l'Astarté phénicienne," *MUSJ* 47: 147-69 (+ pls. I-V).

Sperling, D. 1970. "The Informer and the Conniver," *JANES* 2: 101-4, esp. 104.

Stefanovic, Z. 1992. *The Aramaic of Daniel in the Light of Old Aramaic* (JSOTSup 129; Sheffield, UK: Academic).

Stolz, F. 1970. *Strukturen und Figuren im Kult von Jerusalem* (BZAW

118; Berlin: de Gruyter): 133-37, 149-52.

Swiggers, P. 1983. "The Notation System of Old Aramaic Inscriptions," *ArOr* 51: 378-81.

Tadmor, H. 1961. "Que and Muṣri," *IEJ* 11: 143-50.

------. 1970. "הערות לשורות הפתיחה של החוזה הארמי מספירה" (Notes on the Opening Lines of the Aramaic Treaty of Sefire)," ספר שמואל ייוין: מחקרים במקרא, ארכיאולוגיה, לשון ותולדות ישראל (ed. S. Abramski et al.; Jerusalem: Kiryat Sepher, 1970) 397-405.

------. 1975. "Assyria and the West: The Ninth Century and Its Aftermath," *Unity and Diversity: Essays in the History, Literature, and Religion of the Ancient Near East* (ed. H. Goedicke and J. J. M. Roberts; London/Baltimore: Johns Hopkins University): 36-48, esp. 42-43.

------. 1982. "Treaty and Oath in the Ancient Near East: A Historian's Approach," *Humanizing America's Iconic Book: Society of Biblical Literature Centennial Addresses 1980* (ed. G. M. Tucker and D. A. Knight; Chico, CA: Scholars): 127-52.

------. 1982a. "The Aramaization of Assyria: Aspects of Western Impact," *Mesopotamien und seine Nachbarn: Politische und kulturelle Wechselbeziehungen im alten Vorderasien vom 4. bis 1. Jahrtausend v. Chr.* (XXV. Rencontre assyriologique internationale, Berlin 1978; ed. H.-J. Nissen and J. Renger; BBVO 1/1-2; Berlin: Reimer): 449-70, esp. 455-58.

Tawil, H. 1973. "The End of the Hadad Inscription in the Light of Akkadian," *JNES* 32: 477-82, esp. 478 n. 19.

------. 1977. "A Curse Concerning Crop-Consuming Insects in the Sefîre Treaty and in Akkadian: A New Interpretation," *BASOR* 225: 59-62.

------. 1980. "Two Notes on the Treaty Terminology of the Sefîre Inscriptions," *CBQ* 42: 30-37.

Teixidor, J. 1967. "Bulletin d'épigraphie sémitique," *Syria* 44: 163-95, esp. 165, 178-79;

------. 1968. "Bulletin d'épigraphie sémitique," *Syria* 45: 353-89, esp. 354-55, 377.

Thomas, D. W. 1960. Review of Dupont-Sommer and Starcky, *Inscriptions araméennes*, *JSS* 5: 281-84.

Thompson, J. A. 1965. "Expansions of the *ʿd* Root," *JSS* 10: 222-40.

Timm, S. 1993. "König Hesion II. von Damaskus," *WO* 24: 55-84.

Tsevat, M. 1960. "A Chapter on Old West Semitic Orthography," *The Joshua Bloch Memorial Volume: Studies in Booklore and History* (New York: New York Public Library): 82-91.

Uffenheimer, B. 1977. "*El Elyon*, Creator of Heaven and Earth,"

Shnaton 2: 20-26.
Ussishkin, D. 1971. "Was Bit-Adini a Neo-Hittite or Aramaean State? *Or* 40: 431-37.
Vattioni, F. 1963. "La III iscrizione di Sfiré e Proverbi 1, 23," *AION* 13: 279-86.
------. 1965. "La prima menzione aramaica di ‘figlio dell’uomo,’" *Biblos Press* 6: 6-7.
------. 1966. "A propos du nom propre syriaque Gusai," *Sem* 16: 39-41.
------. 1967. "Recenti studi sull’alleanza nella Bibbia e nell’antico oriente," *AION* 17: 181-226, esp. 202.
------. 1969. "Preliminari alle iscrizioni aramaiche," *Aug* 9: 305-61, esp. 325-28.
Veenhof, K. R. 1963. "An Aramaic Curse with a Sumero-Akkadian Prototype," *BO* 20: 142-44.
Vogt, E. 1958. "Nova inscriptio aramaica saec. 8 a.C.," *Bib* 39: 269-74.
Voigt, R. 1991. "Die sog. Schreibfehler im Altaramäischen und ein bislang unerkannter Lautwandel," *OrSuec* 40: 236-45.
Volkwein, B. 1969. "Masoretisches *‘ēdūt, ‘ēdwōt, ‘ēdōt:* ‘Zeugnis’ oder ‘Bundesbestimmungen’?" *BZ* 13: 18-40.
Vriezen, T. C. 1963. "Das Hiphil von *’amar* in Deut. 26,17. 18," *JEOL* 17: 207-10.
Watanabe, K. 1987. *Die adê-Vereidigung anlässlich der Thronfolgeregelung Asarhaddons* (Baghdader Mitteilungen Beiheft 3; Berlin: Gebr. Mann).
Weinfeld, M. 1965. “Traces of Assyrian Treaty Formulae in Deuteronomy," *Bib* 46: 417-27.
------. 1970. "The Covenant of Grant in the Old Testament and in the Ancient Near East," *JAOS* 90: 184-203.
------. 1971-72. "Bond and Grace -- Covenantal Expressions in the Bible and the Ancient World: A Common Heritage," *Lešonenu* 36: 85-105.
------. 1972. *Deuteronomy and the Deuteronomic School* (Oxford: Clarendon): 59, 103-10, 124-26, 136-42.
------. 1973. "Covenant Terminology in the Ancient Near East and Its Influence on the West," *JAOS* 93: 190-99.
------. 1973-74. "לעניין מונחי ברית ביונית וברומית (Greek and Roman Covenantal Terms and Their Affinities to the East)," *Lešonenu* 38: 231-37.
------. 1975. "The Loyalty Oath in the Ancient Near East," *UF* 8: 379-414 (= *Shnaton* 1 [1975] 51-88).
------. 1982. "The Counsel of the Elders to Rehoboam and Its Implica-

tions," *Maarav* 3: 27-53, esp. 49.

Weippert, M. 1992. "Die Feldzüge Adadniraris III. nach Syrien: Voraussetzungen, Verlauf, Folgen." *ZDPV* 108: 42-67.

Weisberg, D. B. 1967. *Guild Structure and Political Allegiance in Early Achaemenid Mesopotamia* (New Haven, CT: Yale University): 29-42.

Wesselius, J. W. 1980. "Reste einer Kasusflektion in einigen früharamäischen Dialekten," *AION* 40: 265-68.

------. 1984. "A New Reading in Sfire III, 18," *BO* 41: 589-91.

Willi-Plein, I. 1991. "*Šwb šbwt* -- Eine Wiedererwägung," *ZAH* 4: 55-71

Wiseman, D. J. 1958. "The Vassal-Treaties of Esarhaddon," *Iraq* 20: 1-99; repr. *The Vassal-Treaties of Esarhaddon* (London: British School of Archaeology in Iraq, 1958).

Wittstruck, T. 1978. "The Influence of Treaty Curse Imagery on the Beast Imagery of Daniel 7," *JBL* 97: 100-102.

Zadok, R. 1982. "Notes on the Early History of the Israelites and Judeans in Mesopotamia," *Or* 51: 391-93.

------. 1984. "On the Historical Background of the Sefîre Treaty," *AION* 44: 529-34, with bibliography, 535-38.

------. 1985. "Some Problems in Early Aramean History," *ZDMG* Sup 6: 81-85, esp. 84 n. 9.

STELE I

Three preliminary remarks are necessary for the proper understanding of the text of Sf I. First of all, Dupont-Sommer pointed out a feature of the stele in its present state of preservation that was missed by Ronzevalle and all subsequent scholars who had studied it. The left side of the stele, which is not engraved and quite unfinished, is the result of a cutting of the basalt subsequent to its engraving. This cut accounts for the exaggerated slant and dissymmetrical appearance of the stele on the left side, and for the loss of several letters at the end of each line of face A (recto) and the beginning of each line of face B (verso). Earlier studies of the inscription have generally neglected this constant loss of letters. The end of the inscription was engraved on the right side of the stele, face C. It is quite likely that the left side was also engraved, but is now entirely lost.

Second, the stele as reconstructed stands about 51.5 inches high and reveals that three lines have completely disappeared between the sixteenth on the upper part of Face A and the twenty-third on its lower part. Face A therefore had originally 42 lines. Similarly on face B, the reconstruction permits one to arrive at a total of 45 lines. Instead of using, then, the fairly common method of referring to the upper and lower parts of the faces of the steles by a, b (Aa, Ab, Ba, Bb, Ca, Cb), which was first employed by H. Bauer,[1] Dupont-Sommer has simplified the system, numbering all the lines on each face consecutively.

Third, there are no word-dividers in this text; the words follow one another without any greater breaks between them than between the individual letters. This feature provides for a difference of opinion at times as to the separation of words.[2]

---

1 *AfO* 8 (1932-33) 1-16. For the convenience of the reader who may desire a table comparing the two modes of references, the following is supplied:

Old System	*New System*
Aa 1-16	A 1-16
Ab 1-23	A 20-42
Ba 1-15	B 1-15
Bb 1-25	B 21-45
Ca 1-9	C 1-9
Cb 1-12	C 14-25

2 See A. R. Millard, "'Scriptio continua' in Early Hebrew: Ancient Practice or Modern Surmise?" *JSS* 15 (1970) 2-15, esp. 9 and 13.

The following transcription differs slightly from that of Dupont-Sommer and Starcky; the commentary will offer the justification of details which differ. The *editio princeps* should be consulted for the indication of doubtful letters.

TEXT: Sf I

Face A

1 עדי בר גאיה מלך כתך עם מתעאל בר עתרסמך מלך [ארפד וע]

2 די בני בר גאיה עם בני מתעאל ועדי בני בני בר גא[יה ועקר]

3 ה עם עקר מתעאל בר עתרסמך מלך ארפד ועדי כתך עם [עדי]

4 ארפד ועדי בעלי כתך עם עדי בעלי ארפד ועדי חב[ור]

5 ו עם ארם כלה ועם מצר ועם בנוה זי יסקן באשר[ה] ו[עם מלכי]

6 כל עלי ארם ותחתה ועם כל עלל בית מלך ונ[צבא עם ספרא ז]

7 נה שמו עדיא אלן ועדיא אלן זי גזר בר גא[יה קדם אשר]

8 ומלש וקדם מרדך וזרפנת וקדם נבא ות[שמת וקדם אר ונש]

9 ך וקדם נרגל ולץ וקדם שמש ונר וקדם ס[ן ונכל וק]

10 דם נכר וכדאה וקדם כל אלהי רחבה ואדם [... וקדם הדד זי ח]

11 לב וקדם סבת וקדם אל ועלין וקדם שמי[ן וארק וקדם מצ]

12 לה ומעינן וקדם יום ולילה שהדן כל א[להי כתך ואלהי אר]

13 [פד] פקחו עיניכם לחזיה עדי בר גאיה [עם מתעאל מלך]

14 [ארפד] והן ישקר מתעאל בר עתרסמך מל[ך ארפד לבר גאי]

15 [ה מלך כתך וה]ן ישקר עקר מתעאל [לעקר בר גאיה ...]

TRANSLATION[3]

I. *The Title, Introducing the Contracting Parties*

[1]The treaty of Bar-Ga'yah, king of KTK, with Mati'el, the son of 'Attarsamak, the king [of Arpad; and the trea]ty [2]of the sons of Bar-Ga'yah with the sons of Mati'el; and the treaty of the grandsons of Bar-Ga'[yah and] his [offspring] [3]with the offspring of Mati'el, the son of 'Attarsamak, the king of Arpad; and the treaty of KTK with [the treaty of] [4]Arpad; and the treaty of the lords of KTK with the treaty of the lords of Arpad; and the treaty of Ḥa[bur]u [5]with all Aram and with Miṣr and with his sons who will come after [him], and [with the kings of] [6]all Upper-Aram and Lower-Aram and with all who enter the royal palace.

II. *The Gods Who Are Witnesses to This Treaty*

And the st[ele with t]his [inscription] [7]they have set up (as) this treaty. Now (it is) this treaty which Bar-Ga'[yah] has concluded [in the presence of Asshur] [8]and Mullesh, in the presence of Marduk and Zarpanit, in the presence of Nabu and T[ashmet, in the presence of Ir and Nus]k, [9]in the presence of Nergal and Laṣ, in the presence of Shamash and Nur, in the presence of S[in and Nikkal, in the pre]sence of [10]Nikkar and Kadi'ah, in the presence of all the gods of Raḥbah and *Adam* [. . . in the presence of Hadad of A]leppo, [11]in the presence of Sibitti, in the presence of 'El and 'Elyan, in the presence of Hea[ven and Earth, in the presence of (the) A]byss [12]and (the) Springs, and in the presence of Day and Night -- all the god[s of KTK and the gods of Ar]pad (are) witnesses (to it). [13]Open your eyes, (O gods!), to gaze upon the treaty of Bar-Ga'yah [with Mati'el, the king of [14]Arpad].

III. *Curses against Mati'el, if He Violates the Treaty*

Now if Mati'el, the son of 'Attarsamak, the kin[g of Arpad,] should prove unfaithful [to Bar-Ga'yah, the [15]king of KTK, and i]f the offspring of Mati'el should prove unfaithful [to the offpsring of Bar-Ga'yah ...]

---

3 Italics indicate uncertain renderings. Words enclosed in parentheses have been inserted for the sake of the English idiom. Square brackets [ ] indicate editorial restorations of lacunae; angular < > indicate editorial additions to the text.

16 [...והן ישקרן בני] גש כ..[ ]

17 [ ]

18 [ ]

19 [ ]

20 [ ]מן ימ[ ]

21 [.............] שאת ואל תהרי ושבע [מהי]נקן ימשח[ן שדיהן ו]

22 יהינקן עלים ואל ישבע ושבע ססיה יהינקן על ואל יש[בע ושבע]

23 שורה יהינקן עגל ואל ישבע ושבע שאן יהינקן אמר ו[אל יש]

24 בע ושבע בכתה יהכן בשט לחם ואל יהרגן והן ישקר מתע[אל ול]

25 ברה ולעקרהה תהוי מלכתה כמלכת חל מלכת חל מזי ימלך אשר [יסך ה]

26 דד כל מה לחיה בארק ובשמין וכל מה עמל ויסך על ארפד [אבני ב]

27 רד ושבע שנן יאכל ארבה ושבע שנן תאכל תולעה ושבע [שנן יס]

28 ק תוי על אפי ארקה ואל יפק חצר וליתחזה ירק ולי[תחזה]

29 אחוה ואל יתשמע קל כנר בארפד ובעמה המל מרק והמ[ית צע]

30 קה ויללה וישלחן אלהן מן כל מה אכל בארפד ובעמה [יאכל פ]

31 ם חוה ופם עקרב ופם דבהה ופם נמרה וסס וקמל וא[.. יהוו]

32 עלה קק בתן [יש]תחט לישמן אחוה ותהוי ארפד תל ל[רבק צי ו]

[16][... and if the Benê-]Gush should be unfaithful ....] [20][...]from YM[..........] [21][..... and should seven rams cover] a ewe, may she not conceive; and should seven nurses] anoint [their breasts and] [22]nurse a young boy, may he not have his fill; and should seven mares suckle a colt, may it not be sa[ted; and should seven] [23]cows give suck to a calf, may it not have its fill; and should seven ewes suckle a lamb, [may it not be sa]ted; [24]and should seven *hens* go looking for food, may then not *kill* (anything)! And if Mati['el] should be unfaithful <to Bar-Ga'yah> [and to] [25]his son and to his offspring, may his kingdom become like a kingdom of sand, a kingdom of sand, as long as *Asshur* rules! (And) [may Ha]dad [pour (over it) [26]every sort of evil (which exists) on earth and in heaven and every sort of trouble; and may he shower upon Arpad [ha]il-[stones]! [27]For seven years may the locust devour (Arpad), and for seven years may the worm eat, and for seven [years may] [28]TWY come up upon the face of its land! May the grass not come forth so that no green may be seen; and may its [29]vegetation not be [seen]! Nor may the sound of the lyre be heard in Arpad; but among its people (let there rather be) the din of *affliction* and *the noi[se of cry]ing* [30]and lamentation! May the gods send every sort of devourer against Arpad and against its people! [May the mou]th [31]of a snake [eat], the mouth of a scorpion, the mouth of *a bear*, the mouth of a panther And may a moth and a louse and a [... become] [32]to it a serpent's throat! May its vegetation be destroyed unto desolation! And may Arpad become a mound to [house the desert animal]

33 צבי ושעל וארנב ושרן וצדה ו.. ועקה ואל תאמר קר[יתא הא ו]

34 מדרא ומרבה ומזה ומבלה ושרן ותואם וביתאל ובינן ו[.... וא]

35 רנה וחזז ואדם איך זי תקד שעותא זא באש כן תקד ארפד ו[בנתה ר]

36 בת ויזרע בהן הדד מלח ושחלין ואל תאמר גנבא זנה ו[נבשא זא]

37 מתעאל ובנשה הא איכה זי תקד שעותא זא באש כן יקד מ[תעאל בא]

38 ש ואיך זי תשבר קשתא וחציא אלן כן ישבר אנרת והדד [קשת מתעאל]

39 וקשת רבוה ואיך זי יער גבר שעותא כן יער מתעא[ל ואיך ז]

40 [י] יגזר עגלא זנה כן יגזר מתעאל ויגזרן רבוה [ואיך זי תע]

41 [רר ז]נ[יה] כן יעררן נשי מתעאל ונשי עקרה ונשי ר]בוה ואיך ז]

42 [י תקד גברת שעותא זא] וימחא על אפיה כן יקחן [נשי מתעאל ו]

Face B

1 [רסמך מלך אר]פד ועדי בני בר גאיה עם בני מתעאל ועדי [ב]

2 [ני בני בר] גאיה עם עקר מתעאל ועם עקר כל מה מלך זי

3 [יסק וימלך] באשרה ועם בני גש ועם בית צלל ועם אר

4 [ם כלה ועד]י כתך עם עדי ארפד ועדי בעלי כתך עם ע

5 די בעלי א]רפד ועם עמה ועדי אלהי כתך עם עדי א

6 [להי ארפד]עדי אלהן הם זי שמו אלהן טבי מלך

[33]the gazelle and the fox and the hare and the wild-cat and the owl and the [ ] and the magpie! May [this] ci[ty] not be mentioned (any more), [nor] [34]MDR' nor MRBH nor MZH nor MNLH nor Sharun nor Tu'im nor Bethel nor BYNN nor [... nor Ar]neh [35]nor Ḥazaz nor Adam!

IV. *Curses with Accompanying Rites*

Just as this wax is burned by fire, so may Arpad be burned and [her gr]eat [daughter-cities]! [36]May Hadad sow in them salt and *weeds*, and may it not be mentioned (again)! This GNB' and [ ] [37](are) Mati'el; it is his person. Just as this wax is burned by fire, so may Mati['el be burned by fi]re! [38]Just as (this) bow and these arrows are broken, so may Inurta and Hadad break [the bow of Mati'el], [39]and the bow of his nobles! And just as the man of wax is blinded, so may Mati['el] be blinded! [Just as] [40]this calf is cut in two, so may Mati'el be cut in two, and may his nobles be cut in two! [And just as] [41]a [har]lot is stripped naked], so may the wives of Mati'el be stripped naked, and the wives of his offspring, and the wives of [his] no[bles! And just as [42]this wax woman is taken] and one strikes her on the face, so may the [wives of Mati'el] be taken [and]

Face B

V. *The Sacred Character of the Treaty*

[The treaty of Bar-Ga'yah, king of KTK, with Mati'el, son of 'Attarsamak, [1]the king of Ar]pad; and the treaty of the son of Bar-Ga'yah with the sons of Mati'el; and the treaty of the [grandsons of [2]Bar-]Ga'yah with the offspring of Mati'el and with the offspring of any king who [3][will come up and rule] in his place, and with the Benê-Gush and with Bêt-ṢLL and with [4][all] Ar[am; and the trea]ty of KTK with the treaty of Arpad; and the treaty of the lords of KTK with the trea[ty [5]of the lords of Ar]pad and with its people. The treaty of the gods of KTK with the treaty of the g[ods [6]of Arpad]. This is the treaty of gods, which gods have concluded. *Blessed* forever *be the reign of*

7 [בר גאיה לעל]מן מלך רב ומע[די]א אל[ן ...]ושמין ועדיא

8 [אלן כל אלהיא] יצרן ואל תשתק חדה מן מלי ספרא זנ

9 [ה ויתשמען מן] ערקו ועד יאד[י ו]בז מן לבנן ועד יב

10 [רדו ומן דשמ]ק ועד ערו ומ..ו [ומ]ן בקעת ועד כתך

11 [..........ב]ית גש ועמה עם אשרתהם עדיא אל

12 [ן ....]יתה השכ.הוא.. במצר ומרבה

13 [............].. דש ......תם למתעאל בר

14 [עתרסמך ....].ו......למ... ירב[.]

15 [....................]...ע.ש...[........]

16 [ ]

17 [ ]

18 [ ]

19 [ ]

20 [ ]

21 [.......] לביתכם ולישמע מתעאל [ולישמען בנוה ולישמע עמ]

22 [ה ולישמע]ן כל מלכיא זי ימלכן בארפד ל.[............]

23 [.....]..למנין שקרתם לכל אלהי עדיא ז[י בספרא זנה והן]

[7][Bar-Ga'yah], a great king, and *from* this happy treaty [ ] and heaven. [8][And all the gods] shall guard [this] treaty. Let not one of the words of thi[s] inscription be silent, [9][but let them be heard from] *'Arqu* to Ya'd[i and] BZ, from Lebanon to Yabrud, [10]from Damascu]s to *'Aru* and M..W, [and fr]om the Valley to KTK [11][..... in Bê]t-Gush and its people with their *sanctuary*, this treaty [12][.. ....]YTH HŠK.HW'.. in MṢR and MRBH [13][......] DŠ.....TM to Mati'el, son [of 'Attarsamak ....]

(A few letters are legible on lines 14-15; lines 16-20 are missing.)

VI. *The Stipulations of the Treaty*

[21][. . . .] to your house. And (if) Mati'el will not obey [and (if) his sons will not obey, and (if) his people will not o]bey, [22]and (if) all the kings who will rule in Arpad [will not obey] the .[ ] [23][ ]. .LMNYN, you will have been unfaithful to all the gods of the treaty whi[ch is in this inscription. But if]

24 [תשמען ותש]לם עדיא אלן ותאמר גבר עדן הא [אנה לאכהל לא]

25 [שלח יד] בך וליכהל ברי [ל]ישלח יד בבר[ך] ועקרי בעק[רך והן מ]

26 [לה ימלל] עלי חד מלכן או חד שנאי ותאמר ל[כל] מה מלך מה ת[עבד
ויש]

27 [לח יד ב]ברי ויקתלנה וישלח ידה ויקח מן ארקי או מן מקני ש[ק]

28 [רת בעד]יא זי בספרא זנה והן יאתה חד מלכן ויסבנ<י> יאתה ח[ילך]

29 [אלי עם] כל [בעל] חציא וכל מה פ..ך ותקף יקפי ותנתע לי ה[....]

30 [.....]. ופגר ארבא מעל פגר באר[פ]ד ... מן חד מלך לאוין ומות

31 [.....]ם והן ביום זי אלהן ..... מרחיא לתאתה בחילך וא

32 [תם לתא]תון בחילכם לשגב ב[י]תי [והן עק]ר[ך ל]יאתה לשגב אית עקר

33 [י שקרת ל]אלהי עדיא זי בספרא זנה וחב... יעפן עמי ואכהל מי

34 [ביר ....]ל ובירא [ה]א כל זי יסב ליכ[הל ל]פרק ולמשלח יד במי בי

35 [רא ומלכ]א זי יעל וילקח לבכה או ח...... זי ילקח .... בעה .

36 [..... ל]אבדת אנגדה ..מלהם ..מ..כד בקרית אימאם והן להן שק

37 [רת ... ז]נה והן ..ק. לי ...לאכ.ל... להמי .י.בשא תשלח..א.

38 [......]ם והן לתהב לחמי ...[.]שא לי לחם ולתסך שקרת בעדיא אלן

39 [ואת לתכ]הל לתשא לחם אנח כאים יקם לך ותבעה נבשך ותאזל .

[24][you obey and car]ry out this treaty and say, "[I] am an ally," [I shall not be able [25]to raise a hand] against you; nor will my son be able to raise a hand against [your] son, or my offspring against [your] off-[spring. And if] [26]one of (the) kings [should speak a word] against me or one of my enemies (should so speak) and you say to any king, "What are you [going to do?" and he [27]should raise a hand against] my son and kill him and raise his hand to take some of my land or some of my possessions, you will have been unfaith[ful to [28]the trea]ty which is in this inscription. If one of (the) kings comes and surrounds <me>, [your] ar[my] must come [29][to me with every arch[er] and every sort [of weapon], and you must *surround those who surround me* and you must *draw* for me [.... [30]....] and *I shall pile* corpse upon corpse in Ar[pad] ... some king L'WYN WMWT [31][. ...] and if on a day when (the) gods [....] *the rebels*, you (sg.) do not come with your army and (if) [32][you (pl.) do not] come with your (pl.) armies to strengthen my ho[u]se and [if your] off[spring does not] come to strengthen [my] offspring, [33][you will have been unfaithful to] the gods of the treaty which is in this inscription. And (when) [...] Y PN with me, I shall be able [to drink] water [34][of the well of ...]L; whoever *lives around* that well shall not be able to *destroy* (it) or raise a hand against the water of [the] wel[l]. [35][And the king] who will enter and take LBKH or Ḥ......, who will take ... B'H. [36][..... to] destroy 'NGD' .. MLHM .. M .. KD in the town of 'YM'M. And if (you do) not (do) so, you will have been unfaith[ful] [37][to the treaty] <which is in> this <inscription>. And if ..Q. LY ... L'K.L ... LHMY .Y.NŠ', you shall send ..'. [38][... ...]M, and if you do not give (me) my provisions, [or] deduct provisions from me, and do not deliver (them), you will have been unfaithful to this treaty. [39][... You can[not] deduct provisions 'NḤ K'YM YQM LK, and you yourself will seek and will go .

40 [... לקרי]תך ולביתך ינ.. זר א.. לנבשי [ולכ]ל נבש ביתי ולט

41 [........]בה ברך וליגז[רן מ]לה מלכי א[רפד] מנהם זי עדן חי

42 [ן הם ......]ה .... טלל הא וסח הא ובל הא נתרחם לנבשך אם.

43 [........]..........כע.. עמך כן תגזר אפלא והן ......

44 [........] נק.... יעזז קלבת ביתי על ...ל .ח.אי אקל

45 [........]..[על] ברי או על חד סרסי ויקרק חדהם ויאת[ה ...]

Face C

1 כה אמרן [וכה כ]תבן מה

2 כתבת א[נה מתע]אל לזכ

3 רן לברי [ולבר] ברי ז

4 י יסקן ב[אשר]י לטבת

5 [א] יעבד[ו תחת] שמשא

6 [לב]ית מ[לכי ז]י כל לח

7 [יה לתתעבד על] בית מ

8 [תעאל וברה ובר] ברה ע[ד]

9 [עלם ....].ו.[..]

10 [ ]

[40][to] your [cit]y and to your house YN.. ZR'.. for myself [and for eve]ry person of my household and for Ṭ [41][........]*in it your son*; and the kings of Ar[pad] will not cu[t any]thing off from them because *it is a living pact*. [42][...... ..] H.... ṬLL H' WSḤ H' WBL H' NTRḤM for yourself 'M. [43][.......] .... K'.. with you; so you will cut the 'PL'. And if ..... [44][......] NQ.... he will strengthen the QLBT of my house against . . . L.Ḥ.'Y 'QL.... [45][.......].. [against] my son or against one of my courtiers; and (if) one of them flees and com[es ....]

Face C

[1]Thus have we spoken [and thus have we writ]ten. What [2]I, [Mati'‘]el, have written (is to serve) as a reminder [3]for my son [and] my [grand]son who [4]will come a[fter] me. May they [5]make good relations [beneath] the sun [6][for (the sake of) my] ro[yal hou]se that no ev[il may [7]be done against] the house of Mat[i'el [8]and his son and] his [grand]son for[9][ever].

11 [ ]

12 [ ]

13 [ ]

14 ...מ [.........]

15 יצרו אלהן מן יו

16 מה ומן ביתה ומן

17 ליצר מלי ספרא זי בנצבא זנה

18 ויאמר אהלד מן מלו

19 ה או אהפך טבתא ואשם

20 [ל]לחית ביום זי יעב

21 [ד] כן יהפכו אלהן אש

22 [א ה]א וביתה וכל זי [ב]

23 ה וישמו תחתיתה [ל]

24 [ע]ליתה ואל ירת שר

25 [ש]ה אשם

VIII. *Blessings*

. . . . [15]may (the) gods keep [all evils] away from his day [16]and from his house.

IX. *Curses*

Whoever [17]will not observe the words of the inscription which is on this stele [18]or will say, "I shall efface some of its words," [19]or "I shall upset the good treaty-relations and turn (them) [20][to] evil," on any day on which he will d[o] [21]so, may the gods overturn [22]th[at m]an and his house and all that (is) in [23]it. May they make its lower part [24]its upper part! May his sci[on] inherit no name!

COMMENTARY

Face A

1. עדי: "The treaty of." The word is the construct of a noun, used only in the plural, meaning "treaty-stipulations," the things to which a vassal swears an oath. It occurs in Old Aramaic only in these inscriptions. In a generic sense it refers to the treaty or pact as a whole; so it is to be understood at this first occurrence. Only the emph. pl. of this noun (עדיא) is found in Sf III (4, 7, 9, [14], 17, 19, 20, 23, 27), but here one finds the cst. pl. (as in I A 1bis, 2, 3, [3], 4ter, 13; I B 1bis, 4bis, [4bis], 5bis, 6); the emph. pl. (in I A 7bis, I B 7, [7], 11, 23, 24, [28], 33, 38; II B 2, [9], [14], [18]; II C [13]); even the abs. pl. (עדן, in I B 24, 41; II B [5]).

The meaning of this word is certain, for it is related to the Akkadian word *adē*, which is always used in the plural in the same sense.[1] D. J. Wiseman published *The Vassal-Treaties of Esarhaddon* (1958), in which one finds *adē* (always plural) used in the sense of "treaty-terms" or "vassal-treaty stipulations" imposed by the king on his vassals to insure their loyalty to his heirs, Aššurbanipal of Assyria and Šamaššumukin of Babylonia.[2] The fuller Akkadian expression was *adē mamîti*. It is often translated as loyalty oath (I. J. Gelb, *BO* 19 [1962] 162);[3] J. D. Hawkins, "Neo-Hittite States," 407). For B. Frankena (*OTS* 14 [1965] 134-36) *adē* is the specific Akkadian term for a vassal treaty.

The form *adē* is also found in the Akkadian text of the treaty between Aššurnirari V and Mati'ilu (1.13; 4.17-18). Compare the similar beginning of the very fragmentary treaty of Esarhaddon with Baal of Tyre (E. F. Weidner, *AfO* 8 [1932-33] 31), and his vassal treaties (11.1-6). According to W. von Soden (*AHW*, 14), *adē* occurs in middle and new Assyrian, middle and late Babylonian texts. This

---

1 This relation was first proposed by R. Dussaud, *CRAIBL* 1931, 312-21.

2 "Although the general term 'treaty' has been used here for convenience (see p. 3), the more exact meaning is of a law or commandment solemnly imposed in the presence of divine witnesses by a suzerain upon an individual or people who have no option but acceptance of the terms. It implies a 'solemn charge or undertaking on an oath' (according to the view of the suzerain or vassal)" (p. 81).

3 Gelb's conclusion, "From the above examples, and many others . . . , it is clear that *adê* (in plural) or *adû* (in singular) is a pact or agreement imposed by one party upon another and sworn to by the obligated party only. It is not a pact between equals."

affects the decision one must make about the character of these Aramaic treaty-texts. Cf. Noth, *ZDPV* 77 (1961) 139; also *CAD* A, 131-34; K. Deller, *WZKM* 57 (1961) 1-33. In Sf I and Sf III treaty stipulations are preserved; but עדי in Aramaic is scarcely to be restricted to them. It seems to have the wider meaning, "treaty," as can be seen in the expression אלהי עדיא זי בספרא זנה, "the gods of the treaty which is in this inscription."

Actually Akkadian *adē* is a loanword from Aramaic.[4] The failure to recognize this skews Gibson's discussion of the word (*TSSI* 2. 34; see J. C. Greenfield, *IEJ* 28 [1978] 289). More recently Greenfield has suggested that it may even be a loanword in Aramaic from Canaanite, related to the Hebrew root עוד, "see, witness" (*Maarav* 7 [1991] 142).[5] J. Cantineau ("Remarques," 168) related Aramaic עדי to Hebrew עֵדוּת and עֵד, Arabic *wa'ada*, "promise." Since the full publication of the Sefire texts, many others have related the Aramaic word to these and similar OT words.[6] In Isa 33:8 one should probably read *'dym* (instead of *'rym*) in the sense of "treaty," as in this inscription; cf. 1QIsa[a] 27:8.[7]

The use of Aramaic עדי apparently involves the same semantic shift that takes place in Greek ὅρκια τέμνειν, "make a covenant," e.g.

---

4 See H. Tadmor, "The Aramaization of Assyria" [1982a], 456-58. Cf. W. von Soden, "Aramäische Wörter in neuassyrischen und in neu- und spätbabylonischen Texten: Ein Vorbericht: I (*agâ* -- **m*)," *Or* 35 (1966) 1-20; "II (*n* -- *z* und Nachträge)," 37 (1968) 261-71.

5 See also S. A. Kaufman, *Akkadian Influences*, 33.

6 See J. A. Thompson, "Expansions of the *'d* Root," *JSS* 10 (1965) 222-40; F. Vattioni, "Recenti studi sull'alleanza nella Bibbia e nell'antico oriente," *AION* 17 (1967) 181-226; F. O. García Treto, "Genesis 31,44 and Gilead," *ZAW* 79 (1967) 13-17; B. Volkwein, "Masoretisches *'ēdūt, 'ēdwōt, 'ēdōt* -- 'Zeugnis' oder 'Bundesbestimmungen'?" *BZ* 13 (1969) 8-40; M. Parnas, "*'ēdūt, 'ēdōt, 'ēdwōt* in the Bible, against the Background of Ancient Near Eastern Documents," *Shnaton* 1 (1975) 235-46; M. Weinfeld, "*B*[e]*rît* -- Covenant vs. Obligation," *Bib* 56 (1975) 119-28 (actually a review of E. Kutsch, *Verheissung und Gesetz: Untersuchungen zum sogenannten 'Bund' im Alten Testament* [BZAW 131; Berlin: de Gruyter, 1973]); Lemaire-Durand, *IAS*, 91-106; N. Lohfink, "*'d(w)t* im Deuteronomium und in den Königsbüchern," *BZ* 35 (1991) 86-93.

Even earlier Hempel-Bauer (*ZAW* 50 [1932] 178) had related *adē* to *gl'd* of Gen 31:48 and (hesitatingly) to *'d* of Exod 22:12.

Compare B. Couroyer, "*'Édût*: Stipulation de traité ou enseignement?" *RB* 95 (1988) 321-31.

7 Cf. D. R. Hillers, "A Hebrew Cognate of *unuššu/unṯ* in Is. 33:8," *HTR* 64 (1971) 257-59.

Homer, *Il.* 2. 124; *Od.* 24. 483; note the plural of ὅρκιον, "oath."[8] These considerations must prevail in relating the Aramaic עדיא to the Assyrian *adē*, even over the consideration that one would normally expect the *a*-vowel to shift in Akkadian to *e* because of the *'ayin* (e.g. ערב and Akkadian *erēbu*). The lack of such a shift is the best indication of a loanword (cf. Akkadian *adi* and Hebrew-Aramaic *'ad*; Akkadian *aqrabu* and Hebrew *'aqrāb*). A greater difficulty comes from the fact that *adē* is apparently a tertiae infirmae root in Akkadian, whereas עדן עדיא, עדי, in Aramaic apparently do not reflect such a root. But Akkadian may well have secondarily adapted *adē* to the tertiae infirmae system. But in any case, the term עדי as used here reveals the influence of the Assyrian political order on this Aramean kingdom. If the word itself is borrowed from Aramaic into Akkadian, the institution that it represents is Assyrian.

בר גאיה: Or possibly ברגאיה, a one-word name, "Bar-Ga'yah," which means "Son of Majesty." The second element was related to Hebrew גאוה and Syriac *ga'yūtā'* by Cantineau ("Remarques," 178). Bauer (*AfO* 8 [1932-33] 3) compared it to the name-types, Benjamin and Bar-Ṣur. The name should possibly be vocalized *Bir-Ga'yah*, since Aramean names of the Assyrian period with the *br* element are transcribed thus in Akkadian documents: e.g., *Bir-Atar, Bir-Ḫanu, Bir-Ram(m)ān, Bir-Šamaš* (see W. F. Albright, "The Name of Bildad the Shuhite," *AJSL* 44 [1927] 33). On the use of the patronymic alone as a personal name, see A. Alt, "Menschen ohne Namen," *ArOr* 18 (1950) 9-24.

Bar-Ga'yah is otherwise unknown. Since no name of his father is given and the symbolic name may suggest a throne-name, Bar-Ga'yah may have been a usurper (M. Noth, *ZDPV* 77 [1961] 145).[9] But if so, he would scarcely be the partner of Sf III who speaks of his father and his father's house (line 24). Yet *Bar-Ga'yah* must be assumed to be a *Deckname* or a dynastic name. It is hardly a name for the king of Assyria himself; nor could KTK be a code-name for his capital. According to Dupont-Sommer, it is a symbolic name for Sardur III of Urartu, who formed a coalition against Assyria. But it is a genuine Aramean name. So he is probably an Aramean ruler more powerful than Mati'el and king of some city-state in upper Mesopotamia. Malamat and Lemaire-Durand (*IAS*, 37-58) have identified Bar-Ga'yah as Šamši-ilu,

8 See J. F. Priest, "ὅρκια in the *Iliad* and Consideration of Recent Theory," *JNES* 23 (1964) 48-56.

9 Cf. D. J. A. Clines, "X, X *ben* Y, *ben* Y: Personal Names in Hebrew Narrative Style," *VT* 22 (1972) 266-87, esp. 282.

the *turtān*[10] of Assyria, who was a prominent general of the Assyrian armies in the earlier eighth century, in charge of the area called in Assyrian texts *Bīt-Adini*.[11] This is certainly the best proposal made so far, despite their failure to explain KTK properly.

Despite the superficial similarity there is probably no connection between this personal name and the place name *Bīt-Bagaya*, mentioned in a sculpture depicting Sargon's campaigns (see J. E. Reade. "Sargon's Campaigns of 720, 716, and 715 B.C.: Evidence from the Sculptures," *JNES* 35 [1976] 95-104, esp. 103). Cf. *ARAB* 2. 57. The name *Bargai/oi* turns up on a Greek inscription from Palmyra (§48); cf. R. du Mesnil du Buisson, *Inventaire des inscriptions palmyréniennes de Doura-Europos* (Paris: Geuthner, 1939) 60.

מלך: "King of." This use of מלך does not stand in the way of identifying Bar-Ga'yah with a person who is actually a *turtān*, because הדיסעי, who was *šakin māti* [uru]*gu-za-ni* according to the Assyrian form of Fekheriyeh (line 8), calls himself מלך גוזן according to the Aramaic form (line 6; see also line 13). Cf. Isa 10:8, "Are not my commanders all kings?" See Lemaire-Durand, *IAS*, 43-47.

כתך: The name of Bar-Ga'yah's land has been problematic. For various proposed identifications and their relevance, see below. In Sf I A 4, B 4 the phrase בעלי כתך suggests that כתך is a city like Arpad.

מתעאל: "Mati'el," actually *Matī''ēl*. The vassal is the ruler of Arpad, who is the same as *Mati'ilu* (written *ma-ti-'-AN*) of the treaty of Aššurnirari V (754-745) of Assyria (see E. F. Weidner, *AfO* 8 [1932-33] 17-34; *ARAB,* 1.§750-60; M. Noth, *ZDPV* 77 [1961] 127). In this treaty Mati'ilu lacks a title. The campaign of the Assyrian king against him is usually judged to have taken place "im Regierungsantrittsjahre," i.e. 754. He there appears to be a princeling in Syria somewhere between the Euphrates and the Mediterranean, north of Aleppo, in the area called by the Assyrians *Bit-Agūsi* (after the founder of the dynasty). See S. Schiffer, *Die Aramäer* (Leipzig: Hinrichs, 1911) 90 n. 6; 137 n. 9. His capital was Arpad (see E. F. Weidner, *AfO* 15 [1945-51] 101), but he must have exercised control over a considerable number of lesser towns, as appears from this Aramaic treaty. Weidner suggested that Mati'ilu must have soon forgotten his treaty with Aššurnirari and, perhaps under threats from Sardur of Urartu, joined the latter against Assyria. Tiglathpileser III put an end to this alliance, when Arpad

10 The name means "one who is second in command" or "Mann an 2. Stelle" (*AHW* 3. 1332). The Aramaic equivalent would be תנין (= *tinyān*), now found in pap4QTob[a] ar 2:8.

11 See Thureau-Dangin, F. and M. Dunand. 1936. *Til-Barsib*, 141-51.

finally fell to him after a four-year siege. Mati'ilu is mentioned several times in the Annals of Tiglathpileser III (see *ARAB,* 1. §769, 785, 813; cf. P. Rost, *Die Keilschrifttexte Tiglat-Pilesers III.* [Leipzig: Pfeiffer, 1893], Annals, line 60: *Ma-t-'-ilu mar a-gu-us-si*).

The name מתעאל also belonged to a Dedanite king of the sixth century BC (W. F. Albright, "Dedan," *Geschichte und Altes Testament* [BHT 16; Tübingen: Mohr (Siebeck), 1953] 6). It is also found on the Nimrud Bronze Sceptre head: *lmt''l* (R. D. Barnett, "Layard's Nimrud Bronzes," 1*-7*; cf. F. Vattioni, "Frustula epigraphica," *Aug* 9 [1960] 368); also in a Nabatean inscription (N. Glueck, *Deities and Dolphins* [New York: Farrar, Straus and Giroux, 1965] 436).

Bauer noted that in South Arabic the root *mt'* occurs in the meaning, "to save, protect," and he explained the name as meaning "Gott behütet." The name occurs again in a Nabatean inscription published by J. T. Milik (*Syria* 35 [1958] 238) in the form מתעאל, which together with the Assyrian evidence would suggest the vocalization *Matî''ēl* or *Matî''īl*, "protected by 'El" (a *qatīl* type, a passive ptc.). Cf. Hebrew ברוך יהוה (Gen 24:31; 14:20); see D. N. Freedman, *VT* 4 (1954) 192. Compare the name מתעהדד on a deed of sale (BM 123369); see A. R. Millard, "Some Aramaic Epigraphs," *Iraq* 34 (1972) 131-38, esp. 134.

עתרסמך: Mati'el's father's name is "'Attarsamak," an Aramaic form of the Akkadian *Ataršumki*. Some might prefer to vocalize the Aramaic form as 'Attaršumk.[12] It is a compound of the theophoric element *'tr* (the assimilated form of *'Aṯtar* = Akkadian *Ištar*, Hebrew *'aštōret*, Ugaritic *'ṯtrt*) and *smk*: "Athtar has lent support." Cf. the names of similar formation: in Hebrew, אחיסמך (Exod 31:6; 35:34; 38:23); סמכיהו (1 Chr 26:7); יסמכיהו (2 Chr 31:13); in Aramaic, אלסמך (TZerB; LurBr 2); סמכי (*AP* 49:1); עתרעזר (*CIS* 2. 52; Nimrud Bronze Sceptre Head [BM 12179], in ErIsr 8. 1*-7*); in Akkadian, *Atar-idri*, *Atar-bi'di*, *Attar-nūri*, *Attar-ramat*. The name 'Attarsamak is otherwise known from a seal that reads, "Belonging to Nurši, servant of 'Attarsamak," whose reign is usually dated 805-796 (see P. Bordreuil, *Lettre de Jérusalem* 60 [1985] 9). Cf. E. Lipiński, *Studies*, 58-76.

On *'Aṯtar* as the name of a god, see M. J. Dahood, "Ancient Semitic Deities in Syria and Palestine," in S. Moscati (ed.), *Le antiche divinità semitiche* (Studi semitici 1; Roma: Università di Roma, 1958) 85-90; G. Garbini, "'Atar dio aramaico?" *RSO* 35 (1960) 25-28; "Sul nome Athtar/Ashtar," *AION* 34 (1974) 409-10; Caquot, *Syria* 35 (1958) 45-60; Fitzmyer, *JAOS* 86 (1966) 287-88; Vattioni, "Frustula

12 Compare Lipiński, "'Attar-sumki and Related Names," *Studies*, 58-76; also J. D. Hawkins, "Jaḫan," *RLA* 5. 238-39.

epigraphica," *Aug* 9 (1969) 367; Teixidor, "Bulletin d'épigraphie sémitique, 1969," *Syria* 46 (1969) 319-58, esp. 328.

[ארפד וע]די: Dupont-Sommer has shown that six letters have been lost at the end of this line because of the shaving off of the left side of the stele. The restoration of ארפד is certain; see Sf I A 3; B 1.

Arpad, over which Mati'el reigned, was the capital of a small Aramean kingdom or city-state in northern Syria. In Assyrian texts of the ninth and eighth centuries BC the kingdom was called Bīt-Agūsi or Bīt Gūsi in the land of Yaḫan (see note on Sf I A 16; also E. F. Weidner, *AfO* 8 [1932-331 17-26). The same title, apparently a designation of the ruling dynasty, appears in Aramaic form in the fragmentary passages of Sf II B 10 and I B [11], as בית גש. The inhabitants of the area are called בני גש (Sf I B 3; I A [16]). A predecessor of Mati'el is cryptically referred to as בר גש among the kings allied with Bar-Hadad, the son of Haza'el, who leagued together against Zakur, king of Hamath and Lu'ash (Zakur a 5). The title in the latter place is scarcely that of the king who gave his name to the dynasty, because the Zakur stele dates from roughly 780, whereas Bīt Agūsi was already in existence in the preceding century. The capital of this Aramean state was Arpad, the town mentioned in the OT (2 Kgs 18:34; 19:13; Isa 10:9; 36:19; 37:13; Jer 49:23). It is the *Arpaddu* of Assyrian texts, apparently first mentioned in 806 as the goal of a campaign of Adadnirari III; after that it occurs often (see O. A. Toffteen, *AJSL* 21 [1904-5] 86; E. Honigmann, "Arpad," *RLA* 1. 153; A. R. Millard and H. Tadmor, "Adad-nirari III in Syria: Another Stele Fragment and the Dates of His Campaigns," *Iraq* 35 (1973) 57-64, esp. 58-59 (BM 131124, line 5: ^{m}*A-tar-šum-k[i] [*^{uru}*Arpaddāya u šarrani*^{meš}*].*^{ni} *šá māt [ḫat]-ti ša i-si-ḫu-[m]a*, "Ataršumki, [the Arpadite and the kings] of the land of [Ḫat]ti, who had rebelle[d]"); A. R. Millard, "Adad-nirari III, Aram, and Arpad," *PEQ* 105 (1973) 161-64. Situated about 30 km. north of Aleppo, it is identified with modern Tell Refâd (see P. K. Hitti, *History of Syria* [London: Macmillan, 1951] 140 n. 4; R. Dussaud, *Topographie historique de la Syrie antique* [Paris: Geuthner, 1927], p. 468; *KAI*, 2. 243).

Being the capital of a small kingdom, it was often the victim of subjugation by powerful neighbors. During the ninth century Arpad was dominated by Assyria, but in the early part of the eighth century, as Assyria's power declined, Arpad seems to have achieved some independence. We know little of its history in this period, not even whether 'Attarsamak, the father of Mati'el, was actually king just before him. Some earlier king, as mentioned above, was indeed the ally of Bar-Hadad ca. 780. Probably in the year 754-53 Mati'el had to conclude a pact with Adadnirari V, who made a feeble attempt to assert Assyrian domination in the west. Mati'el swore fealty to the Assyrian overlord in a pact, the stipulations of which were not very demanding (see E. F. Weidner, *AfO* 8 [1932-33] 17-26). But at some time during the first part of the eighth century other influence was exerted on Arpad. From about 900 on Urartu had been gradually growing into a powerful kingdom, centered about Lake Van; it profited from the weakness of Assyria at the beginning of the eighth century. About 750, the king of Urartu, Sardur III, son of Argišti I, conquered many city-states to the west of the Euphrates, from Gurgum, Melidh (Melitene), and Kummuḫ (Commagene) to northern Syria. In the latter area he subjugated Ḫalpa (Aleppo), a town to the south of Arpad (cf. the Van Stele, E, lines 40ff.). See A. Goetze, *Kleinasien* (Handbuch der Altertumswissenschaft III/1: 3.3,1; Munich: Beck, 1957) 192. Sardur III thus managed to cut off Assyrian power from Asia Minor and the Mediterranean coastlands. Mati'el, the king of Arpad, apparently broke his pact with Assyria and joined a coalition with Sardur III ca. 743. For Tiglathpileser III records in his third regnal year: "Sardur of Urartu revolted against me and joined Mati'ilu" (*Annals*, line 59; ed. P. Rost, p. 12, cf. *ARAB*, 1 § 769, 785, 813).

Tiglathpileser III, who had come to the Assyrian throne after a revolt in Kalaḫ ca. 745, strove to restore the Assyrian hegemony. After some activity in the area of Babylon he turned to Urartu and Syria. He records the defeat of Sardur at Kištan and Ḫalpi in Kummuḫ on the west bank of the Euphrates. This was the year 743, and Sardur fled to Urartu. Tiglathpileser turned to Syria, subjugating Arpad, 'Umq, and Ya'di. The Eponym List (Cb I) for the year 743 records: "In the city of Arpad: the army of Urartu defeated." Apparently the ultimate defeat of Arpad came only in 740, and its devastation must have impressed the Syrian and Palestinian world. For a few decades later the prophet Isaiah could use it as an example to warn the king of Jerusalem: "the gods of the nations" did not deliver Hamath and Arpad from the hand of the king of Assyria (Isa 36:18-19). "Where is the king of Hamath, the king of Arpad..." (Isa 37:13).[13]

13 See H. Schmökel, *Kulturgeschichte des alten Orient* (Stuttgart: Kröner, 1961) 611-15; G. Goossens, "Asie occidentale ancienne," *Encyclopédie de la Pléiade: Histoire universelle* (ed. R. Grousset et E. G. Leonard; Paris: Gallimard), I (1956) 397-401; P. Naster, *L'Asie Mineure et l'Assyrie aux VIIIe et VIIe siècles av. J.-C. d'après les annales des rois assyriens* (Bibliothèque du Muséon 8; Louvain: Muséon, 1938) 11-27.

2. בני בני: "The grandsons of ...." Occurrence of this formula here confirms the interpretation given below of the phrase in Sf III 21, where Dupont-Sommer sought to take the first בני as a form of the prep. בין.

ועק[ר]ה: "And his offspring." The restoration is suggested by the followrng phrase עם עקר. Literally, עקר denotes the "offshoot of a root." The figurative meaning of this word is now certain, not only from its use in this context, but also from that in Sf I A 3, 15, 25, 41; B 2, 25, 32; II B 6; II C 15; III 1, 3, 11, 12, 15, 16, 21, 22, 25, 26. A similar use of the Hebrew cognate occurs in Lev 25:47, עקר משפחת גר, "a descendant of a stranger's family"; see H. Torczyner (Tur Ṣinai), *Lachish Letters* (London: Oxford University, 1938) 60. J. Cantineau (*RA* 28 [1931] 169) compares the sense of the Latin *stirps*. For its use in Biblical Aramaic, see Dan 4:12, 20, 23; cf. later Aram. *'iqqārā'*.

3. ועדי כתך עם [עדי] ארפד: "And the treaty of KTK with [the treaty of] Arpad." Peculiar though this restoration seems, it is certain, as Sf I B 4 indicates. Does it imply that a similar "treaty" stele was set up in the territory of Bar-Ga'yah?

4. בעלי: "The lords of ...." The word בעל can mean "citizen" or "inhabitant," a meaning found in the Elephantine texts (cf. בעלי יב, "the inhabitants of Yeb," *AP* 30:22; 31:22; בעל קריה, *AP* 5:9; 13:10; 20:10; 46:6), which is paralleled in Hebrew, בעלי יריחו, Josh 24:11 (a passage whose dependence on a vassal treaty for its style and literary structure has been pointed out by G. Mendenhall), and which may still be the correct sense in Sf III 23, 26. See further Judg 9:2-3; 1 Sam 23:11-12; 2 Sam 21:12. Since, however, the בעלי seem to be different here from the עם (Sf I A 29, 30; I B 5, 11; II B 3, C 16), one should probably look on the former word as a designation of the aristocracy in the city of Arpad. Could it denote the remnant of the earlier Mesopotamian *maryannu*? Cf. P. Sacchi, *AANL Rendic.* 8/16/5-6 (1961) 186; M. Noth, *ZDPV* 77 (1961) 130.

חב[ור]ו: "Of Ḥaburu," a place mentioned in Fakh 16, since this text goes on to say that the treaty is with all Aram. The fragmentary word has been understood by Dupont-Sommer as "union," or "federation," after which he restores [ארט]ו, "l'Etat d'Urartu." At first sight, the *waw* at the beginning of line 5 looks like a conjunction, "and," parallel to ועם further on in the line; but Dupont-Sommer suggests that the *waw* is rather the last letter of the proper name of a place, allied to "all Aram." See Sf I B 9-10 for place-names ending in *-w*. That it is a place-name is a plausible suggestion; but that it is Urartu stands or falls with his thesis that Bar-Ga'yah is Sardur III. Possibly the word חבר is the

Aramaic equivalent of Akkadian and Ugaritic *ḫubūru*, "company, community, assembly," a word which Albright ("The Role of the Canaanites in the History of Civilization," in *Studies in the History of Culture* [Leland Volume; Menasha, WI: G. Banta, 1942] 36; cf. *The Bible and the Ancient Near East* [Garden City, NY: Doubleday, 1961] 359) showed to have been used in the Phoenician world to mean a "trading company." Hence, it could easily mean here a "union" or something similar, perhaps "federation;" but scarcely anything so specific as Dupont-Sommer's "état." See Noth, *ZDPV* 77 (1961) 146. Cf. CD 12:8 (ישראל חבור); also 13:15 and Dan 11:6, where the root is used in a context of a treaty. Recall also its use on Hasmonaean coins; see A. Reifenberg, *Ancient Jewish Coins* (3d ed.; Jerusalem: R. Mass, 1963) 13, 40. E. Lipiński (*Studies*, 24-25) prefers not to understand *ḥb[r]* in the abstract sense of "union, federation," but in the sense of an "ally," as in 1QapGen 21:26, 28. Hence he would read the end of the line as: ועדי חב]ר עם חבר[ועם ארם כלה, "and the treaty of one all[y with the other] and with all Aram." Cf. Dan 7:20. That is hardly an improvement.

5. עם ארם כלה: Not only the capital city Arpad, but all Aram is included in the pact. This expresses the extent of the coalition or union which Bar-Ga'yah has set up. While ארם sometimes designates merely a tribal group (see W. F. Albright, *JPOS* 15 [1935] 187), it would appear from line 6 that it is to be understood here in a geographical sense. In the Zakur stele (a 4) Bar-Hadad II, son of Hazael, is mentioned as the king of Aram (ca. 775). For a parallel to the suffixal use of כל, see *A* 12 (אתור כלה), 55; Panammu 17 (אשור כלה), 19 (ביתה כלה). For the possible influence of ארם כלה on the later Κοιλὴ Συρία, see B. Mazar, *BA* 25 (1962) 119-20.

מצר: At first sight, this name might seem to be a place-name because it follows other such names. As such it could refer to one of three different regions: (1) Egypt, which is out of question here; (2) an area east of Assyria in the Zagros mountains, northeast of Nineveh about Jebel Maqlub;[14] this area would not be impossible, but unlikely in the present context; (3) an alleged region of the Taurus mountains between Cilicia and Arpad. The only evidence for the existence of this region seems to be in the *Monolith Inscription* of Šalmaneser III (see III Rawlinson 8.92; *ARAB*, 1 § 611; *ANET*, 278-79). That Assyrian inscription apparently contains the oldest account of the sixth regnal year

14 For cuneiform references and literature on this area, see P. Garelli, "Muṣur (mât Muṣri)," *DBSup* 5. 1468-74, esp. 1469-70; B. Landsberger and Th. Bauer, *ZA* 37 [1927] 76)

of the king and mentions a coalition that was formed against him and was defeated at Qarqar (853): Hadadezer of Damascus, Irḫuleni of Hamath, Ahab of Israel, soldiers of Que, soldiers of Muṣru, soldiers of Irqanata, Matinuba'lu of Arvad, soldiers of Usanata, Adunuba'lu of Si'an, camel-riders of Gindibu', camel-riders of Arabia, Ba'sa son of Ruḫubi from Ammon, "(all together) these were twelve kings." However, other copies of the annals of Šalmaneser III's sixth regnal year merely mention Hadadezer of Damascus, Irḫuleni of Hamath, "together with twelve kings of the sea-coast" (see E. Michel, "Ein neuentdeckter Annalen-Text Salmanassars III.," *WO* 1 (1952) 464-65 (Vs. col. II, 27-28: *a-di 12 šarrānimeš.ni ša pān tam-di*); G. G. Cameron, "The Annals of Shalmaneser III, King of Assyria," *Sumer* 6 (1950) 13: *a-di 12 šarrāni (LUGAL.MEŠ-ni) ša pān tam-di* (Obv. col. II, l. 28); J. Laesse, "A Statue of Shalmaneser III, from Nimrud," *Iraq* 21 (1959) 151:]*ù a-ḫat tam-ti ana A-MEŠ.*[, reading corrected by W. G. Lambert according to the Obelisk inscription; Obelisk inscription *(ANET*, 279); Bull inscription (*ANET*, 279). These copies, which omit the explicit mention of Muṣr, might suggest, nevertheless, the location of it somewhere in the coastal area. It was apparently one of the twelve kingdoms of "the seacoast."[15]

A difficulty, however, arises in taking מצר as a place-name because of the following phrase, ועם בנוה זי יסקן באשר[ה], which suggests rather that the name is personal. Dupont-Sommer edited the text, adding the phrase "<with the king of> Muṣr." That was a better solution than Rosenthal's reference of the suffix on בנוה to Mati'el himself (*ANET*, 504). But Noth (*ZDPV* 77 [1961] 131) had already seen that it had to be a personal name. Now Lipiński (*Studies*, 25) has suggested taking מצר as a shortened form (*Miṣr*), derived from a fuller Neo-Hittite name *Miṣramuwa*, the appellation of a viceroy of Carchemish in the 13th century BC.[16] Hence Lipiński would translate: "and with all Aram and

15 See further A. Alt, "Die syrische Staatenwelt," 255. J. A. Montgomery ("Notes on Early Aramaic Inscriptions," *JAOS* 54 [1934] 424) suggested that מצר be read in 1 Kgs 10:28 instead of מצרים, aligned with קוה (Cilicia). P. Garelli (*DBSup* 5. 1470-71) and Dupont-Sommer (*Les Araméens*, 71) have proposed the same reading for 2 Kgs 7:6. But this is far from certain. In the first case מצרים has probably got into the text by a vertical dittography; the sense is that the horses came from Cilicia and the chariots from Egypt. See R. de Vaux, "Les livres des Rois," *La sainte Bible (de Jérusalem)* (2d ed.; Paris: Cerf, 1958) 74, 156; Albright, *Archeology and the Religion of Israel* (Baltimore: Johns Hopkins University, 1953) 135. Cf. H. Tadmor, "Que and Muṣri," *IEJ* 11 (1961) 143-50.

16 See J. Nougayrol, *PRU IV* (Paris: Imprimerie Nationale, 1956), pl. LXXIII, p.

with Miṣr and with his sons who will come up in [his] place." Similarly Lemaire-Durand, *AIS*, 86-87.

For N. Na'aman, however, מצר would be *Muṣuri*, the king of Damascus ("Looking for KTK"). But that identification is problematic, for one would expect such a name to end in a final *yodh*.

For H. Tadmor, מצר is neither a geographical nor a personal name, but a common noun meaning "border."[17]

בנוה: "His sons." The orthography of this suffix is certain, since it occurs elsewhere in this inscription (Sf I A 39, [41]; C 18); and in Sf III 2, 8, 12, 14-17; Nerab 2:2. It may also persist in later Aramaic in *BMAP* 3:4 (*'grwh*); 6:[9], unless one should rather regard these examples as later scribal misspellings. Cross and Freedman (*EHO*, 29) compared this form with the Syriac *-awhī* and Biblical Aramaic *-ôhî*: "It differs, however, as to the manner in which the secondary suffix has been added: **ayhū* > **ayū* > *aw*, plus the secondary suffix produces **-awh* or **-aweh*. The form can hardly be vocalized **awhī*, because the final *ī* is regularly indicated by the vowel letter in these texts." The preferable vocalization would be *-awh*, with consonantal *he*.

זי יסקן באשר[ה]: "Who will come after [him]," but lit., "who will come up in his place." באשר- is related to the later forms באתר- and בתר-, which have developed the meaning "after." This phrase is used elsewhere (Sf I C 4; I B 3) to designate the successor on a royal throne. Cf. Dan 2:39; 7:6; Deut 29:21; Exod 29:30 and Akkadian *mannu šarru ša i-la-a arkiya* (CT 13. 42-i-20). יסקן is 3d pl. masc. impf. peal of סלק, "go up, ascend." See BLA §43.

ו[עם מלכי] כל עלי ארם ותחתה: "And with the kings of all Upper-Aram and Lower Aram," lit., "and with the kings of all of the upper part of Aram and its lower part." The restoration is plausible. After the mention of ארם כלה in line 5, this expression, which is not found elsewhere, must be intended for greater precision. Bauer ("Ein aramäischer Staatsvertrag," 4) suggested that it referred to the Euphrates River, and Dupont-Sommer followed him in identifying Upper Aram with Syrian Aram, and Lower Aram with Mesopotamian. Alt ("Die syrische Staatenwelt," 254 n. 2) disagreed because what was usually referred to as Mesopotamian Aram was at this period already in the control of Assyria. He preferred to locate both Upper and Lower Aram in Syria: "Oberland"

193 (RS 17.423:6); *PRU V* (1968) 104, 387 (§32) (RS 20.243:8′a and 17′).

17 See "הפתיחה של החוזה הארמי מספירה הערות (Notes on the Opening Lines of the Aramaic Treaty of Sefîre)," ספר שמואל ייוין (ed. S. Abramski et al.; Jerusalem: Kiryat Sepher, 1970) 397-405, esp. 397-401; "Assyria and the West," 36-48, esp. 46 n. 31.

about Damascus, "Unterland" about Arpad. This seems preferable. Noth (*ZDPV* 77 [1961] 131) suggested the possibility that "Lower-Aram" might have meant the area toward the Mediterranean Sea, and "Upper-Aram" what was more inland. Compare Strabo's use of ἡ ἄνω Συρία (*Geogr.* 2.5.38).

עלי and תחתי are sometimes used in Aramaic with the sense of "upstream" and "downstream" (respectively); compare the use of them in Elephantine texts (*AP* 13:13-14; 25:5-7; *BMAP* 3:7-10; 4:9-11), esp. the note in Kraeling, *BMAP*, 77-79. עלי is a substantived gentilic adjective, "the upper part of" (Aram), and תחתה, "its lower part." In this case the prep. תחת is taken as a noun too. See L. F. Hartman, *CBQ* 30 (1968) 256-60, esp. 258.

6. כל עלל בית מלך: "All who enter the royal palace." Ronzevalle's mode of breaking up the words is preferable to that of Dupont-Sommer, who reads כל על לבית מלך. על לביתה of Dan 6:11 might seem to support his reading with the preposition, but the ptc. of the double-'ayin root is *'ālil.* See Dan 4:4; 5:8, where the *kĕtîb* has preserved the older form (עללין). There is no evidence of a ptc. על at this period, similar to the later Aramaic form or even to the Syriac form *bā'ez*, built on an analogy with hollow verbs. This division of words is also preferred by J. Koopmans (*BO* 17 [1960] 52), who compares the Aramaic phrase with באי שער of Gen 23:10 and Akkadian *ērib bīti*. Moreover, in Aramaic verbs expressing motion toward a place are often followed by objects without a preposition: Sf III 5 (ויהכן חלב); Pad I v 5 (כזי תאתון מצרין), I r 3 (בזי לא איתי המו מנפי). Friedrich and Landsberger (*ZA* 7 [1933] 314) suggested that the expression referred to nomads who as subjects would appear from time to time before their prince in his palace. Noth (*ZDPV* 77 [1961] 132) thought that the phrase might designate representatives of subordinate rulers and groups obliged to appear with more or less regularity before the king. McCarthy's explanation (*Treaty and Covenant*, 189), "i.e. take over the rulership," is scarcely correct. On בית מלך, see note on Sf I C 6.

Lipiński (*Studies*, 25) says that "after the *kl 'll byt mlk* one would expect the antithetic verb 'to go down,' so as to express the idea of the totality of the people being in good relationship with the royal palace," i.e. *nḥt*. Hence he would read, *w'm kl 'll byt mlk wn[ḥth bnṣb' z]nh śmw 'dy' 'ln*, "and with anybody entering the royal palace and l[eaving it. On t]his [stele] they have set up this treaty." But נחת is not antithetic to עלל, since it means "go down" and is antithetic to סלק, "go up" -- to say nothing of its intransitive character, which cannot without further ado take an object suffix. Moreover, עלל does not mean "go up," but "enter," and its antithetic form would be נפק. Indeed, one would have to say ונפק מנה, "and going forth from it."

[ונ[צבא: "The stele." This word is restored by Dupont-Sommer on the basis of Sf I C 17. נצב is related to Hebrew נציב, "pillar, column" (see Gen 19:26); it should be vocalized *naṣība'*, as the later Nabatean form indicates (*RES* 1088.1). It is a *qatīl* type, not *qatl*, as P. Joüon maintained (*MUSJ* 5 [1911-12] 414). Cf. Bar Hadad 1; Zakur a 1; Hadad 1; Panammu 1.

7. שמו: "They have set up." This verb is used with עדי in Sf I B 6. I now read this line so with Greenfield (*AcOr* 29 [1965] 1-18, esp. 9; *IEJ* 28 [1978] 288); similarly O. Rössler, *TUAT* 1. 179. Cf. Lemaire-Durand (*IAS*, 113), who read [ומ[ליא instead of Dupont-Sommer's [ונ[צבא (at the end of the preceding line); Gibson (*TSSI*, 2. 28), who reads rather ועןם כל זי נצבא ז]נה שם ועדיא אלן, "and with [all who] have set up [this stele] and this treaty." See H. J. van Dijk, "A Neglected Connotation of Three Hebrew Verbs," *VT* 18 (1968) 16-30, showing the interrelationship of שׂית, שׂים, נתן. Cf. Panammu 1, 20; Ps 81:6 (עדות ביהוסף שמו, "[God] made a pact with Joseph"); and Akkadian *adē šakānu*.

עדיא אלן: There is no need to suspect dittography here; the first instance is an additional direct object of שמו, "(as) this treaty," whereas the second is the subject of a nominal sentence of which זי (compound relative) is the predicate.

גזר: "Has concluded," lit., "has cut in two, divided," as in Sf I A 40. It is here used figuratively, "to conclude a pact or treaty." Undoubtedly the rite alluded to in line 40 is the source of the expression. Dupont-Sommer compared the similar Hebrew and Greek expressions, כרת ברית and *ὅρκια τέμνειν* (Homer, *Il.* 3. 73, 300). To these one may add Latin *foedus ferire* (Virgil, *Aeneid* 10.154; Livy 9.4.5) and Akkadian *TAR be-ri-ti* (see Albright, "The Hebrew Expression for 'Making a Covenant' in Pre-Israelite Documents," *BASOR* 121 [1951] 21-22).[18] Cf. Job 22:28; Gen 15:17; Jer 34:18; Dan 4:14, 21; Neh 10:1.

18 Cf. Noth, "Das alttestamentliche Bundschliessen im Lichte eines Mari-Textes," *Mélanges Isidore Lévy* (AIPHOS 13; Brussels: Editions de l'Institut, 1955) 433-44; J. A. Soggin, "Akkadisch TAR *BERITI* und hebräisch כרת ברית," *VT* 18 (1968) 210-15; O. Loretz, *VT* 16 (1966) 239-41; D. J. McCarthy, *Treaty and Covenant*, 53-54; "Ebla, *ὅρκια τέμνειν*, *ṭb*, *šlm*: Addenda to *Treaty and Covenant*," *Bib* 60 (1979) 247-53; E. Bikerman, "'Couper une alliance,'" *Archives d'histoire du droit oriental* 5 (1950) 133-56; J. Henninger, "Was bedeutet die rituelle Teilung eines Tieres in zwei Hälften?" *Bib* 34 (1953) 344-53; R. Polzin, "HWQY' and Covenantal Institutions in Early

קדם אשר: "In the presence of Asshur." At the end of this line קדם is certainly to be restored, as in the following phrases; the name of a god should also be read, undoubtedly אשר (or אשור), "Asshur," the consort of מלש in the next line. (The Assyrians would have pronounced it "Assur.") There is no need to restore an added verb in the lacuna, as Lemaire-Durand (*IAS*, 113) have done (שם or שמו); similarly E. Puech, "Les traités araméens," 90. For in cognate Assyrian treaties the pact is "concluded" in the presence of the gods. See M. L. Barré, "The First Pair of Deities," 206-7.

Dupont-Sommer had suggested קדם חלד רבא, "in the presence of Ḥaldi the great," the chief god of Urartu. But that again depended on his identification of Bar-Ga'yah as Sardur III. A Mesopotamian or Assyrian god is more likely, given the selection of other divine names and especially the beginning of the list with names of Assyrian gods.

The solemn character of the treaty is indicated by the listing of gods who are witnesses to the making of the pact. Such a list is common to vassal treaties of this type. Those of Esarhaddon have a list of gods that follows the introductory paragraph (and the seal impressions); see D. Wiseman, *Vassal Treaties of Esarhaddon*, 22. Such a list is also found in the treaty of Aššurnirari V with Mati'ilu, in which many of the same pairs of gods are mentioned, but there the list follows the stipulations of the treaty (Rev. VI, 6-27); see McCarthy, *Treaty and Covenant*, 196-97. For oaths sworn "in the presence of" gods, see Esarhaddon's vassal treaties, lines 41-42.

8. מלש: "Mullesh," the consort of Asshur in the Neo-Assyrian period. They are probably the principal gods of KTK. מלש is a form developed from *Mulliššu* or from Neo-Assyrian *Mullissu*, which is in turn a development of *Mulliltu*, the fem. form of *Mullil*, a dialect-form of *Ninlil* (= Enlil). See S. Parpola, "The Alleged Middle/Neo-Assyrian Irregular Verb," 4 n. 13. NIN.LÍL is the common writing of the consort of Asshur in that period. Cf. M. L. Barré, *The God-List*; also W. G. Lambert's review of this book in *JCS* 40 (1988) 120-23; Friedrich and Landsberger, *ZA* 7 (1933) 315; H. V. Hilprecht and A. T. Clay, *Babylonian Expedition* (Philadelphia, PA: University of Pennsylvania, 1898) 9. 50, 77.

In the following list of names of paired gods, the majority is Babylonian, and a few are Syrian or Canaanite. This seems to be an attempt to represent the main areas and peoples covered by the treaty.

Israel," *HTR* 62 (1969) 227-40; F. Vattioni, "Recenti studi sull'alleanza nella Bibbia e nell'antico oriente," *AION* 17 (1967) 181-226, esp. 202.

The first group of gods must be those venerated by Bar-Ga'yah; the second group, beginning with Hadad of Aleppo, must be the gods of Mati'el.

מרדך וזרפנת: "Marduk and Zarpanit." The second pair is the Babylonian god and his consort, also found in the treaty of Aššurnirari V (Rev. VI, 10). In Esarhaddon's vassal treaties (e.g., line 433), Marduk's epithet is "the eldest son"; from earliest times he appears as the son of Enki and as the local god of the city of Babylon, worshipped in the temple of Esagila. His consort here is זרפנת, which in Akkadian is normally spelled *Ṣarpānītu*. Her name has been explained as meaning "shining like silver," but according to B. Meissner, *Babylonien und Assyrien* (Kulturgeschichtliche Bibliothek 4; Heidelberg: Winter, 1925), 2.16, the Assyrians explained it by popular etymology as *Zer-banītu*, "she who creates seed/posterity." Her epithet in Esarhaddon's vassal treaties is "who gives name and seed" (line 435). This etymology accounts for the initial *zayin* in the Aramaic form of the name.

נבא ות[שמת]: "Nabu and Tashmet." The third pair is likewise Babylonian, and the name of the consort is restored with certainty, since Nabu and Tashmet often follow Marduk in lists of gods; see the Nabonidus stele (*ANET* 310b); Aššurnirari V (Rev. VI, 10). The name *Nabû* is often said to mean "the brilliant one," but this is not certain. This god was associated with the planet Mercury, as the planetary god of Borsippa, where his principal temple was Ezida. He was also venerated by Arameans and honored as the scribe of the gods, the one in charge of the learning contained in cuneiform tablets and controller of the destiny of humans.[19] In Mandean texts Nabu is referred to as ספרא חכימא. Dupont-Sommer regarded the Aramaic spelling נבא as curious and suggested the vocalization *Nebâ*, comparing Hebrew *Nĕbô*. In the Egyptian Aramaic ostracon (Clermont-Ganneau §277) published by him (*RHR* 128 [1944] 29), however, the god's name is written as נבו (first half of the sixth century). But both the form on the ostracon and in the Sefire inscription is to be explained as an attempt to write a final long *u*, *Nabū*. Compare the writing הא for the 3d pers. masc. pron. in Sf III 8, 13, 22. Note the similar name in Transjordanian territory, in the Meša inscription, spelled נבה (line 14). The names of the four gods, *Nabū, Tašmetum, Marduk, Ṣarpānītum*, are found together on a late Assyrian cylinder seal discovered at Samaria; see J. W. Crowfoot, G. M. Crowfoot, K. M. Kenyon, *The Objects from Samaria* (London: Palestine Exploration Fund, 1957) 87 §18 (+ pl. XV).

19 See Albright, "Some Notes on the Nabataean Goddess 'Al-Kutba and Related Matters," *BASOR* 156 (1959) 37-38; E. Schrader, *Die Keilinschriften und das Alte*

ך[אר ונש]: "'Ir and Nusk." Bauer suggested the restoration of these names on the basis of their occurrence in the treaty of Aššurnirari V (Rev. VI, 15). Here it is not a god and his consort, as in the foregoing pairs, but a pair of Babylonian gods. Irra was in very early times the god of pestilence, called the "lord of the storm and destruction," who devastated the earth by war, fire, and pestilence; his consort was Ninmug, and he had a temple in Lagash. But he was often identified with Nergal, especially in Kutha. In this inscription, he is associated with Nusk, the god of fire, who drives away darkness and founds cities. His consort was Sadarnunna; both were regarded as the children of Sin and Ningal. Nusk is known as a god worshiped in Aramean lands from the Nerab inscriptions (1:9; 2:9).

9. נרגל ולץ: "Nergal and Laṣ." This pair is the well-known Babylonian god of the underworld and his consort; they too figure in the treaty of Aššurnirari V (Rev. VI, 12), but precede Irra and Nusk. Nergal was originally a manifestation of Šamaš, the sun-god, but in time became god of the underworld. In the latter capacity his consort was normally Ereškigal; but in the temple of Kutha, Laṣ was venerated as his consort; likewise in the temple of Tarbiṣ, built by Sennacherib in honor of Nergal.

שמש ונר: "Shamash and Nur." In the treaty of Aššurnirari V (Rev. VI, 9) one finds Šamaš, the Babylonian sun-god, and his consort Aya. Here the consort נר occurs instead. Earlier commentators, unwilling to accept Ronzevalle's reading, changed it to ור (cf. Zakur a 1). But the reading is certain, and Dupont-Sommer has suggested that it is the name of a god, *Ner*, otherwise found in personal names: Ner (1 Sam 14:50), Abner (1 Sam 14:51), Abiner (1 Sam 14:50). However, H. Donner ("Zur Inschrift," 390-92) has brought together cuneiform evidence to show that *nūru*, an epithet of various gods connected with light (Aya, Nusk), could also be treated itself as a god. This means that we should return to Ronzevalle's original reading of "Šamaš et Nur." Moreover, in Ugaritic *nyr* occurs as an epithet of the moon-god (C. H. Gordon, *UT*, 443). Šamaš was also venerated in Aramean territory, as is clear from Nerab 1,9; Zakur b 24; Hadad 2, 11; Panammu 22. In Esarhaddon's vassal treaties (line 422) he bears the epithet, "light of the heavens and earth" (*nūr šamāmē u qaqqari*).

[סן ונכל]: "Sin and Nikkal." Ronzevalle's restoration is still the best here. In the treaty of Aššurnirari V (Rev. VI, 8) Sin and Ningal precede Šamaš and Aya. Sin was the Babylonian moon-god, worshipped above

---

Testament (2 vols.; 3d ed.; Berlin: Reuther & Reichard, 1902-3) 399-404.

all at Ur, whence his cult spread to Harran. His name occurs in the personal name of the priest of *Śhr* (Nerab 1:1), *Śnzrbn*. In Esarhaddon's vassal treaties (l. 419) he bears the epithet, "brightness of heaven and earth." Sin's consort was Ningal, later pronounced as Nikkal, as in Nerab 1:9; 2:9, and as such should be restored here. See A. F. Key, "Traces of the Worship of the Moon God Sîn among the Early Israelites," *JBL* 84 (1965) 20-26. To fill out the line, Lipiński (*Studies*, 26) would read *wqdm s[n wnkl zy Nbn/Grt*, "in the presence of Sin and Nikkal of Nuban" or "Gurāt." He compares Akkadian *Nin-gal (bēlet) Nubanni* (RS 17.146:51; 17.237:14′; 17.340:20′ [*PRU* 4. 52, 65, 157]). See M. Weinfeld, "The Loyalty Oath in the Ancient Near East," *UF* 8 (1976) 379-414, esp. 395-96.

10. נכר וכדאה: "Nikkar and Kadi'ah." This pair of deities is difficult to identify. Dussaud (*CRAIBL* [1931] 315) mentioned that they occur in a hymn to Tammuz under the names *Nakar* and *Kadi* (IV R 29:1). That identification, however, was rejected by Friedrich and Landsberger (*ZA* 7 [1933] 315) with good reason, because KA.DI is an ideogram in that text. Cf. E. Weidner, *AfO* 9 (1933-34) 98-99. Rosenthal gives "Nikkar and Kada'ah" (*ANET*, 504). J. Cantineau (*RA* 28 [1931] 170) proposed Nikkar and Kadi'a, referring to M. Jastrow, *Die Religion Babyloniens und Assyriens* (Giessen: Ricker, 1905), 1. 162, 185: "Nin-kar is perhaps identical with Nin-karrak, a designation of Gula." See now M. L. Barré, *The God-List*, 24, who identifies Ninkarra(k) and Gula as goddesses of healing and explains *Nikkar* as a development of *Nin-kar*, but he admits that the identification of *Kd'h* is still unsolved.

[ ]כל אלהי רחבה ואדם: "All the gods of Raḥbah and 'Adam." Rosenthal (*ANET*, 504) translated this: "all the Gods of Commons and Land (?)." He obviously related רחבה to the root רחב, "be wide open," and אדם to Hebrew אדמה, "ground, land." Donner-Röllig prefer to translate, "Götter der Wüste und des Fruchtlandes" (*KAI* 2.239). Bauer ("Ein aramäischer Staatsvertrag," 5) had suggested this as a possibility, but also mentioned *Ruḥba* as the name of a place southeast of Damascus. Dussaud ("Nouvelles inscriptions," 321) thought rather that a place called *Raḥeba* or *Raḥbā* on the Euphrates, the modern Meyadin, in whose neighborhood an ancient fortress still preserves the old name, was meant. I have followed Dupont-Sommer in accepting this identification. Such a phrase, "all the gods of X (place-name)," is found in vassal treaties (e.g., Esarhaddon [lines 31ff.: "by all the gods of Asshur, by all the gods of Nineveh, by all the gods of Calah"). See also the treaty of Esarhaddon with Ba'al of Tyre (Rev. II, 8-9; *AfO* 8 [1932-33] 32-33).

In such case, [ ]אדמ must also be a place-name, perhaps like *'Adāmāh* (Josh 19:36) or *'Admāh* (Gen 10:19; 14:2,8), or simply *'Adam* (which seems to appear below in Sf I A 35 as the last of a list of places). In Josh 3:16 אדם should probably be read as *'Adāmāh*; see 1 Kgs 7:46; 2 Chr 4:17; cf. N. Glueck, *BASOR* 90 (1943) 5-6 (= Tell ed-Damieh); W. F. Albright, *JPOS* 5 (1925) 33 n. 37. The name אדם there is possibly related to Hebrew *'Edōm*, or to the Ugaritic *udm* (Keret 277) or the Akkadian *Udūmu*. The phrase, "the gods of KTK," and probably also the "gods of Arpad," is found in Sf I B 5-6.

וקדם הדד זי ח]לב]: "In the presence of Hadad of Aleppo." וקדם הדד חלב was restored by Bauer ("Ein aramäischer Staatsvertrag," 5), since Hadad of Aleppo is mentioned in the treaty of Aššurnirari V (Rev. VI, 18), followed by Palil and the Seven-godhead. L. Hartman (*CBQ* 30 [1968] 258-59) found הדד as a cst. form difficult and suggested the addition of זי, which Lipiński also reads (*Studies*, 26). Šalmaneser III mentions having offered sacrifices before Adad of Aleppo (Monolith inscription, *ANET*, 278-79). On a famous temple of Hadad in Aleppo, see M. J. Dahood, "Ancient Semitic Deities in Syria and Palestine," 77. The town חלב is mentioned in Sf III 5, a town probably belonging to the kingdom of Arpad at this time, a town to which fugitives fled for asylum.[20] Hadad is the West-Semitic (Amorite?) name of the storm-god; he is known as Adad in Babylonian texts from the time of the Amorite dynasty.

11. וקדם סבת: "In the presence of Sibitti," the Seven-godhead, also mentioned in the treaty of Aššurnirari V (Rev. VI, 20), as well as in that of Esarhaddon with Ba'al of Tyre (Rev. II, 5: ^{d}*sibitte ilāni*^{meš} *qardūte*) and in his vassal treaties (line 464). "Le chiffre sacré s'appliquait aux sept dieux des cieux ou aux sept dieux des enfers, avec l'arrière-pensée d'exprimer ainsi la totalité des dieux bienfaisants ou malfaisants. Souvent le nom de 'Sept' terminera une énumération de divinités, comme pour englober celles qu'on a omises. Il existait à Ninive un temple des Sept" (E. Dhorme, *Les religions de Babylonie et d'Assyrie* [Les anciennes religions orientales 2; Paris: Presses Universitaires de France, 1949] 79; also J. Bottéro, "Les divinités sémitiques anciennes," 48-49). Sibitti was a Babylonian deity, here inserted in the second half of the list of gods, where Syrian or Canaanite deities otherwise appear. Normally in Mesopotamian treaties Sibitti ends the god-list.

---

20 For the spelling and derivation of the town's name, see H. T. Bossert, *Or* 30 (1961) 319-20 n. 3. Cf. J. D. Hawkins, "Ḫalab," *RLA* 4. 53.

וקדם אל ועלין: "In the presence of 'El and 'Elyan." This pair of gods is clearly West Semitic or Canaanite. The name *'El* is well known from Ugaritic texts and the OT; it also occurs in Aramaic inscriptions, Hadad 2 (bis), 11, 18; Panammu 22. In the Canaanite pantheon 'El was regarded as the lord of the gods. See R. Dussaud, *Les religions des Hittites et des Hourrites, des Phéniciens et des Syriens* (Les anciennes religions orientales 2; Paris: Presses Universitaires de France, 1949) 360; M. Pope, *El in the Ugaritic Pantheon* (VTSup 2; Leiden: Brill, 1955) 55-58 (with the literature cited there); W. F. Albright, *Archaeology and the Religion of Israel* (Baltimore, MD: Johns Hopkins University, 1953) 72-73. עליון is a name familiar in the OT, as an epithet of אל (Gen 14:18-22; Ps 78:35), of יהוה (Ps 7:18; 47:3), of אלהים (Ps 57:3; 78:56); it is also used in parallelism with אל (Num 24:16; Ps 73:11; 107:11), with יהוה (Deut 32:8-9; 2 Sam 22:14 [= Ps 18:14]; Ps 91:9), with אלהים (Ps 46:5; 50:14), with שדי (Num 24:16; Ps 91:1). It is also used alone (Ps 9:3; 77:11; 82:6; Isa 14:14). In these cases, עליון designates the monotheistic God of Israel. Here in Sf I it appears as one of a pair, along with אל. In the preceding phrases distinct deities were paired, which suggests that אל and עלין are distinct Canaanite gods here too. The relation of the Aramaic אל ועלין to the Hebrew אל עליון is complicated by the fact that in Ugaritic there are divine names sometimes used alone and sometimes connected by *w*-, which apparently denote one god. Contrast *Qdš wAmrr* (Gordon, *UT*, Text 51: IV, lines 8, 13) with *Qdš yuḫdum šb'r / Amrr kkbkb lpnm* (lines 16-17) and *Qdš Amrr* (*'Anat* 6:11); similarly *aḫr mǵy Kṯr wḪss* (Text 51: V, line 106), where the double name is used with a singular verb. See further the same pair in Text 68:7-8 (with a singular verb); 2 Aqht V: 17-18 (contrast lines 10,11); *Nkl wlb* (Text 77:1, to be contrasted with 77:17,18). Recall also the strange *'îr wĕqaddîš* of Dan 4:10,20 (with a sg. ptc.). Cf. G. Levi della Vida, "El Elyon in Genesis 14:18-20," *JBL* 63 (1944) 1-9.

In 1QapGen 12:17; 20:12, 16; 21:2, 20; 22:15, 16bis, 21) עלין appears constantly עליון, which form is to be regarded as a Hebraism. It does not necessarily point to an original *'Elyawn* (*pace* Rosenthal, *ANET*, 504), which would appear in this period with a medial *waw*. Hence the vocalization *'Elyān*, which is to be preferred to *'Elyūn*, suggested by S. Segert, *ArOr* 32 (1964) 125.[21]

21 See further O. Eissfeldt, "El and Yahweh," *JSS* 1 (1956) 25-37; R. Rendtorff, "El, Ba'al und Jahweh," *ZAW* 78 (1966) 277-91; N. Habel, "'Yahweh, Maker of Heaven and Earth': A Study in Tradition Criticism," *JBL* 91 (1972) 321-37, esp. 321-23; B. Uffenheimer, "*El Elyon*, Creator of Heaven and Earth," *Shnaton* 2 (1977) 20-

וקדם שמי[ן וארק]: "In the presence of Heaven and Earth." Calling upon heaven and earth as witnesses to a treaty is also found in Hittite pacts (*ANET*, 206; cf. V. Korošec, *Hethitische Staatsverträge*, 96). A certain numinous character was thus attributed to these natural phenomena, and they were probably objects of worship. A similar usage is found in the OT: Deut 4:26 (העידותי בכם היום את־השמים ואת־הארץ); 30:19; 31:28. For an interpretation of this usage, see H. B. Huffmon, *JBL* 78 (1959) 291 n. 23; L. Moran, *Bib* 43 (1962) 317-20. Cf. Zakur b 25-26.[22]

[וקדם מצ]לה ומעינן: "In the presence of the Abyss and the Springs." צולה has been restored by Dupont-Sommer, as in Isa 44:27; but that creates a problem by introducing a medial long *u* fully written, which, while not without some parallels in the Aramaic of this period (see יעורן, Sf II B 4; שורא, Zakur a 17; רוח, Sf III 2; ימות, Sf III 16), is otherwise rare. For that reason it would be better to restore the alternate suggestion of Dupont-Sommer, מצלה (as in Zech 1:8). מעינן is probably to be vocalized *ma'yānîn*, as in the later Aramaic *ma'yānā'*, and not as in Syriac, *mĕ'înā'*. For parallels in Hittite and Greek writers, see Bauer ("Ein aramäischer Staatsvertrag," 5).

12. וקדם יום ולילה: "In the presence of Day and Night." For parallels to this formula, see Moran, *Bib* 43 (1962) 319 n. 5. The medial *waw* in יום agrees with the normal writing for uncontracted diphthongs in the Aramaic of this period. A propos of לילה Dupont-Sommer remarked, "A lire soit *laylāh*, comme en hébreu, soit plutôt *lêlêh*, ce qui est la forme proprement araméenne (état emph. *lêl*^{e}*yâ*)." Throughout the various phases of Aramaic, however, the form of this noun is seen to be either a reduplicated stem **laylay* or else **layl*. The reduplicated stem could scarcely yield the Hebrew form *laylāh*. Since there is no reason to take לילה here as emphatic, being parallel to the absolute יום, it should be vocalized as *laylêh*. A dissimilation of the diphthongs *laylay* has produced the contraction in the last syllable; and contracted *ê* is indicated by *he*. The same form occurs in 1QapGen 19:14; it is the same phenomenon which appears in סוסה חד קליל, "a swift horse" (*sûsêh* < *sûsay*, *A* 38 [the emph. would be *sûsyā'*]), and probably also in יבעה (< *yib'ay*) in Sf III 2. For this reason the explanation of לילה, given by

26.

22 See M. Delcor, "Les attaches littéraires, l'origine et la signification de l'expression biblique 'prendre à témoin le ciel et la terre,'" *VT* 16 (1966) 8-25; M. C. Astour, "Some New Divine Names from Ugarit," *JAOS* 86 (1966) 277-84, esp. 279-80; N. Habel, *JBL* 91 (1972) 322.

Cross and Freedman (*EHO*, 27), as *laylā* is unacceptable; likewise that of G. Garbini (*AA*, 260) and S. Segert (*ArOr* 32 [1964] 123). It was correctly explained by Bauer; also by Kutscher (*Or* 39 [1970] 183; "Aramaic," 360).

שהדן כל א[להי כתך ואלהי אר]פד: "All the gods of KTK and the gods of Arpad (are) witnesses (to it)." Dupont-Sommer takes שהדן as a noun in apposition to the preceding names, understanding the following כל אלהי כתך ואלהי ארפד as a voc. with the subsequent impv., "(O vous), tous les d[ieux de KTK et dieux d'Ar]pad, ouvrez vos yeux ...." For the restoration of the lacuna, see Sf I B 5-6. That the gods are addressed seems clear; but it is preferable to take the words quoted in the lemma as a nominal declarative sentence, resuming the foregoing. Donner-Röllig also prefer the nominal sentence with the ptc. שהדן as predicate (*KAI*, 2. 246).

Dupont-Sommer called attention to the role of the gods as witnesses in the Hittite treaty of Šuppiluliuma with Mattiwaza (see *ANET*, 205): "We have called the gods to be assembled and the gods of the contracting parties to be present, to listen, and to serve as witnesses." See also the end of the list of gods in the treaty between Mursilis and Duppi-Tessub of Amurru (*ANET*, 205), "Let these be witnesses to this treaty and to the oath." Or the treaty of Mursilis II with Talmišarruma of Aleppo (Rev. 9-10): "May the gods of the land of Hatti and the gods of the land of Aleppo be witnesses to these words." To this Hittite evidence one may add that of the OT: Gen 31:47-50, where Jacob and Laban erected a cairn, which Jacob called in Hebrew *gal'ēd*, but which Laban in Aramaic called *yĕgar śāhădûtā'*, "cairn of testimony." Laban concludes, "Remember that God is witness between you and me," v. 50. Cf. Job 16:19; Panammu 22 (וכל אלהי יאדי).

13. פקחו: "Open," the peal impv. pl. of *pqḥ*, "open the eyes." Vocalize *paqáḥū*. The word עיניכם probably contains two uncontracted diphthongs, *'aynaykum*. For similar notions, see Dan 9:18 (פקח[ה] עניך וראה, "open your eyes and see," in a prayer addressed to God); 2 Kgs 6:20; 19:16; Isa 37:17. Cf. the Hittite treaty of Tudḫaliyas IV with Ulmi-Tessub of Dattasa, obv. 50-51: "Let the gods see and be witnesses" (McCarthy, *Treaty and Covenant*, 184).

לחזיה: "To gaze upon (the treaty)." Dupont-Sommer remarked, "Noter cet infinitif sans *m*- et avec désinence fm. *âh*; cf. III 6 *rqh* (infin. de la racine *rqq* > *r'*')." Garbini (*RSO* 34 [1959] 49, 51) hesitatingly went along with Dupont-Sommer's analysis. There is considerable evidence for the peal infin. without preformative *mem* in early Aramaic; see note on רקה תרקם, Sf III 6 ad fin. The question remains, however, whether לחזיה is peal and whether it has a fem. ending. There is no evidence elsewhere in Aramaic for a peal infin. with a fem. ending. Moreover, the parallel cited (רקה) is not derived from *rqq*, but from a tertiae infirmae root *rqw/y* (with which Rosenthal agrees, *BASOR* 158 [1960] 29). Consequently, חזיה has to be understood as a pael infin. with the normal ending expected of infinitives of derived conjugations in Aramaic: *ḥazzāyāh*. A difficulty with this explanation is alleged in that *ḥzy* is said to be not otherwise attested in pael. Yet the instance in Nerab 2:5 (*KAI*, 226:5) is usually overlooked: ובעיני מחזי אנה בני רבע בכוני והום אתהמו. This does not mean, "and with my eyes, what do I see?" (so Rosenthal, *ANET*, 505), as if מחזה = *mā hāzêh*. Rather it is the pael ptc. (*mĕḥazzêh*), and the phrase should be translated, "and with my eyes I gazed upon my children to the fourth generation."

14. והן: "Now if." This is the normal Aramaic conditional conjunction; see *DISO*, 66. It is also found occasionally in OT Hebrew texts: Jer 3:1; Isa 54:15.

ישקר: "Should be unfaithful to." In Sf III this verb always occurs in the perfect and in the apodosis of a condition expressing a stipulation (likewise in I B 23, 27-28, 36-37, 38; II B 9, 14, 17-18). Here it is found in the imperfect (as also in I A 15, 24; II A 3), where there is no question of treaty stipulations. See note on Sf III 4. Cf. the treaty of Aššurnirari V (Obv. I, 15): *šummu* [I]*Ma-ti-'-lu ina a-di-e ta-mi-ti ilāni[*[meš] *i-ḫa-ṭu]* ... ; Esarhaddon's vassal treaties (line 513).

16. [בני] גש: "The Benê-Gush." So restored on the basis of Sf I B 3; בית גש would also be possible (see Sf I B 11; Sf II B 10). It is the designation of the people of *Bīt Agūsi*, another name for Arpad; or more probably the designation of the ruling dynasty in Arpad. The Assyrians under Aššur-nasirpal II (883-59) knew of the ruler of Gusi in the land of Yaḫan (cf. *ARAB*, 1. §477). In the time of Šalmaneser III (858-24) the people were called *Aramē mār Gusi* (*ARAB*, 1. §614), *Guzi* (*ARAB*, 1. §600, 610), *Agusi* (*ARAB*, 1. §582, 601). In the campaign of Adad-nirari III of 805, *Arpaddu* is referred to as *Bīt-(A)gūsi*. See S. Schiffer, *Die Aramäer*, 90 n. 6; 137 n. 9; M. F. Unger, *Israel and the Aramaeans of Damascus*, 166; R. P. Boudou, *Liste des noms géographiques* (Orientalia 36-38; Rome: Biblical Institute, 1929) 7. Cf. M. Liverani, "Bar-Guš e Bar-Rakib," *RSO* 36 (1961) 185-87.[23] In the Zakur stele (a 5) בר גש denotes the king of Arpad. Before בני גש one can restore confidently והן ישקרן. So Dupont-Sommer, Donner-Röllig.

---

23 Cf. Teixidor, "Bulletin ... 1969," *Syria* 46 (1969) 323-24; Vattioni, "A

21. After the break in which most of lines 17-20 have been lost, the text resumes in the midst of curses, parallels of which have been found in many Assyrian and Hittite treaties: treaty of Šamši-adad V with Marduk-zakir-šumi I (*AfO* 8 [1932-33] 27-29), of Esarhaddon with Baʻal of Tyre (ibid., 29-34); Annals of Aššurbanipal, Cylinder B, ix (*ANET*, 300). Cf. Hos 9:11, 14; Lam 4:3-4; and the extensive study of this subject in Hillers, *Treaty-Curses and the Old Testament Prophets*.

שאת: "Ewe." This is apparently the abs. sg. fem. with the old ending *-at* (another case of which would be בקעת, Sf I B 10, and possibly Sf I C 20, if Dupont-Sommer is correct in interpreting לחית as singular; but the plural is not impossible there). The abs. pl. שאן is found in line 23. Dupont-Sommer is probably correct in relating this word to Hebrew שֶׂה, Ugaritic and Phoenician *š*, Akkadan *šu'*, and Arabic *šā*, even though it appears to be related to later Aramaic תאתא (Sachau, *APO*, pl. 63, §1 i 12; also on an unpublished ostracon [§170] of the Clermont-Ganneau collection, mentioned by Dupont-Sommer) and Ugaritic *ṯat* (Gordon, *UT*, 49:II:7, 29). In such a case one would have to write here *š't*. Is it the same word as *š'h* in Panammu 6:9? Cf. W. F. Albright, *HTS* 22 (1966) 44; S. Segert, *ArOr* 32 (1964) 119. This form which ends in *t* is scarcely the remains of an early Aramaic case-ending (an accusative), *pace* J. W. Wesselius ("Reste einer Kasusflektion").

אל: "Not." In addition to the negative prefix -ל there is also the adv. אל (see Sf I A 22-24, 28-29, 33, 36; I B 8; I C 24; Sf II A 2; III 7, 18, 20; possibly also in Sf III 9). Here it is used in a negative wish (= a curse in a treaty).

תהרי: "May she not conceive." The vocalization of this form is problematic. Should it be *tihray* or *tihrê*? Though no impfs. of tertiae infirmae verbs occur with a final yodh in Sf III (cf. impv. הוי in Sf III 22), there are several cases of this ending in the other two inscriptions (תהוי, Sf I A 25, 32; Sf II A [4], 6; תנש[י]י, Sf II A 4). These forms with final *yodh* must be compared with those with final *he* (יתחזה, Sf I A 28; יאתה, Sf I B 28; Sf III 11; תאתה, Sf I B 31; Sf III 11); esp. יהוה (Sf II A 4); יבעה (Sf II B 8; Sf III 2); תבעה (Sf II B 17); יהונה (Sf II B 16); תרשה (Sf III 9); תרקה (Sf III 18); תכה (Sf III 13). This evidence seems to point to the fact that the final diphthong *-ay* was undergoing contraction at this time, or perhaps had already undergone it in pronunciation, at least in the case of tertiae infirmae roots. For a less likely explanation, see S. Segert, *ArOr* 32 (1964) 124.

---

propos du nom propre syriaque Gusai," *Sem* 16 (1966) 39-41.

I persist in regarding the last syllable of the imperfect of tertiae infirmae verbs as vocalized with an original *a*-vowel, for otherwise it would be impossible to explain such a form as תפנו (Sf III 7). In later vocalization this form would be *tipnô* (compare the Biblical Aramaic form *yibnôn*, Ezra 6:7). This must be derived from *tipnaw* and should be so vocalized in these inscriptions. This would point to a thematic *a*-vowel throughout the imperfect; and this *a*-vowel conveniently explains the forms in final *he* and final *yodh* (= contracted and uncontracted *-ay* diphthongs in a period of transition). There is no valid reason to import from Hebrew the explanation that some forms are built on the active *galay*, and others on the stative *galiy*. This may be adequate for Hebrew, but what is the evidence for it in Aramaic, especially in the imperfect? The same explanation (an *a*-vowel) likewise suits the noun forms: לילה (Sf I A 12 [< *laylay*]), ארבה (Sf I A 27 [< *'arbay*]), צדה (Sf I A 33), גדה (Sf II A 2), אריה (Sf II A 9), צבי (Sf I A 33). Bauer ("Ein aramäischer Staatsvertrag," 7) regarded the root *hry* as "*sonst nicht aramäisch.*" Though it is found in 1QapGen 2:1 (הריאנתא [Kutscher's reading]), 15 (הריונא), one may still ask whether it is a genuine Aramaic verb.

ושבע [מהי]נקן: "Seven nurses." The form of the last word is a haphel ptc. of ינק, "suckle," and hence "nurses." The form is restored on the basis of the words in the following lines.

ימשח[ן שדיהן]: "Anoint their breasts." So restored by Dupont-Sommer. He explained, "En frottant leurs mamelles d'huile ordinaire ou aromatisée, les femmes pensaient sans doute obtenir un lait plus abondant." However, he gave no evidence of such a belief in antiquity. Hillers (*Treaty-Curses*, 61 n. 52) suggests a more prosaic explanation, since it is a common practice of nursing mothers to prevent soreness, cracking, etc. The curse of dry breasts is paralleled in Hos 9:14; Lam 4:3-4. Cf. K. Galling, "Das Salben der Mutterbrust (Sefire I A 21f.)," *ZDPV* 83 (1967) 134-35.

22. עלים: "A young boy." The word is found in 1QapGen 2:2 (עלימא) for a baby boy. It is the diminutive *qutayl* type of noun; hence vocalized as *'ulaym*.

ססיה: "A mare," the abs. sg. fem. form is used here in a collective sense. In later Aramaic (Imperial and Biblical) the noun used with cardinal numbers is usually in the plural; this we find also in line 23 (שאן), 21 (מהינקן). But the verb is plural, *yuhayniqān*. Vocalize: *sūsyāh*.

על: "A colt." Vocalize: *'īl*, as in later Aramaic and Syriac.

23. שורה: "A cow," again the abs. sg. fem. in a collective sense.

Possibly this is the same word as שאה ושורה in Panammu 6:9. Vocalize: *šawrāh*.

שאן: "Ewes." The form is the abs. pl. fem. of שאת (line 21).

אמר: "A lamb." Cf. *'immĕrā'* in later Aramaic (Ezra 6:9, 17; 7:17), and Akkadian *immeru*. Vocalize: *'immar*.

24. בכתה: The reading of this word is certain, but the interpretation of this line is difficult. Dupont-Sommer translated the line, "Et que sept poules aillent en quête de nourriture, et qu'elles ne tuent rien!" The word בכתה was explained by him as related to later Aramaic *'abbakā* and Syriac *bakkā'*, "cock," having, however, a double fem. ending, *-t* and *-āh*, meaning "hen." The parallels that he offered for the double fem. ending are all derived from plural nouns in Hebrew. If he assumes that *bkth* is plural, why should it be emphatic when used with a cardinal, since all the other examples are absolute? It seems to be an abs. sg. fem., but then what is the root and its meaning? The context may seem to demand the mention of some small animal after the mares, cows, and ewes.

Even though Dupont-Sommer's interpretation of this line encounters difficulties, I prefer it to that of Epstein ("Notes on the Sujin Pact," 39), who translated this line, ילכו לפשוט (למטוה) הות הערב ולא יבינו (ולא יצליחו במלאכתם), "(seven weaving women) will go to stretch out weaving yarn and shall not understand (and shall not succeed in their work)." Epstein related בכתה to Syriac *bkt*, "to weave," explained בשט as = *pšṭ*, an infin., and *lḥm* as = Arabic *luḫmatu*ⁿ, "woof, weft," and related הרג to Syriac *hrg*, "ponder over." These suggestions hardly fit the context after the animals mentioned. Moreover, one would expect a *lamedh* before the infin. בשט (cf. Sf I A 13; Sf I B 34). Galling (*ZDPV* 83 [1967] 135) agreed that the mention of weaving women disturbs the context; he also cited G. Dalman[24] for evidence of chickens killing worms, larvae, and bugs.

Hillers (*Treaty-Curses*, 71-74) interpreted the words as a curse involving the loss of men to satisfy the desires of prostitutes. He read ושבע בנתה יהכן בשט לחם ואל יהרגן, "and may his seven daughters go looking for food, but not seduce (anyone)." The reading of בנתה instead of בכתה eliminates grammatical difficulties; and others have preferred to read it so (e.g., Lemaire-Durand, *IAS*, 113). The explanation of יהרגן as a haphel of רגג is attractive (in Syriac the peal means "desire, covet, lust"; cf. also 2 Aqht 6:34-35). Thus translated, the curse would seem

24 *Arbeit und Sitte in Palästina* 7 [Gütersloh: 'Der Rufer' Evangelischer V., n.d.] 248.

to be parallel to the Tell Halaf malediction: "Whoever erases (my) name and puts (his) name, may he burn his seven sons before Adad, may he release his seven daughters as prostitutes for Ishtar" (see B. Meissner, *AfO* Beiheft 1 [Berlin, 1933] 72-73; W. F. Albright, *AnStud* 6 [1956] 75-85). However, this malediction really says just the opposite of the lack of men for prostitutes seeking business and food; in the Tell Halaf malediction the curse is prostitution itself, whereas in Sefire I it would be the lack of men to be seduced by "daughters" turned prostitutes. The parallel of Isa 4:1 is closer, and that of Deut 28:68 even more so. Attractive as Hillers's suggestion is, it should be noted that Bauer ("Ein aramäischer Staatsvertrag," 7) years ago similarly attempted to improve on Ronzevalle's reading: "und seine sieben Töchter mögen in Herumschweifen nach Brot gehen, und sie sollen nicht ...." His comment was: "ist doch wohl 'Hurerei' gemeint." Similarly Lemaire-Durand, *IAS*, 121.

In light of Bauer's suggestion, Dupont-Sommer scrutinized the stone anew and insisted on the certainty of the reading of בכתה: "La lecture de ces 4 lettres est tout à fait sure." The photographs seem to confirm his insistence. Hillers, however, remarks, perhaps too confidently, "If this is so, the error was that of the original stonecutter, who confused *k* and *n*, which in this period are roughly similar in form."[25] In light of all this I prefer to remain tentatively with the Dupont-Sommer's understanding of the line, until something better is proposed. So too Rössler, *TUAT*, 1. 180 (who simply transcribes *bkth*, without translating it).

Garbini also preferred to read בנתה, but interpreted לחם as "war," translating, "e che le sue sette figlie vadano in cerca di lotta e non uccidano" ("Appunti di epigrafia aramaica," 89-92). A. Lemaire compared שט לחם with *pat leḥem* of Gen 18:5 and understood -ב as *beth pretii* (see Ezek 13:19), translating the phrase "for a crust of bread" ("Sfire I A 24," 161-70). Gibson (*TSSI* 2.31) translates, "his seven daughters shall go walking while the bread gets burnt, but let them show no concern!" But he does not explain or justify that translation.

With the discovery of the Assyrian-Aramaic bilingual inscription of Tell Fekheriyeh new light may have been shed on this line. Line 22 of

25 Hillers also mentions a chronological difficulty connected with this interpretation: "The domestic fowl was not introduced in large numbers to the Near East and Europe until the Persian period, and even if hens were sporadically imported before that time -- they had long been raised in India -- they would not have been present in sufficient quantity to figure in an 8th century curse. . . ." (p. 72). How do we know? His footnote about the earliest certain artistic representation of a cock (on the seal of Jaazaniah from Tell en-Nasbeh [ca. 600]) cites an example before the Persian period.

that inscription reads: ומאה נשון לאפן בתנור לחם ואל ימלאנה, "and let a hundred women bake bread in an oven, but not fill it." The parallel of this curse with Lev 26:26 and with this line of Sf I was immediately noticed. Given the foregoing curses about women suckling a child, ewes suckling a lamb, and cows suckling a calf, which are found in both inscriptions, as well as the mention of לחם in both, this line in Sf I may also be speaking of the same sort of curse. Indeed, in light of the Fekheriyeh inscription, S. A. Kaufman has proposed to read this line thus: ושבע בנתה יאפן ב..ט לחם ואל ימלאן, "and may his seven daughters bake bread in an oven(?) but not fill (it)" ("Reflections," 170-72). Similarly E. Puech ("Les traités araméens," 91). That, however, reads several letters differently and remains problematic.

יהכן: 3d pl. masc. impf peal. This form also occurs in Sf III 5, where Dupont-Sommer understood it as a form of הלך. Cf. F. Rundgren, "Zum Lexikon des Alten Testaments," *AcOr* 21 (1950-53) 301-45, esp. 304-16. But it is better taken as a form of הוך, as T. Nöldeke (*ZA* 20 [1907] 142) once suggested; cf. BLA §46b. This root is related to Ethiopic *hôka*. Other occurrences of the same root are in Sf III 6 (אהך), Sf I 24 (יהכן).

בשט לחם: "Looking for food," lit. "in search of food." If correctly read, בשט is to be understood as a peal infin. without preformative *mem* of שוט, "rove about" (see Job 1:7; 2:2). Hillers cites the interesting parallel of Num 11:8.

ואל יהרגן: "May they not kill (anything)." The curse seems to say that the animals shall not find anything to kill. הרג is used in Hebrew of an animal (Job 20:16); it is found in Aramaic in Hadad 26, 33, 34; Panammu 3, 5, 7, and in Moabite (Meša' 11). Cf. H. Tawil (*JNES* 32 [1973] 480-81), who translates [ל]הרגה of Hadad 34, "to destroy it," equating הרג with Akkadian *dâku*.

והן ישקר מתע]אל ול[ברה, "And if Mati'el should be unfaithful <to Bar-Ga'yah> and to his son." At the end of the line there is room for only four letters, two of which must be the end of Mati'el's name, i.e. *'l*, and the other two must be *wl-*, required by the syntax. Something has, therefore, been omitted, to which the suffix on ברה refers, and this can only be the name of Bar-Ga'yah, which is supplied in the translation. Moreover, this addition is confirmed by the fragmentary text of Sf II A 3, where Bar-Ga'yah's name is certain and the context is quite similar to this line.

25. כמלכת חל מלכת חל מזי...: "May his kingdom become like a kingdom of sand, a kingdom of sand, as long as ...." The problem here is the division of words. I prefer this reading, which is basically that of

Bauer ("Ein aramäischer Staatsvertrag," 7-8), to that of Dupont-Sommer, כמלכת חלם לכת חלם זי ימלך, which he translates, "que son royaume soit comme un royaume de songe < >, sur lequel régnera Assur!" He appeals to Ps 73:20; Job 20:8 for a similar use of "dream" and considers the letters לכת חלם as dittographical. Donner-Röllig (*KAI*, 1. 41; 2. 239) prefer to read כמלכת חל מלכת חלם זי, and translate, "dann soll sein Königreich wie ein Sandkönigreich, ein Traumkönigreich werden, das Assur beherrscht." Similarly Lemaire-Durand, *IAS*, 113. Donner-Röllig appeal to the same biblical loci. This is better than Dupont-Sommer's explanation, but it encounters the difficulty that one would expect the retrospective pronoun on *b-* or *'l* to follow the relative *zy*. Dupont-Sommer sensed this difficulty and referred to P. Joüon, *GHB* §158i. But can the prep. *b-* be omitted with *mlk*? It is possible to explain the expression מלכת חל as dittographical, since it occurs before in the line; and a "kingdom of sand" is no more forced than a "dream-kingdom." The sense of Bar-Ga'yah's curse is that, if Mati'el proves unfaithful to the treaty, then may the might of great Assyria fall upon his kingdom, rendering it one of sand. He hopes that it will be a worthless kingdom as long as Asshur is powerfully ruling.

מזי ימלך אשר: "As long as Asshur rules." Dupont-Sommer admitted that the reading of the final *reš* was not certain. If it is correct, then we have a defective writing of *'Aššûr*, which often turns up *plene scriptum* (Bar-Rakkab 9; Panammu 7, 11, 12bis, 13, 15, 16, 17). The *scriptio plena* persisted in later Aramaic: אשור (1QapGen 17:8); אתור (*A* 3, 4, 5, 8). The only other places where it occurs defectively are Kilamuwa 8 and 1 Chr 5:6 (both not Aramaic). It is not impossible here, even though unusual. The form אשר, with a *š*, also is noteworthy. Degen (*WO* 4 [1967] 58 n. 49) raised a question about it, comparing Akkadian *aššur*, Egyptian *'á-śú-ra*, Ugaritic *a̱tr*, Old Aramaic *'šr*, and Imperial Aramaic and Syriac *'twr*. His verdict: "eine semitische Herkunft [des Wortes ist] nicht erwiesen." But who is אשר? Is it the god whose name is now restored at the end of line 7? More likely it refers to the country; but then would Bar-Ga'yah be wishing that Assyria be so strong as to reduce Arpad? What sort of relation between Bar-Ga'yah and Assyria is implied in such case?

I interpret מזי as = *mn zy*, a temporal conjunction; cf. Dan 4:23. The sense seems to be that Bar-Ga'yah is wishing misfortune for Mati'el's kingdom at the hands of Asshur (god or kingdom), if he is not faithful to the treaty. Cf. Z. Ben-Hayyim, *Lešonenu* 35 (1971) 244.

[יסך ה]דד: "May Hadad pour (over it)." The first word is supplied as in the following line. For the restoration of Hadad, see lines 36, 38. The mention of the name of a god is usual in such treaty-curses; cf. the treaty of Aššurnirari V (Rev. IV, 4.8; V, 5); of Šamši-adad V with Marduk-zākir-šumi I (passim); of Esarhaddon with Ba'al of Tyre (Rev. II, 1-19) and his vassal treaties (lines 414-93).

26. כל מה: "Every sort of." The interpretation of this word is now certain. It has nothing to do with כלמה, "disgrace" (so Driver, *AfO* 8 [1932-33] 204; Cross and Freedman, *EHO*, 28), or with a king's name (see note on Sf I B 2); it is simply a compound pronoun. It occurs again in Sf I A 30; I B 2; III 16, 28, 29. See also the Tariff of Palmyra (Cooke, *NSI* §147) i, 12 (*klm' gns klh*). In Bar-Rakkab 15 it is written *kl . mh* (with a word-divider between the pronouns).

לחיה: "Evil." The form is the abs. sg. fem. of a tertiae infirmae root, *lhy*. The word also occurs in Sf I C 7 (לחיה), 20 (לחית), Sf III 2 (לחית); Nerab 1. 10 (לחה), B-M 6 (לחיא), *AP* 30:7; 31:6; 32:6; *AD* 5:7. Cf. Greenfield, *AcOr* 29 (1965) 8-9.

בארק ובשמין: "(Which exists) on earth and in heaven." Cf. the treaty of Aššurnirari V (Rev. IV, 8); 2 Sam 22:8. Cf. H. J. van Dijk, *VT* 18 (1968) 28-29: "over earth and heaven, and every sort of damage; may he pour out [hailst]ones over Arpad." But why should Hadad do this to heaven? It may mean rather "sky," and one may have a parallel in Apoc 16:8 (the fourth plague-bowl poured out over the sun).

[אבני ב]רד: "Hailstones," restored by Dupont-Sommer, comparing Jos 10:11; Isa 30:30.

27. ושבע שנן: "For seven years." שנן is the abs. pl. (masc. form) of the fem. noun שנה, here used adverbially.

ארבה: "The locust." G. Garbini (*AA*, 247) analyzed this form as an emphatic, which is impossible, since the cognates in Hebrew (אַרְבֶּה), Ugaritic (*irby*), and Akkadian (*arbū, erbū, erebū*) show that the word is quadrilitteral and that the final consonant is weak, *-y*. Hence, the *he* represents a contraction from *-ay*; Cross and Freedman (*EHO*, 28) prefer an original *-iy*). Vocalize: *'arbêh*. Cf. Esarhaddon's vassal treaties (lines 442-43): "May the locust that diminishes the land devour your harvest." Note the similar sequence of hail and devouring locusts in Exod 10:5; Ps 105:32-34. Cf. Segert, *ArOr* 32 (1964) 124.

תולעה: "The worm." Cf. the later Aramaic *tôla'tāh*, Syriac *tawla'tā'*, Hebrew *tôlē'āh*. Vocalize: *tawla'āh*. Cf. Deut 28:39; Jon 4:7. Cf. H. Tawil, "A Curse concerning Crop-consuming Insects in the Sefire Treaty and in Akkadian: A New Interpretation," *BASOR* 225 (1977) 59-62.

[יס]ק: "Come up." See Sf I A 5; also possible would be [יפ]ק, from נפק (see line 28).

28. תוי: This word appears here for the first time in Aramaic. Is it perhaps related to Ugaritic *thw*, Arabic *tyh*, or Hebrew *tôhû*, which Koehler-Baumgartner translate as "waterless, impassable desert"? It must refer to some sort of blight, since it follows the attack of locusts and worms and precedes the mention of the lack of vegetation. Koopmans (*BO* 17 [1960] 52) wondered whether it might not be related to Hebrew *t'y* or *t'w* (Deut 14:5; Isa 51:20), which seems to mean "Wildschaf, Wildstier." But does that really fit the context? -- For the sequence *twy, twl'h, 'rbh* (in reverse order), see Deut 28:38-42; cf. M. Weinfeld, "Traces of Assyrian Treaty Formulae in Deuteronomy," *Bib* 46 (1965) 417-27, esp. 424 n. 2, who equates *twy* with "cricket" (Hebrew *ṣlṣl*), comparing Deut 28:38-42. But crickets are not locusts. Greenfield (*JBL* 87 [1968] 241) would rather read ת<ה>וי as a verb and assume a noun in the fem. sg. before it. Cf. Z. Ben-Hayyim, *Lešonenu* 35 (1971) 245; H. Tawil, *BASOR* 225 (1977) 59-60.

ארקה: "Its land," a fem. suffixal form, and not an emphatic (*pace* G. Garbini, *AA*, 247). Vocalize: *'arqah*.

חצר: "Grass." This seems to be a Canaanite loanword, like Hebrew חָצִיר. So E. Y. Kutscher, "Aramaic," 360. But compare the later Aramaic *ḥăṣîrā'*. Also the treaty of Aššurnirari V (Rev. IV. 20): *urqit ṣēri lū uṣṣā*, "may the green of the field not come forth" (see McCarthy, *Treaty and Covenant*, 196); Deut 29:22.

וליתחזה: "So that (no green) may be seen." Dupont-Sommer divided the words thus: ולית חזה, equating the first word with the later Aram. לית (< *l' 'yty*), which he translated, "qu'on n'y voie plus de verdure." He is followed by Koopmans (*AC*, 51). His translation is correct, but he has not explained the form חזה resulting from such a division. Since the prefixed negative *lā-* is abundantly attested in these inscriptions, I prefer to read it here too, with an ithpeel form: *wa-lā-yithazêh*. Rather than understand it as a negative wish (which would rather demand *'l* with impf.), I prefer to regard it as a result clause, "so that there may not be seen ...." The same is true of the restored form at the end of the line. The prefixed *l-* is found also in the Egyptian Aramaic ostracon, Cl-G 137 conv. 1 (Dupont-Sommer, "Note sur le mot *TQM* dans les ostraca araméens d'Eléphantine," *Sem* 14 [1964] 71-72, esp. 72). Cf. Greenfield, "Linguistic Matters in the Sfire Inscriptions," *Lešonenu* 27-28 (1964) 303-13, esp. 308, where he reads rather ולי[שגה], comparing Job 8:11. But other ithpeel forms occur in line 29 (*ytšm'*), line 32 (*yštḥṭ*). See Garbini, "Sefire I A, 28," *RSO* 36 (1961) 9-11, who compares Bar Rakkab 16 and Lev 10:9.

29. אחוה: "Its vegetation." The same word occurs in line 32. Dupont-Sommer related it to Hebrew אָחוּ, "grass" (Gen 41:2, 18; Job 8:11) and Ugaritic *aḫ*, "meadow." T. O. Lambdin ("Egyptian Loan Words in the Old Testament," *JAOS* 73 [1953] 146) regards it as derived from Egyptian; so too J. Vergote, who translates it "fourré de papyrus" (*Joseph en Egypte* [Louvain: Publications Universitaires, 1959] 57-66). But see the remarks of B. Couroyer, *RB* 66 (1959) 588; J. M. A. Janssen, *JEOL* 14 (1955-56) 68. The final *he* is to be taken as a fem. suffix, referring to Arpad; vocalize *'aḥwah*.

יתשמע: "May ... be heard." Note the lack of metathesis here in contrast to ישתחט (line 32). Greenfield fails to note this (*JBL* 87 [1968] 241).

קל כנר: "The sound of the lyre." Dupont-Sommer refers to Ezek 26:13, "The sound of your harps shall be heard no more," and to the treaty of Aššurnirari V (Rev. IV, 19), "then may the farmer in his field not strike up a song." Cf. Apoc 18:22. Vocalize: *qāl kinnār*.

ובעמה: "Among its people." If this reading is certain, then we have an expression parallel to that of line 30. In both cases the suffix is fem., referring to Arpad (fem. in line 35). K. J. Cathcart (*Nahum in the Light of Northwest Semitic* [BibOr 26; Rome: Biblical Institute, 1973] 110) would take ובעמה with the preceding clause, "Nor may the sound of the lyre be heard in Arpad and among its people."

המל מרק: "(Let there rather be) the din of affliction." In interpreting this phrase, I originally followed Dupont-Sommer, even though his solution was not completely satisfactory. It is necessary to supply an adversative conjunction here in the translation, which contrasts this and following nouns with קל כנר. Dupont-Sommer related המל to Hebrew *hămullāh*, "din" (Jer 11:16; Ezek 1:24). The word מרק is to be understood as a noun, "affliction," derived from the root *mrḍ*, related to Hebrew *mrṣ*, "be sick," Akkadian *marāṣu*, Arabic *mariḍa*, and later Aramaic *mĕra'*. This plausible interpretation has been proposed by C. Brekelmans, "Sefire I A 29-30," *VT* 13 (1963) 225-28.

והמ]ית צע[קה: "And the noise of crying." Brekelmans (ibid. 27) proposed this reading, which is preferable to והמ]ון ל[קח read by Dupont-Sommer with an improbable *scriptio plena*. Bauer ("Ein aramäischer Staatsvertrag," 8) read the beginning of line 30 as קה, and the photograph (pl. VI) shows that this is preferable to Dupont-Sommer's reading of קח. Cf. D. Pardee, *JNES* 37 (1978) 197.

30. ויללה: "And lamentation," cf. later Aramaic *yĕlaltā'*, Hebrew *yĕlālāh* (Isa 15:8). Note its similar paralllelism to צעקה in Zeph 1:10.

Cf. Deut 28:47-57.

וישלחן אלהן: "May the gods send." For a similar use of the verb שלח, see Deut 32:24.

מן כל מה אכל: "Every sort of devourer." The use of מן here is peculiar; Dupont-Sommer regarded it as the preposition *min* and took it as "probablement partitif," translating, "des devoreurs de toute espèce." This is correct. *'ākil* is the act. ptc., used as a substantive. For the curse of devouring animals, see Hillers, *Treaty-Curses*, 54-56. Cf. Lev 26:22; Deut 32:24. H. Tawil (*BASOR* 225 [1977] 60) has tried to interpret כל מה differently, this time seeing it as כלמה, an Aramaic word related to Akkadian *kalmatu*, "louse." But that is not to be accepted.

[פ]ם: "Mouth," to be vocalized *pum* (< *pumm*). Compare the repetitious use of *ina pi* in an entirely different context, however, in Esarhaddon's vassal treaties (lines 111ff.).

31. חוה: "Serpent," as in later Aramaic, *ḥiwyā'*, pl. *ḥiwwîn*. The form here is abs. sg. fem., as is the state of most of the other names of animals mentioned. Vocalize: *ḥiwwāh*. Cf. Jer 8:17; Tg. Onqelos, Gen 49:17 (*ḥîwwê*).

עקרב: "Scorpion," as in later Aramaic, *'aqrabbā'*, Hebrew *'aqrāb*, Arabic *'aqrabu*^{n,} Akkadian *aqrabu*. The expression, "the mouth of a scorpion," is strange because the scorpion attacks with its tail; cf. Apoc 9:10.

דבהה: "A bear." Dupont-Sommer says that the reading דבהה is certain, but he prefers to correct it to דברה, comparing the later Aramaic *dabbĕrītā', dibborītā'* and Syriac *debbārtā'*, "bee, wasp." Similarly Lemaire-Durand, *IAS*, 114; Rössler, *TUAT*, 1. 181. I prefer to interpret דבהה as a fem. form of the later Aramaic *dubbā'*, Hebrew *dōb*, for the bear fits better into the context, and the *ursus syriacus* was well known in that part of the world. Cf. 1 Sam 17:34; Hos 13:8. The form דבהה is peculiar; it should be related to כהסי, "my throne" (perhaps *kuhsī* for *kussî*) in Sf III 17. Vocalize: *dubhāh*. Cf. J. A. Rimbach, "Bears or Bees?"; T. Wittstruck, "The Influence of Treaty Curse Imagery."

נמרה: "Panther," the female, since the word is abs. sg. fem. Cf. later Aramaic *nimrā'*, Syriac *nemrā'*, Hebrew *nāmēr*, Akkadian *nimru*, Arabic *nimru*^{n}. Cf. Jer 5:6; Hos 13:7; Hab 1:8.

סס: "Moth," related to later Aramaic and Syriac *sāsā'*, Hebrew *sās*, Akkadian *sāsu*. Cf. *A* 184, 186; Hos 5:12; Isa 51:8; Gilgamesh Epic, 12:93-94.

קמל: "Louse," agreeing with the Arabic *qamlu*^{n}, against the later metathesized form in Aramaic, *qalmĕtā'* and Syriac *qalmā*. But cf. H. Tawil, *BASOR* 225 (1977) 61.

ואז..] יהוו] עלה קק בתן: This part of the sentence is difficult. Dupont-Sommer read ואז[ף יפלן] עלה קקבתן, which he translated, "et, en ou[tre, que s'abbattent] sur elle des perdrix (?)!" He understood עלה as a form of the prep. על (= *'alêha*). If that were correct, there would be a case of the defective writing of a contracted medial diphthong *ay*; but compare *'pyh* (Sf I A 42); *'ly[h]* (Sf III 9). I have no better solution for this word.

It is better to begin a new sentence with וסס וקמל, because they are not preceded by פם, as in the foregoing phrases. Dupont-Sommer related קקבתן to Syriac *qaqbānā'*, "partridge," and Akkadian *qaqabānu*. But the *t* preceding the *nun* creates a problem. Here it can scarcely be a fem. form. More likely there are two words here, as Cantineau (*RA* 28 [1931] 172) once suggested. בתן is related to Ugaritic *bṯn*, "serpent," *bašmu* in Akkadian (cf. *AHW*, 112), but *pitnā'* in later Aramaic, *patnā'* in Syriac, and *peten* in Hebrew. This would mean that Proto-Semitic *tha* is represented here by *t*, as in ירת (Sf I C 24). There is also *b* instead of *p*, as in *nbš* for *npš* (Sf III 5-6; Sf I B 40, 42; Sf II B 5; Hadad 17, 21, 22; Panammu 18), and possibly in *'lb* for *'lp* (Hadad 34). Cf. Garbini, "Considerazioni sulla parola ebraica *peten*," *RivB* 6 (1958) 263-65. קק is, furthermore, not the word for "pelican," but the early form of *qō'ā'*, "throat, neck," found in the Babylonian Talmud. An interesting parallel occurs in *b. Berakot* 49a (Goldschmidt 1. 175): זקפיה רב ששת לקועיה עלי כחוויא, "da reckte R. Šešeth seinen Hals gegen mich wie eine Schlange." Hence "towards it the throat of a serpent." In this curse a wish is probably being expressed that even small insects may become far more voracious toward Arpad than was ordinary. So, restore יהוו (= *yihwaw*). Cf. P. Nober, *VD* 39 (1961) 112; W. F. Albright, *The Protosinaitic Inscriptions and their Decipherment* (HTS 22; Cambridge, MA: Harvard University, 1966) 39. Cf. Deut 32:24 for a similar evil: ואשלח בם שן בהמות, "and I shall send against them the tooth of beasts."

Rosenthal (*ANESTP*, 224) translates, "[There shall be no] *foliage. Defoliated,* it will be laid waste." He understands עלה as "leaf, foliage," and קקבתן as an adj. that ends in *-tn*, from the Arabic (root) *qḍb* or (Hebrew) root *qṣb/p*. Similarly, Gibson, *TSSI*, 2. 31, 41.

32. [יש]תחט: "May it be destroyed." Dupont-Sommer restored this verb, explaining it is an alternate form of *šḥt* and claiming that the confusion of the two roots is attested in Syriac. But Greenfield maintains that the two roots are kept distinct there (*JBL* 87 [1967] 241). In any case, the form is an ithpaal jussive with metathesis. Cf. The Treaty of Aššurnirari V (Rev. V, 5-6).

לישמן: "Unto desolation," lit. "for a desert." Cf. Hebrew *yĕšîmôn*. Vocalize: *yašīmān* (*qatīl-ān* type of noun). Cf. Deut 32:10; Ps 68:8.

תל: "A mound," i.e., a tell. Cf. Hebrew *tēl,* later Aramaic *tillā'*, Akkadian *tillu*.

לרבק צי]: Lit., "for the roost of the desert animal." Dupont-Sommer compared Hebrew *rbṣ* and later Aramaic *rb'*, "lie down," often used of animals. The restored form would be a noun, the *nomen regens* of an extended construct chain. צי is restored by Dupont-Sommer on the basis of Isa 13:21; see also 34:11-15; Zeph 2:13-15.

33. צבי: "Gazelle"; cf. Hebrew *ṣĕbî*, Akkadian *ṣabītu*, Arabic *ẓabyu*ⁿ, and later Aramaic *ṭabyā'*. The last mentioned points to a form like *ṣabay* here. See the note on תהרי (line 21 above).

שעל: "Fox"; cf. Hebrew *šû'āl*, later Aramaic *ta'ălû*, Arabic *ṯu'ālu*ⁿ. Cf. Ezek 13:4; Lam 5:18.

ארנב: "Hare"; cf. Hebrew *'arnebet*, Syriac *'arnĕbā'*, Arabic *'arnabu*ⁿ, and Akkadian *annabu*. The *reš* is probably a secondary substitute for the doubled *n*; compare *Darmeśeq* and *Dammeśeq*; *korsĕya'* and *kussu*.

שרן: "The wild-cat," well-known as a devourer of fowl and a general pest. Dupont-Sommer related the word to Akkadian *šurānu*. Subsequently, Fensham ("The Wild Ass in the Aramean Treaty") maintained that the final *n* was not clear and could be read as *m*. Hence שרם could be understood as the equivalent of Akkadian *sirrimu*, "wild ass," an animal that plays a part in ancient Near Eastern maledictions.[25] However, Greenfield ("Three Notes," 98-100) adequately disposed of Fensham's suggestion and brought together additional data to support Dupont-Sommer's interpretation of the word as "wild-cat."

צדה: Probably the "owl"; cf. Arabic *ṣadâ*, later Aramaic *ṣadĕyā'*. The latter word, however, can mean in Aramaic either an "unclean bird" or a type of "grasshopper." Either meaning could be defended here, but the meaning "owl" is preferred in the context. Vocalize: *ṣadêh* (abs. sg., from **ṣaday*).

עקה: "Magpie," so Dupont-Sommer, relating it to Arabic *'aq'aqu*ⁿ. Perhaps to be vocalized as *'aqāh* (abs. sg. fem.).

אל תאמר: "May . . . not be mentioned," 3d sg. fem. short impf. (= jussive) passive of אמר, a yuqtal-type, also attested in Sf I A 36 (*t'mr* ?), 38 (*tšbr*), 40 (*ygzr, ygzrn*), 41 (*t'rrn* ?); 42 (*[tqḥ], yqḥn*); Sf II C 3 (*y[r]šmn*). Dupont-Sommer compared a similar use of אמר in Hebrew

25 Cf. J. Nougayrol, "*Sirrimu* (non **purîmu*) 'ane sauvage,'" *JCS* 2 (1948) 203-8; D. J. Wiseman, *Vassal Treaties of Esarhaddon*, 59-60 (*kima sirrimme*). Cf. Isa 32:14.

(Ps 40:11; Neh 6:19) in the sense of "mention." It also occurs in Sf I A 36.

קר]יתא הא]: This restoration of Dupont-Sommer makes good sense, as it would refer to Arpad, and the following list of names connected by *waw* makes the suggestion all the more plausible. They are probably the "daughter-cities" of Arpad (cf. Num 21:25, 32), towns (or perhaps regions) that were subject to Mati'el. Noth (*ZDPV* 77 [1961] 136 n. 51) observed that the words beginning with *mem* might seem to be appellatives rather than proper names; but since they are coordinated to obvious names, they too should undoubtedly be so regarded.

34. מדרא: A town whose location is unknown. The root in the name may be like that of *Dūrā* (Dan 3:1) or like Akkadian *Dūru*. S. Segert (*ArOr* 32 [1964] 122) considered this name to be an emphatic state of a common noun, "settlement."

מרבה: A place-name perhaps like the biblical *Mĕrîbāh* (Exod 17:7; Ps 95:8.). Its location is unknown.

מזה: Perhaps *Mazêh*. Dupont-Sommer preferred to refer it to *Mazî*, the name of a place near Tyre attested in the Talmud.

מבלה: An unknown site.

שרן: "Sharun." This is probably the town of *Sa-ru-na* mentioned in an inscription of Tiglathpileser III as one of the *alāni ša* ^{mat}*Bīt A-di-ni* (see S. Schiffer, *Die Aramäer*, 71). Cf. W. F. Albright, *The Vocalization of the Egyptian Syllabic Orthography* (American Oriental Series 5; New Haven: American Oriental Society, 1934) 55. It is probably to be identified with modern *Sārîn*, about 49 km. NNE of Tell Refâd, on one of the tributaries of the Sājûr River. Cf. *ARAB*, 1, §821; K. Elliger, *Festschrift Otto Eissfeldt* (Halle an der S.: Niemeyer, 1947) 93.

תואם: "Tu'im." Dupont-Sommer compared this name with *Tu-'-im-mi* in the Annals of Tiglathpileser III (III. 24, 148; ed. P. Rost). Cf. *ARAB*, 1. §772. If this identification be correct, then we have another instance of a medial long *u* written with *waw*. Degen, however, would vocalize the name as *Taw'am*, a name related to the word for "twin" (*AG*, 27 n. 10).

ביתאל: Though no Bethel is known in Aramaic territory, this name is probably the same as the biblical name (cf. Gen 12:8; 13:3).

בינן: An unknown site.

35. [א]רנה: Understood by Dupont-Sommer as Arne, one of the principal towns of the kingdom of Arpad, perhaps the modern Erwin, situated ca. 21 km. SW of Arpad; see R. Dussaud, *Topographie historique de la Syrie*, 468. Noth (*ZDPV* 77 [1961] 137) suggested that this might be uru*Ḫaurāni* (*Ḫa-u-ra-a-ni*) of Tiglathpileser III's list (Kleine Inschrift, 2.26); it has been identified by K. Elliger (*Festschrift Otto Eissfeldt*, 93) with Ḥawart en-Nahr, ca. 14 km. ENE of Arpad.

חזז: "Ḥazaz." Most likely the *Ḫazazu* of various Akkadian texts; see S. Schiffer, *Die Aramäer,* 71; *ARAB*, 1. §821; J. D. Hawkins, "Ḫazazu," *RLA* 4. 240. It lay east of the upper course of the River Afrin, ca. 13 km. NNW of Arpad. The modern Arabic name, however, is ʿAzaz.

אדם: "Adam." Probably the same place as that mentioned in line 10 (see note there).

איך זי: "Just as." The same formula is found in lines 38, [39]; but in line 37 we have איכה זי. The latter should not be taken as evidence that the form found here was pronounced *'aykā*, with the difference being merely graphic. It is more likely a fuller form with the adverbial ending *-ā*; cf. *LFLAA*, §47b. It is a formula used to introduce curses which are to affect Matiʿel and his people; they are accompanied by some dynamistic rite, symbolizing the gravity of the oaths sworn. Cf. the passage in the treaty of Aššurnirari V (Obv. I, 15 ff.), where Mati'ilu is compared with a ram taken from the herd at the head of which he will no longer stand. The Akkadian equivalent of איך זי is *ki ša*, a formula also used in a series of similar curses in Esarhaddon's vassal treaties (line 530). Cf. M. Weinfeld, *UF* 8 (1976) 400. 9.

תקד: "Is burned." 3d sg. fem. impf. peal of יקד (stative formation); vocalize: *tiqqad*.

שעותא: "Wax." The meaning is clear, but the vocalization and orthography present a problem. In Syriac the form attested is *šĕʿôtā'* or *šĕʿûtā'*, whereas Jewish Aramaic has preserved it as *šaʿawtā', šĕʿûtā'*, or *šaʿăwātā'*. The Hebrew form is *šaʿăwāh*, and the Arabic *saʿwatu*n. Hence the question: Do we have here *šaʿawta'* or *šaʿūta'*? It is hard to say. It seems better to take the form as diphthongal, given the preponderance of evidence for the *scriptio plena* of the uncontracted diphthongs over against that for medial long *u*. Segert (*ArOr* 32 [1964] 125) prefers to regard it as a fem. in *-ut*. Bauer ("Ein aramäischer Staatsvertrag," 9) pointed out the similarity of these ritual formulas involving wax figurines to the Hittite military oaths (see J. Friedrich, "Der hethitische Soldateneid," *ZA* 35 [1924] 163: I, 41-45; II, 1-3 [*ANET*, 353]). Here the figurine was roughly in the form of a town; in line 37 it would represent Matiʿel (cf. line 39, "man of wax"). See also Esarhaddon's vassal treaties (lines 608-10). For references relating this practice to the larger context of magic, see J. Cantineau (*RA* 28 [1931] 174); C. Picard, "Le rite magique des εἴδωλα de cire brulés, attesté sur trois stèles araméennes de Sfiré," *RArch* 2 (1961) 85-88.

זא: "This." K. R. Veenhof (*VT* 22 [1972] 383) comments: "That the act described in the curse was actually performed to impress those taking the oath, is clear from the use of the demonstrative pronoun (*z'*) in the Sfiré-inscriptions; but a similar pronoun is also occasionally used in the text of the Esarhaddon treaty (*Iraq* 20, 1958, 76 line 612: 'Just as *this* charriot [sic!] . . .') and in that of Aššurnirāri's treaty (*AfO* 8, 1932f., 18, 10 and 21)."

באש: "By fire." Dupont-Sommer calls attention to the masculine form of the noun used here, whereas in later Aramaic it is usually fem., אשה (AšOstr 17; *AP* 30:12; *A* 103, 104, 222), *'iššātā', 'eššātā'* (Syr.). Cf. Akkadian *išātu*, Ugaritic *išt*. The form of Dan 7:11, אשא, with an *aleph*, not a *he*, is usually taken as fem. sg. abs. There is no reason why this masc. form could not be fem. in function. For a similar expression, see Ps 68:3.

At the end of this line Dupont-Sommer supplies ו[בנתה ר]בת, which he translates, "et [ses filles nom]breuses," referring to the daughter-cities of Arpad (see note on line 33). The first word is plausible, but the restoration of [ר]בת is questionable, as even Dupont-Sommer sensed. Can the abs. pl. fem. (archaic form as in Sf III 2, 22) modify a suffixal form? Does the adj. רב ever have the meaning "many" in Aramaic? Normally, it means "great," and if the restoration were correct, it would have to be so translated.

36. ויזרע בהן הדד מלח: "May Hadad sow salt in them." For the practice of spreading salt on a devastated town, see Judg 9:45 (Abimelech treats Shechem in this fashion); Deut 29:22; Jer 17:6; Zeph 2:9; Job 39:6. The practice is attested in Assyrian annals; see the Cylinder Inscription of Tiglathpileser I, VI: 14; cf. E. A. W. Budge and L. W. King, *Annals of the Kings of Assyria* (London: British Museum, 1902), l. 79; E. Weidner, *AOB* 1 (1926) 116-17; *AfO* 5 (1928-29) 90-91 (line 39). Is this merely "un geste magique," as Dupont-Sommer suggests? Is it not rather a wish expressed that the god Hadad will render the area of the towns completely unproductive -- an idea which is expressed by the figure of "sowing salt?"[26]

שחלין: "Weeds." Dupont-Sommer translates this word as "cresson" (watercress), comparing it with Mishnaic *šiḥlayīm*, *šĕḥālîm*, later Aramaic and Syriac *taḥlê* (identified by I. Löw, *Aramäische Pflanzennamen* [Leipzig: Engelman, 1881] 396, as *lepidium sativum*). The word

26 Cf. F. C. Fensham, "Salt as Curse in the Old Testament and the Ancient Near East," *BA* 25 (1962) 48-50; W. L. Moran, *Bib* 39 (1958) 71; J. Friedrich and B. Landsberger, *ZA* 41 (1933) 316-18; A. M. Honeyman, *VT* 3 (1953) 192-95.

seems to be related to the Akkadian *saḫlê*, which is used in an identical way in one of the Annals of Aššurbanipal: *nagê* [kur]*Elamti*[ki] *ušaḫrib ṭābta* [ú]*saḫlê ušappiḫa ṣiruššun*, "the districts of Elam I laid waste, salt and cress (or tares) I strewed thereon" (G. R. Driver, *AfO* 8 [1932-33] 204); see Rassam-Cylinder, VI. 78-80; *ARAB* 2. §811; VAB 7.56-57. The context of both the Akkadian and Aramaic texts demands the name of some destructive weed. The form of the word is also problematic. Is it *šaḥlīn* (with medial long *i* fully written) or *šaḥlayin*? Even the first consonant may be questioned; if it is related to the Mishnaic and Syriac words, it would be *š*. Cf. also the occurrence of the word in the Elephantine Ostracon (Cairo Museum, No. 35468b): ושחלין טב כסא זעירא (*RES* 3. 1296; *AC* 35). Cf. R. C. Thompson, *A Dictionary of Assyrian Botany* (London: British Academy, 1949) 55-61; B. Landsberger, *OLZ* 25 (1922) 343 n. 3.

ואל תאמר גנבא זנה ו[נבשא זא] מתעאל ונבשה הא: "And may it not be mentioned (again)! This GNB' and [...] (are) Mati‘el; it is his person." This is the reading of Dupont-Sommer, which he translates, "et qu'on n'en parle plus! Ce bandit(?)-ci et [cette âme-ci], c'est Mati'el et son âme." Similarly Rössler (*TUAT* 1. 181). In such an interpretation תאמר is taken as 3d sg. fem. impf. pass. (*yuqtal* type; see note on line 33 above). The identification of Mati‘el with a figurine would then be the burden of the next sentence. It has in its favor a similar statement of identity found in the treaty of Aššurnirari V (Obv. I, 21-22): "This head is not the head of the ram; it is the head of Mati'ilu." The difficulty is the meaning of the word גנבא. Normally, it would mean "thief" (*gannābā'*); Dupont-Sommer mentions another meaning found apparently only in Jewish Aramaic, "tail" (*gōnĕbā* or *gĕnūbtā'*). The latter meaning does not fit the context at all; the meaning of the former is not too satisfactory either. But there is a further difficulty. The sentence beginning with ואל תאמר seems to have גנבא זנה as its subject (or object?). Could it not possibly be, "And you shall not mention this GNB'; the GNB' is Mati‘el, and it is his person," reading ואל תאמר גנבא זנה ו[גנבא הא] מתעאל ונבשה הא? For prohibitions in the treaty, cf. Sf III 9.

37. נבשה: "His person," or "his life." If נבשה is correctly read, this would be another case of נבש instead of נפש; see note on Sf I A 31 (בתן) and I B 39, 40, 42; II B 5; III 6. Cf. Bar-Rakkab 8:7; Hadad 17, 21, 22; Panammu 18. The following הא (singular) is hardly the copula for both מתעאל and נבשה, as Dupont-Sommer seems to have taken it. Vocalize: *hī'*. Lipiński (*Studies*, 31) would rather read מבשה, a *mem* noun-form from the root *bwṯ*, "be ashamed"; he would translate: "And may you not say: ‘This thief with [this shame of his] is Mati‘-’el with his shame." Lemaire-Durand (*IAS*, 114) read rather: ואל תאמר גברא זנה ו[כנותה?] מתעאל ורבוה הא, "et qu’il ne soit fait plus mention de cet *homme*-ci [*ni de ses collègues?*], c’est (à dire) de Mati‘él et de ses *grands*!" (122).

כן יקד מ[תעאל בא]ש: "So may Mati‘el be burned by fire." Cf. Esarhaddon’s vassal treaties (lines 608-11): "Just as they burn an image (made) of wax in the fire and dissolve one of clay in water, so may your figure burn in the fire and sink in water." Cf. Ps 68:3, כהמס דנוג מפני־אש, "as wax melts before fire," as suggested by A. Caquot (*RHR* 175 [1969] 211).

38. תשבר: "Is broken." The form is 3d sg. fem. impf. pass. (*yuqtal* type; see note on line 33). The verb that precedes is sg., even though the subject is compound, קשתא (fem. sg.) and חציא (masc. pl.), "bow and arrows."

חציא: "Arrows," the cognate of Hebrew חֵץ and later Aramaic חט (*A* 126, 128), Arabic *ḥazwatu*ⁿ , Akkadian *uṣṣu*. See below, I B 29.

אנרת: "Inurta," i.e., Ninurta. According to Dupont-Sommer the reading אנהת is "practically certain," even though he does mark the *he* with a dot. Ronzevalle and Bauer had both taken it as *reš*, whereas Driver preferred a *šin*. The latter is in my opinion definitely excluded as a reading, even though the reading adopted here comes substantially to what Driver was aiming at. Dupont-Sommer interpreted אנהת as the name of the goddess Anahita, the Persian goddess of fertilizing waters, who is here coupled with Hadad. He claimed that she was later identified with Ishtar and became quite popular in the Semitic world. In the Hellenistic world she was known as Anaitis. In favor of this identification he cited the similar "smashing of a bow" ascribed to Ishtar, "the lady of battle and war," in Esarhaddon’s vassal treaties (see line 453). Cf. McCarthy, *Treaty and Covenant*, 202. Even though the preceding verb (ישבר) is again singular (see note above on תשבר), the copula before Hadad’s name calls for the name of some other deity preceding it. In this regard, Dupont-Sommer’s suggestion is plausible; but it is otherwise linked to his questionable thesis that KTK is Urartu, which he maintains was under early Median influence. This would explain the presence of Anahita there. But, as Noth pointed out (*ZDPV* 77 [1961] 165), one would hardly expect the name of Persian goddess here, in a text coming from mid-eighth century? Noth rightly rejects this identification and would rather read אנגת as the name of an otherwise unknown deity (see his restoration of I A 7). But his suggested reading is scarcely convincing. Greenfield ("Three Notes," 100-103) has brought together several telling arguments against the reading אנהת and its interpretation as Anahita: (1) This name is first attested epigraphically only about three centuries later. (2) The identification of Anahita with Ishtar is highly questionable at this period, even if admissible in Hellenistic syncretism. (3) The preceding verb ישבר (3d sg. masc.) would call for a masc. name as the first deity of a pair. Consequently, Greenfield proposes to return to the reading of Ronzevalle, אנרת, and interpret it as "Inurta," i.e., Ninurta, a god of both fertility and of battle (see D. Edzard, "Ninurta," *Wörterbuch der Mythologie* [ed. H. W. Haussig; Stuttgart: Klett, 1961] 1. 114-15). He is known particularly as a god who breaks the weapons of the enemy (*dNinurta qardu ašārid ilāni giškakkēšunu ušebbir*, "warlike Ninurta, eminent among the gods, broke their weapons"; cf. E. Ebeling, *MAOG* 12/2, p. 8, line 31). Moreover, Greenfield has found Ninurta and Hadad (called Zababa and Adad) closely related in the curse formulas of the *Narû* inscriptions (cf. *CH* rev. xvii, 61-90). The spelling of the name, אנרת is also found on an Aramaic (Ammonite?) stamp-seal, published by N. Avigad ("Seals of Exiles," *IEJ* 15 [1965] 222-32, esp. 222-28): חתם מנגאנרת ברך למלכם, "seal of Mannu-ki-Inurta, blessed by Milkom." The form אנרת represents the Assyrian phonetic pronunciation of the name which appears as אנושת (= Inušta) in Aramaic dockets on Babylonian tablets.[27] Cf. R. Borger, "Die Aussprache des Gottesnamens Ninurta," *Or* 30 (1961) 203.

[קשת מתעאל]: "The bow of Mati'el." This reconstruction is demanded by the phrase at the beginning of line 39. For parallels to the breaking of weapons by a god, see the CH, R 28,3-4 (G. R. Driver and J. C. Miles, *Babylonian Laws* [Oxford: Clarendon, 1955] 2. 104-5; R. C. Thompson, *The Prisms of Esarhaddon and Ashurbanipal* [London: British Museum, 1931] 12, line 75); treaty of Esarhaddon with Ba'al of Tyre (Rev. II, 18); Hos 1:5 (ושברתי את־קשת ישראל); Jer 49:35.

39. רבוה: "His nobles." For the suffix, see note on Sf I A 5.

יער: "Is blinded." This form is 3d sg. masc. impf. pass., not of the simple, but the causative stem of עור (= is caused to be blind). A few hophals are recognized in Biblical Aramaic (see BLA §36r,t). This form would rather be an 'ophal, since there is no *he* present before the *'ayin*. 'Ophal perfects have turned up in a text from Qumran Cave 4; see J. T.

27 See A. T. Clay, "Aramaic Indorsements on the Documents of the Murašu Sons," *Old Testament and Semitic Studies in Memory of William Rainey Harper* [Chicago: University of Chicago, 1908] 1. 285-322; see esp. §27, 31, 14, 25; L. Delaporte, *Epigraphes araméens* [Paris: Geuthner, 1912] §51, 52, 62, 75; *Ephem*. 3. 63; H. Tadmor, "A Note on the Seal of Mannu-ki-Inurta," *IEJ* 15 [1965] 233-34).

Milik, *The Books of Enoch: Aramaic Fragments of Qumrân Cave 4* (Oxford: Clarendon, 1976): אחזית, 4QEn[e] 1 xxvii 1, 21; [אחלפ[ת, 4QEn[e] 1 xxvi 19; אעברת, 4QEn[e] 1 xxvi 19). Cf. the Hebrew impf. pass. Hoph. (?) יודש from the hollow root *dwš*. Vocalize: *yu'ar*. -- For similar cases of the blinding of figurines, see the treaty of Aššurnirari V (Rev. VI, 2) and the Hittite military oath (III, 2-10). See F. E. Deist, "The Punishment of the Disobedient Zedekiah," *JNSL* 1 (1971) 71-72 (cf. Jer 39:6-8).

40. יגזר: "Is cut in two," the 3d sg. masc. impf. pass. (*yuqtal*-type). The cutting up of a calf in a rite of covenant-making resembles the scene found in Gen 15:9-18; see further Jer 34:18, where a calf is cut in two and the contracting parties pass between the bloody parts of the sacrificial victim, symbolizing their readiness to suffer the same fate if they violate the pact. For a full discussion of the possible meanings of this rite, see J. Henninger, "Was bedeutet die rituelle Teilung eines Tieres in zwei Halften?" *Bib* 34 (1953) 344-53; A. González Nuñez, "El rito de la alianza," *EstBíb* 24 (1965) 217-38; R. Polzin, "*Hwqy'* and Covenantal Institutions in Early Israel," *HTR* 62 (1969) 227-40; E. Bickerman, "'Couper une alliance,'" *Studies in Jewish and Christian History* (AGJU 9; Leiden: Brill, 1976) 1-32, esp. 15. Cf. the figurative use of גזר in line 7 above. In the treaty of Aššurnirari V (Obv. 1, 13-14) a ram is mentioned as being brought up precisely to conclude the pact (*ana a-di-e* [d]*Aš-šur-nirāri . . . itti* [I]*Ma-ti-'-ilu ša-ka-ni*); the enumerated parts of the ram (head, hind leg, blood) suggest dismemberment. Cf. Esarhaddon's vassal treaties (lines 551-54). These parallels make the translation given by Bauer and Rosenthal, "castrate," rather unlikely.

עגלא זנה: "This calf." The same animal is used in the rite of Jer 34:18 (העגל) and of Gen 15:9 (עגלה).

רבוה "His nobles," see note on line 39.

[ואיך זי תערר ז]נ[יה]: "And just as a harlot is stripped naked. . . ." I have used here the suggestion of Hillers (*Treaty-Curses*, 58-60), which has pressed to its logical conclusion the suggestion that Bauer had made. I prefer to read a form of ערר at the end of line 40 to correspond with יעררן in the following line. Dupont-Sommer read יעבד and יעבדן and translated, "[Et de même que sert ce]lui-[ci], qu'ainsi servent les femmes. . . ." He admitted, however, the difficulty that עבד does not have the meaning of "serve, be a slave," in Aramaic, even though the noun עבדא, "slave" is found. Only the tops of the letters בד are preserved, and they could just as easily be read רר. This reading was suggested long ago by Bauer ("Ein aramäischer Staatsvertrag," 10), and it has much to commend it. It is better than עבד in the context, and there are the biblical parallels in Neh 3:5; Jer 13:26-27; Ezek 16:37-38; Hos 2:5 to support Hillers' contention that one should read זניה, "harlot," instead of the demonstrative pronoun זנה, which otherwise lacks a noun that it would modify. תערר is the 3d sg. fem. impf. pass. (*yuqtal*-type) and יעררן is the 3d pl. fem. of the same form; vocalize *yu'rar* and *yu'rarūn*. Bauer mentioned the practice of Assyrian kings that parallels this curse. Hillers is undoubtedly right in suggesting that this curse was probably not accompanied by any ritual action. Degen (*AG* §58) consider יעררן to be a pual, "because the third radical is written." But that would be a strange form in Aramaic.

42. [תקח]: 3d sg. fem. impf. pass. (*yuqtal*-type), agreeing with the restored fem. subject. The assimilated form of the impf. of לקח is also found in Sf I B 27; Sf III 2. The unassimilated form occurs in Sf I B 35 (ילקח). Apropos of such forms appearing in the same inscription, see the discussion of K. Petráček and S. Segert, *ArOr* 24 (1956) 131-34, esp. 133 ("so zeigt es sich, dass im Altaramäischen das Verbum *lqḥ* nicht assimiliert wurde . . ."). Cf. *ArOr* 32 (1964) 120; *AP* 67:18; *CIS* 2.141:3.

ימחא: "One strikes." This form is the 3d sg. masc. impf. peal active, not the passive, as Dupont-Sommer would have had it, for it would have to be fem. to be treated as passive. The subject is impersonal. Degen (*AG* §57) has also understood it as peal active.

אפיה: "Her on the face," lit. "(strikes) against her face." The ending of the form אפיה is written fully (contrast עלה in line 32), and it is probably to be vocalized as *'appayh*. For other examples, see Sf III 9, 23.

יקחן: 3d pl. fem. impf. pass. (*yuqtal*-type) of לקח, with assimilated *lamedh*; see note above on תקח.

There is scarcely any connection between the end of face A and the beginning of face B. The relation of the treaty (or treaties) on the two sides of this stele is still a matter of dispute. Dupont-Sommer was inclined to think that the preamble and the beginning of the stipulations of the treaty on face B began on the left side (= face D), the side that was subsequently shaved off. Noth (*ZDPV* 77 [1961] 122-23), however, considered Dupont-Sommer's view to be quite improbable; he prefered to regard Sf I as the base of some sculpture or relief, on which the inscription of Sf I B really began. In his opinion, face B is more probably the beginning or the front of the monument (further reasons for the priority of face B are given by him on pp. 124, 135, 169 of his article). He is accordingly inclined to date Sf I B before 754 and Sf I A after that year, when Mati'el concluded a pact with Aššurnirari V. The text of Sf

I A would then be "eine (neugefasste) Erneuerung von I B" (p. 169 n. 161). Whereas the view of either Dupont-Sommer or of Noth is possible, there is nothing inherent in the text of Sf I A or B that makes it imperative to date either one before the other. The precise relationship of the two treaties, or the two parts of one treaty, is still a matter of debate. Moreover, one has to recall the opinion of Van Rooy about the structure of the treaty and the order of the elements in it, already discussed in the introduction above.

Face B

The reverse side of the inscription, especially in its lower half, is badly preserved. Dupont-Sommer and Starcky have done an excellent job in clearing up many of the obscure points that previously existed. However, many difficulties still remain, and I have not been able to solve all of them. Some of the following remarks may help in the understanding of this difficult part of the Sefire treaty. The first line of face B begins in the middle of a sentence, and we are possibly dealing with a new section of the treaty, in which the contracting parties are once again listed. The beginning of the lines on this side of the stele are lost, corresponding to the loss of the end of the lines on face A. But even the loss of seven or eight letters (as calculated by Dupont-Sommer) cannot account for the whole of the beginning of this section. It must have begun on some other part of the monument, possibly on the lost left side, or face D.

1. רסמך מלך אר[פד]: ". . . Attarsamak, the king of Arpad." This phrase was restored by Dupont-Sommer, who argued that something like **עדי בר גאיה מלך כתך עם מתעאל בר עת** must have preceded. Bauer ("Ein aramäischer Staatsvertrag," 12) was of the opinion that face B represented a renewal of the treaty by the sons of Bar-Ga'yah and Mati'el, which took place after the capture of Arpad by Tiglathpileser III in 740. However, it is certain that Mati'el was still one of the contracting parties (see Sf I B 13, 21), and since the stipulations of the treaty are entirely lacking on face A, the introduction which we have at the beginning of face B must be understood as the solemn introduction to the section (lines 1-13) that stresses the sacred character of the treaty.

... ועדי בני: See Sf I A 2 and the notes there.

2. [בני בני בר] גאיה: "The grandsons of Bar-Ga'yah." Restored as in Sf I A 2, corresponding to **עקר** there; note the similar telescoping of expressions for descendants there.

כל מה מלך: "Any king." See note on Sf I A 26. Cf. Sf III 28. There is no question here of a king named פלמה. Cf. J. A. Montgomery, *JAOS* 54 (1934) 425; J. Friedrich, "Kein König פלמה in der Stele von Sudschin," *ZA* 9 (1936) 327-28. This detail of dynastic succession is probably insignificant; it is formulaic and absent in Sf I A. Cf. Noth, *ZDPV* 77 (1961) 130.

3. [יסק וימלך] באשרה: Dupont-Sommer read simply [ימלך] appealing to Sf I B 22. But the reading of this line in his note does not agree with the reading he gives of the line itself, where we read not כל מלכיא זי ימלכן באשרה, but בארפד. The verb usually construed with -באשר is סלק (see Sf I C 3-4; Sf I A 5); we expect it here, but it is too short to fill out the whole lacuna. Hence I prefer to read [יסק וימלך] באשרה. This gives a restoration of eight letters, whereas Dupont-Sommer admits that "il y a place normalement pour 7 signes." Degen (*AG*, 13 n. 58) thinks that [יסק] באשרה should be read alone and that I have mixed up two syntagmemes. Is that true?

ועם בני גש: "And with the Benê-Gush." See note on Sf I A 16. Bauer ("Ein aramäischer Staatsvertrag," 12) was the first to identify this expression with Bīt-Agūsi of Assyrian texts.

ועם בית צלל: "And with Bêt-ṢLL." Though the reading is not certain here, Dupont-Sommer depended on Sf II B 10: ובית גש ובית צלל, where it is certain and where בית גש is coordinated with בית צלל. Dupont-Sommer identified the name בית צלל as topographical, the Aramaic form of [kur]*A-ṣal-li* (*ARAB*, 1. §475, 480). Since, however, this district lies on the route from Calah to Carchemish, to the west of Bīt-Baḫiani, there is the problem, which Dupont-Sommer recognized, of Arpad extending its power so far to the east. Noth (*ZDPV* 77 [1961] 129) preferred to regard the name as dynastic, being parallel to בית גש. Both here and in Sf II descendants of Mati'el are mentioned in the immediately preceding context. This might suggest that בית צלל is the name of a prominent family in Arpad.

Lemaire-Durand (*IAS*, 56-66) have shown that בית צלל is to be understood as "une appellation dynastique du royaume de Kit(t)ika; autrement diṭ, *byt ṣll* semble le nom de la maison royale à laquelle se rattachait Šamši-ilu fils ou petit-fils de Ga'yah/Ga'uni." They have also shown that the location of (A)ṣallu was between Guzana (Tell Halaf) and Bīt Adini, to the west of Haran.

ועם אר[ם כלה]: "And with all Aram." Restored according to Sf I A 5. This seems to imply that the title of Mati'el was really "king of Arpad and of all Aram." Cf. Bar-Hadad 3 (= *KAI* 201:3).

4. ועד[י] כתך: "And the treaty of KTK." Cf. Sf I A 3.
בעלי: "The lords of (Arpad)." See note on Sf I A 4. Here the "lords" are clearly distinct from the "people" (עמה), mentioned in the next clause in line 5.

5. ועדי אלהי כתך עם עדי א[להי ארפד]: "And the treaty of the gods of KTK with the treaty of the gods of Arpad." The sacred character of the treaty is stressed in the statement that it is not merely concluded in the presence of the gods (Sf I A 6 ff.), but is a treaty of the gods themselves of the contracting peoples. Cf. Sf I B 23, 33; Sf III 4, 14, 17, 23; and McCarthy, *Covenant and Treaty*, 40.

6. עדי אלהן הם זי שמו אלהן: "A treaty of gods, which gods have concluded." See the comment of P. Grelot, *RB* 75 (1968) 283. For the idiom עדיא שים, see note on Sf I A 6-7.
טבי מלך [בר גאיה לעל]מן: The restoration and the interpretation of the last part of this line and most of line 7 are quite debatable. Dupont-Sommer read: טב ימלך at the end of this line, "Qu'heureusement régne [Bar-ga'ayah à jam]ais." This is not an impossible solution, but the adverbial use of טב, modifying a verb, is strange and otherwise unattested, as far as I know. A wish seems to be expressed, as Dupont-Sommer acknowledges. Another possibility is to divide the letters differently: טבי מלך. Then there would be the construct pl. *ṭūbay* (from *ṭūbā*, "goodness"), often used in wishes and macarisms in the targums, akin to Hebrew אשרי. In such an interpretation one would expect מלכא, if the second word meant "the king." Possibly, however, מלך means rather "reign, kingship" and is a construct itself. Hence one might translate, "Happy forever be the reign of B." Vocalize: *ṭūbay mulk*. See note on Sf I C 6. Degen (*AG* §44 and 71) took טב as adverbial; on p. 13 n. 59 he calls טבי a "nicht existenten Nominalform"! Perhaps he should consult 4QTob[a] ar 18:3 (= Tob 13:14), where Greek Sinaiticus translates טובי as *μακάριοι*; or Tg. Jonathan on 1 Kgs 10:8.
Lemaire-Durand (*IAS*, 114) read at the end simply עדי מלך, "les serments du roi," without filling in the lacuna at the beginning of line 7.

7. [לעל]מן: The more usual Aramaic expression for "forever" is עד עלם (Sf III 24, 25) or לכל עלמין (1QapGen 20:12; 21:10, 12 [with the Hebrew ending *-m*]). But in Dan 2:4, 44; 3:9; 5:10 we find לעלמין, the phrase restored here. The wish refers to the everlasting character of the pact to which one has sworn, especially in the presence of gods; cf. Gen 9:16 (ברית עולם); Exod 31:16; Lev 24:8; 2 Sam 23:5.
מלך רב: "A great king." At first sight the expression, coming after

the name of a king (if correctly restored), reminds one of the common Akkadian title, *šarru rabû*. The phrase is in the absolute state, and Dupont-Sommer interprets it as a predicate, "(en tant que) roi grand." He remarks, "S'ils étaient en apposition, il faudrait l'état emphatique: מלכא רבא." Donner-Rollig (*KAI*, 2. 253) also sense the syntactic problem and prefer to regard the phrase as an adverbial construction, rather than an appositive. That is forced. It seems that much depends on the nuance to be conveyed. In fact, the absolute is often used with proper names as an appositive; see ביתאל אתר די אנתה יתב, "Bethel, the place where you are dwelling" (1QapGen 21:9); אסרוך בר פלטו כמר זי חנ[ום], "Esrok son of Palṭu, priest of the god Khnum" (*AP* 13:15); ענני בר עז[ריה ל]חן ליהו, "Anani son of Azariah, a sacristan of Yahu" (*BMAP* 1:2; see further 2:2; 3:3, 25; esp. 12:20). Contrast המלך הגדול (2 Kgs 18:28), which precedes מלך אשור. The expression would refer, according to Noth (*ZDPV* 77 [1961] 146), to Bar-Ga'yah as head of the חבר, possibly mentioned in Sf I A 4 (if the reading of Dupont-Sommer is used). It is, moreover, the classic title of the suzerain in Hittite treaties (see McCarthy, *Covenant and Treaty*, 29; cf. *ANET*, 203). See further J. C. Greenfield, "Some Aspects," 117-19, where Greenfield relates this Aramaic phrase, מלך רב, to the similar Ugaritic title *mlk rb*, used by Niqmad of Ugarit of his suzerain (*UT* 1018:3; *PRU* 2.18.3), to the Old Babylonian *šarru rabû*, to the form in Dan 2:10 (*melek rab wĕšallîṭ)*, to a Hebrew instance (מלך גדל) on an inscription from Nimrud (see A. R. Millard, *Iraq* 24 [1962] 45-49), as well as to the Hittite usage. -- Cf. *RES* 1785G.

ומע[די]א אל[ן] ושמין: An almost unintelligible phrase owing to the lacuna. Lemaire-Durand (*IAS*, 114) read: ועדיא אלן [ש]מע שמין, "et ces serments ont *[en]tendus* les cieux." This is plausible, but can one construe שמין with a sg. verb?

8. יצרן: "And all the gods shall guard this treaty." The verb is 3d pl. masc. long impf. peal of נצר, "guard, keep." Vocalize: *yiṣṣarūn*. Cf. Sf I C 15, 17. Being the long impf. with *nun*, it scarcely expresses a wish here. The same root occurs unassimilated in Nerab 1:12-13; the old orthography (with ṣ, as here) is also preserved in the Adon Letter, line 8 (*Sem* 1 [1948] 44; cf. *Bib* 46 [1965] 52-54), whereas the later form *nṭr* begins to appear at Elephantine (*AP* 27:1; *A* 98, 192, 209). -- Greenfield (*AcOr* 29 [1965] 9) compares Hebrew נצר עדות of Ps 25:10; 119:2 and Akkadian *adē naṣāru*.

ואל תשתק חדה מן מלי ספרא זנ[ה]: "And let not one of the words of this inscription be silent." The verb תשתק is the 3d sg. fem. juss. peal; vocalize: *tištuq*. On מלי ספרא זנה, see Sf I C 17; cf. K. F. Euler, *ZAW*

14 (1937) 281-91.

9. [ויתשמען]: "Let them be heard." So restored by Dupont-Sommer; if correct, it must be vocalized as 3d pl. fem. impf. ithpeel: *yitšam'ān*, since the subject is מלי ספרא זנה. However, a short impf. is really needed here, something like יתשמעה, but I hesitate, since such a form is apparently not otherwise attested in this period. Donner-Röllig (*KAI*, 2. 254) think that this expression reveals that the inscription was regarded "magically as a witness," for it can not only hear (cf. Josh 24:26-27), but also speak. That the expression is figurative is clear, but that it is intended in a magical sense is questionable. See McCarthy, *Covenant and Treaty*, 66, who thinks that "the text is conceived of as an active divine agent which proclaims the treaty by its own power."

[מן] ערקו ועד יאד[י ו]בז: "From 'Arqu to Ya'di and BZ." For the prepositional formula ועד . . . מן, see Dan 2:20 (of time); Ezra 4:15, 19; in Hebrew, Gen 10:19 (of space); 15:18. Here I have followed the restoration of Dupont-Sommer as modified by B. Mazar (*BA* 25 [1962] 118). *'Arqū* has been identified by Mazar as 'Arqa in the vicinity of Ṣumur on the coast; cf. Gen 10:17 (*'rqy*). It is known from inscriptions of Tiglathpileser III (Kleine Inschrift I, line 2; *ARAB*, 1. §772, 815, 821) and is undoubtedly the city Irqata mentioned in the Amarna letters (cf. J. Knudtzon, *EA*, 75:26; 100:3, 8). It has been identified as Tell 'Arqa not far from the basin of the Nahr el-Kabir; it is thus a southern limit in this descriptive expanse over which the words of the treaty are to be heard. Given the space for the restored *'ayin*, the name has nothing to do with *Raqqu*.

Lemaire-Durand (*IAS*, 81-82, 114) read rather: [מן] קרקר ועד יאדי [ו]בז, "[depuis] Qarqar et jusqu'à Ya'ady [et] Baz" (123). This would refer to Qarqar, an important town in the kingdom of Hamath and often mentioned in Assyrian texts; Baz would be for them the town of Bazu on the Upper Euphrates.

Ya'di is the kingdom known from the inscriptions of Hadad (1, 9, 21, 25) and Panammu (1, 2, 5, 7, 8, 12), as well as from Kilamuwa I.2 (= *KAI* 24. 2). This identification has been accepted by almost all commentators on the Sefire inscriptions. It indicates that Mati'el, as "king of all Aram," had annexed even the kingdom of Ya'di; it is presented here as the northern boundary of his realm.

The vocalization of the name *Y'dy* is still problematic. The often-used vocalization, *Ya'udī*, was based on what many regard as an originally false identification: *Yaudu* in Assyrian inscriptions. But this should preferably be interpreted as Judah (in the south). H. Winckler (*Altorientalische Forschungen, I* [Leipzig: Pfeiffer, 1897], 1-23) identified the Assyrian *Ya-u-du/i* with the northern district *Y'dy* of Aramaic and Phoenician texts; his identification led to the vocalization of the Aramaic name as *Ya'udî*. However, it has since been shown that this identification is highly questionable. See W. F. Albright, *BASOR* 100 (1945) 18, n. 8; E. R. Thiele, *JNES* 3 (1944) 156-61 (who showed that Izriyau of *Ya-u-di* in Assyrian texts is none other than Azariah [Uzziah] of Judah); B. Landsberger, *Sam'al*, 22 n. 42; 36 n. 76 (who insisted that *Y'dy* in the Kilamuwa inscription must have been pronounced *Ya'adiya* and would scarcely have been represented in Assyrian texts as *Ya-u-du*; when the latter refer to the northern district, they call it *Sam'alla*); and especially H. Tadmor, "Azriyau of Yaudi," *ScrHier* 8 (1961) 232-71. Despite the efforts of Garbini ("Sul nome Y'dy," *RSO* 31 [1956] 31-35) to relate the name *Y'dy* to the Assyrian *Yaudu* and to derive from the latter its vocalization, the convincing arguments are all for the contrary view. Hence my vocalization *Ya'dī* in Aramaic and *Ya'diya* in Phoenician.

A further problem that this line raises calls for comment. According to most commentators יאדי has been regarded as the designation of the land, whereas *Śam'al* has been taken as the name of the capital or principal town of יאדי (e.g., Donner-Röllig, *KAI* 2. 32, 207, 216). Part of the reason for this view is the occurrence of the name *Sa-ma-al-la* with the determinative [uru], indicating it as the name of a town or city. In Kilamuwa I. 2 the name יאדי also occurs in a phrase suggesting that it is a country or land (מלך גבר על יאדי). If, however, the identification of ערקו is correct and it is the town of 'Arqa, then one would expect that the other term of the comparison would also be the name of a town. The identification is further complicated by the fact that מלך שמאל occurs in Zakur a 7 as the designation for the king along with the kings of several other lands or countries (מלך, מלך ארם, מלך קוה, מלך עמק, מלך גרגם, מלז).

בז: The identification of this name has not yet been established. It may be a name like *Bûz* (Jer 25:23; Gen 22:21), though the latter location is out of the question here, for it lies in the region of Têma and Dedan and is apparently the same as the Assyrian proper name *Bāzu*, "the Arabian hinter-land of the island of Tilmun, modern Bahrein" (W. F. Albright, "Dedan," in *Geschichte und Altes Testament* [Alt-Festschrift; BHT 16; Tübingen: Mohr [Siebeck] 1953] 8 n. 2). One would expect it to be the name of a place in the north near Ya'di, and so the suggestion of Lemaire-Durand mentioned above becomes more plausible.

מן לבנן ועד יב[רדו]: "From Lebanon to Yabrud." This phrase suggests a geographical extension similar to the previous one. It probably refers to Mt. Lebanon, often used in the OT as the north border of the land of Canaan (see Deut 11:24; Josh 1:4). Here it would designate the northwestern border of "lower Aram," and it seems preferable to that of Noth (*ZDPV* 77 [1961] 152-53) that it would refer to the Anti-Lebanon. Yabrud is situated on the road from Damascus to Aleppo, near el-Nebq. In Hellenistic and Roman times it was called τὰ Ἰαβρουδά (Ptolemy, *Geography*, 5.15). For יב[..] Dupont-Sommer suggested a name like *yb[nh]* or *yb[l'm]*. My suggestion that it might be *Yabrūd*, mentioned in the Annals of Aššurbanipal (see S. Schiffer, *Die Aramäer*, 139; *ARAB*, 2. §818) has found support in the geographical discussion of B. Mazar (*BA* 25 [1962] 118); and in Lipiński's translation (*Studies*, 51). Donner-Röllig (*KAI*, 2. 254) make no attempt to restore the lacuna; nor does Degen (*AG*, 13) or Lemaire-Durand (*IAS*, 82-83, 114). Vocalize: *Yabrūdu* and *Libnān*; cf. Syriac *Lebnān*, Hebrew *Lĕbānôn*, Akkadian *Labnānu*.

10. [ומן דמש]ק ועד ערו ומ..ו: "From Damascus to 'Aru and M..W." At the beginning of this line the lacuna is one of ten letters according to the transcription of Dupont-Sommer. The first two letters are restored as the end of the name *Yabrud*. Even if the final *-w* is read (with Mazar), there is still room for seven letters. Hence Mazar's restoration of the beginning of the line is insufficient. He proposed: [רדו ודמש]ק וערערו ומ[נצ]ות, "(from Lebanon to) Iab[rud, and Damas]cus, and Aroer and Ma[ns]uate, . . ." (*BA* 25 [1962] 118). He was led to this interpretation by the association of Damascus and Aroer in Isa 17:1-2. He has been followed by Lipiński (*Studies*, 51). But on closer inspection there are several difficulties that must be faced: (a) the need for more letters to fill up the lacuna; this calls for ומן before the name דמשק; (b) if the restoration of ומן is correct, then there must be a corresponding ועד, as in line 9. If this is right, then Dupont-Sommer's otherwise plausible reading is called in question: וערערו, which he understood as *'Arâ'iru* and related to the name for three different cities mentioned in the OT: one in Moab (Num 32:34), the ערער of Meša 26; another in Transjordan east of Rabbat Ammon (Josh 13:25; Judg 11:33); a third in Judah (1 Sam 30:28, perhaps = *Araru* of the Amarna letters (*EA*, 256.25). But if we read the first three letters of this complex as ועד, then we are left with a name ערו, coordinated with a topographical name ומ..ו. Here Mazar reads ומ[נצ]ות, and although he italicizes the final *t*, there is no possibility of reading it. Dupont-Sommer made no provision for an extra letter at this point and there is no trace of a *taw* in the photograph. Consequently, his restoration is implausible. So I prefer to leave this lacuna blank, as do Lemaire-Durand (*IAS*, 114).

As for ערו, which emerges from the division of the words proposed above, is it not possibly the town called *Arā* in the Annals of Tiglath-pileser III, line 128 (see *ARAB*, 1. §770)? It was the town later called Arra in Chalcidice, thirty-two km. south of Chalcis, and identified with modern Ma'arrat en-No'man, SSE of Aleppo. See E. Ebeling, *RLA*, 1. 125. This would give yet another expanse in the present context, from Damascus to 'Aru.

ומ[ן] בקעת ועד כתך: "And from the Valley to KTK." The fem. noun בקעת (abs. sg.) must be related to the Hebrew *biq'āh*, "valley." But to what valley does it refer? It seems to be used here as a proper name. In the Bible, as Dupont-Sommer has noted, the Hebrew word can designate the valley of the Jordan (Deut 34:3), the plain of Esdrelon (Zech 12:11), "valley of the Lebanon" (Josh 11:17; 12:7; cf. Amos 1:5 בקעת און), and the plain of Shinar (Gen 11:2). Dupont-Sommer hesitated between the last two, but preferred the latter because he identified KTK with Urartu. The expression would thus indicate the extent of the Urartian-Aramean coalition against Assyria. This depends, once again, on the correctness of the identification of KTK as Urartu. The mention of Lebanon in the previous line and of בקעת here seems to point to a region closer to what is called today the Beqa'. The words of the treaty are to be heard from an area near the land of Arpad; hence it seems better to look for the places introduced by מן in the region around Arpad. Since Noth (*ZDPV* 77 [1961] 154) eventually identified KTK with Kisik in southern Mesopotamia, he understood בקעת to refer to a river-plain of the middle Euphrates. This is implausible; see the discussion of KTK below.

11. [ב]ית גש: See note on Sf I A 16.

אשרתהם: "Avec leur sanctuaire(?)." So Dupont-Sommer interpreted this word, which is not read with certainty. He related it to the Akkadian *aširtu*, "sanctuary." For אשר, meaning "sanctuary," see Pyrgi 1 (cf. *JAOS* 86 [1966] 288-89); *CIS* 1. 3779:6. But does the word ever occur elsewhere in this sense in Aramaic?

12. במצר ומרבה: Possibly two places, one of which occurs above in Sf I A 34. But see the note on מצר in Sf I A 5.

21. The lower half of face B seems to deal entirely with treaty-stipulations. Certain phrases show that in general they are of the same type as those in Sf III, which thus aids somewhat in the interpretation of this face.

ולישמע: "And ... will not obey." An example of the prefixed negative *lā*-. See Appendix, Morphology, IV.2. The introductory conjunction "if" does not appear here, but probably occurred in the foregoing lacuna; it is demanded by the sense. It is, however, possible, as Dupont-Sommer suggests, that the *waw* has conditional force, as sometimes in Hebrew (Exod 16:21; 33:10; 1 Kgs 18:10; Jer 18:4, 8). Note the similarity of this part of the treaty with Sf II B 2-3. Lemaire-Durand (*IAS*, 115) restore thus: ולישמען רבוה ולישמע עמה ולישמ]ען], "[ni écoutent ses grands, ni écoute son peuple, ni écou]tent ...."

22. כל מלכיא זי ימלכן בארפד: "All the kings who will rule in Arpad," as D. Pardee has suggested (*UF* 9 [1977] 219), since the prep. *b-* more properly indicates the seat of the reign rather than the territory ruled over. He compares Josh 13:21 (אשר מלך בחשבון).

23. למנין: Unintelligible in the context; perhaps one should read לשמין. Lemaire-Durand (*IAS*, 115) so read: למ[לי ספרא זנה זי יתשמען תחת כ]ל שמין, "les pa[roles de cette inscription qui ont été entendues sous to]us les cieux."

שקרתם: "You will have been unfaithful." Undoubtedly 2d pl. masc. pf. pael; the plural is used probably because the king and his people are enivsaged. But in most cases the singular is used of the king alone. Formerly I thought that the form used here was sg. with an enclitic *mem*, which is well attested in Ugaritic and Biblical Hebrew; see H. D. Hummel, "Enclitic *mem* in Early Northwest Semitic, especially Hebrew," *JBL* 76 (1957) 85-107. His remark on the scarcity of such an enclitic in Aramaic is significant. See also note on Sf I A 14. The verb שקר is followed by the prep. ל- when persons are the object of the treachery (see Sf I A 24, [14, 15]; Sf I B 23; Sf II A 3; Sf II B 9, 18; Sf III 4, 14, 16, 23; cf. Gen 21:23), but by prep. ב- when the treaty itself is the object (Sf I B 38; Sf II B 14; Sf III 7, 9, 19, 20, 27; cf. Ps 44:18).

[ז]י בספרא זנה]: "Which is in the inscription," restored as in Sf I B 28, 33. ספרא denotes the text of the inscription engraved on the stone; there is no reason to suppose that it was written at first on some soft material. In Sf I C 17 we find מלי ספרא זי בנצבא זנה, "the words of the inscription which (is) on this stele." Such a use of the root ספר to express an inscription engraved on stone sheds light on the expression ספר הברית in Exod 24:7; 2 Kgs 23:2; 2 Chr 34:30, and especially in 2 Kgs 23:21: ככתוב על ספר הברית. See also Josh 8:32; Isa 30:8; Deut 27:2-8; Kilamuwa I. 14-15; Ahiram Sarcophagus 2. Cf. D. R. Hillers, *Treaty-Curses*, 45-49, who would include Isa 34:16-17. But compare S. M. Paul, "Heavenly Tablets and the Book of Life," *The Gaster Festschrift* (= *JANES* 5 [1973]), 345-53, esp. 347 n. 18.

24. [תשמען ותש]למן: "You obey and fulfill." This phrase is restored according to the sense of the context, which demands the opposite of the preceding stipulation. See also Sf II B 4 (תשמע פהן). תשלמן should probably be understood as aphel; vocalize: *tašlimūn*. See F. C. Fensham, "Clauses of Protection in Hittite Vassal-Treaties and the Old Testament," *VT* 13 (1963) 133-43, esp. 137-38.

גבר עדן הא [אנה]: "I am an ally." Dupont-Sommer takes only the first three words together, translating, "C'est un homme (avec qui j'ai conclu) des pactes." גבר עדן seems, however, to be the Aramaic equivalent of Akkadian *bēl adē*, used of a vassal in Sennacherib's Annals (*Oriental Institute Prism* [H^2] 2. 74; cf. *ANET*, 287). But it makes better sense to take the restored אנה as the subject: "I am an ally." עדן is the abs. pl. of עדי and עדיא; see note on Sf I A 1.

הא: Vocalize: *hū'*. This form occurs in Sf III 8, 13, 22; Hadad 22; Panammu 11; Meša' 6. Note the same spelling in the Hebrew text of the Nehemiah ostracon from Arad, line 12 (Y. Aharoni, "אוסטרקון 'נחמטהו' מערד (The Nehemiah Ostracon from Arad)," *Nelson Glueck Memorial Volume* [ErIsr 12; Jerusalem: Israel Exploration Society, 1975] 72-76), a restudy of the second ostracon originally published in *W. F. Albright Volume* (ErIsr 9; Jerusalem: Israel Exploration Society, 1969) 10-21, esp. 15-17.

[לאכהל לאשלח יד] בך: "I shall not be able to raise a hand against you," lit. "to send a hand." This restoration is based on Sf II B 6 (פלאכהל לאשלח י[ד בך]). אכהל is the 1st sg. impf. peal of כהל; and אשלח is 1st sg. impf. peal of שלח. The use of a finite complement to the verb כהל (or יכל), instead of a complementary infin. (see Sf I B 34, [ל]פרק ולמשלח), is often found in later Aramaic: *BMAP* 2:13 (לא אכל אנצל לפלטי מן תחת לבבך, "I shall not be able to take Palti away from you"); 3:14, 17; 4:13, 14; 6:15; 7:38, 40, 41. For idiom שלח יד ב-, see Zakur b 21 (מן ישלח ב]ה אית ידה]); Gen 37:22; Exod 22:7, 10; 1 Sam 24:11; Esth 2:21; Dan 11:42. Cf. Esarhaddon vassal treatises, lines 66-67, 365. See H. Tawil, "Two Notes on the Treaty Terminology of the Sefire Inscriptions," *CBQ* 42 (1980) 30-37, esp. 32-37.

25. [מלה ימלל] עלי: "Should speak a word against me." Dupont-Sommer restored מללה ימלל, in which מללה is the pael infin. used as an infin. abs. would be in Hebrew, a usage that is attested in Sf III 18. But there is no need for an intensifier here, and the idiom seems to be closer to that of Sf III 1-2. Hence restore simply מלה, "a word."

חד מלכן: "Any king." Note the use of the abs. pl.; the same phrase occurs in line 28. See note on Sf III 1; contrast Sf I B 8.

מה ת[עבד]: "What are you going to do?" This conjectural restoration should be understood of a hostile suggestion made by Mati'el or his descendants to some ill-disposed third party, tempted to rebel against the suzerain. Vocalize: *ta'bid*; the thematic vowel in later Aramaic is *i*.

27. ויקתלנה: "And kill him." This is the 3d sg. masc. energic impf. peal of קתל with a suffix; vocalize: *wa-yiqtulinneh*. For energic forms of the impf. before suffixes, see Sf III 17 (יעברנה), 20 (תעשקני). For קתל instead of קטל, i.e., without emphatic *ṭ*, see Sf II B 9; Sf III 11, 18, 21; Panammu 8; cf. Arabic *qatala*.

ויקח: "And take." The 3d sg. masc. impf. peal of לקח. See note on Sf I A 42.

מן: "Some of (my land)." Dupont-Sommer rightly took this prep. in the partitive sense, comparing Gen 8:20 (ויקח מכל הבהמה).

מקני: "My possessions." This word is related to the Hebrew *miqneh*, "possession, cattle." Vocalize: *miqnay* (pl.); cf. Exod 17:3. It could also be the collective sg. *miqnī*.

ש]קרת בעד[יא: "You will have been unfaithful to the treaty." Cf. Sf I B 23 (2d pl.). For the formula, see the treaty of Mursilis II and Niqmepa of Ugarit (J. Nougayrol, *PRU* 4. 97), IV D 2, lines 21, 28, 37, 40.

28. זי בספרא זנה: "Which is in this inscription." See note on I B 23.

יאתה: "Comes." The 3d sg. masc. impf. peal of אתי; vocalize: *yi'têh* (< *yi'tay*) and see note on תהרי in Sf I A 21.

חד מלכן: See Sf I B 26.

ויסבנ<י>: "And surrounds me." Dupont-Sommer read ויסבן and translated, "et qu'il m'encercle." For such a translation one would expect ויסבני because the final *ī* is usually represented by *yodh* in these inscriptions; cf. תעשקני (Sf III 20). Since the next word begins with a *yodh* (יאתה), one should probably reckon with haplography. Vocalize: *yissubinnī*.

ח]ילך[: "Your army." Restored on the basis of the same word in lines 31-32.

29. This line is badly preserved. Dupont-Sommer read it as follows: [אלי עם] כל [..]חציא וכל נאפ..כות קפי קפי ותנת עליה [....] and marked ל נא and כו as doubtful letters. But has he divided the letters correctly toward the end of the line? Since the vassal is being addressed, it is more likely that ות goes with קף, yielding a 2d sg. masc. verbal form. My attempt to read the line, which may suggest to someone else a still better solution, is as follows: [אלי עם] כל [בעל] חציא וכל מה פ..ך ותקף יקפי ותנתע לי ה[....], "to me with every archer and every sort [of weapon], and you must surround those who surround me, and you must draw for me [...]." For the restoration of בעל, cf. the Hebrew expression *ba'ălê ḥiṣṣîm* (Gen 49:23). For *p..k*, I have no solution, unless the uncertain *waw* is to be read as a *yodh* together with the preceding *kaph*, yielding *ky*. Could it be *pgz*, like the later Aramaic *pāgōzā'*, "battering projectile" (Jastrow, 1132, a word not listed in M. Sokoloff's new dictionary)? תקף יקפי might be regarded as 2d sg. masc. impf. peal of יקף and the peal ptc. pl. with the 1st sg. suffix from the same verb. יקף would be a byform of נקף, "to go around, surround" (like *yṣb* and *nṣb*, *y'b* and *n'b* [Bar-Rakkab 14]). תנתע might be the 2d sg. masc. impf. peal of נתע (attested in Syriac in the sense "to draw"; in Hebrew, "to knock out" [Job 4:10]). The difficulty with the last suggestion is that this would be a rare case of an unassimilated Pe Nun verb; but cf. *tnṣr* (Nerab 1. 12). *Pace* Donner-Röllig (*KAI*, 2. 256), if it is written with an *'ayin* in Old Aramaic, it can scarcely be related to Hebrew *nts*.

Lemaire-Durand (*IAS*, 115) read rather: אתה ב[כל חילך וב[כל חציא וכל מאפק[י]ך ותקף יקפי ותמתע לי[..], "viens avec [toute ton armée et avec] tous [..]..... et tous tes brav[es,] et tu attaqueras ceux qui m'attaquent et tu me délivreras" (124). They maintain that the verb מתע, "save, protect," is involved here, a verb attested only in the name "Mati'el." That might be acceptable, but the sign of the accusative ל would be just as problematic as in Sf I C 4.

30. ופגר ארבא מעל פגר באר[פ]ד: "And I shall pile corpse upon corpse in Arpad." The final *mem* of ארבאם, as read by Dupont-Sommer, is not clear; it could be a *nun*. This badly preserved clause must mean something like, "and I shall pile (lit., "multiply") corpse upon corpse in Arpad." Part of it is found again in Sf II B 11: ופגר..[[ ]ך על פגר.., which confirms the division of words here. ארבאן could be some form of the verb רבי, "increase, multiply." Greenfield ("Three Notes," 103-5) explained it as the 1st sg. impf. pael with energic nun. For instances of the latter he appeals to *A* 82 (אשבקן, where the suffix *-k* is to be understood from the context). Similar forms are found in *AP* 35:5 (אשלמן, "I shall pay in full," viz., "it"); *A* 119 (תלקחן, "you shall take"); *AP* 8:10 (תנתנן); see *LFLAA*, §19d-e. Greenfield's explanation of the verbal form in *-n* may be correct, but it is quite anomalous outside of Egyptian Aramaic. If the *mem* is retained, is it not possible that it is part of the following prep., like Hebrew מעל? Cf. Ps 108:5. Greenfield cites a number of interesting parallels to the saying itself: an Akkadian Amorite example in a Mari letter (A 1121, obv. 19-21; cf. A. Lods, "Une tablette inédite de Mari," *Studies in Old Testament Prophecy* [ed. H. H. Rowley; Edinburgh: Clark, 1950] 103-10); biblical examples (Ps

61:7, ימים על־ימי מלך תוסיף; Isa 30:1; Jer 4:20; Job 16:14); a Phoenician example (Karatepe [*KAI*, 26], A I 6-8).

מן חד מלך: "Some king." The phrase מן חד is the same as the indefinite expression found seven times in Sf III 9-10; there it is followed by a plural *nomen rectum*, at least in sense. Perhaps then מלך has a collective sense here.

לאוין: As yet unexplained. Donner-Röllig (*KAI*, 2. 256) consider the word to be related possibly to Hebrew און, "trouble, sorrow, wickedness," which seems unlikely in the context. Could it be a proper name? Lemaire-Durand (*IAS*, 115) would read: לכל אוין ומות [יהמת?]ן, "pour tout .... et à mort [ils seront mis à mort]" (124). But what form would יהמתן be? Lipiński (*Studies*, 38) also restores it, but does not explain it.

ומות: S. Segert (*ArOr* 32 [1964] 125) suggested that מות might be the infin. and would vocalize it *mawt*. If it is the infin., it would rather be vocalized *mūt* and would be another case of a medial long *u* being fully written? Cf. Sf III 16, ימות (*yamūt*).

31. ... והן ביום זי אלהן: "And if on a day when (the) gods...." One would perhaps expect the emph. state (ביומא), but the almost identical expression occurs in Sf I C 20 (ביום זי יעב[ד] כן). Cf. *AP* 30:28 (מן גבר זי).

מרחיא: "The rebels," as suggested by Greenfield.

וא[תם לתא]תון: "You (pl.) do not come." The form אתם (2d pl. masc. independent pers. pron.) is not otherwise attested. The forms, however, of הם for the 3d pl. masc. (Sf III 5-6) and ־כם (Sf III 5, 7, 21) for the 2d pl. masc. suffix suggest that the independent form would have had *mem* at this period, as found here. Later one finds אתון or אנתון.

32. לשגב: "To strengthen." This form has been related by Dupont-Sommer to the later Aramaic שגב (pael), "to strengthen, fortify." It is also taken as a pael infin. by Donner-Röllig (*KAI* 2. 256). But the form here cannot be a pael infin., since it lacks the usual ending, *-ūt* or *-āh*). It must be a peal infin. without the preformative *mem*. Cf. Ezra 5:3, 13 (לבנא); Hadad (*KAI* §214) 14 (לבנא), 34 ([ל]הרגה). R. Degen (*AG*, §57) agrees that it is peal.

אית: This sign of the accusative occurs elsewhere in these inscriptions: Sf II B 8; Sf II C 5(bis), 14; Sf III 11, <13>; see also Zakur b 5, 10, 15, 16, 27. Since it is also attested in Phoenician in the same form, the second letter must be regarded as a consonant. Instead of the vocalization *'ayat*, which I originally proposed (*CBQ* 20 [1958] 466), I follow the suggestion of Friedrich (*PPG* §256) and vocalize it as *'iyyāt*, changing Friedrich's short *a* to a long one in view of the later Aramaic form *yāt-* and the forms *lĕwāt* or *kĕwāt* in Syriac, to which ותה (Hadad 28) must be related. Segert (*ArOr* 32 [1964] 126) would simply vocalize it *'īt*, which is problematic. The syntactical function of this particle remains a mystery in these inscriptions, since it is not always used, and the reason why it is used does not clearly emerge.

33. וחב: Both the ח and the ב are marked as doubtful letters. After the foregoing phrase, one would normally expect והן. In fact, Lemaire-Durand (*IAS*, 115) now propose to read: והן טפף יטפן עמי, "mais s'ils se joignent à moi, alors je pourrai ..." (125).

[... ואכהל מי [ביר: "I shall be able [to drink] water [of the well of ...]." There is apparently question of the use of the water of some well for Bar-Ga'yah's army. Can one restore the lacuna at the beginning of line 34 thus: [ביר בית צל]ל?

34. יסב: "Whoever lives around." Lit. "as for that well, whoever surrounds (it)." The form יסב is the 3d sg. masc. impf. peal of סבב, "surround." See line 28.

[ל]פרק ולמשלח יד: "Will not be able to destroy (it) or raise a hand against ...." Apparently two infins. are used as complements to [ליכ]הל, whereas a finite complement is used in lines 25 and 39. If [ל]פרק is correctly read, we have a peal infin. without preformative *mem* (contrast למשלח); cf. לשגב (line 32 above); רקה (Sf III 6).

[בי[רא: "The well." The word is related to the Hebrew *bĕ'ēr*, Moabite *br*, later Aramaic באר (*AP* 27:6), ברא (*AP* 27:8), Syriac *bīr'*, Jewish Palestinian Aramaic *bĕ'ērā'* (a Hebraism). In fact, the Hebrew form is often regarded as a hypercorrection. Vocalize: *bīra'* (with *scriptio plena* of medial long *i*). Segert (*ArOr* 32 [1964] 126) rather vocalizes it as *bayr-*.

35. ....לבכה או ח: Perhaps proper names.

ילקח: "Will take." Note the double occurrence of the unassimilated form of ילקח, the impf. of לקח, with which should be compared יקח (Sf I B 27), תקח (Sf III 2), יקחן (Sf I A 42). See note on Sf I A 42.

36. [ל]אבדת: "To destroy." Pael infin. of אבד. The *-ūt* ending is found both with and without a suffix (Sf III 11, 15, 16 המתתי, המתת). Vocalize: *'abbādūt*. The same form occurs in Sf II B 7. Cf. *hitnaddābūt*, an infin. without a suffix (Ezra 7:16). I can make nothing of the majority of this line, except for the three words at the end.

והן להן: "And if (you do) not (do) so." This expression, which also occurs in Sf III 4, 9, 14, 20, seems to mean something like, "And if you do not do so," since the usual conclusion is "you will have been unfaithful to all the gods of the treaty," or "you will have been unfaithful to this treaty." It is a negative protasis, referring to the foregoing stipulation, couched either in the form of a command or of a prohibition. In Sf III 4, 14 it follows a positive command; in the other two cases (lines 9, 20), it follows a prohibition. According to Dupont-Sommer the first הן is the usual Aramaic conditional conjunction, the ל is the negative adverb (usually prefixed in these inscriptions; cf. Sf I B 21), whereas the second *hn* is the 3d pl. fem. pers. pron., used in a neuter sense, "this." He also suggested the possibility of considering the second הן as the interjection, "voici" (cf. Gen 3:22; 4:14; 11:6). Then the meaning would be, "Et sinon, voici ...." Donner-Röllig (*KAI* 2. 256) follow him in this explanation. But Dupont-Sommer recognizes that "voici" in Aramaic is generally הא, הלו, אלו, ארו, sensing the difficulty of his explanation. Whereas להן occurs in later Aramaic as a subordinate conjunction, meaning "if not, except" (*A* 107, 120, 154; *AP* 8:11; *BMAP* 4:20) and also as a coordinate conjunction, meaning "but" (*AP* 9:6, 7, 9; *BMAP* 4:16; Ezra 5:12), neither use seems to fit here, if the preceding הן means "if." In favor of the first הן meaning "if" in this stele we have the use of והן, "and if," elsewhere (Sf I A 14; Sf III 4, 6). The second הן, then, is better taken as an emphatic adverb, such as occurs in the Sabbath ostracon published by Dupont-Sommer ("L'ostracon araméen du Sabbat [Clermont-Ganneau 152]," *Sem* 2 [1949] 31), concave side, lines 3, 7. A similar word is also found in *AD* 6:2; 2:3 (which Driver translates "lo," and would like to change to הא). In these texts the meaning of the adverb הן seems to be "surely;" but in the abbreviated phrase of these Sefire inscriptions it must mean something like "so." Hence והן להן should be understood, "and if not so." Jean-Hoftijzer (*DISO*, 66) also prefer this explanation.

37. There is not enough space for any of the usual formulae found in these inscriptions with the word שק[רת], if it is to end so soon in [ז]נה. Dupont-Sommer restored the sg. בעדא, which is most unlikely, since such a sg. is unattested. Either another formula, otherwise unknown, was used, or the engraver has skipped part of the usual formula. We should probably read שק]רת בעדיא <זי בספרא> ז[נה.

והן: This word begins a new stipulation, but most of the line is illegible. The stipulation must deal with the furnishing of food and provisions for Bar-Ga'yah's army. Perhaps להמי on this line should be read as לחמי, as in line 38.

38. לתהב: "You do not give." Apparently this form is the 2d sg. masc. impf. peal of יהב with the prefixed negative. It is a rare occurrence of the impf. of this verb, which in later Aramaic is usually replaced by the impf. of נתן. Vocalize: *lā-tihab* (< *tihhab*). See W. Kuhnigk, *Nordwestsemitische Studien zum Hoseabuche* (BibOr 27; Rome: Biblical Institute, 1974) 11: "und wenn du mir keine Lebensmittel gibst." He takes the suffix as dative, rejecting my translation and that of *KAI*. He compares Sf III 7: ותסך להם לחם, "und (wenn) du ihnen Lebensmittel zukommen lässt." Cf. Hos 2:7b: *nōtĕnê laḥmî ūmêmay ṣamrî ûpištî*.

[.]...שא לי לחם: "Deduct provisions from me." Dupont-Sommer suggested restoring והן [ת]שא לי לחם, "and if you take food away from me."

ולתסך: "And do not deliver." Cf. Sf III 5, 7 (לתסך להם לחם). The verb must come from the root נסך, which normally means "pour a libation." But it is used in these inscriptions in a generic sense with לחם, "provide food." Rosenthal (*BASOR* 158 [1960] 29 n. 3) compared Akkad. *nasāku*, but that is a questionable comparison, according to Greenfield (*AcOr* 29 [1965] 8 n. 21). Cf. Dan 2:46.

39. לתשא: "You cannot deduct," the 2d sg. masc. impf. peal of נשא. Another case of a finite complement to the verb כהל; see note on Sf I B 24-25; contrast line 34.

אנח כאים יקם לך: ??

ותבעה נבשך: "And you yourself will seek," lit. "and your soul will seek." For נבש, instead of נפש, see note on Sf I A 37.

40. The lacuna probably contained some words expressing the object of the verb of "going" at the end of line 39. The first two letters preserved suggest a fem. noun with the suffix *-k*, some word coordinated with לביתך, perhaps something like לקריתך. Given the space at the end of line 39 and that at the beginning of line 40, I suggest: ותאזל [נבשך לקרי]תך ולביתך, "and will yourself go to your city and to your house."

לכ[ל] נבש ביתי: "And for every person of my household." Dupont-Sommer compares *napšôt bêtô* (Gen 36:6).

41. וליגז[רן מ]לה מלכי א[רפד]: "The kings of Arpad will not cut anything off from them." This restoration is conjectural. However, one should note the occurrence of the phrase מלכי א[רפד], the restoration of which is quite likely; cf. Sf II C 15; Sf III 1, [3], 27. Noth (*ZDPV* 77 [1961] 135 n. 48) rejected this obvious restoration in favor of a hypothetical historical reconstruction, which is itself problematic.

[זי עדן חי[ן הם: Dupont-Sommer suggested the translation, "Parce que [ce sont] des pactes viv[ants] (?)." If correct, we have another example of the abs. pl. of עדיא; see Sf I B 24 and the note on Sf I A 1.

42. Unintelligible except for לנבשך.

43. כן תגזר אפלא: "So you will cut the 'PL'." The last word looks like אף לא at first sight, but it cannot be the conjunction and the negative, since והן, "and if," follows it and the negative is usually written as a prefix. So it must be a noun, the object of תגזר, or its subject (if fem.). Is אפלא possibly a metathesis for אלפא? See note on Sf I A 40. Lemaire-Durand (*IAS*, 115) reads rather אף לי, "ainsi tu trancheras aussi pour moi" (125).

44. יעזז: Dupont-Sommer suggested that this word was a pael impf., "he will strengthen." Lemaire-Durand (*IAS*, 115) read: יעזז קל בר ביתי [...] על[י או על ברי] או על, "et si s'élève la voix d'un fils de ma maison contre [moi ou contre mon fils] ou contre[...]" (125).

45. Dupont-Sommer reads this line as follows: [.....] פדיאכעלחבסרחי [.]ויקחקח בהם ו.נת. However, a number of the letters can be read differently. I find here a sentence related to a stipulation in Sf III 4-5. Read [.....]..[על] ברי או על חד סרסי ויקרק חדהם ויאת[ה...] and translate, "against my son or against one of my courtiers; and (if) one of them flees and com[es...]." In the case of *b* instead of *p*, there seems to be a cross-bar discernible in the photograph. The *waw* of או seems quite clear. The traces of the doubtful ח might just as well be the second *s* in סרסי. There is nothing against taking the vertical shaft between the two *qoph*s as a *reš* (יקרק). Similarly read by Lemaire-Durand (*IAS*, 115). See the note on Sf III 4.

Face C

The engraving of the inscription on this face of the stele is coarser and less carefully executed.

1. כה אמרן: Probably the 1st pl. pf. peal, "thus we have spoken." There is no indication that the final long *a*, found in later Aramaic, was written or pronounced. There is fluctuation in this regard in Elephantine texts: *AP* 30:16 (חוין) and *AP* 31:15 (חוינא). See *LFLAA* §25a. The first plural refers to both Bar-Ga'yah and Mati'el. T. Vriezen ("Das Hiphil von *'Amar* in Deut. 27,16.18," *JEOL* 17 [1963] 207-20) would rather read: כ האמר [עדן נ]קבן מה, "als wir den Worten der Verträge zugestimmt haben, bestimmten wir, was ich, M., zur Erinnerung für meinen Sohn schreiben sollte ... " (209). He admits, however, that the verb נקב, "bestimmen, festsetzen," is not yet attested in Aramaic, apart from Nabatean (210).

וכה כ]תבן]: "And thus have we written." Dupont-Sommer left the lacuna vacant and read a *t* before *bn* only with some hesitation. However, the context seems to call for something like this restoration, which had previously been suggested.

מה: "What." The interrogative pron. used as an indefinite relative; it serves as the subject of the nominal sentence of which לזכרן is the predicate.

2. כתבת: "I have written," the 1st sg. pf. peal of כתב. Mati'el is thus named as the one who has ordered the engraving of the addendum to this inscription as a reminder of the pact concluded with Bar-Ga'yah.

לזכרן: "As a reminder." Vocalize: *la-zikrān*. Cf. Hebrew *zikkārôn*. Cf. W. Schottroff, *Gedenken im Alten Orient und im Alten Testament* (WMANT 15; Neukirchen-Vluyn: Neukirchener V., 1964): cf. Exod 32:13; Deut 9:27; Isa 26:14; Ps 111:4.

4. יסקן: Cf. Sf I A 5; Sf I B 3. Vocalize: *yissaqūn*.

לטבת[א] יעבד[ו תחת] שמשא: "May they make good relations beneath the sun." Dupont-Sommer translated this clause, "en vue du bien qu'ils agissent devant le soleil," reading קדם instead of תחת, which he also admitted as possible. He sensed the difficulty in the expression קדם שמשא, even though he could appeal to *A* 93 (יקיר [קד]ם שמש), because קדם would normally suggest the presence of a deity, and the name *Šamaš* would scarcely be in the emphatic, if it were meant. For this reason I prefer תחת שמשא, which is closer to *taḥat haššemeš* of Qoh 1:3, 9, 14; 2:11; Tabnit 7; Ešmun'azor 12, even though these occurrences are of later date. See B. Peckham *The Development of the Late Phoenician Scripts* (HSS 20; Cambridge, MA: Harvard University, 1968) 79-80.

Dupont-Sommer also suspected that שמשא might be a royal title; see *AH* 1/2. 7. Hillers appealed to a Hittite inscription from Carchemish of Arara (Yariri), a ruler in the first half of the eighth century: A 6 = No. 11 in Piero Meriggi, *Manuale di Eteo geroglifico: Parte II, Testi* (Incunabula graeca 14; Rome: Ateneo, 1967).

The real problem in this clause, however, is the meaning of טבת[א]. Dupont-Sommer understood it as the fem. sg. emph., preceded by the prep. *l*-, "pour le bien;" similarly Donner-Röllig (*KAI*, 2. 257).

However, Moran ("A Note on the Treaty Terminology," 173-76) proposed for טבת[א] the meaning of "friendship, good relations," or more specifically "amity established by treaty." He appealed to Akkadian parallels that make this interpretation plausible: *ṭūbtu u šulummû*, "friendship and peace" (cf. L. W. King, *Chronicles Concerning Early Babylonian Kings, II* [London: Luzac, 1907] 58:6; D. J. Wiseman, *Chronicles of Chaldaean Kings (626-556 B.C.) in the British Museum* [London: British Museum, 1956] 59:29; *CT* 34:29 ii 27), and *tābūta* (*tābutta*) *epēšu*, "to make (a treaty of) friendship" (Amarna letters, *EA* 136:8-13; 138:53; 11 r 22; cf. C. Virolleaud, *RA* 38 [1941] 2:9-13); and in the Mari letters the semantic parallel of *damqātum* (lit., "good things"; cf. G. Dossin, *RA* 36 [1939] 51). The same Aramaic expression occurs in Sf I B 19-20 and Sf II B 2, where the fitness of this interpretation is more evident than here. It is also found in the Adon Letter, line 8 (וטבתה עבדך נצר, "your servant has kept his good relations"); see *Bib* 46 (1965) 52-54. Cf. McCarthy, "Covenant 'Good' and an Egyptian Text," *BASOR* 245 (1982) 63-64. Moran, however, attempted no translation of this line of the treaty because the text is so damaged. What we have suggested is not without its difficulties, because the form טבת[א], as restored by Dupont-Sommer, is emphatic; and I have construed the prefixed *lamedh* as the sign of the accusative (since the phrase seems to be the equivalent of the Akkadian *tābūta epēšu*), even though elsewhere in these inscriptions that sign is rather אית. But cf. Sf I C [23]. Degen (*AG*, 109) understood the *l-*, not as the sign of the accusative, but, as in לזכרן ("as a reminder"), in the sense "of, about."

Hillers also pointed out that this interpretation illuminates several OT passages as well ("A Note on Some Treaty Terminology," 46-47): Deut 23:7 (cf. Ezra 9:12); 2 Sam 2:6. Cf. 1 Sam 25:30; 2 Sam 7:28; 1 Kgs 12:7; Jer 33:9, 14; Hos 3:5; 8:3, and possibly also 2 Kgs 25:28; 2 Chr 24:16. These comparisons have been suggested by G. Buccellati, *BeO* 4 (1962) 233; A. Malamat, *BA* 28 (1965) 64; M. Weinfeld, *Lešonenu* 36 (1971-72) 10-13; M. Fox, *BASOR* 209 (1973) 41-42.

6. [לב]ית מ[לכי]: "For the sake of my royal house." If this reconstruction of Dupont-Sommer is correct, then we must vocalize it *labayt mulkī*, for the last word cannot be *malk*, "king," and is probably the abstract noun, *mulk-*, "kingship, reign, kingdom." Possibly it also occurs in Sf I B 6. According to Ginsberg, this word occurs in the Adon Letter (*Sem* 1 [1948] 44), line 1: מרא מלכן, "lord of kingdoms," equalling the Ptolemaic title κύριος βασιλειῶν ("An Aramaic Contemporary of the Lachish Letters," *BASOR* 111 [1948] 25); but see *Bib* 46 (1965) 45-47; E. G. Kraeling, *BMAP*, 17-18 n. 69. At any rate, *mulk* is found in Ugaritic and Phoenician in the same sense; see *BASOR* 87 (1942) 35, n. 20; *JBL* 56 (1937) 142; *AJSL* 57 (1940) 71-74. The vocalization with *u* is found in Arabic *mulku*^{n}, "sovereignty, Herrschaft"; it is also reflected in the Wen-Amun Report 2:19 (*mrk.f*, "his dominion"), compared with 2:12 (*mu-r-ku*), as G. S. Glanzman informed me.

כל לח[יה]: "No evil may be done." On לחיה (fem. sg. abs.), see note on Sf I A 26.

15. יצרו: "May they keep away"; the 3d pl. masc. short impf. (= juss.) peal of נצר. Vocalize: *yiṣṣarū*. Since this verb is usually construed with a direct object, Dupont-Sommer concludes that the two following instances of מן cannot be that of the preposition, but must either be particles (meaning "en verité, certes") like מת in the Hadad and Panammu inscriptions, or else the interrogative-indefinite pron. *man* used in the sense of "ceux-ci, ceux-là." He translated accordingly, "que des dieux gardent qui ses jours et qui sa maison!" יומה and ביתה thus become the direct objects of the verb יצרו. As a parallel he appealed to Kilamuwa 10-11 (ואנך למי כת אב ולמי כת אם, "and I was as a father to some and as a mother to others"). However, it is not impossible that the direct object of יצרו been lost in the preceding lacuna. In Hebrew there are a number of cases of נצר with a direct object and מן in the sense of "guard from (dangers), preserve" (see Ps 12:8; 32:7; 64:2; 140:2, 5). Moreover, the distributive use of מי in Phoenician is clear, but the parallel is not exact; for מי ... מי is not used in apposition to a noun already expressed, as would be the case here, if Dupont-Sommer's interpretation were correct.

יומה: "His day," i.e., his life-time. Dupont-Sommer interpreted this form as a plural noun with a suffix (= *yômôhi*). This cannot be correct, for all other cases of plural nouns with the 3d sg. masc. suff. are written fully, thus *-wh*. The defective writing should not be admitted until a clear, undisputed case of it is recognized. Vocalize: *yawmeh*. For a Hittite parallel to this blessing, see the treaty of Mursilis II with Duppi-Tessub, 21** (*ANET*, 205).

17. ליצר: "Will not observe," lit., "keep, guard." Prefixed negative; 3d sg. masc. impf. peal of נצר. The Akkadian cognate, *naṣāru* is used in the identical sense of "guarding the treaty" in Esarhaddon's vassal treaties (line 291); cf. *Bib* 46 (1965) 52-54. See further K. Cathcart, *Nahum in the Light of Northwest Semitic* (BibOr 26; Rome: Biblical Institute, 1973) 42-43. Cf. M. Weinfeld, *UF* 8 (1976) 398.

בנצבא זנה: "On this stele." See note on Sf I A 6. For a similar Hittite formula, see the treaty of Mursilis II and Duppi-Tessub, 20**

(*ANET*, 205).

18. אהלד: "I shall efface." The reading of this word is certain and is confirmed by Sf II C 1-2, [מן י]אמר להלדת ספריא אלן מן בתי אלהיא, "and whoever will give orders to efface these inscriptions from the bethels." Two other passages must also be considered: ויזחל הא מן לד ספר]י[א מן בתי]א[להיא, "should that (person) be frightened from effacing the inscriptions from the bethels" (Sf II C 6-7); and ו]י[אמר לד]ספ[ריא אלן מן בתי]א[להיא, "and order (him), 'Efface these inscriptions from the bethels'" (Sf II C 8-10). The various forms of the verb that occurs in these places suggest that we have both haphel and peal forms of the same root, meaning "efface." Dupont-Sommer suggested that the root was either לוד or לדד. I believe that לוד is preferable. אהלד is the 1st sg. impf. haphel (vocalize: *'uhalīd*); whereas הלדת is haphel infin. (vocalize: *halādūt*), and לד is peal impv. (vocalize: *lūd*). The root *lwd* is otherwise unattested in Aramaic and Hebrew, unless it is the cognate of *lwz* in Prov 3:21; 4:21, as suggested by Dupont-Sommer. Gevirtz (*VT* 11 [1961] 144) compared it with *lwz* of Mishnaic Hebrew, but is this really the same root? Note that in Prov 3:21 it is parallel to נצר (as here), and in 4:21 to שמר. If the root is correctly analyzed as *lwd* and is related to Hebrew *lwz*, then there is an interesting case of the early shift of *z* > *d* in the writing attested here.

מן מלוה: "Some of its words." The suffix might refer either to ספרא or to Mati'el; my translation has favored the former. For the partitive use of מן, see Sf I B 27. Garbini (*RSO* 34 [1959] 47) strangely reads מלוך, which is perhaps only a typographical error.

19. אהפך: "I shall upset," the form is 1st sg. impf. peal of הפך, "overturn, upset." Cf. Deut 23:6, where the verb is also used in a figurative sense; in line 21 it has a more literal force. See N. Lohfink, "Zu Text und Form von Os 4,4-6," *Bib* 42 (1961) 303-32, esp. 315; cf. Karatepe III. 12-18, esp. lines 13, 18.

טבתא: "The good relations," i.e., treaty relations or amity. See note on Sf I C 4. Moran notes ("A Note," 176) that the contrast with generic "evil," which plays on the etymology of טבתא, is no real difficulty for the specific meaning he attaches to the latter.

ואשם: "And I shall turn." This is the 1st sg. impf. peal of שים, "set," lit., "I shall set (them, i.e., the good relations [fem. emph. pl.]) for evil things." Vocalize: *'aśīm*. Lemaire-Durand (*IAS*, 116) read rather ואשנ]ה[לחית, "je change[rai] le mal" (126). But what would that mean? They do not seem to recognize the technical sense of טבתא.

20. [ל]לחית: "To evil." The form is the abs. pl. fem.; see note on Sf I A 26. Cf. Panammu 4 (קירת חרבת ישבת), 8 (קתילת), 13 (מחנת).

ביום זי: See note on Sf I B 31.

21. אש[א ה]א: "That man." If the reading and restoration are correct, we have another very early attestation of the noun אש, "man, human being," in Aramaic. Cf. Zakur a 2; Hadad 11(?), 34. On אש זר (Hadad 34), see H. Tawil, *JNES* 32 (1973) 477-82. It is found in this form (אש) in both Phoenician and Moabite, and the form איש is abundantly attested in later Aramaic (*AP* 8:11, 12, 16; 20:10, 12, 13, 14; *A*, passim). Vocalize: *'īša'*. This is the first occurrence, however, of the emph. state, if the restoration is correct.

23. תחתיתה [לע]ליתה: "May they make its lower part its upper part," an explanation of the preceding verb יהפכו. Cf. E. Herzfeld, "Summa imis confundere," *AMI* 5 (1933) 143-48; the words are probably fem. forms of the gentilic adjectives *taḥtāy* and *'illāy*. Lemaire-Durand (*IAS*, 116) read rather: וישנו, "et qu'ils changent son bas en haut." That is possibly an improvement.

24. ואל ירת: "And may he not inherit." If this form is interpreted correctly, we have an early example of a Proto-Semitic *tha* appearing in Aramaic as *t*, whereas it normally is *š* in these inscriptions. Vocalize: *yirat* (< *yirrat*). See note on *btn* (Sf I A 31). In thus reading this line, I have followed Dupont-Sommer, but W. R. Garr (*Dialect Geography*, 119, 158 n. 276) reads, ואל ירתשה [ל]ה אשם, "may a name not be acquired by him," a questionable reading, introducing into this stage of Aramaic an otherwise unknown expression of agency with the prep. *l*-.

שר[ש]ה: "His scion." Vocalize: *šuršeh*. This noun, related to Hebrew *šōreš*, "root," is used in the sense of "scion" (cf. Isa 14:29). *šuršu* in Akkadian also has the meaning of "sprout, scion" (used in parallelism to *līpu*). For a similar idea, see Eshmun'azor 11; Isa 37:31 (= 2 Kgs 19:30); Zakur b 28; Karatepe (*KAI* 26) A I 10; Larnax Lapethou III.3 (A. M. Honeyman, *Muséon* 51 [1938] 286). Cf. Apoc 5:5 (ἡ ῥίζα Δαυίδ, allusion to Isa 11:10, where the LXX uses ῥίζα as = *šōreš*). See A. R. Millard, "Notes: II. Isaiah 53:2," *Tyndale Bulletin* 20 (1969) 127; H. L. Ginsberg, "'Roots Below and Fruit Above' and Related Matters," *Hebrew and Semitic Studies Presented to G. R. Driver ...* (ed. D. W. Thomas and W. C. McHardy; Oxford: Clarendon, 1963) 72-76.

אשם: This word for "name" is also found elsewhere with a prothetic *aleph* in Aramaic: Sf II B 7; Hadad 16, 21; *RES* 1786, 10(?).

STELE II

Stele II was obtained by the Damascus Museum in a very fragmentary form, consisting of about a dozen pieces. When put together, they yielded the middle portion of three sides of a monument which must have been similar in shape to stele I. The left side, which is preserved in this case with its entire width, equals the width of the side of stele I (35 cm.). For further particulars about the physical state of this stele, see the remarks of Dupont-Sommer (pp. 293-94).

The names of the parties who have made the treaty which is recorded on this stele are the same as those on stele I, viz. Bar-Ga'yah (II A 3, B [5]) and Mati'el (II C 14). The character of the curses on face A recalls that of the curses inscribed on Sf I A 21-31, even though there are slight differences. The utterances regarding the fulfillment or the non-fulfillment of the treaty stipulations also remind one of those of Sf I B 21-45. The concluding lines of the treaty on face C resemble those of Sf I C 18ff. The differences, slight though they are, show that stele II is not simply a second copy of stele I. Segert (*ArOr* 32 [1964] 111) calls it a "second recension ... with numerous variants." Because of the bad state of preservation of this monument it is really impossible to specify further the relation of steles I and II. They are both closely related to each other, and more so than either of them is to stele III.

TEXT: Sf II

Face A

1 [יהינקן על ואל ישבע ושבע שורה יהינקן עגל וא]ל ישבע ושבע
2 [שאן יהינקן אמר ואל ישבע ושבע עזן יהי]נקן גדה ואל יש
3 [בע ושבע בכתה יהכן בשט לחם ואל יהרגן והן יש]קר לבר גאיה ול
4 [ברה ולעקרה תהוי מלכתה כמלכת חל ואשמה י]תנשי ויהוה קב
5 [רה..........................וש]בע שנן שית שב
6 [..........................וש]בע שנן תהוי [.]
7 [..........................]. בכל רברבי .
8 [..........................].ואת. [....]. וארקה וצע
9 [קה.................ויאכל] פם אריה ופם [..]. ופם נמר[ה] ..
10 [ ]..הו....פ[..].ח .. מ[...]
11 [ ]אד....בד ב[...].....[...]
12 [ ].א זי בית ...[..].פ.נ.י
13 [ ]..זי .נב...[...].....
14 [ ]...ו.צ...[.....]...

Face B

1 ....[ ]
2 עדיא וטבתא ז[י] עבדו אלהן ב[ארפד ובעמה ולישמע מתעאל]
2b ולישמען בנוה
3 לישמען רבוה ולישמע עמה ולי[שמען כל מלכי ארפד.......]
4 ים זי יעודן פהן תשמע נחת מ[.................. ו]
5 הן תאמר בנבשך ותעשת בלבב[ך גבר עדן אנה ואשמע לבר גאיה]
6 ובנוה ועקרה פלאכהל לאשלח י[ד בך וברי בברך ועקרי בעקרך]
7 ולחבזתהם ולאבדת אשמהם ו[הן יאמר מן חד בני אשב על כרסא]
8 אבי ויב ויזקן ויבעה ברי א[ית ראשי להמתתי ותאמר בנבשך י]
9 קתל מן יקתל שקרתם לכל אלה[י עדיא זי בספרא זנה ....]

TRANSLATION

Face A

... [and should seven mares [1]suckle a colt, may it not be sated; and should seven cows give suck to a calf, may it n]ot have its fill; and should seven [2][ewes suckle a lamb, may it not be sated; and should seven goats suck]le a kid, may it not be sa[ted; [3]and should seven *hens* go looking for food, may they not *kill* (anything). And if (Mati'el) should be un]faithful to Bar-Ga'yah and to [4][his son and to his offspring, may his kingdom become like a kingdom of sand; and may his name be for]gotten, and may [5][his grav]e be ...... [and for se]ven years thorns, ŠB[...] [6][... and for se]ven years may there be [..] [7][...] among all the nobles of ... [8][...] and his land. And a cry [9][... and may] the mouth of a lion [eat] and the mouth of [a ...] and the mouth of a panther [10][....] (Lines 10-14 are practically illegible.)

Face B

[1] . . . . [2]the treaty and the amity whi[ch] the gods have made in [Arpad and among its people; and (if) Mati'el will not obey], and (if) his sons will not obey, [3](if) his nobles will not obey, and (if) his people will not obey, and (if) [all the kings of Arpad] will not o[bey ...] [4]YM who bear witness. But if you obey, (may) tranquility [... And] [5]if you say in your soul and think in your mind, ["I am an ally, and I shall obey Bar-Ga'yah] [6]and his sons and his offspring," then I shall not be able to raise a ha[nd against you, nor my son against your son, nor my offspring against your offspring], [7]either to rout them, or to destroy their name. And [if one of my sons says, "I shall sit upon the throne] [8]of my father, for he is *babbling* and growing old," or (if) my son seeks [my head to kill me and you say in your soul, [9]"Let him kill whomever he would kill," (then) you will have been unfaithful to all the gods [of the treaty which is in this inscription ....]

10 [..].נך ובית גש ובית צלל ו[ ]
11 [......]..י ופגר ..ך על פגר[ ]
12 [......].י וביום חרן לכל [ ]
13 .... יאתה אל ברי ובני בנ[י]
14 מן יד שנאי ו....ון שקרתם [בעדיא אלן]
15 רבאב.. כמי ...שמרובשק .[ ]
16 ולאש יהוננה הן יהונה בקר[ ]
17 .להו.ה... הן תבעה ולת.[שק]
18 [ר]ת לכל [אלהי ע]דיא זי בספר[א זנה]
19 [.]ליע[.....]לך יגבר עד..[ ]
20 [.]הנ[.......]זי יעז מנך [ ]
21 [.].[...........]..... [ ]

Face C

1 ....[ומן י]א
2 מר להלדת ספריא [א]לן מן ב
3 תי אלהיא אן זי י[ר]שמן ו
4 [י]אמר אהאבד ספר[י]א ולמ[ג]
5 ן אהבד אית כתך ואית מלכ
6 ה ויזחל הא מן לד ספר
7 [י]א מן בתי אלהיא ויאמר ל
8 זי לידע אנה אגר ו[י]
9 אמר לד [ספ]ריא אלן מן בת
10 י [א]להיא ובלחץ עלב י[מת הא]
11 וברה
12 ....את.......מ....
13 [ישא]ן כל אלה[י עד]יא זי בספרא
14 [זנ]ה אית מתעאל וברה ובר ברה
15 ועקרה וכל מלכי ארפד וכל רב
16 וה ועמהם מן בתיהם ומן
17 יומיהם

[10][...]NK and Bêt-Gush and Bêt-ṢLL and [...] [11][...] and corpse ... upon corpse [...] [12][...] and on a day of wrath for all [...] [13][...] will come to my son and [my] grandsons [...] sons of [my] sons [...] [14]from the hand of my enemies and [...], you will have been unfaithful [to this treaty ....] [15]RB'B..KMY ... ŠMR WBŠQ. [...] [16]and let *no one* oppress him. If he oppresses (him) in QR[...] [17]LHW.H... if you should seek and not ..[...] [18]you [will have been unfaithful to] all the [gods of the trea]ty which is in [this] inscription [...] [19][.]LY' [...] he will surpass *you* until [20][.]HN [....] who will be stronger than you [...]

Face C

[1]... ... [and whoever will] give [2]orders to efface [th]ese inscriptions from the [3]bethels, where they are [wr]itten, and [4][will] say, "I shall destroy the inscript[ion]s and *with impunity* [5]shall I destroy KTK and its king," [6]should that (man) be frightened from effacing the inscript[ion]s [7]from the bethels and say to [8]someone who does not understand, "I shall engage (you) indeed," and (then) [9]order (him), "Efface these inscriptions from the bethels," [10]may [he] and his son die in oppressive torment. [12] [...] [13]and all the gods of the [trea]ty which is in [this] inscription will [...] [14]Mati'el and his son and his grandson [15]and his offspring and all the kings of Arpad and all its nobles [16]and their people from their homes and from [17]their days.

COMMENTARY

Face A

1. The few words, which are preserved on lines 1-2, suggest a text similar to that of Sf I A 21-25, the curses of the treaty. For line 1, see Sf I A 22-23. Dupont-Sommer utilized these lines for the reconstruction here. There is not an exact agreement, however, so that any reconstruction will be questionable. Greenfield expressed grave doubt about the restoration of lines 1-4 on the basis of Sf I A 21-25 (*JBL* 87 [1968] 241), but he did not give a different set of curses. He called attention, however, to the two different series of curses in the vassal treaties of Esarhaddon (lines 414-493 and 518-688), to which these may correspond.

2. Cf. Sf I A 23-24.

ושבע עזן יהי]נקן גדה]: "And should seven goats suckle a kid." It is possible to restore either עזן (fem. abs. pl.; vocalize: *'izzān*), as Dupont-Sommer has done, or עזה (fem. abs. sg.) in a collective sense, like שורה. עזה is the assimilated form of *'nz*, "goat," which occurs in *AP* 33:10 and as the cst. st. in Syriac (*'ănez*); cf. also Arabic *'anzu*ⁿ. גדה is abs. sg. of גדיא, "kid." Vocalize most probably: *gadêh* (< *gaday*); see *LFLAA* §54 and §43w' (*qatal*-type).

3. Cf. Sf I A 24. This line would be read otherwise by those who read I A 24 differently from Dupont-Sommer. Note that at the end of this lime Bar-Ga'yah's name is read with certainty and confirms the addition of it at the end of Sf I A 24, where it is otherwise almost certainly demanded by the context.

4. תהוי מלכתה כמלכת חל]: "May his kingdom become like a kingdom of sand." This reconstruction depends upon my reading of Sf I A 25; Dupont-Sommer read מלכת חלם.

ואשמה י]תנשי]: "And may his name be forgotten," the plausible restoration of Dupont-Sommer. יתנשי is the 3d sg. masc. impf. ithpeel of *nšy*, "forget." Vocalize: *yitnašê* (< *yitnašay*); cf. יתחזה (Sf I A 28: *yitḥazêh*). Nothing in Sf I A corresponds to this or the following curse.

ויהוה קב[רה]: "And may his grave be (or become unknown) ...." The form יהוה should be noted and contrasted with תהוי (Sf I A 25, 32; Sf II A 6); the former points to the contraction of the final diphthong, *yihwêh*. קברה should be vocalized *qabreh*, since the *a*-vowel is preserved in the first syllable in later Aramaic and Syriac; cf. also Arabic *qabru*^{n}. Cf. K. Cathcart, *Nahum*, 66.

5. [...]ושבע שנן שית שב[...]: "And for seven years thorns ...." This and the following line contain curses that are similar to those of Sf I A 27-28, but the word שית does not occur there. It is apparently otherwise unknown in Aramaic. Dupont-Sommer related it to Hebrew *šayit*, "thorns," which certainly would suit the context as known from Sf I A.

7. בכל רברבי: "Among all the nobles of." Perhaps related to Sf I A 29 (בארפד ובעמה); if so, ארפד can be supplied after רברבי, which is the reduplicated form of the plural of רב, normal in later Aramaic. Elsewhere in these inscriptions one finds only רבוה (Sf I A 39, 40, 41; Sf II B 3; Sf II C 15).

8. [צע]קה: "And a cry." See Sf I A 29. Cf. Gen 27:34; Ps 9:13.

9. Cf. Sf I A 30-31. אריה: "Lion." Vocalize: *'aryêh* (< *'aryay*). Cf. Segert, *ArOr* 32 (1964) 124. For a lion in a treaty curse, see the treaty of Esarhaddon with Ba'al of Tyre (Rev. IV 6-7); Jer 5:6; Hos 13:7-8. Cf. Hillers, *Treaty-Curses*, 54-56.

Face B

2. עדיא וטבתא: "The treaty and the amity." For this meaning of טבתא, see note on Sf I C 4. Moran ("A Note," 176) would translate, "a treaty and friendship ...."

[זי] עבדו אלהן: "Which gods have made." Moran (ibid.) recalls the Akkadian use of *epēšu* (with *ṭābūta*), which parallels the use of עבד.

[לישמע מתעאל]: "And (if) Mati'el will not obey." Restored by Dupont-Sommer as the logical antecedent of the following רבוה, בנוה, and עמה. The sentence is similar to Sf I B 21-22. There is no need to restore a *waw* at the end of this line, for one precedes the first word of line 2b.

2b. This line consists of only two words.

4. –ים זי יעודן: "Who bear witness." This is the end of a sentence. Dupont-Sommer admits that the last word can also be read יעודן. This has been adopted by Lemaire-Durand (*IAS*, 117) and now seems better than the form יעורן, which created problems discussed in the first edition of this book. Both Segert and Degen (*AG*, 76) follow Dupont-Sommer in taking the form as a pual impf. of עור.

פהן: "But if." The conjunction -פ (lit., "and") occurs also in line 6 below. It was previously thought that this conjunction was a peculiarity of the dialect of Ya'di, since it occurs frequently enough in the form -פ and פא in both the inscription of Hadad (-פ: 3, 13, 14, 30, 31; פא: 17, 33) and Panammu (פא: 22, 11[?]). In fact, Garbini ("La congiunzione semitica *pa-*," *Bib* 38 [1957] 422 n. 2) considered its occurrence in the Bar-Rakkab inscription as owing "al permanere di elementi ya'udici nel nuovo dialetto aramaico, di provenienza assira, che sotto Bar-Rkb venne introdotto nello stato di Šam'al." But the occurrence of the conjunction here shows that its use was more widespread than previously-known evidence allowed us to believe. To the evidence listed by Garbini one should add an occurrence in the Nabataean contract from the Judean Desert, published by J. Starcky (*RB* 61 [1954] 163, line 3).

נחת: "Tranquility." Though this looks at first sight like the familiar Aramaic verb, "descend," that meaning hardly fits the broken context. Dupont-Sommer may, therefore, be right in regarding it as a noun, "tranquility, peace," related to the Hebrew *naḥat* (Isa 30:15; Qoh 4:6) and the cognate Phoenician word (Aḥiram Sarcophagus 2; Karatepe A I 18, A II 8). Cf. Ugaritic *nḫt* (UT 95:14). This word would belong to a blessing pronounced over Mati'el on condition that he remains faithful to the treaty.

5. ותעשת בלבב[ך]: "And think in your mind." The verb עשת occurs in *BMAP* 5:3; 9:2; *A* 25, 68; Dan 6:4; in the ithpaal form: *AP* 30:23; 31:[22]; *AD* 8:3; frg. 3:13. Greenfield (*AcOr* 29 [1965] 6) maintained that the verb עשת did not simply mean "think," but rather "plot against." He compared Hebrew חשב בלבב (Zech 7:10; 8:17) and targumic Aramaic (on Isa 32:6).

[גבר עדן אנה]: See Sf I B 24. This restoration makes better sense than that of Dupont-Sommer: גבר עדן הא.

6. לאשלח י[ד בך]: "I shall not be able to raise a hand against you." Finite complement to פלאכהל; see note on Sf I B 24, 34. For the conj. -פ, see note on line 4 above.

7. ולחבזתהם: "Either to rout them ...." This verb occurs also in Sf III 24, but is otherwise unknown in Aramaic. Dupont-Sommer wrote apropos of its occurrence in Sf III 24 (*BMB* 13 [1956] 35): "Cette racine חבז semble devoir être rapprochée de la racine חבט "frapper", attestée en araméen, en hébreu, en éthiopien, en arabe (*ḫbṭ*). Rapprocher encore akkadien *ḫabatu*, ugaritique *ḫbt* "piller"; judéo-araméen (et hébreu post-biblique) *ḥbs* "broyer"; syriaque *ḥbṣ* "presser," hébreu post-biblique *ḥbṣ* "battre le lait"; arabe *ḫbz*, "broyer (le grain), faire le pain" (cette derniere racine est exactement identique à notre חבז). Nous traduisons donc: quand les dieux *frappèrent* la maison [de mon père ...]'." Except for the last-mentioned Arabic root the other etymological connections mentioned by Dupont-Sommer are far-fetched. As far as I know, a *z* in Aramaic never represents a *t*, *ṭ*, *s*, or *ṣ* in the other Semitic languages. The Arabic root *ḫbz* may give enough of the idea of "striking" to admit it here as the cognate of this Aramaic word. But Hartman (*CBQ* 30 [1968] 259) queried this connection, for the Arabic root really means "bake bread," and only secondarily "grind, strike." Hence he preferred Rosenthal's interpretation (*BASOR* 158 [1960] 30), which related חבז to Hebrew הפז, "flee in a hurry," and Arabic *ḥfz*, "push." Hence pael חבז would mean "rout, drive out," a solution that could be admitted since there are other cases of the shift *p* > *b* in these inscriptions. Cf. Greenfield, *AcOr* 29 (1965) 5 n. 12. In view of the infin. form here, ending in *-t*, it is preferable to interpret both forms as pael; hence vocalize: *ḥabbāzūthom* and *ḥabbizū*. See now H. Tawil, *CBQ* 42 (1980) 30-37, esp. 30-32.

ולאבדת: "Or to destroy." Pael infin.; vocalize: *'abbādūt*.

אשמהם: "Their name." The prothetic *aleph* is also found on this word in Sf I C 25; II A 4. Cf. Deut 2:3; 7:24.

ו]הן ...: The conjectural restoration of this sentence by Dupont-Sommer is based on Sf III 17. The first personal form is demanded by אבי at the beginning of the next line.

8. ויבע ויזקן: "For he is babbling and growing old." The meaning of the first verb is not clear. Dupont-Sommer suggested that the root is נבע, "speak," attested in both Hebrew (Ps 19:3; 59:8) and Aramaic in the causative stem. The specific nuance of "babbling" is derived from the context and the collocation of this verb with the next, יזקן, "grows old," which is not otherwise attested. And yet it is scarcely dittographical, *pace* D. W. Thomas, *JSS* 5 (1960) 284.

ויבעה ברי א]ית ראשי להמתתי: "Or (if) my son seeks my head to kill me." Cf. Sf III 11; but note that אית does not occur there.

9. י]קתל מן יקתל: "Let him kill whomever he would kill." For קתל instead of קטל, see note on Sf I B 27. The words are a sort of soliloquy put on the lips of Mati'el, who would be secretly siding with the rebellious son of Bar-Ga'yah. Cf. Exod 33:19; 2 Sam 15:20.

שקרתם: "You will have been unfaithful." See notes on Sf I A 14;

Sf I B 23.

10. ובית גש ובית צלל: See note of Sf I B 3.

11. [...] ופגר..ך על פגר: See note on Sf I B 30. Lemaire-Durand (*IAS*, 117) read: [פרך על פ]גרי ופגר ברך על פגר [ברי], "[ton cadavre sur mon ca]davre et le cadavre de ton fils sur le cadavre [de mon fils]" (127).

12. וביום חרן: "And on a day of wrath." Dupont-Sommer related חרן to Hebrew *ḥārôn*; cf. Isa 13:13 (ביום חרון אפו).

13. Dupont-Sommer believed that this line was parallel to Sf I B 31-32. This suggestion is, however, problematic. אל is almost certainly correct as the restored preposition; cf. Sf III 1. [בנ]יך, read by Dupont-Sommer, is not convincing. I prefer to restore simply [בנ]י; cf. Sf I A 2.

14. מן יד שנאי: "From the hand of my enemies." The same expression occurs in Sf III 11.

15. Unintelligible.

16. ולאש יהוננה: "And let no one oppress him." Dupont-Sommer may have been right in translating, "et personne ne l'opprimera," but the position of the negative is rather peculiar. One would expect ואש ליהוננה. On the defective writing of אש, see note on Sf I C 1. The verb is 3d sg. masc. energic impf. haphel of ינ׳, well attested in later Aramaic and Hebrew. Vocalize: *yuhawninneh*. The ordinary impf. follows in *yuhawnêh*. The final vowel is shortened before the energic ending; cf. pael form *yĕhawwinnanī* (Dan 5:7).
[...]בקר: Perhaps [בקר[יתא, "in the town."

18. Cf. Sf III 4, 14, 16, 23; Sf I B 23; Sf II B 9.

19. ... לך יגבר עד[ ]: "He will surpass you until ...." But it is not certain that לך is an independent word; it may be the suffixal ending of some noun, which is the subject of יגבר. Dupont-Sommer suggested [חי]לך, "your army." Perhaps "your army will be strong." However, this phrase may be related to the only legible one in line 20.

20. זי יעז מנך: "Who will be stronger than you." The form יעז is the 3d sg. masc. impf. peal of עזז, "be strong." Vocalize: *ya'uz* (< *ya'uzzu*). Cf. BLA §48b-c. Contrast מנך with מך (Sf III 22).

Face C

2. להלדת: "To efface," or "to destroy." See note on Sf I C 18. For parallels to [י]אמר, see Exod 2:14; 2 Sam 21:16.

ספריא: "Inscriptions." One wonders about the plural here. Could it refer to Sf I and Sf II?

בתי אלהיא: "Bethels," lit. "the houses of the gods." This expression is found below in lines 7, 9-10. Since the context may show that this expression refers to the steles themselves on which the inscriptions are written, Dupont-Sommer translated the phrase as "bétyles," i.e. sacred stones (sometimes considered as the dwelling of a god or even as the god himself). The noun "bethel" can be used in this sense in English (see J. A. H. Murray, *A New English Dictionary on Historical Principles* [Oxford: Clarendon], I [1888] 829). One should contrast this expression with the use of נצבא זנה, "this stele" (Sf I C 17). Dupont-Sommer cited the words of Philo Byblius, quoting Sanchuniaton, about the βαιτύλια invented by the god Uranus and considered to be "animate stones," ἔτι δὲ (φησιν) ἐπενόησεν Θεὸς Οὐρανὸς βαιτύλια, λίθους ἐμψύχους μηχανησάμενος (Eusebius, *Praep. Evang.* 1.10.23; ed. K. Mras, GCS 43/1 [1954] 48). But is this the first known instance of this expression in a Semitic text to designate the sacred stone itself? See Gen 28:18-22, where Jacob anoints the stone he had used as a pillow, set it up as a sacred pillar (*maṣṣēbāh*) and said, והאבן הזאת אשר שמתי מצבה יהיה בית אלוהים (v. 22). On Gen 28:18-22, see H. Donner, *ZAW* 74 (1962) 68-70; O. Eissfeldt, "Der Gott Bethel," *ARW* 28 (1930) 1-30 (repr. in *Kleine Schriflen* [Tübingen: Mohr [Siebeck], 1962], 1. 206-33); E. Meyer, *ZAW* 49 (1931) 11-12. Moreover, in the treaty of Esarhaddon with Ba'al of Tyre there is in the list of the gods after [Ištar], Gula, and Sibitti a deity named *Ba-a-a-ti-ilani*^{meš} (Rev. II, 6), "Baiti-ilāni." This deity was related by Harris (*GPL*, 86) to βαίτυλος of Hesychius and βαιτύλιον of Sanchuniaton. Besides C. Clemen, *Die phönikische Religion nach Philo von Byblos* (MVAG 42/3; Leipzig: Hinrichs, 1939] 27), referred to by Dupont-Sommer, see K. Tümpel, "Baitylia," *RE* II/2. 2779, 81; N. Turchi, "Betìlo," *Enciclopedia cattolica* II. 1514-15. Cf. B. Soyez, "Le bétyle dans le culte de l Astarté phénicienne," *MUSJ* 47 (1972) 147-69; M. J. Mulder, *Kanaänitische goden in het Oude Testament* (Exegetica 4/4-5; The Hague: Vorheen van Keulen, 1965) 20-23.

However, Greenfield (*JBL* 87 [1968] 241) has preferred to interpret בתי אלהיא as "temples of the gods" and to understand the verb לוד, not as "efface," but as "remove." If this is correct, there would be a warning against the removal of the inscription from the temple wherein it was deposited, which is a standard stipulation in many treaties. Lemaire-Durand (*IAS*, 128) literally translate "maisons des dieux."

3. אן זי י[ר]שמן: "Where they are written." The interrogative adverb אן is well attested in later Aramaic. ירשמן is the 3d pl. masc. impf. pass. (*yuqtal*-type) of רשם, "scratch, make a mark; write"; see note on Sf I A 33.

4. אהאבד: "I shall destroy," lit. "I shall cause (it) to be lost," 1st sg. impf. haphel of אבד, "be lost." Vocalize: *'uha'bid*.

ולמ[ג]ן: Dupont-Sommer read ולמ[ל]ן and took this phrase as an adverbial expression with distributive sense, "et, mot par mot(?), je supprimerai KTK et son roi." He compared the Hebrew expressions לבקרים, "à chaque matin," Ps 73:14) or לרגעים ("à chaque instant," Isa 27:3). But these are temporal expressions, which is not the case with למלן. I read here rather the adverb מגן, which is found in Palmyrene Aramaic (see Cooke, *NSI* §116:4) and the targums (as the equivalent of *ḥinnām*; see Tg. Onqelos on Gen 29:15) with the meaning "gratis, for nothing"? (Suggestion of G. S. Glanzman).

5. אהבד: "Shall I destroy." This form seems to be an alternate form of אהאבד (line 4). Was the *aleph* in the second syllable lost by quiescence or simply by scribal omission? Donner-Röllig too confidently opt for the former (*KAI* 2. 263).

אית: Two clear uses of the sign of the accusative; see note on Sf I B 32.

6. ויזחל: "Be frightened." 3d sg. masc. impf. peal of זחל, "be frightened, fear." Cf. the later Aramaic דחל, construed with מן (Dan 6:27); also Job 32:6; Zakur a 13. See K. R. Veenhof, "An Aramaic Curse with a Sumero-Akkadian Prototype," *BO* 20 (1963) 142-44.

לד: See note on Sf I C 18.

7. בתי אלהיא: See note on Sf II C 2 above.

ויאמר לזי לידע: "And say to someone who does not understand." Dupont-Sommer translated: "(et qu'il dise) à qui ne sait rien." Dupont-Sommer's interpretation of this part of the sentence is certainly superior to that of Donner-Röllig (*KAI*, 2. 259). The *l* is the prefixed negative; *yd'* is the peal act. ptc. ("who does not know"). H. Tawil (*JNES* 32 [1973] 480) translates, "and command an idiot," comparing Akkadian *qabû* with Aramaic אמר and Akkadian *lā mudû* with Aramaic זי לידע.

8. אנה אגר אגר: "I shall engage (you) indeed," i.e., pay you a salary. The first אגר should be understood as a peal infin., intensifying the main verb, the second אגר. The latter is 1st sg. impf. peal from the root אגר (related to the word for "salary," cf. *DISO*, 4). Attempts to explain אגר as a form of גור, "be afraid," are unconvincing. See further K. R. Veenhof, "An Aramaic Curse," where parallels to this curse in Sumerian and Akkadian treaties are given.

9. לד: "Efface." See note on Sf I C 18. Veenhof (ibid., 144) denied that there was room for the final ת, read by Dupont-Sommer.

10. ובלחץ עלב י[מת]: "And may he die in oppressive torment." The noun לחץ (cst. st.) is not otherwise attested in Aramaic, but it seems to be related to the biblical Hebrew *laḥaṣ*, "oppression" (Exod 3:9; Deut 26:7). Nor is עלב found as a noun in Aramaic (except in the derived form עלבנא, "torment, oppression"); cf. 1QapGen 2:17 (עליבא). The two nouns express the same idea in a cst. chain.

י[מת]: So restored plausibly by Dupont-Sommer. Note that the form is written *ymwt* in Sf III 16. This restoration is more in accord with the normal orthography of these inscriptions.

11. וברה: "His son." Dupont-Sommer read ובנה, marking the *nun* as a doubtful letter, translating it, "et ses fils," and explaining it as equal to בנוה. Similarly S. Segert, *ArOr* 32 (1964) 126 n. 111. This defective writing of the 3d sg. masc. suff. on a plural noun, however, is problematic, not being attested elsewhere in early Aramaic. I have hesitated to read it in Sf I C 15-16 too, where it is no more certain. In this case the *nun* is far from certain and might just as well be a *reš*, which would yield a normal form, "his son." See the comments of P. Grelot, *RB* 75 (1968) 284.

13. [ישא]ן: The restoration of the verb is problematic; this is the form given by Dupont-Sommer, apparently as the 3d pl. masc. impf. peal of נשא. Whatever verb is to be restored, it should be noted that the last letter is a nun, which precludes its being understood as a jussive; it is more likely the long impf. The end of the sentence, מן בתיהם ומן יומיהם (line 16) reminds one of the blessing in Sf I C 15-16: יצרו אלהן מן יומה ומן ביתה, where the direct object of the verb is lost. As Dupont-Sommer understood this last section of the inscription, it deals with some crime committed in violation of the treaty or with some damage done to the steles. This is certainly possible, and in such case the restoration of ישאן is not wholly improbable. But could not the last paragraph be a blessing? Admittedly, we cannot simply restore some form of נצר here (as in Sf I C 15-16), because the direct object expressed would not suit that verb. But possibly some other verb should be restored.

כל אלה[י עד]יא: See Sf I B 23, 33; Sf II B 9; Sf III 4, 14, 17, 23.

14-16. מתעאל וברה ובר ברה ועקרה וכל מלכי ארפד וכל רבוה ועמהם: "Mati'el and his son and his grandson and his offspring and all the kings of Arpad and all its nobles and their people." Cf. Sf III 1, 3, 14-16 for similar formulae. Noth (*ZDPV* 77 [1961] 132 n. 40) believed that the suffix on רבוה really referred to Arpad; and that, though in form it is masc., it should really be treated as a fem.

16. מן בתיהם ומן יומיהם: "From their homes and from their days." See Sf I C 15-16.

STELE III

Stele III was acquired by the Beirut Museum in 1956 and consists of nine fragments. Pieced together, they yield an extended text of 29 lines, of which the last three lines are quite fragmentary. A few letters have been lost from the middle of most lines, but they are in most cases easily restored. Unlike steles I and II this inscription was engraved on a broad slab and apparently only on one face of it. What remains, therefore, of the inscription is a surface roughly 102 cm. x 72 cm.

When Ronzevalle published the so-called Sujin stele (Sf I) in 1931, he gave notice of the existence of two other fragmentary steles belonging to a group which had been set up in the neighborhood of Sefire. Stele III is to be identified with what he then called a "seconde stèle, très fragmentaire, [qui] n'a laissé d'elle qu'une trentaine de lignes, toutes très incomplètes et mutilées.[1]

On the relation of stele III to the other steles, see above pp. 00-00. It should be recalled that, though Bar-Ga'yah's name is plausibly restored in III 25, that restoration is not certain and has, in fact, been contested. Mati'el's name does not occur in this stele either. Yet it does mention the "kings of Arpad" (lines 1, 3, 16, 27). Moreover, as Dupont-Sommer remarked, there is in it "the same type of stone, the same handwriting, the same absence of word-dividers, the same mention of the "kings of Arpad" and the same general contents."[2]

My transcription of this text differs only slightly from that of Dupont-Sommer: חד instead of כל (line 3), אעבד instead of אעבר (3), רחם הא לי instead of רחמה אלי (8), לשלם instead of לשלח (8), נגדי instead of נגרי (10), תכה instead תפה (13), זי לה instead of זי להם (20), והוי חלפה instead of הו יחלפה (22).[3]

Neither the beginning nor the end of the inscription has been preserved. It contains only a list of stipulations imposed on the king(s) of Arpad. In only one instance does the suzerain promise anything: to return fugitives, provided his own are sent back.

---

1 *MUSJ* 15 (1931) 237.

2 *BMB* 13 (1956) 24.

3 Returning from Jerusalem to the United States via Beirut in July 1958, I was able to inspect the stele itself. In my opinion, one must read אעבד (3), וארק (6), and נגדי (10). Generally, the *daleth* is clearly distinguished from the *reš* in this inscription, the vertical shaft of the latter being longer than that of the former. In line 13 שגבוה is almost certainly to be read שרבוה. Though the reading is in any case doubtful, I prefer לשלם to לשלח (8) and תכה to תפה (13). See further comments on the respective lines.

TEXT: Sf III

1 או אל ברך או אל עקרך או אל חד מלכי ארפד וי[מל]ל [ע]לי או על ברי
או על בר ברי או על עקרי כים כל גב

2 ר זי יבעה רוח אפוה וימלל מלן לחית לעלי [את ל]תקה מליא מן ידה הסכר
תהסכרהם בידי וב

3 רך יהסכר לברי ועקרך יסכר לעקרי ועקר [חד מ]לכי ארפד יהסכרן לי מה
טב בעיני אעבד להם ו

4 הן להן שקרתם לכל אלהי עדיא זי בספרא [זנה] והן יקרק מני קרק חד
פקדי או חד אחי או חד

5 סרסי או חד עמא זי בידי ויהכן חלב לתס[ך ל]הם לחם ולתאמר להם שלו
על אשרכם ולתהרם נ

6 בשהם מני רקה תרקהם ותהשבהם לי והן לי[שב]ן בארקך רקו שם עד אהך
אנה וארקהם והן תהרם נבשה

7 ם מני ותסך להם לחם ותאמר להם שבו לתחתכ[ם] ואל תפנו באשרה
שקרתם בעדיא אלן וכל מלכיא זי ס

8 חרתי או כל זי רחם הא לי ואשלח מלאכי א[ל]וה לשלם או לכל חפצי או
ישלח מלאכה אלי פתח

9 ה לי ארחא לתמשל בי בזא ולתרשה לי עלי[ה ו]הן להן ש[ק]רת בעדיא אלן
והן מן חד אחי או מן חד בי

TRANSLATION

I. *Concerning the Surrender of Plotters*

[... And whoever will come to you] [1]or to your son or to your offspring or to one of the kings of Arpad and will s[pea]k [ag]ainst me or against my son or against my grandson or against my offspring, *indeed,* any man [2]who *rants* and utters evil words against me, [you] must [not] accept such words from him. You must hand them (i.e., the men) over into my hands, and your son [3]must hand (them) over to my son, and your offspring must hand (them) over to my offspring, and the offspring of [any of the ki]ngs of Arpad must hand (them) over to me. Whatever is good in my sight, I will do to them. And [4]if (you do) not (do) so, you shall have been unfaithful to all the gods of the treaty which is in [this] inscription.

II. *Concerning the Surrender of Fugitives*

Now if a fugitive flees from me, one of my officials, or one of my brothers, or one of [5]my courtiers, or one of the people who are under my control, and they go to Aleppo, you must not gi[ve th]em food or say to them, "Stay quietly in your place"; and you must not incite [6]them against me. You must *placate* them and return them to me. And if they [do] not [dwell] in your land, *placate* (them) there, until I come and *placate* them. But if you incite them [7]against me and give them food and say to them, "Stay where [yo]u are and do not (re)turn to his region," you shall have been unfaithful to this treaty.

III. *Concerning Freedom of Passage*

Now (as for) all the kings of my [8]vicinity or any one who is a friend of mine, when I send my ambassador to him for peace or for any of my business or (when) he sends his ambassador to me, [9]the road shall be open to me. You must not (try to) dominate me in this (respect) or assert your authority over me concerning [it]. [And] if (you do) not (do) so, you shall be unfaithful to this treaty.

10 ת אבי או מן חד בני או מן חד נגדי או מן חד [פ]קדי או מן חד עמיא
זי בידי או מן חד שנאי ו

11 יבעה ראשי להמתתי ולהמתת ברי ועקרי הן אי[ת]י יקתלן את תאתה ותקם
דמי מן יד שנאי וברך יאתה

12 יקם דם ברי מן שנאוה ובר ברך יאתה יקם ד[ם ב]ר ברי ועקרך יאתה יקם
דם עקרי והן קריה הא נכה

13 תכוה בחרב והן חד אחי הא או חד עבדי או [חד] פקדי או חד עמא זי בידי
נכה תכה אי<ת>ה ועקרה ושר

14 בוה ומודדוה בחרב והן להן שקרת לכל אלהי [ע]דיא זי בספרא זנה והן
יסק על לבבך ותשא על ש

15 פתיך להמתתי ויסק על לבב בר ברך וישא על שפתוה להמתת בר ברי או הן
יסק על לבב עקרך

16 וישא על שפתוה להמתת עקרי והן יסק על [ל]בב מלכי ארפד בכל מה זי
ימות בר אנש שקרתם לכ

17 ל אלהי עדיא זי בספרא זנה והן ירב בר[י] זי ישב על כהסאי <עם> חד
אחוה או יעברנה לתשלח לש

18 נך בניהם ותאמר לה קתל אחך או אסרה ו[אל] תשריה [ו]הן רקה תרקה
בניהם ליקתל וליאסר

19 והן לתרקה בניהם שקרת בעדיא אלן ו[מ]לכן [זי סחר]תי ויקרק קרקי אל
חדהם ויקרק קר

IV. *Concerning Vengeance to be Taken in the Case of Assassination*

Now if any one of my brothers or any one of my [10]father's household or any one of my sons or any one of my officers or any one of my [of]ficials or any one of the people under my control or any one of my enemies [11]seeks my head to kill me and to kill my son and my offspring -- if they kill m[e], you must come and avenge my blood from the hand of my enemies. Your son must come [12](and) avenge the blood of my son from his enemies; and your grandson must come (and) avenge the blo[od of] my grandson. Your offspring must come (and) avenge the blood of my offspring. If it is a city, you must [13]strike it with a sword. If it is one of my brothers or one of my slaves or [one] of my officials or one of the people who are under my control, you must strike him and his offspring, his *nobles*, [14]and his friends with a sword. And if (you do) not (do) so, you shall have been unfaithful to all the gods of the [tr]eaty which is in this inscription.

V. *Concerning Plots against the Suzerain*

If the idea should come to your mind and you should express with your lips (the intention) [15]to kill me; and if the idea should come to the mind of your grandson and he should express with his lips (the intention) to kill my grandson; or if the idea should come to the mind of your offspring [16]and he should express with his lips (the intention) to kill my offspring; and if the idea should come to the [mi]nd of the kings of Arpad, in whatever way anyone shall die, you shall have been unfaithful to all [17]the gods of the treaty which is in this inscription.

VI. *Concerning Duty in a Strife for Succession to the Throne*

If [my] son, who sits upon my throne, quarrels <with> one of his brothers, and he would *remove* him, you shall not interfere [18]with them, saying to him, "Kill your brother or imprison him and do no[t] let him go free." But if you really *make peace* between them, he will not kill and will not imprison (him). [19]But if you do not *make peace* between them, you shall have been unfaithful to this treaty.

VII. *Concerning the Reciprocal Return of Fugitives*

And as for [k]ings [of my vicin]ity, if a fugitive of mine flees to one of them, and a fugitive of theirs flees

20 קהם ויאתה אלי הן השב זי לי אהשב [זי לה וא]ל תעשקני את והן להן
שקרת בעדיא א

21 לן ולתשלח לשן בביתי ובני בני ובני א[חי ובני ע]קרי ובני עמי ותאמר
להם קתלו מרא

22 כם והוי חלפה כי לטב הא מך ויקם חד [דמי והן ת]עבד מרמת עלי או על
בני או על עקר[י]

23 [ש]קרתם לכל אלהי עדיא זי בספא זנ[ה ותלאי]ם וכפריה ובעליה וגבלה
לאבי ול

24 [ביתה מן] עלם וכזי חבזו אלהן בית [אבי הא ה]ות לאחרן וכעת השבו
אלהן שיבת בי

25 [ת אבי ורבה בית] אבי ושבת תלאים ל[בר גאי]ה ולברה ולבר ברה ולעקרה
עד עלם ו

26 [הן ירב ברי וירב בר ב]רי וירב עקרי [עם עקרך ע]ל תלאים וכפריה
ובעליה מן ישא

27 [............... מל]כי ארפד [............]לנה שקרת בעדיא
אלן והן

28 [................................] וישחדן כל מה מלך זי י

29 [...................................כל מה ז]י שפר וכל מה זי
ט[ב..]

[20]and comes to me, if he has restored mine, I will return [his; and] you yourself shall [no]t (try to) hinder me. And if (you do) not (do) so, you shall have been unfaithful to this treaty.

VIII. *Concerning Plots against the Suzerain's Household*

[21]You shall not interfere in my house or (with) my grandsons or (with) the sons of my bro[thers or (with) the sons of my off]spring or (with) the sons of my people, saying to them, "Kill your lord, [22]and be his successor! For he is not better than you." Someone will avenge [my blood. If you do com]mit treachery against me or against my sons or against [my] offspring, [23]you shall have been [unfaith]ful to all the gods of the treaty which is in th[is] inscription.

IX. *Concerning the Territory of Tal'ayim*

[Tal'ay]im, its villages, its lords, and its territory (once belonged) to my father and to [24][his house from] of old. When (the) gods struck [my father's] house, [it came to belong] to another. Now, however, (the) gods have brought about the return of my [25][father's ho]use, [and] my father's [house has grown great], and Tal'ayim has returned to [Bar Ga'y]ah and to his son and to his grandson and to his offspring forever. [26][If my son quarrels and (if)] my [grand]son quarrels and (if) my offspring quarrels [with your offspring a]bout Tal'ayim and its villages and its lords, whoever will raise [27][...... the ki]ngs of Arpad [.............]LNH, you shall have been unfaithful to this treaty.

X. *Concerning Gifts (?)*

And if [28][ ] and they bribe in any way a king who will [29][.... all th]at is beautiful and all that is go[od] [30][....].

COMMENTARY

1. או: "Or." The first word, being a coordinate conjunction introducing a series, shows that we do not have the beginning of this inscription. Dupont-Sommer believed that the verso of the stele alone was preserved and that the formal introduction has been lost.

אל: The preposition אל, common in Hebrew, but rare in later Aramaic, is found several times in this inscription; see lines 8 (אלוה, אלי), 19 (אל), 20 (אלי). It also occurs in Zakur a 11, 12 and frequently in the address of a letter in the Elephantine texts (*AP* 40:1, 5; 41:1, 9; 30:1; *BMAP* 13:1, 6). Note that in *AD* (2:1; 3:1; etc.) it is usually replaced by על. On the basis of the verb אתה used with אל in line 20 we may restore: [ומן יאתה אליך] או אל ברך. Dupont-Sommer suggested: וכל זי יאתה אלי, but the last word is a printing error; see his translation.

עקרך: "Your offspring." See note on Sf I A 2. The series of son, grandson, offspring, or any other king (usurper?) is intended to guarantee the perpetuity of the pact that is being made. It is but another way of expressing עד עלם (Sf III 25). One should recall in this connection the attempts of Esarhaddon to insure the succession of this two sons on the throne in his vassal treaties. Cf. 2 Sam 7:11-14 and M. Tsevat, "Studies in the Book of Samuel, III: The Steadfast House," *HUCA* 34 (1963) 71-82.

חד: "One of." The indefinite use of the numeral in the sense of "a" or "one" is frequent in this stele; see line 4, 5, 9, 10, 13, 17, 19 (with a suffix), 22. It is usually construed as the *nomen regens* in a construct chain and not coupled with מן; cf. *A* 33; and note on Sf I B 26.

מלכי: "The kings of." This word most likely refers to kings of a dynasty (so Dupont-Sommer, E. Vogt); but Noth thought that it referred to kings allied in some way to the king of Arpad.

ארפד: "Arpad." The mention of Arpad constitutes one of the important links between this stele and Sf I, where Mati'el appears as the king of Arpad, upon whom Bar-Ga'yah, the king of KTK, imposes a vassal treaty. See note on Sf I A 3.

וי[מ]ל[ל] [ע]לי: "Speak against me," in the sense of plotting against. Restored as in line 2. This refers to a conspiracy against the overlord. See H. Tawil, "The End of the Hadad Inscription in the Light of Akkadian," *JNES* 32 (1973) 477-82, esp. 478 n. 19, where he compares *ana/ina muḫḫi dabābu*. See *ABL* 965:8: *ša ina muḫḫika idbubu gabbišunu ina qā[tēka] ašakkan*, "I shall hand over to you all those who plotted against you."

כים: "Indeed." Dupont-Sommer considered this word to be an

adverb, "so, likewise," comparing the Akkadian *kîam;* see Bezold-Goetze, *BAG*, 133. Though this is plausible, it may, however, be a conjunction, like Akkadian *kīma* (cf. W. von Soden, *Grundriss der akkadischen Grammatik,* §114g, 1.1.6e), "just as." Rosenthal: "in the manner of any one man" (*BASOR* 158 [1960] 28).

2. גבר זי יבעה רוח אפוה: "Any man who rants," lit., "who causes the breath of his nostrils to boil." This obscure expression Dupont-Sommer translated, "qui suppliera pour sa vie." His literal translation, "who seeks the breath of his nostrils," is understood as "'qui demandera qu'on lui laisse le souffle vital ...'; le texte viserait un suppliant, menacé de mort." He appeals to Lam 4:20 to support this interpretation. But that hardly fits the context. Would one expect a suppliant to speak evil things against a king? The expression rather indicates the reason for the evil words; hence the phrase is better taken as meaning a transport of arrogance or anger, as the other biblical expression mentioned by Dupont-Sommer would indicate, רוח אפים (Exod 15:8). Hence, "becomes enraged." Rosenthal (*BASOR* 158 [1960] 28 n. 1) related the phrase to Prov 1:23 (אביעה לכם), explaining it as an expression of strong emotion; he noted that both here and in Prov 1:23 the phrase is followed by a reference to speaking. The basic meaning of the verb בעי, "cause to swell, cause to boil." The phrase then would mean: "who causes his breath to boil, who breathes heavily" (as in anger or overweening pride). M. J. Dahood showed me the difficult passage in Isa 11:15, where the same idiom may occur. He read בעום רוחו, "causing his wrath to well up" (an infin. absol. with enclitic mem; cf. H. D. Hummel, *JBL* 76 [1957] 94-95).[4] Lemaire-Durand (*IAS*, 128) translate literally "qui cherchent le souffle de ses narines," and appeal to Exod 15:8 to explain it as "se mettre en colère."

רוח: Because of the use of this word with אפוה, it seems necessary to understand it as the equivalent of the biblical Hebrew רוח, even though the *scriptio plena* of a long vowel in a medial position is rare in an Aramaic inscription of the eighth century. One cannot understand רוח as related to Hebrew *rewaḥ*, *pace* P. Nober (*VD* 37 [1959] 173-74), since it does not fit the context.

אפוה: See note on Sf I A 5 (בנוה) for the suffix; the form is probably a dual, "his nostrils."

4 Cf. F. Vattioni, "La III iscrizione de Sfiré A 2 e Proverbi 1,23," *AION* 13 (1963) 279-86; R. J. Williams ("Some Egyptianisms in the Old Testament," *Studies in Honor of John A. Wilson* [Studies in Ancient Oriental Civilization 35; Chicago, IL: University of Chicago, 1969] 93-94) compared Egyptian *pꜣ ṯꜣw n fnd.m*, "breath of our

ימלל: "Utters evil words against me." The form is the 3d sg. masc. impf. pael.

מלן: "Words." The form is abs. pl. masc., but the gender is fem., as shown by the adj. לחית. Vocalize: *millīn laḥyāt.*[5]

לחית: "Evil," usually in a moral sense. This word is found also in Sf I A 26; Sf I C 7, 20; Nerab 1.10, B-M 6, *AP* 30:7; 31:6; 32:6; *AD* 5:7 (see Driver's note). The form is the abs. pl. fem., which has preserved the archaic ending *-āt*, instead of the later *-ān*. The same ending is found on מרמת (line 22). The word occurs in a non-moral sense in the contract published by J. T. Milik, recto line 8 (*Bib* 38 [1957] 255-64, esp. 263). Cf. J. C. Greenfield, *AcOr* 29 (1965) 8-9.

לעלי: Dupont-Sommer filled in the lacuna thus: לעלי[לותי ו]תקח, which he translated, "relativement à ma conduite (?) et ...." This restoration, however, is hardly convincing. I originally preferred to leave it simply as "against me." The form לעלי would be the compound prep. known at least three times in unpublished Aramaic texts of Qumran Cave 4. Cf. 1QapGen 2:26. It is apparently used here as the equivalent of the simple preposition על with the verb מלל. H. Tawil (*JNES* 32 [1973] 478 n. 20) explains the compound prep. as the semantic equivalent of Akkadian *ina/ana muḫḫi PN dabābu.* He compared Akkadian *amat lemutti qabû/dabābu*, "plot, conspire against" (lit., "speak evil words against").

תקח: "Accept." The lacuna unfortunately makes the understanding of this word quite difficult. The context seems to demand a negative, "you must [not] accept." It seems to be the 2d sg. masc. impf. peal of לקח.

מליא: "Such words." The emph. masc. pl. ending occurs here in a determinate sense on a fem. noun; the form obviously refers to the aforementioned מלן, hence "such words." Vocalize: *millayyā'*. The same ending is found on עדיא (lines 4, 7, 9, 14, 17, 19, 20, 23, 27), מלכיא (7), עמיא (10).

מן ידה: "From him," lit., "from his hand," as the immediate source.

הסכר תהסכרהם: "You must hand them over," lit., "you must really hand them over." The first word is the haphel infin., used to intensify the finite form of the same verb in the manner of the Hebrew infin. absol. The same use of the infin. is found in line 6 (רקה תרקהם), 12-13 (נכה ת[כ]וה־ת[כ]ה), 18 (רקה תרקה). Dupont-Sommer noted that this use

nostrils." Cf. Akkadian *ša-ri balāṭi-ia*, "breath of my life."

5 See H. L. Ginsberg, "Aramaic Dialect Problems," *AJSL* 52 (1936) 99-101. Cf. A. Goetze, "The Akkadian Masculine Plural in *-ānū/ī* and its Semitic Background," *Language* 22 (1946) 121-130, esp. 126-28.

was frequent in Hebrew and was known in Phoenician, but that it had not been met before in Aramaic. However, it very probably also occurs in Nerab 2:6: והום אתהמו (see the note in Cooke, *NSI*, 191). The construction is also found commonly in Ugaritic; see Gordon, *UT* 9:27; Driver, *CML*, 132. The root *skr* in the sense of "hand over, deliver" is found in Hebrew in the piel; see Isa 19:4. It is possibly related to *sgr*, which has the same meaning in Hebrew in the hiphil (1 Sam 23:11), in Phoenician (see *GPL*, 126), and in Qumran Aramaic (1QapGen 22:17). Is הם a suffix or an independent pron.? In later Aramaic the 3d pl. suff. on verbs is often avoided and an independent form (sometimes enclitic, as in Syriac) is used. In this case we cannot tell; but see the note on תרקהם (line 6). הם occurs as a suffix on a noun in lines 6-7 (נבשהם) and on a pron. in line 19 (חדהם). Cf. Zakur a 9 (ומחנות־הם); Meša' 18 (ואסחב־הם) with word-dividers. See M. Weinfeld, "The Loyalty Oath in the Ancient Near East," *UF* 8 (1976) 379-414, esp. 387.

3. יסכר: Dupont-Sommer remarked: "Noter la syncope de la préformante *h* du hafel; cf. un peu plus haut יהסכר." But since both haphel and aphel causative stems occur in later Aramaic (see BLA §36; *LFLAA* § 35i, 38k, 40s; in Qumran Aramaic: יושע, 4QpsDan[a] 16:2 [*RB* 63 (1956) 413; תשלט, 4QTLevi 1 i 17 [*RB* 62 (1955) 400]; ישכח, אשגה, 1QapGen 21:13; ינפק, 1QapGen 20:32; יתיבו, 1QapGen 20:25), it is better to regard this form as an early instance of an aphel impf. Segert (*ArOr* 32 [1964] 121), Degen (*AG* 19 n. 79), and Greenfield (*AcOr* 29 [1965] 9 n. 24) called יסכר rather a scribal mistake.

עקר ... יהסכרן: "The offspring of any of the kings of Arpad must hand (them) over." Dupont-Sommer found this construction strange, as the subject is sg., while the verb is pl. Though he translated, "et la descendance [de tous les r]ois d'Arpad devra me (les) livrer," he thought that עקר might be the result of dittography. Then מלכי ארפד would become the subject of יהסכרן, "ce qui serait plus conforme à la syntaxe et donnerait un sens meilleur." But there is nothing wrong with a plural verb being construed with a collective singular subject. Hence... עקר יהסכרן is to be so understood.

[חד]: "Any," lit. "one." Restored according to line 1. Dupont-Sommer preferred to read כל; Noth (*ZDPV* 77 [1961] 133 n. 42) also read חד.

אעבד: "I shall do." Dupont-Sommer read אעבר, saying, "Le ר est tout à fait sûr," and translating, "je leur pardonnerai." For such a meaning of עבר, he appealed to Amos 7:8; 8:2 and to the aforementioned suppliants, to whom the vassal is supposed to show mercy. Granted that such a meaning of עבר suits the passages in Amos (see *HALAT* 736a), it is not yet attested in Aramaic, as far as I am aware. However, it scarcely fits the construction of the subordinate clause, מה טב בעיני, where it would be necessary to twist the meaning of מה to "if," to suit such a conclusion: "I shall pardon them, if it seems good in my sight." But with the normal meaning of the compound rel. pron. מה, used in a generic sense, one would expect something like, "I shall pardon or punish," or better still, "I shall do." Again, the context of "suppliants," to which Dupont-Sommer referred is questionable, as already noted. But from a careful examination of the photos, a squeeze, and the stone itself, I prefer to read a *daleth*. The vertical shaft of the letter is rather broad down to a certain point (making a good *daleth*); after that it thins out. The thinning belongs to a chipping of the stone produced probably when the stone was damaged. The chipped spot is visible in pl. IV published by Dupont-Sommer, just above the *yodh* of אחי (line 4). When אעבד is read, the compound relative functions normally: as the subject of the nominal relative clause and the object of the main transitive verb. It is then the Aramaic equivalent of the expression in 2 Sam 19:38: ועשה־לו את אשר־טוב בעיניך; see also Josh 9:25; 2 Sam 3:19; 1 Kgs 14:8; 2 Kgs 10:5; Esth 3:11. The word is so read by Greenfield too (*JBL* 87 [1968] 241); Lemaire-Durand (*IAS*, 118); Gibson (*TSSI*, 2. 46).

4. והן להן: See note on Sf I B 36.

שקרתם: "You shall have been unfaithful." See notes on Sf I A 14; I B 23. Interesting for the light it may shed on several OT passages (especially Ps 89:34; also 44:18; Isa 63:8) is the use of the root שקר, meaning "break faith" (in a covenant).

עדיא: "Treaty." Only the emph. pl. of this word occurs in Sf III; the cst. pl. עדי occurs often in Sf I. See note on Sf I A 1.

ספרא: "Inscription." The emph. state before the dem. adj. is supplied as in the same expression in lines 14, 17, 23; Sf I B 28, 33; Sf I C 17; Sf II B 18; Sf II C 13. See note on Sf I B 23.

יקרק: "Flees." Dupont-Sommer noted that the same form is found in *AD* 3:5 and in AšOstr (9, 13, 16, 17, 18). I read it also in Sf I B 45. See *KAI*, §233; D. H. Baneth, *OLZ* 22 (1919) 55-58. In later Aramaic the form is ערק, as in Syriac. Now that this etymology is established, there can no longer be question of a relation between Aramaic ערק and Arabic *'araqa* (see Brockelmann, *Lexicon syriacum*, 550), or with Job 30:3, 17.

קרק: Though Dupont-Sommer regarded this form as an infin. absol., he did mention another more probable explanation, viz., a participle, "fugitive" (*qāriq*). Cf. קרקי and קרקהם on lines 19-20, which must be regarded as participles. Moreover, in the other cases of an intensifying infin. in this inscription, it always precedes the finite verb; see note on הסכר (line 2). For provisions concerning fugitives in earlier Syrian treaties, see D. J. Wiseman, *The Alalakh Tablets* (London: British Institute of Archaeology at Ankara, 1953), 3:5-15 (p. 31); 1 Kgs 2:39-40.

פקדי: "Officials." See lines 10, 13 for the same word. Cf. Hebrew פקיד, Akkadian *pāqidu* and *paqūdu*, Aramaic פקיד (*AD* 2:2, 3; 4:1; 6:1). Note the *scriptio defectiva* of the medial long *i*. In Egyptian Aramaic texts פקיד denotes an officer highly placed under the satrap in Egypt (*AD* 1:2; 7:1; 13:1), who has עבדן or עלימן under him. But vis-à-vis the satrap, he is also עלים. He expected obedience from the commander of a חיל, "army," and had mercenary troops under him (*AD* 12:1-5).

5. סרסי: "My courtiers," lit., "eunuchs"; cf. Hebrew סריס, later Aramaic סרס (*NSI* 150:2; *CIS* 2:75). The word is sometimes explained as related to Akkadian *ša rēši šarri*, "he who is by the head of the king."

זי בידי: "Who are under my control," lit., "who are in my hands."

יהכן: "They go." See note on Sf I A 24.

חלב: "Aleppo." See note on Sf I A 10. Why would fugitives flee to Aleppo and not to Arpad? Greenfield ("Asylum at Aleppo") answers that Aleppo was the place where the fugitives would find asylum, presumably in the temple precinct, and thus be safe from extradition to the territory of the overlord. For the details about the importance of Aleppo in this capacity, see Greenfield's discussion.

לתס[ך ל]הם לחם: "You must not give them food." Restored as in line 7. The verb must come from נסך, which normally means "pour a libation." It is used here in a generic sense with לחם, "provide food." Rosenthal (*BASOR* 158 [1960] 29 n. 3) compared Akkadian *nasāku*, "throw down food, meals." Cf. Dan 2:46. But the comparison is weak. For the prefixed negative *l-*, see note on Sf I A 28.

שלו: "Stay quiet"; the form is the pl. impv. peal of שלי. Cf. Jer 12:1; Ps 122:6; Lam 1:5. This would refer to the providing of domicile to the fugitive.

ולתהרם: "You must not incite them." The form is the 2d sg. masc. impf. haphel of רום. Dupont-Sommer translated it, "tu ne me soustrairas pas leur âme," but the literal meaning seems to be, "you shall not make their soul higher than me"; hence, you must not incite or embolden them. Cf. רם לבו (Jer 48:29; Hos 13:6; Deut 8:14; Ezek 31:10; and esp. Deut 17:20, which uses the prep. מן of the person toward whom the insolence would be displayed). Rosenthal (*BASOR* 158 [1960] 29) translated, "you must not cause them to be disdainful of me." The expression denotes reckless elation and disdain. Cf. Dan 5:20, כדי רם לבבה.

6. נבשהם: See note on Sf I A 37.

רקה תרקהם: "You must placate them." For the use of the infin., see note on הסכר (line 2). The same root is also found in רקו and ארקהם of this line and lines 18-19. Dupont-Sommer regarded the verbs in this line as forms of רקק, "broyer, contraindre," whereas those of lines 18-19 as forms of רקה, "être bienvaillant, vouloir." In favor of such a distinction one should note the transitive use of the verbs in this line and the use with בן with the forms in lines 18-19. Here he translated, "tu devras les capturer ... capturez(-les) là-bas, jusqu'à ce que j'(y) aille moi-même et que je les capture." The form רקה was explained by him as an infin., without preformative *mem*, but with the fem. ending *-h* (cf. the now certain reading of Sf I A 13: לחזיה). However, I fail to see how one can regard רקה as the peal infin. of רקק, related to Hebrew רצץ, "crush," in this context. The forms רקה and תרקה point rather to a *tertiae infirmae* root, an originally *lamedh waw* root. This analysis was suggested to me by F. M. Cross, who compared the Moabite forms, ויענו and אענו (*Meša'* 5, 6; *KAI* 181:5-6; S. R. Driver, *Notes on the Hebrew Text and the Topography of the Books of Samuel* [Oxford: Clarendon, 1913] lxxxv), and the South Arabic *rḍw*. Hence, the Aramaic verb used here must be רקי, related to Hebrew רצי, "be acceptable, pleasing." The forms are probably pael, "make acceptable to them," hence, "prevail upon" (their wills). Rosenthal (*BASOR* 158 [1960] 29) compared the pael usage in Syriac and translated, "placate" or "pacify." Vocalize: *raqqiw*, *turaqqīhom*, *'uraqqīhom* (< *'uraqqiyhom*).

For the infin. without preformative *mem*, see רקה (line 18); נכה (lines 12-13); לנצב, לבני (Hadad 10); לאמר (*AP* 2:3; 5:3, 12; *BMAP* 1:3; 2:3); contrast לממר (*AP* 32:2; 43:2). Since this use of the infin. in this Aramaic inscription is probably owing to Canaanite interference, the instances should perhaps be vocalized rather as in Phoenician or Hebrew. Thus *raqqēh* (as in Hebrew piel *gallēh*); *haskir* (line 2), *nakeh* (?). Cf. Garbini, *RSO* 34 (1959) 50-51.

תהשבהם: "You must return them." The form is the haphel impf. of שוב, cognate of the later Aramaic תוב. For a parallel to the apodictic style found here, see the Hittite treaty of Mursilis II with Manapa-Dattas 1.52.

לי[שב]ן: "They do not dwell." This is the 3d pl. masc. impf. peal of ישב, cognate to later Aramaic יתב. Vocalize: *yiššibūn*; cf. biblical Aramaic *yittibūn* (BLA § 45j).

רקו: "Placate." The form is the pl. impv. pael of רקי. Vocalize:

raqqiw. The direct object is understood.

שם: "There," as in Hebrew *šām*. In later Aramaic it is תמה, and in Syriac, *tmn*.

ארקהם: "I placate them." Though I hesitated at first between *r* and *d* in this word, having seen the stele, I am convinced that Dupont-Sommer is correct in reading *r*. The same chipping that makes the *lamedh* of שלו (5) difficult has effaced the top of the *reš* here. But the long vertical shaft remains. Hence, we have a suffixal form of the 1st sg. pael impf., *'uraqqīhom*.

7. שבו: "Stay where you are." The form is the masc. pl. impv. of ישב. Dupont-Sommer translated it, "Résidez au lieu où vous êtes." The substantival use of תחת, "place," together with the verb ישב occurs in Exod 16:29, שבו איש תחתיו (as J. Strugnell pointed out to me); cf. Josh 5:8; Greenfield, *ZAW* 73 (1961) 226-28. Dupont-Sommer noted that the context excludes the sense of "return" (root שוב); so the verb must be ישב.

ואל תפנו באשרה: "And do not (re)turn to his region." See note on Sf I A 21. Rosenthal (*BASOR* 158 [1960] 29) would translate this phrase, "and pay no attention to him," noting that "to turn after him" means "to look after him." He compares the use of פני in Hebrew with the corresponding prep. אחרי "to turn, look behind oneself." But the meaning of this phrase is not quite the same (with the suffix of a different person), and the sense of the Hebrew parallel scarcely fits the present context. Cf. Greenfield (*AcOr* 29 [1965] 7), who compares Ugaritic *a<u>t</u>r* and targumic פני בתר.

וכל מ̄לכיא: "As for all the kings." A new section begins here, but there is no verb with which מלכ̇יא can be construed; hence it must be a *casus pendens* or a nominative absolute.

זי: "Of." Whereas זי is used elsewhere in this inscription as a rel. pron., it appears here as a determinative, expressing a genitive relationship, the substitute for a construct chain.

8. סחרתי: "My vicinity." This word is related to the later Aramaic סחר, "go about (as a trader), go around." Dalman (*ANHW*, 287b) lists a noun סחרנין (masc. pl.), "Umgebung, Nachbarschaft." It has turned up also in 4QTob[b] ar 4 i 14 in a different sense, יסחרון סחרתהו[ן] [לא] לעלם, "and their encounters will never occur again." The word "vicinity" undoubtedly refers here to the lands contiguous to that of Bar-Ga'yah, with whose rulers he had made a pact of trade and commerce, and consequently of friendship or amity. See J. J. Rabinowitz, *Bib* 39

(1958) 401; cf. Gen 34:9-10; 42:34; Isa 47:15; Ezek 27:12, 21. Compare Akkadian *saḫāru*, Hebrew סחר. W. F. Albright (*Yahweh and the Gods of Canaan* [Garden City, NY: Doubleday, 1968] 89 n. 92) translated the clause: "All the kings of my trading area" (i.e., all the kings who trade with me).

כל זי רחם הא לי: "Anyone who is a friend of mine," i.e., an ally. Dupont-Sommer broke up the letters differently: כל זי רחמה אלי and explained רחמה as "graphie défective pour רחמוה, du nom pluriel רחמין." He translated, "quiconque dont l'affection (se portera) vers moi." Similarly S. Segert, *ArOr* 32 (1964) 126 n. 111. But the defective writing of such an ending seems impossible in this inscription; see note on אפוה (line 2). Consequently, רחם must be a ptc.; הא, the 3d masc. pers. pron. used as copula, and לי the object of רחם. For הא (= *hu'*), see Hadad 22; Panammu 11; Meša' 6, and the note on Sf I B 24. Cf. G. Schuttermayr, "*RḤM* -- Eine lexikalische Studie," *Bib* 51 (1970) 499-525, esp. 516.

ואשלח: "When I send." As in line 17, a *waw* follows *casus pendens*, which may have conditional force (so Vogt, *Bib* 39 [1958] 272), or even better a temporal force. Cf. Meša' 4-5 (*KAI*, 181:4-5). For the idiom שלח מלאכי, see AšOstr 19; 1 Kgs 20:2. M. J. Dahood (*CBQ* 22 [1960] 403-4) noted that 1QIsa[a] 18:6 read for Isa 23:2b, עברו ים מלאכיך (instead of the MT עבר ים מלאיך) and that the *RSV* had adopted this reading, "your messengers passed over the sea." He further suggested that מלאך, being in parallelism here with סחר, "merchant," might bear the meaning, "salesman." See further W. F. Albright, *BASOR* 150 (1958) 38 n. 14.

א[ל]וה: "To him." This prep. is restored on the basis of אלי, which is parallel to it.

לשלם: "For peace." The reading here is doubtful. Dupont-Sommer read לשלח, translating, "pour (lui) envoyer (un message)," noting that שלח is attested in Aramaic in the sense, "to send a message, order." Aside from the fact that the expression is cumbersome, the last letter is doubtful, judging both from the photos and the squeeze. J. T. Milik has suggested the reading שלם, which suits the context well. J. Starcky told me that this was his original reading, but that he yielded to Dupont-Sommer who had returned to Beirut to verify several readings and maintained that the ח was certain. Having seen the stele, I know that the letter is quite doubtful. There is a vertical line on the left and a horizontal one on the top, but it is hard to say whether these are primary or secondary cuts. Greenfield (*JBL* 87 [1968] 241) also reads לשלם. Cf. Ps 107:23.

חפצי: "My business." The meaning of the word is clear, but does it refer to diplomatic or commercial business? Cf. Isa 58:3; Qoh 3:1, 17; 8:6.

9. פתחה: "Open." This is the pe'īl ptc. fem. sg., "opened." Vocalize: *patīḥāh*. Dupont-Sommer, while preferring this explanation, mentioned another "moins probable": impv. with paragogic *-h*. However, he gives no parallel for this in Aramaic, and it is rather unlikely.

ארחא: "The road." Dupont-Sommer read, as I do, פתחה לי ארחא לתמשל בי. Since the negative in this inscription is either the prefix -ל or אל, it is difficult to say whether one should read, ארח אל תמשל בי, or as above. The context would seem to demand the emph. state of ארחא. Though all other cases of the emph. sg. are followed by a dem. adj. in this stele, one does find the emph. pl. alone (מליא, line 2). Hence it is better to retain Dupont-Sommer's division of the words. On the fem. gender of the masc. form, see G. Garbini, *RSO* 34 (1959) 46. Note the apodictic form, or better the prohibitive form, of the stipulation, which throws light on the forms in the OT Decalogue.

בזא: "In this respect," lit., "on it," i.e., on the road, since ארחא is fem.

ולתרשה: "Or assert your authority over me concerning it." The negative is repeated in Aramaic. Dupont-Sommer noted that the root רשי is frequent in the Elephantine papyri in the sense "to sue for" or "to lay a claim to," and also in Syriac in the meaning "to reproach." But the meaning of תרשה is rather that found in Nabatean, "to have authority over." Cf. רשי (*NSI* 89:4), רשין (*NSI* 90:3). It seems to occur also in this sense in Hadad 27; Karatepe A III 26. Cf. also Hebrew רשיון, "permission," Ezra 3:7. In later Aramaic one finds רשאי, "allowed, authorized."

והן להן: See note on Sf I B 36.

מן חד: "Any one." Compound indef. pron. מן = *man*. See note on Sf II B 9.

אחי: "My brothers." Does this mean "blood brothers" or "kinsmen"? See *JNES* 21 (1962) 17; Kutscher, *Lešonenu* 26 (1962) 8-9.

10. נגדי: "My officers," or "my military commanders." Dupont-Sommer read נגרי, comparing the Akkadian *nāgiru*. But an examination of the squeeze and the stele suggests rather that נגדי was originally written and that the lengthened vertical shaft of the letter is either a slip or a secondary cut. It is neither as deep as the upper first part nor does it continue in the same direction. Cf. Hebrew נגיד, the interesting parallel use of פקיד נגיד in Jer 20:1, and its use as applied to Saul (1 Sam 9:16) and David (1 Sam 13:14). Important is the position occupied here by the נגד (= later Aram. *nĕgîdā'*) among the royal princes and the "officials" (*paqīday*). See further W. F. Albright, *Samuel and the Beginnings of the Prophetic Movement* (Cincinnati: Hebrew Union College, 1961) 15-16; cf. Noth, *ZDPV* 77 (1961) 150, who looks with skepticism on the reading נגדי. An attempt to support the reading נגדי by an appeal to Adon Letter 8 is nothing more than *obscurum per obscurius*; see *Bib* 46 (1965) 44, 54-55; R. A. Bowman, *AJSL* 58 (1941) 303 (B7). Cf. F. M. Cross, "An Interpretation of the Nora Stone," *BASOR* 208 (1972) 13-19, esp. 16-17. Cross translates נגד לפמי (lines 7-8) as "general of (king) Pummay" (= Pygmalion of Tyre, 831-785). Cf. 1 Chr 12:28 (הנגיד לאהרון).

[פ]קדי: "My officials." Cf. *AD* 1:2; 2:3; 4:1; *RES* 1798A. The form is basically passive (*qatīl*-type), expressing one who is under a command; but he is himself a commander or officer of some sort. Cf. Matt 8:9.

עמיא: "The people," or possibly "the peoples." The noun is pl. here, whereas in lines 5, 13 (which are parallel) the sg. occurs.

-ו: I had originally proposed to delete this conjunction. J. Hoftijzer (*VT* 9 [1959] 316 n.2) identified it as a "waw of apodosis." Koopmans (*AC*, 66) objected to this explanation of it, and I agree, because it introduces, not the verb in the apodosis, but the verb in the conditional clause itself after a long series of subjects. More than likely it should be explained either as anacoluthon, with the *waw* added because of a similar conditional use of *waw* found elsewhere in these texts, or as a pleonastic *waw* (on which see P. Wernberg-Möller, *JSS* 3 [1958] 321-26).

11. להמתתי: "To kill me." Vocalize: *la-hamītūtî* or possibly *la-hamātūtî* (cf. BLA §46z). The haphel infin. appears here with the fem. ending *-ūt* before the pronominal suffix; the same form occurs also on a non-suffixal infinitive, המתת (cf. BLA §65p). These forms are found again in Sf III 15-16; cf. Sf II B 8. For a similar Hebrew idiom, see Jer 26:21; Ps 37:32; for possible Akkadian parallels, see Greenfield, *AcOr* 29 (1965) 7.

אי[ת]י: "Me," the sign of the accusative; see note on Sf I B 32.

ותקם: "And you must avenge." The form is the 2d sg. masc. impf. peal of נקם, "avenge." Cf. 2 Kgs 9:7.

יקתלן: "They kill me." The form is the 3d pl. masc. impf. peal of קתל (with non-emphatic *t*); see note on Sf I B 27.

את: "You." The emphatic use of the independent pers. pron. before the verb; cf. lines 6, 20 (after the verb).

12. יקם: "Will avenge." Note the asyndetic collocation of the verbs here, in contrast to תאתה ותקם in line 11. The omission may be merely the engraver's mistake.

והן קריה הא: "If it is a city." The pron. הא serves as a predicate-copula. Vocalize: *hī'*.

נכה: "You must strike it with a sword." The peal infin. נכה is used as an intensifier; see note on הסכר, Sf III 2. For a biblical parallel to striking a city with a sword, see Deut 13:16; Josh 11:11; 1 Sam 22:19.

13. ת(כ)וה: Dupont-Sommer read תפוה, taking the form as the pl. impv. with suffix (3d sg. fem.) of the root תפף, "strike." This form, however, must be considered with תכה further on in the line. In the latter case the reading תפה is, in my opinion, doubtful. But תפוה at the beginning of the line is read with certainty. Since the infin., which precedes the finite verb in both cases, is clearly נכה, and one can read תכה in the second instance, I prefer to read תכוה at the beginning of the line too, regarding תפוה as the engraver's error. All the other cases of an intensifying infin. in this inscription are of the same root as the finite form that they modify. This reason is not, of course, absolutely conclusive, but it does strengthen an otherwise problematic reading. Cf. Deut 13:16; Josh 11:11; 1 Sam 22:19. But what form is תכוה? If from נכי, it looks like a 2d sg. impf. pael with a fem. suffix, perhaps *takkiwah* (suggestion of F. M. Cross). See further the note on רקה תרקהם (line 6). Cf. Greenfield, *JBL* 87 (1968) 241, where he agrees with my interpretation; also *AcOr* 29 (1965) 5 n. 11; *DISO*, 333. Similarly Lemarie-Durand (*IAS*, 119). Degen (*AG* §78) read: נכה תפוה and נכה תפה, translating, "schlagt sie [fem. sg.] gewiss!" and "schlag ihn [mask. sg.] gewiss!" He understood תפה and תפוה as forms of תפף. Similarly Gibson (*TSSI*, 2. 48). For an example of an infin. absol. of a different root, but related in meaning, as an intensifier of a finite verb, see Deut 9:21: ואכת אתו תחון היטב, "and I crushed it very fine" (lit., "pulverizing it very well, I crushed it"). Or does the infin. absol. in such a case, being postpositive, continue the action instead of intensifying it? Cf. Joüon, *GHB* §123r and n. 1 on p. 354. See further K. Cathcart, *Nahum*, 100.

תכה: "You must strike." This form is the 2d sg. masc. impf. peal of נכי. Dupont-Sommer explained תפה, which he read here, as a defective spelling for *toppeh* (sg. impv. with suffix) or for *toppūhī* (pl. impv. with suffix). But that cannot be right. First of all, the *yodh* is always found in this inscription for a final *ī*; hence his latter vocalization is excluded. Second, there is no reason to explain *h* as a suffix, if his explanation of the following word (איה) is correct.

אי<ת>ה: "Him." "Tel quel, ce mot ne nous semble offrir ici aucun sens. Nous supposons qu'un *t* a été accidentellement omis: אי<ת>ה, *eum* (cf. 1.11: איתי), reprise du pronom suffixe *-h* devant l'énumération ועקרה ושגבוה ומודדוה." Thus Dupont-Sommer. But is it not better to regard the corrected איתה as the first element of the compound direct object, thus eliminating the doubtful suffix?

שרבוה: "His nobles." Dupont-Sommer read ושגבוה and compared the Hebrew root שגב, "be lofty," and took the word as a synonym for רבוה (Sf I A 40), translating it, "ses grands." The reading of ג at the end of the line is doubtful and should be read as ר. In favor of שגבוה one can cite the Akkadian *sagbu*, "guard, protection" (G. Dossin, *ARM*, 5.1, 12 and p. 124 n.; see also Noth [*ZDPV* 77 (1961) 150], "Wächter"). But שרבוה, "his nobles," must be read and one can compare Akkadian *šurbû*, "gross, hoch, erhaben" (BAG, 253) or Syriac *šarbtā'* (Rosenthal, *BASOR* 158 [1960] 29 n. 8).

14. והן להן: See note on Sf I B 36.

יסק על לבבך: "(The idea) should come to your mind," lit. "it should ascend to your heart." On the form יסק, see note on Sf I A 5. Cf. Ps 139:8, and the Hebrew equivalent עלה על לב (Isa 65:17; Jer 3:16); and 1 Cor 2:9. Note the use of the 3d sg. masc. here as impersonal; cf. Sf I A 42.

ותשא: "You should express with your lips (the intention)," the 2d sg. masc. impf. peal of נשי; lit., "if you should raise to your lips"; cf. Zakur a 11 and Aḥiqar (passim) for the same verb in Aramaic. Cf. Ps 16:4.

15. שפתוה: See note on אפוה Sf I A 5.

16. כל מה: See note on Sf I A 26. Here the expression is pronominal and neuter.

ימות: "Shall die." Vocalize: *yamūt*. Note the *scriptio plena* of a medial long vowel; see the note on רוח, Sf III 2. Bange (*A Study*, 91) understood this form to be pual (*yĕmuwwat*), "if he is slain." He compares יעורן, "are blinded" (Sf II B 4). Cf. Degen, *AG* 28, 75. But are there pual forms in Aramaic?

בר אנש: "A man" or "a human being." This inscription attests the early use of this phrase in a generic sense. Cf. Dan 7:13; 1QapGen 21:13; 11QtgJob 9:9; 26:3. See F. Vattioni, "La prima menzione aramaica di 'figlio dell'uomo,'" *Biblos-Press* 6/1 (1965) 6-7. E. Sjöberg (*AcOr* 21 [1950-53] 57-65, 91-107), who wrote before the publication of the instances mentioned, was able to cite no instance of בר אנש in Aramaic texts between the eighth century BC and the third century AD. This is now changed. Cf. G. Garbini, *RSO* 34 (1959) 47; and my discussion in *WA*, 143-60.

17. ירב: "Quarrels with." Vocalize: *yarīb*. Contrast this form with the fully written ימות of line 16; it is the 3d sg. masc. peal impf. of ריב. Hartman (*CBQ* 30 [1968] 259) noted that this is a strange instance of ריב governing a direct object; possibly the engraver forgot to insert the prep. עם. See the restoration in Sf III 26. Cf. Job 13:19; 23:6. It is, however, possible that ירב has here a more technical meaning, "carries out a lawsuit (against)" or "makes a complaint (against)." See J. Limburg, "The Root ריב and the Prophetic Lawsuit Speeches," *JBL* 88 (1969) 291-304, esp. 299-301.

ישב: See note on ישבן, Sf III 6.

כהסאי: "My throne." The reading of this word is certain. Dupont-Sommer regarded the *h* as a stonecutter's error for *r*. This would give כרסאי, "my throne," a meaning that is favored by the context. The word כרסא is found in the Bar-Rakkab inscription I.7. BLA (p. 233 n. 1) explain *korsê* as a word taken over directly from the Akkadian *kursē*: through a false analogy *kursê* > *kursay* and with a suffix *korsĕyeh* (Dan 7:9). The form with the *aleph* preserved is also found in *AP* 6:2. The Arabic form is *kursiyu*^{n}, whereas Hebrew and Phoenician have כסא, and Akkadian has a second form *kussû* (probably the original form, from Sumerian GU-ZA). Dupont-Sommer suggested that, if the form כהסאי is not to be regarded as an error, then it must represent a transitional form between the Aramaic-Arabic word and that of Phoenician-Hebrew. Cf. the form דבהה in Sf I A 31, another doubled consonant resolved by use of *he*? Segert (*ArOr* 32 [1964] 121) is undoubtedly right in saying that these two isolated instances scarcely argue for a weakened or uvular articulation of *reš*. The *reš* is secondary, the resolution of a doubling by a liquid, *pace* KB (1087).

זי ישב ...: "Who sits upon my throne." I have taken this clause as a relative attributive to ברי; so too Rosenthal (*BASOR* 158 [1960] 30). ישב is scarcely a ptc. (so G. Garbini, *RSO* 34 [1959] 49), given the impf. forms in the vicinity (ירב and יעברנה). The expression has an Akkadian counterpart: *ina kussi ašābu* (see D. J. Wiseman, *Chronicles of Chaldaean Kings (626-556 B.C.) in the British Museum* [London: British Museum, 1961] 50, lines 14-15; *OIP* 2. 41: col. 5:14-16). It is also used in Hebrew (Deut 17:8; 1 Kgs 1:20, 27, 46; 2:12, 24; 8:20; Jer 22:2), Phoenician (*KAI* 214:8), Amarna Akkadian (*EA* 33:10-1, *ašbāta eli kussî abīka*).

יעברנה: "And he would remove him," or "would exile him," as Greenfield (*AcOr* 29 [1965] 6) has understood the word. This form is the 3d sg. masc. energic impf. aphel (not haphel) with a suffix, from עבר, lit., "pass over." Cf. Jon 3:6; Zech 13:2; 2 Chr 15:8. This explanation of the form seems preferable to the proposal of Rosenthal (*BASOR* 158 [1960] 30), "conceives a hatred of him," who related the word to Hebrew עברה and Arabic *ǵibru*^{n}. Rosenthal has been followed by Degen, *AG* §57: "er zürnt ihn."

לתשלח לשנך: "You shall not interfere with them," lit., "you shall not send your tongue." For the figurative use of the tongue as an instrument of slander or strife, see Hadad 9; Ps 140:12; 101:5; 15:3; Ugaritic *lšn* (Driver, *CML*, 158). Cf. Ps 50:19. Compare Akkadian *lišāna w/mu'uru*, "send/direct a tongue." See further D. Sperling, "The Informer and the Conniver," *JANES* 2 (1970) 101-4; cf. H. Tawil, *CBQ* 42 (1980) 32, esp. n. 15.

18. בניהם: The same word occurs twice again in this inscription: once in this line and once in the following. The reading is certain in each case. From the context the meaning seems to be "between them." Dupont-Sommer took it so too. But if it is a form of the prep. *byn*-, then we have a case of a medial diphthong contracted and written defectively, whereas one would expect ביניהם according to the usual explanation of the orthography of Aramaic at this period (see Cross and Freedman, *EHO*, 24 §4). The same defective spelling is found later in *AP* 13:14; 25:7; *BMAP* 4:10, 11 (see *LFLAA* §4g). J. T. Milik thought that we rather have here a form of the adverb/preposition בנ-, which is found in Phoenician (meaning "inside, within"); see Karatepe Portal Inscription 2.18; 3.8; Ešmun'azor (*CIS* 3) 5; *PPG*, §254 Ia. Until further evidence is found that this word is also used in Aramaic, בניהם has to be understood as the well-known prep. *byn*-, even if written defectively. Cf. Prov. 6:19b.

ותאמר: "Saying to him," lit., "and you shall (not) say to him." The negative is supplied from the previous, coordinated verb, לתשלח (line 21).

אחך: "Your brother." Vocalize: *'aḥūk*.

אסרה: "Imprison him." The form is the masc. sg. impv. peal with 3d sg. masc. suff.

וא[ל]: Restored as in line 7. Part of the *aleph* is still visible on the stele.

תשריה: "Do not let him go free." Vocalize: *tišrayeh*. The form is probably the 2d sg. masc. impf. peal of שרי, "loose, set free," but could it be aphel? Note that the suffix, in either case, is not added to the energic form of the imperfect. This clear case of a suffix added to a *tertiae infirmae* verb should be considered in the analysis of תרקהם (line

6).

והן רקה תרקה: "But if you really make peace." For the explanation of רקה תרקה, see note on הסכר (Sf III 2) and that on the same root in Sf III 6. The restored *waw* before הן has adversative force; there is no need to read להן, "but," as J. W. Wesselius would have it ("A New Reading"), because that would then suppress the needed conj. הן.

ליקתל וליאסר: "He will not kill and will not imprison." The direct object is to be supplied from the context. Dupont-Sommer had an alternate explanation: impf. pass. *yuqtal* forms. But that is less likely, since it would demand a change of subject in this otherwise very dense style.

19. ו[מ]לכן [זי סחר]תי: "As for kings of my vicinity," a *casus pendens* or nominative absolute. This restoration of Dupont-Sommer has proved to be the best, despite the absol. pl. form instead of the expected emphatic. Lemaire-Durand (*IAS*, 130) translate rather, "et quant aux rois de mes [relations]," without explaining it.

ויקרק: "If a fugitive of mine flees." The *waw*, used after the *casus pendens*, must have conditional force, as suggested by Vogt (*Bib* 39 [1958] 273), comparing line 8.

קרקי, קרקהם: Participles (used substantively) with suffixes; see line 4.

חדהם: "One of them." The numeral with a suffix is not extraordinary in view of the fact that חד in this inscription is regularly construed in a construct chain (and not with the prep. מן). For the use of suffixes on numbers in Aramaic, see C. Brockelmann, *Grundriss*, I. 249b.

20. השב, אהשב: "He has restored ... I shall restore." Haphel act. forms of שוב; note the change of tense from perfect to imperfect. Garbini (*RSO* 34 [1959] 48) thought that השב was a passive form of the haphel perfect.

זי לי: "Mine." Perhaps these words should be written as one, זילי, for the expression has all the earmarks of the stereotyped possessive so familiar in the Elephantine texts (*AP* 5:4; *BMAP* 3:16, 19; *A* 172), Arsames correspondence (*AD* 1:2; 2:2, 3), and in Syriac (*dyl-*).

[זי לה]: "His." Dupont-Sommer restored זי להם, "clairement suggeré par le contexte." But it is rather the sg. suffix that the context demands, as חדהם ("one of them"), השב (3d sg. masc. pf. haphel) show. Greenfield (*JBL* 87 [1968] 241) agrees.

תעשקני: "You yourself shall not try to hinder me." The form is the 2d sg. impf. peal (jussive) of עשק, "oppress, wrong," with the 1st sg. suff. Cf. Agbar 8. Cf. Hartman, *CBQ* 30 [1968] 259.

21. **לתשלח לשן**: See note on Sf III 17.

בביתי: "In my house." The prep. *b-* is to be repeated in sense with the nouns coordinated with this one. Literally, the expression means, "you shall not send your tongue into my house or (among) the sons of my sons, or (among) the sons of my brothers, etc." But Dupont-Sommer takes the first בני in each group as a form of the prep. *bên-* "between," translating, "Et tu ne mettras pas la langue dans ma maison ni entre mes fils ni entre [mes] frè[res ni entre] ma [des]cendance ni entre mon peuple." Such an interpretation is not impossible. If it were correct, we would have three more cases of the defective writing of a contracted diphthong (or four, counting the restoration, which is certain). However, it is strange to see a shift from one prep. (*b-*) to another (*bên-*) with the same verb in the same sentence. My interpretation seems more natural, but it is admittedly more cumbersome; however, in view of the line-up of kin found in the earlier part of the inscription such a cumbersome expression does not seem impossible. See note on Sf I A 2.

ותאמר: "Saying to them," lit., "you shall not say." One has to understand the negative prefix from the preceding coordinated verb, as in lines 17-18.

מראכם: "Your lord." In the Hazael inscription of Arslan-Tash, in Panammu (13, 16,17) and in Bar-Rakkab (5, 6, 9) the word מרא is used as a title for a sovereign. The *aleph* is still consonantal. See the Assyrian transcription: ^{m}*ma-ri-'i ša* ^{kur}*Imeri-šú*. Cf. F. Vattioni, "Frustula epigraphica," *Aug* 9 (1969) 366-67.

22. **והוי חלפה**: "And be his successor." The division of the letters into words is crucial here. Dupont-Sommer read them thus: והו יחלפה, translating, "et qu'un tel le remplace," and he was followed in this by Vogt (*Bib* 39 [1958] 269-74), Koopmans (*AC* 2. 15), I. N. Vinnikov (*PS* 4 [1967] 219). Garbini (*RSO* 34 [1959] 44-45) and Segert (*ArOr* 32 [1964] 124) also take הו as a pron., though with some hesitation. Since the usual orthography of the 3d sg. masc. pron. at this period is הא (Sf III 13, 22; Hadad 22, 30; Panammu 11, 22; Bar-Rakkab 17, 18, 19), whereas הו occurs in later Aramaic texts (especially at Elephantine), this reading cannot be right. Milik suggested the reading used here: הוי is the masc. sg. impv. peal and חלפה is the act. ptc. with a suffix, *ḥālipeh*, "his successor." His suggestion has been adopted by Rosenthal (*BASOR* 158 [1960] 30), Nober (*VD* 37 [1959] 171-72), and Donner-Röllig (*KAI* 1.45; 2. 270). Another possibility was suggested by Rosenthal, to understand חלפה as a suffixal form of the prep. -חלפ, "and be in his place." Either of these seems better than my original suggestion (followed by Donner-Röllig, *KAI*, 2. 270) to take חלפה as a noun, "and let there be a change" (*ḥalīpāh*); cf. 1 Kgs 5:28; Ps 55:20; Job 10:17; 14:14. But Milik's suggestion is better, not only because in later Aramaic the prep. -חלפ usually takes suffixal endings in the plural form, but also because of the impv. הוי. Cf. *A* 18, 21. For the plural form of the ending of the prep. -חלפ, see also *AD* 2:2-3. See further Fitzmyer, "A Further Note," *JSS* 14 (1969) 197-200; Greenfield, "The 'Periphrastic Imperative,'" 201; Teixidor, *Syria* 48 (1971) 477. Cf. *DISO*, 63. See note on Sf I A 21. Cf. M. J. Dahood, "Isaiah 51,19 and Sefîre III 22," *Bib* 56 (1975) 94-95.

כי לטב הא מך: "For he is not better than you." This is Rosenthal's interpretation (*BASOR* 158 [1960] 30) for this difficult phrase. The assimilated suffixal form of the prep. מן is peculiar and may be only an engraver's mistake. Should one rather write מ<נ>ך? Cf. 1 Kgs 19:4; Hos 5:13 (*mikkem)*; Gen 42:16; Lev 1:2; 17:12; 19:34.

ויקם: If this is the same verb as in lines 11-12, then Dupont-Sommer was right in restoring a form of -דמ.

חד: "Someone." This is the absol. state of the numeral used as a pron., whereas all the other instances of it in this inscription are in the construct.

מרמת: "Treachery." The form is the fem. absol. pl., as in the case of מלן לחית (line 2); the idea is indefinite. Cf. Hebrew מרמה (Dan 11:23).

23. [ותלאי]ם: "Tal'ayim." Restored as in lines 25-26. From the words that follow it must be the proper name of a place, belonging to the royal house of the suzerain. Noth (*ZDPV* 77 [1961] 156) had identified it with *Talḫayum*, repeatedly mentioned in the Mari letters (see *ARM* 2.4,9; 5.51,12-15; 1.53,11; C.-F. Jean, *Sem* 1 [1948] 18-21). It would seem to have lain in the Khabur region, but a location in the more westerly Balikh area is not excluded. Grelot (*RB* 75 [1968] 285) argued that it must be a neighboring city-state rather than a distant state in Urartu. Lemaire-Durand (*IAS*, 68-72) have noted that *Talḫayum* in the Mari texts is close to Emar, probably between Emar and Carchemish; and that *Tl'ym* in this inscription is an object of contestation between Arpad and KTK. All points to an identification of the two names as Noth once proposed, even though the location still remains uncertain.

וכפריה: "And its villages." This word occurs again in line 26 and in Hadad 10, Panammu 10. In the last two instances it is spelled כפיר; see also Neh 6:2. Noth (*ZDPV* 77 [1961] 155) understood the word to mean "storehouses" ("ihre Vorratshäuseranlagen"), in which semi-nomads stored their harvests. Cazelles ("Tal'ayim, Tala et Muṣur") compared the Mari expression, *Talḫim u kapranišu,* "Talḫayim and its villages." Cf. 4QpNah 3-4 i 9, 11 (כפיריכה in parallelism with ה[רובכ], "your abundance").

בעליה: "Its lords," or possibly "its citizens." See note on Sf I A 4.

גבלה: "Its territory." Vocalize: *gabūlah*. Garbini (*RSO* 34 [1959] 47) wrongly takes גבלה as a fem. noun. The form must be suffixal, given the preceding words כפריה and בעליה.

24. ל[ביתה מן] עלם: "To his house from of old." Originally I restored this lacuna thus: ל[ביתה עד] עלם, " ... (belong) to my father and to his house forever." But this restoration seemed to Hartman (*CBQ* 30 [1968] 260) to involve a contradiction. He proposed rather to read ולביתה מ]עלם], "[Tal'ay]im ... (belonged) to my father and to [his house from] of old." This is clearly a better solution, and it is still better to restore מן, rather than simply -מ.

וכזי: "When." This conjunction appears often in Elephantine texts: *AP* 6:1; 13:4; 27:2.

חבזו: "Struck." See note on Sf II B 7.

אלהן: "(The) gods." Vocalize: *'ilāhīn*; see note on מלן in Sf III 2.

[ה]ות: "It came to belong." The form is the 3d sg. fem. pf. peal הוי, the subject of which is הא (vocalize: *hī'*), referring to Tal'ayim.

אחרן: "To another." This other person or city-state is unknown. For the idiom, see Deut 24:2 (היתה לאיש־אחר).

השבו: "Have brought about the return." The form is the 3d pl. masc. pf. haphel of שוב, which is followed by a cognate accusative, שיבת, with the medial long *i* fully written. Dupont-Sommer compared Ps 126:1: בשוב יהוה שיבת ציון. In this verse several commentators have wanted to read *šĕbût* or *šĕbît* (cf. Jer 33:7) instead of *šîbat*, which is to be retained, being now supported by this extrabiblical attestation of the same expression (even though in Aramaic). Moreover, the significance of this expression for the understanding of the biblical Hebrew expression *šûb* or *hēšîb šĕbût* should not be missed. The Hebrew noun has always been puzzling, and some interpreters have wanted to derive it from שבי, "capture," whereas others from שוב, "return." The Aramaic expression shows that the noun is a cognate accusative and so supports the interpretation that derives *šĕbût* from *šwb*. The context, moreover, is one of restoration. See further Greenfield, *AcOr* 29 (1965) 4. Cf. Meša' 8-9, where one should read ו[יש]בה כמש, "but Kemosh restored it." See P. D. Miller, "A Note on the Meša' Inscription," *Or* 38 (1969) 461-64. Segert (*ArOr* 32 [1964] 126) suggested the possibility of vocalizing שיבת as *šayyābat*. But what is the basis for such a vocalization?

25. ושבת: "Has returned." Vocalize: *šābat*. The form is the 3d sg. fem. pf. peal.

תלאים ל[בר גאי]ה: "Tal'ayim has returned to Bar-Ga'yah." Dupont-Sommer supplied בר גאיה, thus reading the name of the suzerain known from Sf I. Here only the last letter is preserved of what is obviously a proper personal name, to judge from the following phrases. There is just space for five letters, and the conjecture is plausible. Noth (*ZDPV* 77 [1961] 118-72) was quite skeptical of this restoration. It is not accepted by Rosenthal, but has been used by Donner-Röllig (*KAI* 2. 271). Even though it is not certain, no better restoration has been proposed. If correct, it establishes a relation between Sf III and Sf I and II.

26. The first part of this line is restored according to line 17.

מן: "Whoever." The interrogative pron. is here used as an indefinite relative.

ישא: "Will raise." The form is the 3d sg. masc. impf. peal of נשי, the same verb as in line 14-16.

27. Dupont-Sommer suggested as a possible restoration: מן ישא [על שפתוה להשבתה לחד מל]כי ארפד [תקתלנה והן לתקת]לנה שקרת ...

28. ישחדן: "They bribe," lit., "they give presents." .Dupont-Sommer thought that this last section (beginning with והן) expressed a hope for the prosperity of the vassal, provided that he remained loyal to the suzerain. But see Greenfield (*AcOr* 29 (1965) 10; "Some Aspects of the Treaty Terminology," 117-19) for the more correct sense, "send gifts."

כל מה מלך: "Every king." See note on Sf I A 26.

29. שפר: "Beautiful." Vocalize: *šappīr*.

AFFINITY OF THE SEFIRE INSCRIPTIONS TO HITTITE AND ASSYRIAN TREATIES

During the course of the foregoing discussion comments on various lines of the Aramaic treaties of Sefire called attention to parallels in Hittite and Assyrian treaties of a similar nature. Since these Aramaic treaties come from a general area where the Hittites once had influence and the Assyrians were neighbors, it is not surprising that a certain amount of similarity would be found in Aramaic, Assyrian, and Hittite treaties. However, because the last-named come from several centuries earlier than the others, there are also differences.

The classical analysis of the Hittite treaties was published by V. Korošec in 1931.[1] He distinguished treaties of two sorts: *parity treaties*, in which both parties were mutually bound to obey similar stipulations, and *suzerainty treaties*, in which an inferior king was bound by oath as a vassal to obey the stipulations imposed on him by the suzerain or great king. It is with the suzerainty or vassal treaty that Dupont-Sommer compared the Sefire Aramaic inscriptions.[2] Korošec described the general form of the Hittite suzerainty treaty as follows:

(1) the preamble, which identifies the author of the pact (the "great king") and gives his titles and attributes;

(2) the historical prologue, which recounts the benevolent deeds of the suzerain on behalf of the vassal, because of which the latter is obligated to obey forever the suzerain's stipulations;

(3) the stipulations, which set forth in detail the obligations imposed on the vassal;

(4) the provisions for the deposit of the treaty in a shrine or temple and for periodic public readings of it;

(5) the list of the gods, who are summoned as witnesses of the pact;

(6) curses and blessings, which are invoked on the vassal.

The various subheadings interspersed throughout my translation of the Aramaic treaties will enable the reader to make a quick comparison with the above list of details which characterize the Hittite suzerainty treaty. The Aramaic treaties are unfortunately fragmentary, and it is difficult to say whether they ever contained all six parts, a scheme which was not rigidly followed in any case, even in the Hittite treaties. One

1 *Hethitische Staatsverträge: Ein Beitrag zu ihrer juristischen Wertung* (Leipziger rechtswissenschaftliche Studien 60; Leipzig: Weicher, 1931).

2 See *BMB* 13 (1956) 36: Sf III was characterized as a vassal treaty, and it was compared (pp. 37-38) in particular with the Hittite treaty of Mursilis II and Duppi-Tessub of Amurru from the fourteenth century (*ANET*, 203-5).

element in particular is significantly absent, the historical prologue. Whatever reason may be assigned for the omission of this element in the Aramaic treaties, the absence of it constitutes a major difference between the Aramaic and Hittite treaties. This element is basic to the Hittite conception of the pact; it constitutes the "legal framework" of the Hittite suzerainty treaty. Hittite suzerains recalled the favors shown to their vassals as well as those of their predecessors in order to establish the obligation of the vassal's loyalty and service.

Indeed, precisely this element is absent from pacts of the first millennium BC, whether they be Aramaic or Assyrian. This qualification seems to be necessary in view of the claim made by D. J. Wiseman that the treaty form "remained basically unchanged through Neo-Assyrian times."[3] W. L. Moran pointed out that more recently published material has confirmed the thesis that G. E. Mendenhall tried to establish by his comparison of certain covenants described in the OT with the legal form of the Hittite treaties.[4] Basing his investigations mainly on the Hittite treaties of the fifteenth to thirteenth centuries, Mendenhall made a case for the derivation from them of a form of covenant-relationship that characterizes much of the Yahweh-Israel relationship in the OT. In particular, he pointed to the covenant-tradition containing the Decalogue (Exodus 20) and the narrative of the renewal of the covenant at Shechem (Joshua 24). In the case of the Decalogue, specific obligations are imposed on the tribes of Israel without Yahweh being bound to any at all. As for Joshua 24, "it is very difficult to escape the conclusion that this narrative rests upon traditions which go back to the period when the treaty form was still living, but that the later writer used the materials of the tradition which were of importance and value to him, and adapted them to his own contemporary situation."[5] It was crucial to Menden-

3 *Iraq* 20 (1958) 28.

4 G. E. Mendenhall, *Law and Covenant in Israel and the Ancient Near East* (Pittsburgh, PA: Biblical Colloquium, 1955); cf. *BA* 17 (1954) 25-46, 50-76; and the review by Moran, *Bib* 41 (1960) 297-99.

5 *BA* 17 (1954) 67. Further support for Mendenhall's thesis can be found in the independent work conducted along the same lines by K. Baltzer, *Das Bundesformular* (WMANT 4; 2d ed.; Neukirchen-Vluyn: Neukirchener-V., 1964); in English, *The Covenant Formulary in Old Testament, Jewish and Early Christian Writings* (Philadelphia, PA: Fortress, 1971). It is beyond the scope of my discussion to go into a detailed study of the relevance of such treaty-forms to the OT covenants. Though Mendenhall's thesis has found widespread acceptance, dissenting voices have raised difficulties in some areas. For further details, see E. Gerstenberger, "Covenant and Commandment," *JBL* 84 (1965) 38-51; D. J. McCarthy, "Covenant in the Old Testament: The Present

hall's thesis that the OT covenant forms were related to the Hittite style of the suzerainty treaty. For him this was an indication of the date of the tradition and of the legal pattern that were being used; they must have been introduced into the history of Israel at an early date. In stressing the influence of such an early literary form derived from Hittite sources, Mendenhall stands in sharp contrast to the usual Wellhausenian explanation of the origin of the covenant relationship: that it was the product of prophetic religious thought in the eighth and seventh centuries.[6] Moran has also made much of the difference between the Hittite and later treaties, precisely in their absence of the historical prologue.[7] The more recently published material from the second millennium BC, to which he has appealed, are Ugaritic and Akkadian texts.[8]

It is also significant that in the Assyrian treaties of Esarhaddon, dating from the first millennium BC, there is no historical prologue, just as there is none in the Aramaic treaties of Sefire. Another difference that characterizes the later first-millennium treaties is the tendency to use more elaborate and colorful curses.[9]

When, however, one prescinds from these differences, one cannot fail to notice the otherwise striking similarity existing between the Aramaic treaties of Sefire and the Hittite and Assyrian vassal treaties. The detailed comparison has been made in many cases in the comments on the lines in the foregoing treatment. It may be, however, useful to recall some of the similarities. Several of the stipulations in the Hittite treaty between Mursilis and Duppi-Tessub of Amurru end with a formula quite similar to the concluding clauses in these steles: If you do (or do not do) such things, you act in disregard of your oath. This is the Hittite counterpart of the Aramaic והן להן clause. Still more significant

State of Inquiry," *CBQ* 27 (1965) 217-40; also his *Treaty and Covenant*; and *Old Testament Covenant: A Survey of Current Opinions*; H. B. Huffmon, "The Exodus, Sinai and the Credo," *CBQ* 27 (1965) 101-13, esp. 109-10; P. B. Harner, "Exodus, Sinai and Hittite Prologues," *JBL* 85 (1966) 233-36.

6 For the espousal of a view very close to that of J. Wellhausen, see C. F. Whitley, "Covenant and Commandment in Israel," *JNES* 22 (1963) 37-48.

7 *Bib* 41 (1960) 298-99.

8 See J. Nougayrol, *Le palais royal d'Ugarit IV* (Mission de Ras shamra 7; Paris: Imprimerie Nationale, 1956); D. J. Wiseman, *The Alalakh Tablets* (London: British Institute of Archaeology at Ankara, 1953).

9 See H. B. Huffmon, "The Exodus" (n. 5 above), 109 n. 41. Greater detail for the purpose of comparison can be found in McCarthy, *Treaty and Covenant*, part I, chaps. 7-8.

is the alternate formula, You act in disregard of the gods of the oath. Cf. Sf I B 27, 33; Sf II B 9; Sf III 4, 14, 16, 23. Dupont-Sommer has also called attention to the striking parallel in Sf III 4-7 to the Hittite treaty of Mursilis with Duppi-Tessub §13: "If anyone of the deportees from the country of Kinzu, whom my father removed and I myself removed, escapes and comes to you, (if) you do not seize him and turn him back to the king of the Hatti land, and even tell him as follows, 'Go! Where you are going, I do not want to know,' you act in disregard of your oath" (*ANET*, 203-5).

There is also the question whether the Sefire treaties are vassal treaties at all. This question was raised by Noth,[10] and undoubtedly in dependence on him by Donner-Röllig.[11] Noth recalled that we have only the texts found in the area of Mati'el of Arpad. Sf I and Sf II may represent the treaty of Bar-Ga'yah, king of KTK, setting forth only his understanding of the pact with the stipulations that he has imposed on Mati'el. It is not impossible that a similar text had been drawn up from the standpoint of the latter, imposing similar (but not identical) stipulations on Bar-Ga'yah, a text that is unfortunately lost to us. If so, then the Sefire inscriptions would really represent a parity treaty, and not a vassal treaty at all. Moreover, Noth insisted that four essentials were needed in a vassal treaty, which appear in the study of the Hittite treaties carried out by V. Korošec.[12] These are: (a) the setting up (or confirmation) of the vassal by the overlord; (b) the imposition of an obligation on the vassal to appear regularly before the overlord; (c) a regularized payment of tribute to the overlord; and (d) the supply of a number of armies or troops by the vassal to the overlord in the case of a war. According to Noth, the first three elements in this list are lacking in the Sefire inscriptions; though (d) appears in Sf I B 28-33 and Sf II B 5-7.

Noth, however, fell into the same trap that he complained about when others who were using the Hittite treaties as norms to say that the Sefire inscriptions were vassal treaties, for he derived certain elements from the Hittite treaties and, not finding them present in the later Aramaic treaties, questioned whether they were really vassal treaties. It seems to me that the relationship of Mati'el to Bar-Ga'yah cannot be understood, at least on the basis of the material now available, in any other way than as that of a vassal to his overlord, or "great king." McCarthy has also disagreed with Noth's estimate of the Sefire treaties in this regard. He insisted that

10 *ZDPV* 77 (1961) 138-45.

11 *KAI* 2. 271-72.

12 Noth (*ZDPV* 77 [1966] 139) refers to the following pages of Korošec's

Mati'el's throne clearly depends on KTK (Stele I, B, 24-25; II, B, 5-7) and this is the essential thing. Furthermore, Noth mentions that parity treaties appeared in different editions for each party, and he thinks Sfiré is Mati'el's edition, while there might have been another with more emphasis on the king of KTK's duties. However, each edition of the typical parity treaty, Ramses II-Hattusilis III, details the obligations of both parties. There is no question of different texts of the clauses for each, and we have seen that the parity treaty normally applied an obligation now to one, now to the other party, and only then moved on to the next obligation. The obligations of each were not listed separately. There is an instance of a double edition of a vassal treaty (Mattiwaza) and there each edition makes clear the inferiority of the lesser party.[13]

Until further evidence is brought to light to change this judgment, I prefer to regard the Sefire inscriptions as examples of vassal or suzerainty treaties.[14]

Hethitische Staatsverträge, 8-10, 72-85.

13 *Treaty and Covenant*, 64 n. 39. It might also be good to recall here McCarthy's more general thesis that there is basically no difference in the vassal and the parity treaty from the point of their form: "Formally, parity and vassal treaty are one" (ibid., 27). The judgment, therefore, will have to be made on the contents, the stipulations, and the general treatment of the underling.

14 See further M. Weinfeld, "Traces of Assyrian Treaty Formulae in Deuteronomy," *Bib* 46 (1965) 417-27; "The Covenant of Grant in the Old Testament and in the Ancient Near East," *JAOS* 90 (1970) 184-203; J. C. Greenfield, "Some Aspects of Treaty Terminology in the Bible," 117-19; L. Perlitt, *Bundestheologie im Alten Testament* (WMANT 36; Neukirchen-Vluyn: Neukirchener-V., 1969).

THE LAND OF KTK

The major problem in the interpretation of the Sefire inscriptions is the identification of the land of KTK over which the suzerain Bar-Ga'yah ruled in the middle of the eighth century BC. KTK is mentioned in Sf I (A 1, 3, 4, [12], [15]; B 4bis, 5, 10) and in Sf II (C 5), but not in Sf III. Various attempts to identify it have been made by writers since the first publication of Sf I in 1931. The present discussion is an attempt to survey the various proposals and assess them.

(1) Ronzevalle, the original editor of Sf I, sensed the problem and gave only a generic description of the locality where KTK should be found, between Aleppo and the Euphrates.[1]

(2) Shortly after Ronzevalle's publication, J. Cantineau proposed the interpretation that KTK was Assyria and understood Bar-Ga'yah as a second name for Aššurnirari V (or a name for a general in the Assyrian army),[2] because of the Assyrian treaty of Aššurnirari V that mentioned Mati'ilu of Arpad.[3] Since the latter is certainly to be identified with Mati'el, son of 'Attarsamak, the vassal in the Sefire inscriptions, Cantineau suggested that Sf I was an Aramaic version of the same pact. Accordingly, he regarded KTK as "une graphie volontairement fautive" for Kalaḫ, the capital of the Assyrian kingdom. This sort of interpretation of KTK was pushed still further by G. Dossin who proposed that it was a cryptogram for *KUR.AŠ.KI*, equalling *māt Aššur*.[4]

The obvious difficulty that such an interpretation encounters is to explain why KTK should be a cryptogram or a deliberately false writing of the name of the suzerain's country in the text of a state treaty. This is scarcely the sort of document in which one conceals the identity of the country or of the king involved. Now, however, אשר is certainly restored in the list of the gods who are witnesses to the treaty. If Sf I A 25 is correctly read and interpreted, then "Assyria" (אשר) is explicitly mentioned and seems to be distinct from KTK.[5]

(3) A. Alt proposed the vocalization of the name as *Katikka* and located it in the region between Lake Jebbûl, to the east of Aleppo in

1 *MUSJ* 15 (1930-31) 252.

2 *RA* 28 (1931) 178.

3 See E. F. Weidner, *AfO* 8 (1932-33) 17-34.

4 *Muséon* 57 (1944) 151-53. See also G. Contenau, "La cryptographie."

5 See further the remarks of Dupont-Sommer, *BMB* 13 (1956) 39.

Syria, and the Euphrates, an area mentioned in one of the inscriptions of Tiglathpileser III.[6] He maintained that the steles had been erected by the Aramean princeling Bar-Ga'yah in his own territory. Unfortunately, the Assyrian text is broken, and one has only the beginning of the geographical name to which he referred, *Ka[ ]*.[7] On the basis of the spelling of the Aramaic name KTK, Alt proposed to restore *Ka-[ti-ik-ka]*, a name which would resemble *Ḫatarikka*, the Akkadian form of the biblical Hadrach. Indeed, Alt apparently regarded the territory as "ein unselbstständiger Teil des Reiches Arpad." This proposal has not met with much acceptance because of the many problematic elements in it: the broken text of Tiglathpileser III, the likelihood that the region around Lake Jebbûl belonged rather to the territory of Mati'el, and the implication of Sf I C 1-3, that it was rather Mati'el who had erected the steles in his territory.[8]

(4) B. Landsberger equated KTK with Ḫatarikka, which is the same as *Ḥazrak* of the Zakur stele (a 4, 9, 10; b 1, 4) and *Ḥadrak* of Zech 9:1.[9] He suggested that Bar-Ga'yah was king over the united kingdom of Ḥamath and Ḫatarikka, and the successor to Zakur, who was king of Ḥamath and Lu'ash, according to the Zakur stele.[10]

The difficulty with this suggestion is to show that there is a linguistic connection between KTK and Ḫatarikka or a political connection between KTK and Ḥamath in this period. Again, why would Babylonian-Assyrian gods and Syrian gods both be mentioned in such an understanding of the inscription?

(5) Dupont-Sommer at first identified KTK with *Kaška*, the king of which is mentioned in the Annals of Tiglathpileser III as *Da-di-i-lu* uru*Kaš-ka-ai*.[11] In this context *Kaška* is mentioned after Sam'al,

6 *ZDMG* 88 (1934) 237; *Kleine Schriften* 3 (1959) 216.

7 See P. Rost, *Die Keilschrifttexte Tiglat-Pilesers III.*, Kleinere Inschriften II, line 28 (p. 85).

8 See also H. Genge, *Nordsyrisch-südanatolische Reliefs* (Copenhagen: Munksgaard, 1979) 33-34.

9 *Sam'al*, 59 n. 147.

10 N. Na'aman has followed Landsberger and changed some of the explanation ("Looking for KTK").

11 *Les Araméens*, 59-60. See P. Rost, *Die Keilschrifttexte*, 26 (*Annals*, lines 152-53); *ARAB*, 1. §772; *ANET*, 283. A place called Kasku is mentioned along with Tabal, Ḫilakku (Cilicia), Musku, and Muṣur in an inscription of Sargon II; see H. Winckler, *Die Keilschrifttexte Sargons* (Leipzig: Pfeiffer, 1889), I. 148-49; II, pl. 38; *ARAB*, 2.

Gurgum, and Melidh, but before Tabal, Tuna, and Tuḫana. From this collocation Dupont-Sommer concluded that *Kaška* lay somewhere between Gurgum, Melidh, and Tabal. It pointed to a northern locality, which was plausible in light of the references to Muṣr (= Muṣri), Arpad, and "all Aram" in Sf I A 5. The name *Dadi-ilu* is Aramaic and suggests that the dynasty of *Kaška* was Aramean. Since the name Bar-Ga'yah is also Aramaic, Dupont-Sommer proposed that he was the father of Dadi-ilu in the time of Aššurnirari V (or possibly even the same person, Dadi-ilu bar Ga'yah). Aside from the last element in this proposal, this identification encounters only one major difficulty. Dupont-Sommer was apparently aware of it, when he later wrote,

> Du point de vue linguistique, la graphie KTK, au lieu de KSK-KŠK, ne ferait pas difficulté; c'est ainsi, par ex., que, dans les documents assyriens, le mot *Luḫuti* (avec *t*), designant une région située en Syrie, correspond au mot *L'Š* (avec *š*) de l'inscription araméenne de Zakir.[12]

How can the Aramaic *t* equal the Assyrian *s* (pronounced *š*). If Arameans heard the name *Kaška*, why would they not have written it *KŠK*? After all, it is the Proto-Semitic *tha*, apparently still pronounced as such by the Arameans who wrote these inscriptions,[13] who used *š* to represent it. When *ṯ* > *t* eventually, it was then written as *t*, as in Imperial Aramaic and later. Noth also questioned the identification of Luḫuti with Lu'ash, but he tried to justify the *š-t* shift by pointing to the identification of *Ḥzrk* (in the Zakur stele) with *Ḥdrk* (in Zech 9:1) and with Assyrian *Ḫa-ta-rik-ka*.[14] But this is not very convincing either, for the anomaly is the Assyrian *t* for the West Semitic *z-d*; the parallel limps. If one were to object and say that the Arameans heard the Assyrian *Kašk* precisely as *Kaṯk*, then the problem still remains to explain why they did not write this as *Kašk*, as *ṯ* is represented in the majority of cases in these inscriptions. The only way that this could be saved would be to postulate that in this instance too there is another case of the shift of *ṯ* to *t*.[15] Moreover, the place *l'š* in the Zakur stele is most probably to be identified with *Nuḫašše* and not with *Luḫuti*.

---

§99; *ANET*, 284.

12 *MPAIBL* 15 (1958) 22 n. 1.

13 Two exceptions apparently occur in these inscriptions, in which the shift from *ṯ* to *t* seems to have taken place: *yrt* (Sf I C 24) and *btn* (Sf I A 32).

14 *ZDPV* 77 (1961) 166.

15 See n. 13 above. Then another instance would have to be added to the list in the Appendix, B. Phonology, 1. Cf. R. Degen, "Zur Schreibung des Kaška-Namens." Kutscher ("Aramaic," *Linguistics*,368) seems to agree with Degen on this.

The identification of KTK with Kašk was also adopted by W. F. Albright.[16] He located it at Sakcegözü, east of Zinjirli, where Garstang partially excavated a Syro-Hittite royal city. Segert (*ArOr* 32 [1964] 112 n. 21) has preferred the identification of KTK with Kašk ("wohl mit dem Königreich Kasku [Kašku] nördlich von Syrien identisch"). Similarly, Greenfield (*JBL* 87 [1968] 241) understands it as *Kaška* despite the phonetic problems. More recently this identification with Kaška has been developed and defended by E. Schuler.[17]

(6) Later, however, Dupont-Sommer adopted another identification on a conjectural basis,[18] preferring to regard Bar-Ga'yah as a second or imperial throne-name of Sardur III, son of Argišti I, the king of Urartu. Being Aramaic in form and meaning "son of majesty," it would have been preferred by the Urartian king in his dealings with his Aramean allies; in this sense, then, it can be regarded as a *Deckname* for Sardur. Having brought his kingdom of Urartu to the peak of its power, Sardur consolidated his rule over the Araxus area, collected tribute from Melidh and Commagene, and conquered Aleppo. He then sought to influence the king of Arpad despite the latter's treaty with Assyria to revolt from the latter and to join him in a coalition against Assyria. Dupont-Sommer thinks that he must have succeeded in this because in the third year of his reign Tiglathpileser III (ca. 743) recorded: "Sardur of Urartu revolted against me and joined Mati'ilu."[19] Apropos of the same year we read in the Eponym List, "In the city of Arpad: the army of Urartu defeated."[20] These two texts show Arpad and Urartu were leagued against Assyria and were defeated by Tiglathpileser III. Dupont-Sommer concluded that the Sefire steles may well have been the treaty between Mati'ilu and Sardur III of Urartu. In this proposal KTK would be the name of an important city in Urartu in SE Asia Minor, possibly a city founded by Sardur himself, but not attested elsewhere. The name KTK would equal *Kasku-i* or *Kašku-i*. Once again we are confronted with the difficulty that the list of gods who witness the pact in Sf I A 8-13 contains none that are Urartian. E. Vogt pointed out a further difficulty that this identification encounters, when account is taken of Sf III 24. The king there says that

16 "Syrien, Phönizien und Palästina," *Historia mundi* (ed. F. Kern; Munich: Lehnen), 2 (1953) 370-71.

17 *Die Kaskäer*.

18 *BMB* 13 (1956) 39-40; *MPAIBL* 15 (1958) 22.

19 *Annals*, line 59; see P. Rost, *Die Keilschrifttexte*, 12; *ARAB* 1. §769, 785, 813.

20 See A. Ungnad, *RLA* 2 (1938) 430; H. Tadmor, *ScrHier* 8 (1961) 252-58.

his father's house had been struck by the gods and that Tal'ayim had been lost to it. This town, whose locality is not certain, was almost certainly in northern Syria.[21] The situation, described in Sf III 24 and involving it, would scarcely suit the reign of Argišti I, the father of Sardur III and former ruler of Urartu.[22]

(7) Noth made still another attempt to establish the locality of KTK, identifying it with *Kissik* (= *[Ki-is]-sik*^{ki}), mentioned in the *Annals* of Tiglathpileser III (line 13).[23] Though very little can be learned from these annals about the place, the name appears elsewhere in a stereotyped list of cities in southern Mesopotamia (along with Ur, Uruk, Eridu, etc.).[24] This would suggest that Kissik was a not unimportant eighth-century town in the lower region of Mesopotamia, on either the Euphrates or the Tigris. But its precise location is apparently impossible to establish.[25] The Eponym List (Cb 1 and Cb 2) indicates that Aššurnirari III had earlier (ca. 786) undertaken a campaign against Kiski (= Kissik), just as he had done against Arpad and Damascus. To the obvious question whether a king with an Aramaic name would be ruling in an area in southern Mesopotama in the eighth century, Noth answered confidently that Tiglathpileser III had recorded his campaign against "all the Arameans" in the plains of that region. Again, he argued that the list of gods in Sf I A 8-13 is Mesopotamian in part and that the name of the obscure god Mullesh is particularly decisive.

It is, however, an identification of KTK that is not very convincing. The distance of over 500 km. between the two places is a factor that must be considered. There is, further, the linguistic difficulty that is similar to that mentioned above (under § 5).

21 *Bib* 39 (1958) 270. Noth (*ZDPV* 77 [1961] 161) acknowledged the validity of Vogt's argument, but he linked to it his own objections to the Sefire inscriptions as examples of vassal treaties and to the identification of the main king of Sf III as Bar-Ga'yah. If the latter is not the king of Sf III who is contracting the pact with the "king(s) of Arpad" (see the problematic restoration of Sf III 25), then the pertinence of this inscription to the land of Urartu is even less. See further his remarks on p. 167 n. 154.

22 Gibson (*TSSI*, 2. 21-22) follows Dupont-Sommer to a certain extent in this identification.

23 *ZDPV* 77 (1961) 166-67. See P. Rost, *Die Keilschrifttexte*, 4; *ARAB*, 1. §764.

24 For instance, in the records of Sargon II. See H. Winckler, *Die Keilschrifttexte Sargons*, 1. 54-55, 60-61, 96-97, 124-25, 146-47. Cf. A. Ungnad, *RLA* 2 (1938) 429, 431.

25 See A. Falkenstein, "Zur Lage des südbabylonischen Dūrum," *AfO* 21 (1966)

(8) Y. S. Kassouny suggested the identification of KTK with a place called Katuk in Syriac and Armenian sources,[26] viz., in the Syriac *Chronicle* of Michael the Great, the Jacobite patriarch of Antioch (AD 1126-99).[27] This work was utilized by Gregory Abû'l Faraj (Bar Hebraeus) in his *Chronography.*[28] There exists also an Armenian translation of the *Chronicle* of Michael the Great, the work of a priest Ischok.[29] Bar-Hebraeus's text runs as follows in Wallis Budge's translation: "And in the year fourteen hundred and seventy-six of the Greeks (= AD 1165), Kelej Arslan, Sûltân of Iconium, reigned over Gâdûg and Ablestîn, and Tûrandâ, and he began to persecute the sons of Dânishmand. And Nûr ad-Din reigned over Bânyâs and he fortified it strongly. And Tôrôs the Armenian pillaged Mar'âsh and captured four hundred Turks."[30] Though Kassouny identified KTK with the name *Katuk*,[31] the Syriac text of Bar Hebraeus reads the name as *g'dwg*, which most of the translators have transcribed as *Gâdûg.*[32] It is, in effect, identifying KTK with an area in Gurgum, near Marash.

50-51.

26 *Nakhahaygagan Hayastan* (Beirut, 1950), 417 [= *Prearmenian Armenia: A Critical HIstory of Armenia from the Neolithic Age to 600 B.C.*]. Kassouny wrote the name as *katouk.*

27 J.-B. Chabot (ed.), *Chronique de Michel le Syrien, Patriarche jacobite d'Antioche (1166-1199)* (4 vols.; Paris: Leroux, 1899, 1901, 1905, 1910; réimpression anastatique, Brussels: Culture et Civilisation, 1963).

28 See E. A. Wallis Budge, *The Chronography of Gregory Abû'l Faraj the Son of Aaron, the Hebrew Physician Commonly Known as Bar Hebraeus, Being the First Part of His Political History of the World, Translated from the Syriac* (2 vols.; London: Oxford University, 1932); P. J. Bruns and G. G. Kirsch, *Bar-Hebraei chronicon syriacum* (2 vols.; Leipzig: Boehm, 1788-89); P. Bedjan, *Gregorii Barhebraei chronicum syriacum* (Paris: Maisonneuve, 1890).

29 See V. Langlois, *Chronique de Michel le Grand, patriarche des Syriens jacobites, traduite pour la première fois sur la version arménienne du prêtre Ischôk* (Venice: Académie de Saint-Lazare, 1868). Unfortunately the manuscript on which the modern edition of Michael the Great's *Chronicle* depends lacks the page in which Book 18, chap. 11 should appear, and the editor J.-B. Chabot has substituted for it the corresponding passage of Bar Hebraeus's *Chronography.*

30 See E. A. Wallis Budge, *Chronography*, 1. 289. The Syriac text can be found in the photo of fol. 103r, col. 1, line 9 of the Bodleian Ms. Hunt No. 52 in the second volume of Wallis Budge's edition. Other editions of Bar Hebraeus give the same spelling of the name, *g'dwg*. See P. Bedjan, *Gregorii*, 331; Bruns and Kirsch, *Bar-Hebraei*, 1. 354.

The difference may simply be a phonetic shift from the voiced to the unvoiced velar and dental. But which came first? Did KTK > GDG, or vice versa? There is, moreover, a time lapse of almost 2000 years between the Sefire inscriptions and these sources, which must not be forgotten. This identification has little to be said for it.

(9) In 1972 H. Farzat proposed that Bar-Ga'yah was a name for *(Nabû)-Mukîn-zēri/Ukin-zer* (or his father), who was an Aramean prince of *Bīt-Amukkāni* in Babylonia (*Le royaume araméen d'Arpad*).

(10) In 1976 A. Malamat[33] suggested that KTK was *Ki-i[t?]-qa*, a royal city of Bit-Adini on the east side of the Euphrates, the name used by its indigenous Luwian people, and that Bar-Ga'yah was a dynastic name for Šamši-ilu, the *turtān*, who held power for more than fifty years, and whose seat was in Til-Barsip (modern Tell Ahmar). This proposal has been further adopted by Lemaire-Durand (*IAS*, 23-58) and worked out in great detail. This is the most promising identification of Bar-Ga'yah that has emerged. It has much to be said for it, even though it is contested.[34] Šamši-ilu is known by such titles as *nāgiru* and *šāpir māt ḫatti* in Assyrian texts. Til-Barsip was conquered by Šalmaneser III and given the new name of Kar-Šalmaneser (Šalmaneser's Port); it continued to be Assyrian-controlled. For Šamši-ilu it was the city of his governance (*āl bēlūtiya*), or as Amos (1:5) puts it, "the sceptre-bearer of Beth Eden (= Bit-Adini)."

But the identification of KTK still remains a problem, because it is far from certain that it is the same as Til-Barsip. It was thought that KTK was a way of writing the Hittite form of the name of that town. But now J. D. Hawkins has shown that the Hittite name was quite different, being Masuwari.[35] This, then, creates a major problem in adopt-

31 *Nakhahaygagen Hayastan*, 417-18.

32 *Chronique*, 324. Even the French version of the Armenian, done by V. Langlois, gives the name as *Gadoug*. Cf. F. Haase, "Die armenische Rezension der syrischen Chronik Michaels des Grossen," *Oriens christianus* ns 5 (1915) 60-82, 271-84.

33 "הצער חדשה לזיהויה של 'כתך' בכתובות ספירה (A New Proposal for the Identification of KTK in the Sefire Inscriptions)." The name *Ki[..]qa* is found in the Kurkh Monolith of Shalmaneser III (858-824); *ANET*, 277.

34 See the reviews of *IAS* by F. M. Fales, H. D. Galter, M. Krebernik, E. Lipiński, F. Malbran-Labat.

35 "The Hittite Name of Til-Barsip: Evidence from a New Hieroglyphic Fragment from Tell Ahmar." The name was written *ma-su-wa/i-ra/i-na*(URBS), "(the city)

ing the entire proposal of Lemaire-Durand, attractive as is their identification of Bar-Ga'yah.

(11) Y. Ikeda, while accepting the identification of Bar-Ga'yah with Šamši-ilu, has proposed that KTK is an acronym or the designation of a federation of three north Syrian neighbors, Kummuḫ, Til-Barsip, and Carchemish (כרכמיש).[36] Šamši-ilu, known to the people of these territories by the Aramaic name Bar-Ga'yah ("Son of Majesty") and מלך רב, would then have concluded a treaty with Mati'el, hoping that Arpad would not share in any anti-Assyrian moves to attack the member states of his federation. This might have occurred about the time of the treaty between Aššurnirari V and Mati'el (754) or perhaps even earlier. This is an interesting proposal, but one wonders what the evidence would be for the use of acronyms in antiquity.

Masuwari."

36 "Once Again *KTK* in the Sefire Inscriptions."

APPENDIX

GRAMMAR OF THE SEFIRE INSCRIPTIONS

APPENDIX

In this appendix is presented a comprehensive view of the grammatical features of the Sefire inscriptions. Even though these inscriptions scarcely reflect all aspects of Aramaic grammar in the period of "Old Aramaic,"[1] they are quite representative because of their length. There is, then, reason to study the language of these texts, which represent an important group in the division of Old Aramaic. Since the first edition of this book, other studies of the grammar of Old Aramaic have appeared,[2] which better situate the language of the Sefire inscriptions in the context of Old Aramaic as a whole, but there is still room for a detailed study of these texts in and for themselves. This will also give me the opportunity to agree or disagree with explanations found at times in these grammars, as well as in other specific studies.

A. ORTHOGRAPHY

An explanation of the orthography of the inscriptions of Sefire depends to some extent on the vocalization of the words appearing in them. I shall say a word, first, about the method used to determine the vocalization of the words in the inscriptions. In general, the vocalization of later Aramaic is the norm, especially when this exists in a vocalized form that can be predicated of the consonantal text of these inscriptions. In particular, we refer to what is known as Aramaic in the Bible, in rabbinic literature, and in Syriac. Yet it must be emphasized that this later Aramaic has often developed forms that cannot be easily transferred to consonantal texts of this early period; it is necessary to make an effort to discern what is late and secondary. There are, indeed, times when the full consonantal writing of words gives us a clue to the vocalization of these early texts. When this vocalization not only agrees with later patterns but also with contemporary (early) data from the cognate Semitic languages, it should be regarded as certain. But the norm for vocalization should be a judicious mixture of the indications derived from later Aramaic and the early cognate material. This is why I have often cited in the commentary cognate Semitic forms of the words that appear in the text.

---

1 For my understanding of this term, see *The Genesis Apocryphon of Qumran Cave I: A Commentary* (BibOr 18A; Rome: Biblical Institute, 1971) 22-23 n. 60; also "The Phases of the Aramaic Language," *WA*, 57-84.

2 See R. Degen, *AG*; S. Segert, *AAG*. The latter uses the adjective "altaramäisch" in a sense wider than either Degen or I do.

I persist in regarding the Aramaic family as a unit in that I give preference to forms of words according to the later Aramaic vocalization rather than to Hebrew or Phoenician or Ugaritic forms. For instance, because the word for "night" turns up almost always in various stages of Aramaic either as a form **layl* or as the reduplicated form **laylay*, I regard this as a distinctive Aramaic development, and accordingly vocalize the consonants לילה as a form of the latter: **laylay* > *laylêh*, with the dissimilation of the diphthong and the representation of it by final *h*, rather than as a form similar to the Hebrew *laylāh*. The Aramaic of this period is under Canaanite influence, and a priori one cannot exclude the possibility that the word for "night" in Aramaic is a Canaanite borrowing, but it seems advisable to analyze the form as Aramaic, when that can be done, even if it means appealing to later Aramaic vocalization. In this case, no principle is being compromised by such an appeal, for it is obvious that, whereas the vast majority of diphthongs in Old Aramaic are uncontracted, there are exceptions. No thesis about the vocalization of the Aramaic of this period should create a procrustean bed.

When the evidence for a particular word is lacking in the Aramaic family, then we are forced to have recourse to cognate languages. The main difference, which the reader will note between the vocalization of the Aramaic of these early texts attempted below and later Aramaic, is the reluctance to make use of the reduced vowel in the open pretonic syllable. It is a well established principle in Aramaic phonology that a short vowel in such a syllable is reduced to shewa. The only difficulty is that we do not know at what period this reduction to shewa became operative. I have already discussed this question briefly in the sketch of Qumran Aramaic, which forms part of my commentary on that text.[3] Because of this difficulty I have preferred here to retain the full short vowel for convenience. Those who prefer to reduce the vowel even at this period can easily make the slight adjustment which that entails. But then the principle should be carried out consistently. One should avoid using, now the full short vowel, now the shewa without any apparent reason for the difference (e.g., as in Cross and Freedman, *EHO*, 21-34).

In the following tables the number within parentheses behind the suggested vocalization of the form refers to one instance in which the given form can be found; the references are not meant to be exhaustive for each form. But the subsequent list of forms occurring in these inscriptions is intended to be complete.

In an earlier form of this grammatical study I made frequent use of the circumflex accent in attempted vocalizations. In what follows there

3 See n. 1 above. Appendix II, pp. 173-174

is a slight difference. The circumflex is now restricted to those vowels which arise from a contraction of a diphthong. Otherwise the macron is used to designate a long vowel. The reason behind this decision to use the macron is that there is really no evidence in Aramaic aside from Masoretic Hebraisms in Biblical Aramaic of tonal long vowels. Tonal and pretonic lengthening is a characteristic of Hebrew. The macron, therefore, designates what would be an original long vowel in Proto-Semitic or in the Aramaic noun or verb types that are being used. In this regard, one should beware of interpreting the *ṣere* in Biblical Aramaic as a long *e*. Such an interpretation might seem plausible in the light of the tonal lengthening in Hebrew, e.g., in the piel. But the corresponding form in Aramaic is either pael or pail, which shows that in reality the *e* or *i* is merely an allophone of the same basic phoneme, which in this case is short. The same is to be said for the peal participle, *qātel* or *qātil*; both forms are found in Biblical Aramaic and correspond to the Hebrew *qôtēl*.

In this discussion of the orthography of the Sefire inscriptions I continue to recognize the validity of the thesis first set forth by Cross and Freedman in their book, *Early Hebrew Orthography*, even though I disagree with the interpretation of a given word at times. What they established there has continued to prove itself over the years. For this reason I look with skepticism on the work of L. A. Bange, *A Study of the Use of Vowel Letters in Alphabetic Consonantal Writing*. That was intended to be a corrective of the Cross-Freedman thesis, but its dissent from that thesis is wrongheaded, and the following discussion conducted along the principles of the Cross-Freedman thesis will set forth the reasons why.[4]

(1) *Final Long a Is Indicated by He*[5]

br g'yh (Bar Ga'yāh Sf I A 1); *znh* (zināh I A 6); *kd'h* (? kadi'āh I A 10); *rḥbh* (Raḥbāh I A 10); *mṣlh* (maṣūlāh I A [11]); *ḥzyh* (ḥazzāyāh I A 13); *ssyh* (sūsyāh I A 22); *šwrh* (šawrāh I A 23); *bkth* (? bakkatāh

4 For reviews of Bange's book, see K. Beyer, *BZ* 18 (1974) 139-40; W. Röllig, *WO* 8 (1975-76) 155-57; G. Fohrer, *ZAW* 84 (1972) 118. The thesis of Cross and Freedman has also been called in question by D. W. Goodwin, *Text-Restoration Methods in Contemporary U.S.A. Biblical Scholarship* (Ricerche 5; Naples: Istituto Orientale di Napoli -- Pubblicazioni del Seminario di Semitistica, 1969).

5 When a line-number is given in square brackets [ ], it means that some restoration of the word is involved; the reader should then consult the text. A question mark preceding or following a suggested vocalization means that the form is problematic; the reader should consult the commentary.

I A 24); *mh* (māh I A 26); *lhyh* (laḥyāh I A 26); *twl'h* (tawla'āh I A 27); *ṣ'qh* (ṣa'aqāh I A [29]); *yllh* (yalalāh I A 30); *ḥwh* (ḥiwwāh I A 31); *dbhh* (? dubhāh I A 31); *nmrh* (nimrāh I A 31); *'qh* ('aqāh I A 33); *mrbh* (? Maribāh I A 34); *mzh* (? I A 34); *mblh* (? I A 34); *znyh* (zāniyāh I A [41]); *'ykh* ('aykāh I A 37); *ḥdh* (ḥadāh I B 8); *'nh* ('anāh I B [24]); *lbkh* (? I B 35); *mlh* (millāh I B [41]); *kh* (kāh I C 1); *ptḥh* (patīḥāh III 8); *qryh* (qiryāh III 12).

For the negative *lā* one finds only *l*-, without a final consonant, which suggests that it is a prefix. Cf. *lhn* (lāhen III 4); *ltsk* (lātissuk III 5); *lṭb* (lāṭāb III 22). Two forms should be noted here, *'mrn* and *ktbn* (I C [1]), which lack a final *he* and so were probably not pronounced *'amarnāh* and *katabnāh*. For a different, less convincing, explanation, see P. Grelot, *RB* 75 (1968) 285.

(2) Final long i Is Indicated by Yodh

zy (zī I A 5); *twy* (? I A 28); *ṣy* (ṣī I A [32]); *y'dy* (Ya'dī I B 9); *bry* (barī I B 25); *'qry* ('iqqārī I B 25); *'rqy* ('arqī I B 27); *byty* (baytī I B 32); *'my* ('immī or 'ammī I B 33); *lḥmy* (laḥmī I B 38); *ly* (lī I B 38); *nbšy* (nabšī I B 40); *'šry* ('ašrī I C 4); *mlky* (mulkī I C [6]); *'by* ('abī II B 8); *r'šy* (ri'šī II B 8); *hmtty* (hamītūtī or hamātūtī I B 8); *sḥrty* (saḥratī III 7); *ml'ky* (mal'akī III 8); *ḥpṣy* (ḥapṣī III 8); *dmy* (damī III 11); *qrqy* (qāriqī III 19); *khs'y* (? kuhsa'ī? III 17); *mny* (minnī III 4); *by* (bī III 9); *ky* (kī III 22); *kzy* (kazī III 24); *'yty* ('iyyātī III 11); *t'šqny* (ta'šuqinnī III 20); *'my* ('ammī III 21).

(3) Final Long u Is Indicated by Waw

[...]w (? I A [5]); *pqḥw* (paqaḥū I A 13); *śmw* (śamū I B 6); *'rqw* ('Arqū I B 9); *ybrdw* (yabrūdū I B [9-10]); *'rw* (? 'Arū I B 10); *m..w* (? I B 10); *y'bdw* (ya'bidū I C [5]); *yṣrw* (yiṣṣarū I C 15); *yhpkw* (yahpukū I C 21); *yśmw* (yaśīmū I C 23); *'bdw* ('abadū II B 2); *šbw* (šibū III 7); *qtlw* (qitlū or qitulū? III 21); *ḥbzw* (ḥabazū III 24); *hšbw* (hašībū III 24).

(4) Final aw Is Represented by Waw

'w ('aw I B 26); *yhww* (yihwaw I A [31]); *tpnw* (tipnaw III 7); *šlw* (šilaw III 5). Garbini (*RSO* 34 [1959] 42) prefers to vocalize *'w* as *ô*.

(5) Final ay Is Indicated by Yodh:

'dy ('aday I A 1); *bny* (banay I A 2); *b'ly* (ba'alay I A 4); *mlky* (malakay I A [5]); *'lhy* ('ilāhay I A 10); *'bny* ('abanay I A 26); *'py* ('appay I A 28); *nšy* (našay I A 41); *ṭby* (ṭūbay I B 6); *mly* (millay I B 8); *'ly* ('alay I B 26); *śn'y* (śāni'ay I B 26); *mqny* (miqnay I B 27); *'ly* ('elay I B 29); *yqpy* (yāqipay I B 29); *my* (may I B 33); *srsy* (sarīsay I B 45); *rbrby* (rabrabay II A 7); *bty* (bāttay II C 7); *ydy* (yaday III 5); *'yny* ('aynay III 3); *'ḥy* ('aḥay III 4); *pqdy* (paqīday III 4); *ngdy* (nagīday III 10); *'bdy* ('abaday III 13).

The gentilic ending *-āy* (e.g., *'ly* ['illāy I A 6]) should not be confused with this final diphthong *-ay*, for the *yodh* there is consonantal, following a long *a*.

(6) Final Long e Is Represented by Both He and Yodh

(a) *He:*

lylh (laylêh < laylay I A 12); *'rbh* ('arbêh I A 27); *ytzḥh* (yitḥazêh < yitḥazay I A 28); *ṣdh* (ṣadêh I A 33); *'rnh* (? I A 34); *y'th* (yi'têh < yi'tay I B 28); *t'th* (ti'têh I B 31); *tb'h* (tib'êh I B 39); *gdh* (gadêh II A 2); *yhwh* (yihwêh II A 4); *'ryh* (? 'aryêh II A 9); *yb'h* (yib'êh II B 8); *yhwnh* (yuhawnêh II B 16); *tršh* (tiršêh III 9); *trqh* (turaqqêh III 18); *tkh* (tikkêh III 13); *rqh* (? raqêh III 6); *nkh* (nakêh III 13).

Garbini (*RSO* 34 [1959] 42) strangely lists the verb forms *yb'h*, *tršh*, *t'th*, *y'th*, *'rqh*, and *trqh* under *he* as a *mater lectionis* for long *a*.

(b) *Yodh*:

thry (tihrê <tihray I A 21); *thwy* (tihwê I A 25); *ṣby* (ṣabê I A 33); *ytnšy* (yitnašê II A 4); *hwy* (hawê III 22). On the problem that these forms present for the study of early Aramaic orthography, see note on *thry* (I A 21). Cf. the dissertation of a student of F. M. Cross who concludes that "all in all, a mixed paradigm seems called for by the evidence" (M. E. Sherman).[6] Perhaps the form *'lh* (I A 32) should be considered here too; see below §11. Dupont-Sommer restored *krs'* (II B 7; see note there); if correct, this would be a case of final *ê* represented by *aleph*.

N.B. In the following sections dealing with medial vowels the form is not repeated if it occurs merely with a different suffix.

---

6 *Systems of Hebrew and Aramaic Orthography: An Epigraphic History of the Use of Matres Lectionis in Non-Biblical Texts to ca. A.D. 135* (Cambridge, MA: Harvard Divinity School, 1966) 23 [cf. *HTR* 59 (1966) 455-56].

(7) Medial Long a Is Never Represented by a Vowel Letter

'rm ('Arām ? [or 'Aram < Aramm?] I A 5); *'ily* ('illāy I A 6); *'ll* ('ālil I A 6); *śm* (śām I A 7); *qdm* (qudām I A 8); *'lhy* ('ilāhay I A 10); *'lyn* ('elyān I A 11); *m'ynn* (ma'yānīn I A 12); *śhdn* (śāhidīn I A 12); *ḥzyh* (ḥazzāyāh I A 13); *mhynqn* (muhayniqān I A 21); *ymšḥn* (yimšaḥān I A 21); *yhynqn* (yuhayniqān I A 22); *ś'n* (śa'ān I A 23); *yhkn* (yahākān I A 24); *yhrgn* (yihragān I A 24); *ḥl* (ḥāl I A 25); *ql* (qāl I A 29); *knr* (kinnār I A 29); *mrq* (māriq I A 29); *'lhn* ('ilāhīn I A 30); *'kl* ('ākil I A 30); *ss* (sās I A 31); *qāq* (qāq? I A 32); *yšmn* (yašīmān I A 32); *šrn* (šurān I A 33); *bnth* (banātah I A 35); *gnb'* (? I A 36 [perhaps gannābā']); *znyh* (zāniyāh I A [41]); *y'rrn* (yu'rarān I A 41); *yqḥn* (yuqqaḥān I A 42); *śmw* (śāmū I B 6); *'lmn* ('ālamīn I B [7]); *ytšm'n* (yitšama'ān I B [9]); *lbnn* (Libnān I B 9); *bk* (? bāk I B 25); *brk* (barāk I B [25]); *'qrk* ('iqqārāk I B 25); *śn'y* (śāni'ay I B 6); *yqpy* (yāqipay I B 29); *ḥylk* (ḥaylāk I B 31); *'yt* ('iyyāt I B 32); *'bdt* ('abbādūt I B 36); *zkrn* (zikrān I C 2); *'lm* ('ālam I C [9]); *ṭbt* (ṭābāta' [perhaps sg. ṭabata'?] I C 4); *lḥyt* (laḥyāt I C 20); *tḥtyth* (taḥtāyteh I C 23); *'lyth* ('illāyteh I C [24]); *'zn* ('izzān II A [2]); *p-* (? pā- II B 4); *ḥbzthm* (ḥabbāzūt-hum II B 7); *ḥrn* (ḥarān II B 12); *mnk* (minnāk II B 20); *hldt* (haladūt II C 2); *bty* (? bāttay [< bahtay] II C 2); *'n* ('ān II C 3); *ld* (lād II C 6); *šlm* (šalām III 8); *śptyk* (śapātayk III 14); *'nš* ('unāš III 16); *mrmt* (mirmāt III 22); *'ḥrn* ('uḥrān III 24); *qrq* (qāriq III 4); *rḥm* (rāḥim III 8); *hmtty* (perhaps hamātūtī III 11); *ḥlph* (ḥālipeh, or possibly ḥalāpeh III 22[?]); *šbt* (šābat III 25).

The only apparent exception to this list is *'hbd* (II C 5), which is not clearly a case of a long *a*. It must be contrasted with *'h'bd* (II C 4), in which the *aleph* of the root is preserved. It is difficult to say whether it has disappeared in the first form due to quiescence or to mere scribal omission. Dupont-Sommer noted that in later Aramaic the haphel of *'bd* appears as *tĕhôbed*, a form built on analogy with Pe Waw verbs.

(8) Medial Long i Is Usually Not Indicated by a Vowel Letter

mt''l (Matī''el I A 1); *nṣb'* (naṣība' I A [6]); *zrpnt* (zarpanīt I A 8); *m'ynn* (ma'yānīn I A 12); *śhdn* (śāhidīn I A 12); *'l* ('īl I A 22); *šmyn* (šamayīn I A 26); *šnn* (šanīn I A 27); *ḥsr* (ḥaṣīr I A 28); *'lhn* ('ilāhīn I A 30); *yšmn* (yašīmān I A 32); *h'* (hī' I A [33]); *mrbh* (? Marībāh I A 34); *'lmn* ('ālamīn I B [7]); *'dn* ('adīn I B 24); *mlkn* (malakīn I B 26); *ḥyn* (ḥayyīn I B 41); *srsy* (sarīsay I B 45); *'hld* ('uhalīd I C 18); *'śm* ('aśīm I C 19); *'š'* ('īša' I C [21]); *yśmw* (yaśīmū

I C 23); *hmtty* (hamītūtī [possibly hamātūtī? II B 8); *mln* (millīn [see note on III 2]); *ngdy* (nagīday III 10); *pqdy* (paqīday III 4); *srsy* (sarīsay III 5); *ptḥh* (patīḥāh III 8); *špr* (šappīr III 29); *kpryh* (? kapīrayh III 23); *yrb* (yarīb III 17); *hšbw* (hašībū III 24); *hšb* (hašīb III 20); *'hšb* ('ahašīb III 20); *thšbhm* (tuhašībhum III 6); *'rqhm* ('uraqqīhum III 6); *trqhm* (turaqqīhum III 6); *thrm* (tuharīm III 5, 6).

But *šybt* (III 24) stands for *šībat*, and medial long *i* is written with *yodh*. Another case of the full writing of medial long *i* is found in *byr'* (I B 34). *Kym* (III 1) is best understood as *kīm*, probably < *kī-'im*, the particle found in *AP* 34:6; 13:11, compounded with *'ap* in *'pm* in *AP* 6:15. Here the *yodh* represents the final *i* of *kī*. The word *šḥlyn* is also problematic. Is it *šaḥlīn*, with medial long *i* fully written, or *šaḥlayin* (I A 36)?

(9) Medial Long u Is Usually Not Indicated by a Vowel Letter

ysqn (yissaqūn I A 5); *nb'* (Nabū' I A 8); *mṣlh* (maṣūlāh I A [11]); *yšqrn* (yušaqqarūn I A 16); *ssyh* (sūsyāh I A 22); *mlkt* (malkūt I A 25); *'šr* ('aššūr I A 25); *yšlḥn* (yišlaḥūn I A 30); *ygzrn* (yugzarūn I A 40); *ṭby* (ṭūbay I B 6); *yṣrn* (yiṣṣarūn I B 8); *yšm'n* (yišma'ūn I B [21]); *ymlkn* (yimlukūn I B 22); *tšm'n* (tišma'ūn I B [24]); *tšlmn* (tašlimūn I B [24]); *h'* (hū' I B 24); *lygzrn* (lāyigzarūn I B [41]); *ḥbzthm* (ḥabbāzūthum II B 7); *'bdt* ('abbādūt II B 7); *hmtty* (hamītūtī or hamātūtī II B [8]); *hldt* (halādūt II C 2); *yršmn* (yuršamūn II C 3); *ld* (lūd II C 9); *ymt* (yamūt II C [10]; cf. III 16); *yś'n* (yiśśa'ūn II C [13]); *yhskrn* (yuhaskirūn III 3); *yhkn* (yahākūn III 5); *yšbn* (yiššibūn III 6); *yqtln* (yiqtulūn III 11); *yšḥdn* (yišḥadūn III 28); *hmtt* (hamītūt or hamātūt III 11); *'ḥk* ('aḥūk III 18).

But medial long *u* is represented by *waw* in several cases: *tw'm* (? Tū'im I A 34); *rwḥ* (rūḥ III 2); *ymwt* (yamūt III 16); *y'wdn* (ya'ūdūn II B 4; but Segert [*ArOr* 32 (1964) 125] took the form *y'wrn* as pual). These forms must now be considered in connection with *'šwr* ('Aššūr) in Panammu 7, 11, 12, 13, 15, 16, 17, 17; Bar-Rakkab 9; Agbar 7 (*šmwny*); Zakur a 17 (*šwr'*, "wall," in contrast to *šr*, a 10). The form *'šwr*, being a name, is precious evidence for the fact that the phenomenon of representing an internal long vowel by a vowel-letter was known to the Arameans of this period. For in writing a foreign name they would be expected to record it in accordance with their own orthographic habits. In none of these cases is there any reason to look for a diphthong; we simply have an extension of the use of vowel-letters from the final position to a medial position.

(10) Medial aw Is Represented by Waw

bnwh (banawh I A 5); *ywm* (yawm I A 12); *šwrh* (šawrāh I A 23); *twl'h* (tawla'āh I A 27); *š'wt'* (ša'awta' I A 37); *rbwh* (rabbawh I A 39); *t'twn* (ti'tawn I B [32]); *mlwh* (millawh I C 18); *yhwnnh* (yuhawninneh II B 16); *yhwnh* (yuhawnêh II B 16); *ywmyhm* (yawmayhum II C 17); *'pwh* ('appawh III 2); *śn'wh* (śāni'awh III 12); *šrbwh* (? šarabawh III 13); *mwddwh* (mawdidawh III 14); *'ḥwh* ('aḥawh III 17); *'lwh* ('elawh III 8); *śptwh* (śapātawh III 15).

(11) Medial ay Is Represented by Yodh

byt (bayt I A 6; III 21); *'dy'* ('adayya' I A 7); *lylh* (laylêh I A 12); *šmyn* (šamayīn I A 11); *'ynykm* ('aynaykum I A 13); *mhynqn* (muhayniqān I A [21]); *šdyhn* (šadayhen I A [21]); *'lym* ('ulaym I A 22); *byt'l* (bayt'el I A 34); *'yk* ('ayk I A 35); *'ykh* ('aykāh I A 37); *šḥlyn* (šaḥlayin? [see note at the end of §8]); *ḥṣy'* (ḥiṣṣayya' I A 38); *'pyh* ('appayh I A 42); *'lhy'* ('ilāhayya' I B [8]); *mlky'* (malakayya' I B 22); *ḥylk* (ḥaylāk I B 31); *mrḥy'* (? māriḥayya' I B 31); *ḥyn* (ḥayyīn I B [41]); *šyt* (šayt II A 5); *spry'* (siparayya' II C [4]); *btyhm* (bāttayhum II C 16); *ywmyhm* (yawmayhum II C 17); *mly'* (millayya' III 2); *'yny* ('aynay III 3); *'my'* ('ammayya' III 10); *śptyk* (śapātayk III 14); *kpryh* (kapīrayh III 23); *b'lyh* (ba'alayh III 23); *'lyh* ('alayh III 9).

But *bnyhm* (III 18-19) is problematic. According to Cross and Freedman (*EHO*, 24 §4), "There is no evidence for the contraction of diphthongs, ay and aw, in Old Aramaic under any circumstances." That would prevent us from vocalizing this word as *bênayhom* and from deriving it from the prep. *bên-*. Yet the sense of the context forces us to regard the word as a form of this prep. (and not of *bn-*, known in Phoenician and suggested by J. T. Milik). Consequently, the statement of Cross and Freedman has to be modified. Together with this word one should consider the form *tgltplsr* in Panammu 13, 15, 16 and *tgltplysr* in Bar-Rakkab 3, 6. The remarks of Garbini (*AA*, 246) concerning their treatment of *tgltplsr* now seem justified. There is the further case of *'lh* ('alêh, I A 32; cf. III 9 [*'lyh*]). Compare *BMAP* 4:10, 11 (*bnyhm* for *bynyhm*). The reason for maintaining that the diphthong was normally uncontracted in both the case of *ay* and *aw* is the general thesis of Cross and Freedman, who have gathered the pertinent orthographical evidence for the various Northwest Semitic languages. The material of the Sefire inscriptions confirms their general thesis, although it has brought to light some scattered Aramaic examples that show that the treatment of the final diphthong *ay* (especially on *tertiae infirmae* roots) and of medial long vowels and diphthongs was beginning to fluctuate somewhat.

(12) Consonantal Aleph

About the existence of consonantal *aleph* in Old Aramaic there is a difference of opinion between Cross and Freedman, on the one hand, who maintain that final *aleph* is consonantal, and Garbini and Segert, on the other, who regard it as a *mater lectionis*. See also M. Tsevat, "A Chapter on Old West Semitic Orthography."[7]

Commenting on a form like *nṣb'*, Cross and Freedman say, "The article is indicated by aleph, which is of course consonantal. As will be seen, there is no evidence for the early quiescing of aleph in Aramaic" (*EHO*, 24, 33-34). This position is criticized by Garbini who maintains that "l'aramaico antico usava la ' come *mater lectionis* in fine di parola col valore di -*â*, e che conseguentemente lo stato determinato, almeno nel periodo della lingua a noi noto, consisteva in una determinazione di natura vocalica" (*AA*, 247). Most of the examples cited by Garbini there to support his contention, however, are questionable (e.g., *'rbh* certainly represents *'arbêh* [< *'arbay*; cf. Ugaritic *irby*]; the final *he* has nothing to do with the emph. state; *'rqh* is not the emph. state but has the 3d sg. masc. suffix; the enigmatic *rḥbh* is most likely a proper noun [cf. R. Dussaud, *CRAIBL* 1930, 155-56]; *š'wth* is simply not written with final *he*, but with *aleph* [see the plates]!). Indeed, not one of the instances cited is valid evidence to show that the word concerned was written with a final long *a*.

In these inscriptions, prescinding from cases in which *aleph* is used as the first consonant of a word (as in *'l*, either the negative adv. or the prep.), one finds it in both the final and medial position.

(a) *In the final position*:

nṣb' (naṣība' I A [6]); *'dy'* ('adayya' I A7); *nb'* (Nabū' I A 8); *qryt'* (qiryata' I A [33]); *h'* (hī' I A [33]); *mdr'* (? I A 34); *š'wt'* (ša'awta' I A 35); *z'* (za' I A 35); *nbš'* (nabša' I A 36); *h'* (hū' I A 37); *qšt'* (qašta' I A 38); *ḥṣy'* (ḥiṣṣayya' I A 38); *'gl'* ('igla' I A 40); *ymḥ'* (yimḥa' I A 42); *'lhy'* ('ilāhayya' I B [8]); *spr'* (sipra' I B 8); *mlky'* (malakayya' I B 22); *mrḥy'* (? māriḥayya' I B 31); *tś'* (tiśśa' I B 39); *mlk'* (malka' I B [35]); *'pl'* (? I B 43); *ṭbt'* (ṭābāta' I C 4); *šmš'*

7 *The Joshua Bloch Memorial Volume: Studies in Booklore and History* (New York: Public Library, 1960) 82-91.

(šamša' I C 5); *'š'* ('īša' I C [21]); *spry'* (siparayya' II C 2); *'m'* ('amma' III 5) ; *'rḥ'* ('urḥa' III 9); *mly'* (millayya' III 2); *'my'* ('ammayya' III 10); *yś'* (yiśśa' III 15).

(b) *In the medial position*:

br g'yh (Bar-Ga'yāh I A 1); *kd'h* (? I A 10); *ś't* (śa'at I A 21); *ś'n* (śa'ān I A 23); *y'kl* (yi'kul I A 27); *t'kl* (ti'kul I A 27); *t'mr* (tu'mar I A 33); *tw'm* (Tū'im I A 34); *y'dy* (Ya'dī I B 9); *t'mr* (ti'mar I B 24); *śn'y* (śāni'ay I B 26); *y'th* (yi'têh I B 28); *t'th* (ti'têh I B 31); *t'twn* (ti'tawn I B [32]); *t'zl* (ti'zil I B 39); *y'mr* (yi'mar I C 18); *'h'bd* ('uha'bid II C 4 -- cf. *'hbd* II C 5 [see note above §7]); *yś'n* (yiśśa'ūn II C [13]); *r'šy* (ri'šī III 11); *khs'y* (kuhsa'ī, see note on III 17); *y'sr* (yi'sar III 18); *śn'wh* (śāni'awh III 12).

In the case of *h'* (hū' or hī') the *aleph* is clearly consonantal; probably also in *nb'* (Nabū'). The same seems to be true of *z'*. As far as the other words with final *aleph* are concerned, it might seem at first sight that it is impossible to decide whether the *aleph* is consonantal or not. Here we must consider the evidence of the negative *lā*-, which is never written with an *aleph* in these inscriptions. The fact that it is a prefix does not militate against the argument here. If final long *a* were represented by *aleph*, one would certainly find it in the negative (judging from later Aramaic and cognate languages).

In the case of *śn'y* and *śn'wh* the medial *aleph* is clearly consonantal. In most of the other medial cases listed it appears at the end of a closed syllable, where it seems to have retained its character as a radical. Moreover, there are a number of cases of medial long *a* not represented by a vowel letter (see §7 above). Hence, I find no reason to regard *aleph* in these early inscriptions as anything but consonantal, and consequently the emph. ending as *-a'*.

(13) Consonantal He

(a) = *-eh*:

'qrh ('iqqāreh I A [2]); *'šrh* ('ašreh I A 5); *brh* (bireh I A 25); *mlkth* (malkūteh I A 25); *nbšh* (nabšeh I A 37); *yqtlnh* (yiqtulinneh I B 27); *ydh* (yadeh I B 27); *ywmh* (yawmeh I C 15); *byth* (bayteh I C 16); *bh* (beh I C [22]); *tḥtyteh* (taḥtāyteh I C 23); *'lyth* ('illāyteh I C [24]); *šršh* (šuršeh I C [24]); *'šmh* ('ašumeh II A [4]); *qbrh* (qabreh II A [4]); *'rqh* ('arqeh II A 8); *'mh* ('ammeh II B 3); *yhwnnh* (yuhawninneh II B 16); *ml'kh* (mal'akeh III 8); *lh* (leh III 18); *'y<t>h*

('iyyāteh III 13); *tšryh* (tišrayeh III 18); *'srh* ('asureh III 18); *y'brnh* (yi'barinneh III 17); *ḥlph* (ḥālipeh III 22).

(b) = *-ah*:

klh (kullah I A 5); *tḥth* (taḥtah I A 6); *'rqh* ('arqah I A 28); *'ḥwh* ('aḥwah I A 29); *'mh* ('ammah I A 29); *mlkh* (malkah II C 5); *gblh* (gabūlah III 23); *tkwh* (? takkiwah III 13).

(c) = part of *-awh*:

bnwh (banawh I A 5); *rbwh* (rabbawh I A 39); *mlwh* (millawh I C 18); *'pwh* ('appawh III 2); *śn'wh* (śāni'awh III 12); *śgbwh* (? śagbawh III 13); *mwddwh* (mawdidawh III 14); *'ḥwh* ('aḥawh III 17); *'lwh* ('elawh III 8); *śptwh* (śapātawh III 15).

(d) = part of *-ayh*:

'pyh ('appayh I A 42); *kpryh* (kapīrayh III 23); *b'lyh* (ba'alayh III 23); *'lyh* ('alayh III 9 [see note on *'lh* above, §11]).

B. PHONOLOGY

(1) Interdentals: Treatment of the interdentals in these inscriptions conforms entirely to that found in other Old Aramaic inscriptions.[8]

Protosemitic	*Old Aramaic*	*Later Aramaic*	*Canaanite*
ḏ	z	d	z
ṯ	š	t	š
ḏ̣	q	'	ṣ
ṯ̣	ṣ	ṭ	ṣ

ḏ: *zy*, *znh*, *z'*, *zkrn*, *zqn*, *zḥl* (but *ld*)
ṯ: *'šr*, *šwb*, *yšb*, *šm*, *šybt*, *šwrh*, *šbr*, *š'l*, *šḥlyn*(?), *šdyhn*, *yšmn*

8 See G. Garbini, *AA*, 248; S. Moscati, *Il sistema consonantico delle lingue semitiche* (Roma: Istituto Biblico, 1954) 46-47. See also W. Diem, "Das Problem von שׂ im Althebräischen und die kanaanäische Lautverschiebung," *ZDMG* 124 (1974) 221-52, esp. 244-45 (§19); F. M. Fales, "A Cuneiform Correspondence to Alphabetic שׂ in West Semitic Names of the I Millennium B.C.," *Or* 47 (1978) 91-98.

ḏ̣: *qrq*, *'rq*, *rqh*(?), *qq*, *rbq*, *prq*(?), *mrq*
ṯ̣: *ḥpṣ*, *ṣby*, *ḥṣ*, *nṣr*

At the period of these inscriptions the Arameans were most likely still using the Proto-Semitic sounds *ḏ*, *ṯ*, *ḏ̣*, *ṯ̣*, which they represented in writing by the closest-sounding letters of the borrowed Phoenician alphabet. This feature gives to Old Aramaic orthography a peculiar Canaanite quality, which it later lost as the pronunciation of the interdentals evolved. However, certain anomalies are to be noted. For instance, *zrpnt* instead of the usual Akkadian *ṣarpanītu*; the *zayin* reflects the Assyrian popular etymology of the name (see note on Sf I A 8), not a different treatment of an interdental. If Dupont-Sommer's reading and interpretation of *yrt* (I C 24) are correct, and if I am right in dividing *btn* as I have (Sf I A 32), and in explaining it as related to Ugaritic *bṯn*, then one has here the earliest known examples of a Protosemitic *tha* turning up in an Aramaic text as *t*. Cf. AšOstr 11 (*yhtb* = *yhšb*). There is also the uncertain case of *lwd* (instead of *lwz*) in Sf II C 6 and I C 18 (see notes). They are exceptions to the otherwise consistent treatment of the interdentals in these (and other early Aramaic) inscriptions. Perhaps the name of Mati'el's father, *'trsmk*, should be included here too, for it may be an assimilation of *'ṯtrsmk* (< *'štrsmk*).

(2) Assimilated Consonants: In the case of Pe Nun verbs the first consonant is always assimilated to the following consonant, when it has closed a syllable: *ysk*, *tsk* (nsk); *ypq* (npq); *yṣr*, *yṣrw*, *yṣrn* (nṣr); *yś'*, *tś'* (nś'); *yb'* (nb'); *tkh* (nkh); *tqm* (nqm). The only exception is *tnt'* (I B 29, if my division of the letters is correct; see note). Pe Yodh verbs form their impf. on an analogy with the Pe Nun verbs, as in certain cases in later Aramaic: *tqd*, *yqd* (yqd); *'šb* (yšb); *thb* (yhb); *tqp* (yqp); *yrt* (yrt). In each case the second radical must be considered doubled. Assimilation is also found in *'pwh* and *'pyh* ('np). It is hard to say whether analogy or real assimilation is at work in the following forms: *ysq*, *ysqn* (slq); *yqḥ*, *tqḥ*, *yqḥn* (lqḥ), with which one must compare *ylqḥ* (I B 35). On *'hk*, *yhkn*, see note on Sf III 5. *'trsmk* (I A 1) probably belongs here too; see §1 immediately above.

(3) Varia: I have already called attention in the notes to the peculiar word *khs'y* (III 17), which may be an engraver's error or possibly a transitional form. Likewise to be noted is the form *nbš* for the usual *npš* (III 5-6) and *qtl* for the usual *qṭl* (III 11, 18, 21).[9] A new instance of

9 See Garbini, *RSO* 34 (1959) 43; *Ant* 31 (1956) 310-11.

the *b/p* shift is found in *btn* for later Aramaic *ptn* (I A 32). There is also the lack of metathesis of *š* and *t* in the reflexive forms of verbs (I A 29; I B [9]), which are to be contrasted with *yšthṭ* (I A [32]).

C. MORPHOLOGY

I. Pronouns

(1) Personal

(a) *Independent forms*

'nh (Sf I B [24]; I C [2]; II B [5]; II C 8; III 6); *'t* (I B [39]; III 11, 20); *h'* (hū' I B 24, 42ter?; III 8, 13, 22); *h'* (hī' I A 37; III 12, [24]); *'tm* (I B [31]); *hm* (I B 6, [42]). I consider *hw* (III 22, as read by Dupont-Sommer, Garbini) to be erroneous.

(b) *Suffixal forms*

on nouns:

-y (I B 25bis, 27bis, 32, [33], 38, 40bis, 44, 45; I C 3bis, 4, [6]; II B [6bis], 8bis, [8], 13; III 1ter, 3); *-k* (I B [25], 31, [32], 39, 40, 41, 42; II B 5, [5], [6bis], [8]; III 1bis, 3, 6, 11, 12bis, 14, 15bis, 18, [26]); ---; *-h* (-eh I A [5], 25ter, 28, 41; I B 3, 11, [21-22], 27; I C [8], 8, 16bis, 22, 23, 24, 25; II A [4quater], [5], 8; II B 3, 6; II C 14bis, 15; III 7,8); *-h* (-ah I A 5, 6, 28, 29bis, [35]; I B [4], 5; II B [2]; II C 5; III 23); ---; *-km* (I B 21, 32); ---; *-hm* (I B 45; II B 7; II C 16).

-y (-ay I B 26, 27, 29?, 45; II B [13], 14; III 4, 10quinquies, 11, 13quater, 21, [21], 22); *-yk* (-ayk III 14); ---; *-wh* (-awh I A 5, 39, 40, [41]; I B [21]; I C 18-19; II B 2, 3, 6; II C 15; III 2, 13, 14, 15, 16); *-ayh* (-ayh I A 42; III 23bis, 26); ---; *-km* (? I A 13; III 5, 7, 21); ---; *-hm* (II C 16, 17; III 5, 6); *-hn* (I A [21]).

on prepositions:

-y (I B 29?, 33, 38; III 3, 4, 6, 7, 8, 9ter); *-k* (I B 25, 39?, 43; II B [6], 19?, 20; III 22?); ---; *-h* (-eh I C 22; III 18, [20]); ---; *-y* (-ay I B 26, [29]; III 1, 2, 8, 20, 22); *-wh* (III 8); *-yh* (III 9); ---; ---; *-hm*

(III 3, 5, 7, 18, 19, 21); *-hn* (I A 36).

on finite verbs:

-ny (nī I B <28>; III 20); ---; ---; *-h* (-eh I B 27; II B 16; III 17, 18bis); *-h* (III 13?); ---; ---; ---; *-hm* (II B 7; III 26ter); ---.

on infinitives:

-y (II B [8]; III 11, 15).

(2) Demonstrative

znh ("this" masc.): I A 7, 36, 40; I B 8, [23], 28, 33, 37; I C 17; II B [9], [18]; II C [14]; III [4], 14, 17, 23. *z'* ("this" fem.): I A 35, [36], 37, [42]; III 9. *'ln* ("these"): I A 7bis, 38; I B 7, [8], 11, 24, 38; II B [14]; II C 2, 9; III 7, 9, 19, 20, 27.
h' (hū', "that" masc.): I C [22]; II C 6, [10]. *h'* (hī', "that" fem.): I A [33]; I B [34].
'ln ("these, those"): I A 7bis, 38; I B [7], [8], [11], 24, 38; II B [14]; II C [2], 9; III 7, 9, 19, 20, 27.

(3) Determinative-Relative

determinative: *zy* (I A [10]; III 7, [19]).
relative: *zy* (I A 5, 7; I B 2, 6, 22, 23, 28, 31, 33, 34, 35bis; I C 3, 17, 20, 22; II B 2, 4?, 18, 20; II C 8, 13; III 2, 4, 5, 8, 10, 13, 14, 16, 17bis, 20bis, 23, 28, 29bis).
compounded: *mzy* (I A 25); *'yk zy* (I A 35, 38, 39bis, [40], [41); *'ykh zy* (I A 37); *'n zy* (II C 3); *kzy* (III 24); *zyly* (III 20).
conjunction: *zy* (I B 41?; I C 6).

(4) Indefinite

interrogative used as indefinite: *mn* (I B 30; I C 16; II B [7], 9; II C [1]; III 9bis, 10quinquies, 26); *mh* (I A 26bis, 30; I B 2, 26bis, 29?; I C 1; III 3, 16, 28, 29).
'ḥrn (III 24).
kl (cst. st.): I A 6bis, 10, 12, 26bis, 30; I B 2, [8], 22, 23, [26], 29bis, 34, 40; I C 6, 22; II A 7; II B 3, 9, 12, 18; II C 13, 15bis; III 1, 4, 7, 8bis, 14, 16bis, 23, 28, 29, [29].
klh (suffixal): I A 5; I B [4].

kl mh: I A 26bis, 30; I B 2, 26, 29; III 16, 28, 29.

ḥd (abs. st.): III 22; *ḥdh* (fem.): I B 8.

ḥd (cst.): I B 26bis, 28, 30, 45; II B [7]; III 1, [3], 4ter, 5, 9bis, 10quinquies, 13quater, 17.

ḥd (suffixal): *ḥdhm* I B 45; III 19.

II. Nouns and Adjectives

(1) States

Masculine Forms

	Sg.	Pl.
Abs.	*mlk* (I A 6)	*mlkn* (I B 26)
Cst.	*mlk* (I A 1)	*mlky* (I B 41)
Emph.	*spr'* (I B 8)	*mlky'* (I B 22)

Feminine Forms

	Sg.	Pl.
Abs.	*ssyh* (I A 22)	*ś'n* (I A 23)
	ś't (I A 21)	*lḥyt* (I C 20)
Cst.	*qšt* (I A 39)	----
Emph.	*qšt'* (I A 38)	*ṭbt'* (II B 2)
		bkth (? I A 24)

N.B. The archaic ending (*t*) is found for both the abs. fem. sg. (= at) and pl. (= āt).

Abs. sg.: (masc.) *mlk* (I A 6; I B 2, 7, 26, 30?; III 28); *ywm* (I A 12; I B 31; I C 20); *lylh* (I A 12); *'lym* (I A 22); *'l* (I A 22; II A [1]); *'gl* (I A 23; II A [1]); *'mr* (I A 23; II A [2]); *lḥm* (I A 24; I B 38, 39; II A [3]; III 5, 7); *ḥl* (I A 25bis; II A [4]); *'ml* (I A 26); *brd* (I A 26); *'rbh* (I A 27); *twy* (? I A 28); *ḥsr* (I A 28); *yrq* (I A 28); *knr* (I A 29); *mrq* (I A 29); *'qrb* (I A 31); *ss* (I A 31); *qml* (I A 31); *btn* (I A 32); *yšmn* (I A 32); *tl* (I A 32); *ṣy* (I A [32]); *š'l* (I A 33); *'rnb* (I A 33); *šrn* (I A 33); *ṣdh* (I A 33); *'š* (I A 35, 37, [37]); *mlḥ* (I A 36); *rb* (I B 7); *pgr* (I B 30bis; II B 11bis); *byr* (I B [34]); *zkrn* (I C 2); *'lm* (I C [9]; III 24, 25); *'šm* (I C 25); *gdh* (II A 2); *śyt* (II A 5); *'ryh* (II

A 9); *nḥt* (? II B 4); *ḥrn* (II B 12); *ʻlb* (II C 10); *gbr* (III 1); *šlm* (III 8); *ḥrb* (III 13, 14); *'nš* (III 16); *lšn* (III 21); *ṭb* (III 3, 22, 29); *špr* (III 29); *qrq* (III 4); *rḥm* (III 8).

(fem.) *'rq* (I A [11], 26); *mṣlh* (I A [11]); *ś't* (I A 21); *ssyh* (I A 22); *śwrh* (I A 23; II A [1]); *bkth* (? I A 24; II A [3]); *lḥyh* (I A 26; I C [6]); *twlʻh* (I A 27); *ṣʻqh* (I A [29]; II A [8]); *yllh* (I A 30); *ḥwh* (I A 31); *dbhh* (? I A 31); *nmrh* (I A 31; II A [9]); *ʻqh* (I A 33); *bqʻt* (I B 10); *yd* (I B [25], 25, [27], 34; II B [6]); *mlh* (I B [25]); *qryh* (III 12).

Cst. sg.: (masc.) *mlk* (= malk I A 1bis, 3, [13], 14, [15]; I B [1]); *br* (I A 1, 3, 14; I C [3], [8]; II C 14; III 1, 12bis, 15bis, 16, 25, [26]); *ʻqr* (I A 3, 15, [15]; I B 2bis; III 3); *ḥbr* (? I A [4]); *ʻly* (I A 6); *byt* (I A 6; I B 3; I C [6], 7; II A 12?; II B 10bis; III 9, 24bis, [25]); *šṭ* (? I A 24); II A [3]); *ql* (I A 29); *hml* (I A 29); *pm* (I A 30, 31ter; II A 9ter); *qq* (I A 32); *rbq* (I A 32); *gbr* (I A 39; I B 24; II B [5]); *mlk* (= mulk I B 6); *bʻl* (I B [29]); *krs'* (II B [7]); *ywm* (II B 12); *yd* (II B 14; III 11); *lhṣ* (II C 10); *dm* (III 12ter); *lbb* (III 15bis, 16).

(fem.) *nbš* (I B 40); *yd* (II B 14; III 11); *rwḥ* (III 2); *mlkt* (I A 25bis; II A [4]); *hmyt* (I A [29]); *qšt* (I A [38], 39); *gbrt* (I A [42]); *qryt* (? I B 36); *šybt* (III 24).

Emph. sg.: (masc.) *nṣb'* (I A [6]; I C 17); *spr'* (I A [6]; I B 8, [23], 28, 33; I C 17; II B [9], 18; II C 13; III 4, 14, 17, 23); *gnb'* (I A 36); *ʻgl'* (I A 40); *mlk'* (I B [35]); *ngd'* (? I B 36); *'pl'* (I B 43); *šmš'* (I C 5); *'š'* (I C 21); *ʻm'* (III 5, 13).

(fem.) *nbš'* (I A [36]); *qryt'* (I A [33]); *šʻwt'* (I A 35, 37, 39, [42]); *qšt'* (I A 38); *byr'* (I B 34bis); *'rḥ'* (III 9 [see note on gender]).

Suffixal sg.: *bry* (I B 25, 27, 45; I C 3bis; II B [6], 8, 13; III 1bis, 3, 11, 12bis, 15, 17, 26bis); *ʻqry* (I B 25, [32]; II B [6]; III 1, 3, 11, 12, 16, 21, 22, 26); *byty* (I B 32, 40, 44; III 21); *lḥmy* (I B 38); *'šry* (I C [4]); *mlky* (I C [6]); *'by* (II B 8; III 10, 23, [24], [25], 25); *r'šy* (II B [8]; III 11); *ḥpṣy* (III 8); *ml'ky* (III 8); *qrqy* (III 19); *dmy* (III 11, [22]); *khs'y* (III 17); *ʻmy* (III 21).

(fem.) *'rqy* (I B 27); *nbšy* (I B 40); *sḥrty* (III 7).

brk (I B 25, 41; II B [6]; III 1, 2, 11, 12, 15); *ʻqrk* (I B [25], 32; II B [6]; III 1, 3, 12, 15, [26]); *ḥylk* (I B [28], 31); *bytk* (I B 40); *lbbk* (II B [5]; III 14); *lšnk* (III 17); *'ḥk* (III 18).

(fem.) *nbšk* (I B 39, 42; II B 5, [8]); *'rqk* (III 6).

ʻqrh (I A [2], 25, 41; II A [4]; II B 6; II C 15; III 13, 25); *'šrh* (I A [5]; I B 3; III 7); *tḥth* (I A 6); *brh* (I A 25; I C 8bis; II A [4]; II C

11, 14bis; III 25bis); *'mh* (I B 11, [21]; II B 3); *ywmh* (I C 15); *byth* (I C 16, 22; III [24]); *tḥtyth* (I C 23); *'lyth* (I C 24); *šršh* (I C [24]); *'šmh* (II A [4]); *qbrh* (II A [4]); *ml'kh* (III 8).

(fem.) *'rqh* (II A 8); *ydh* (I B 27; III 2); *mlkth* (I A 25; II A [4]); *nbšh* (I A 37); *'ḥwh* (I A 29, 32); *'mh* (I A 29, 30; I B 5; II B [2]); *gblh* (III 23).

(fem.) *'rqh* (I A 28).

bytkm (I B 21); *ḥylkm* (I B 32); *'šrkm* (III 5); *mr'km* (III 21); *tḥtkm* (III 7).

'šmhm (II B 7); *'šrthm* (I B 11); *'mhm* (II C 16); *qrqhm* (III 19).

(fem.) *nbšhm* (III 5, 6).

Abs. pl.: (masc.) *šmyn* (I A 11, 26; I B 7); *m'ynn* (I A 12); *'lhn* (I A 30; I B 6bis, 31; I C 15, 21; II B 2; III 24bis); *šḥlyn* (I A 36); *'lmn* (I B [7]); *'dn* (I B 24, 41; II B [5]); *mlkn* (I B 26, 28); *ḥyn* (I B [41]).

(fem.) *ś'n* (I A 23; II A [2]); *šnn* (I A 27bis, [27]; II A 5, 6); *'zn* (II A [2]); *mln* (III 2); *mrmt* (III 22); *lḥyt* (I C 20; III 2).

Cst. pl.: (masc.) *'dy* (A I 1bis, 2, 3, [3], 4ter, 13; I B 1bis, 4quater, 5bis, 6); *bny* (I A 2quater, [16]; I B 1bis, [1], [2], 3; II B 13; III 21quater); *b'ly* (I A 4bis; I B 4, [5]); *mlky* (I A [5]; I B 41; II B 3; II C 15; III 1, 3, 16, 27); *'lhy* (I A 10, [12bis]; I B 5, [5], 23, 33; II B [9], [18]; II C [13]; III 4, 14, 17, 23); *'bny* (I A [26]); *'py* (I A 28); *ṭby* (I B 6); *my* (I B 33, 34); *rbrby* (II A 7); *bty* (II C 2, 7, 9).

(fem.) *nšy* (I A 41ter, [42]); *mly* (I B 8; I C 17).

Emph. pl.: (masc.) *'dy'* (I A 7bis; I B 7bis, 11, 23, 24, [28], 33, 38; II B 2, [9], [14], 18; II C [13]; III 4, 7, 9, 14, 17, 19, 20, 23, 27); *ḥsy'* (I A 38; I B 29); *'lhy'* (I B [8]; II C 3, 7, 10); *mlky'* (I B 22; III 7); *mrḥy'* (I B 31); *spry'* (II C 2, 4, 6, [9]); *mly'* (III 2); *'my'* (III 10).

(fem.) *ṭbt'* (I C [5, possibly sg.], 19; II B 2).

Suffixal pl.: *śn'y* (I B 26; II B 14; III 10, 11); *mqny* (I B 27); *srsy* (I B 45; III 5); *bny* (II B [7], [13]; III 10, 21, 22); *pqdy* (III 4, 10, 13); *'ḥy* (III 4, 9, 13, 21); *ngdy* (III 10); *'bdy* (III 13).

(fem.) *'yny* (III 3); *ydy* (III 2, 5, 10, 13).

śptyk (III 14).

bnwh (I A 5; I B [21]; II B 2, 6); *rbwh* (I A 39, 40, [41]; II B 3; II C 15); *śn'wh* (III 12); *šrbwh* (III 13); *mwddwh* (III 14); *'ḥwh* (III 17); *'pwh* (III 2).

(fem.) *mlwh* (I C 18); *śptwh* (III 15, 16).

'pyh (I A 42); *kpryh* (III 23, 26); *b'lyh* (III 23, 26).
(fem.) *bnth* (I A [35]);
(fem.) *'ynykm* (I A 13).
btyhm (II C 16); *ywmyhm* (II C 17).

(2) Gender

Some feminine nouns have masculine forms: *yd* (I B 25; III 11); *ydy* (III 2, 5, 10, 13); *ydh* (I B 27; III 2); *'yny* (III 3); *'ynykm* (I A 13); *'rq* (I A 26); *'rqk* (III 6); *nbš* (I B 40); *nbšy* (I B 40); *nbšk* (I B 39); *nbšh* (I A 37); *nbšhm* (III 5, 6); *mln* (III 2); *mly* (I B 8); *mlwh* (I C 18); *nšy* (I A 41); *šnn* (I A 27); *byr'* (I B 34bis); *'rḥ'* (III 9); *'* ("fire," I A 35, 37, [37]).

III. Verbs

(1) Conjugations and Forms Attested

Pf.	Impf.	Impv.	Infin.	Ptc.
			Peal	
gzr (I A 7)	*ymlk* (I A 25)		*śgb* (I B 32)	Act.:
hwt (III 24)	*tštq* (I B 8)		*mšlḥ* (I B 34)	*'kl* (I A 30)
	tmšl (III 9)	*qtl* (III 18)	*nkh* (III 12)	*znyh* (I A [41
				śhdn (I A 12
ktbt (I C 2)	*'šlḥ* (I B 24)			*yqpy* (I B 29
śmw (I B 6)	*y'bdw* (I C 5)			
	tpnw (III 7)			Pass.:
				ptḥh (III 8)
	ymlkn (I B 22)			
	ymšḥn (fem. I A 21)			
	tš'mn (I B 24)	*qtlw* (III 21)		
ktbn (I C 1)				
			Yuqtal	
	ygzr (I A 40)			
	tšbr (I A 38)			
	ygzrn (I A 40)			
	y'rrn (I A 41)			

Ithpeel

yṫšm‘ (I A 29)
tt‘bd (I C [7])
ytšm‘n (I B [9])

Pael

ymll (III 1)
ḥzyh (I A 13)
’bdt (I B 36)
rt (I B 38) *trqh* (III 18)
zw (III 24) *’rqhm* (III 6)
rtm (III 4)
rqw (III 6)

Ithpaal

yštḥt (I A [32])

Haphel

šb (III 20) *yhskr* (III 3)
yhwnh (II B 16)
thrm (III 5, 6)
’hld (I C 18)
šbw (III 24) *yhskrn* (III 3)
yhynqn (fem. I A 22)
hskr (III 2)
hmtt (III 11)
hmtty (III 11)
mhynqn (I A [21])

Aphel

yskr (III 3)
y‘brnh (III 17)
tšlmn (I B 24)

Ophal

y‘r (I A 39)

(2) Suffixal Forms

Peal: *yqtlnh* (I B 27); *ysbn<y>* (I B 28); *y‘brnh* (III 17); *t‘šqny* (III

20 ?); the foregoing forms are energic imperfect. But the suffix is also found on the ordinary impf.: *tkwh* (III 13?); *tšryh* (III 18). On the impv.: *'srh* (III 18); on the ptc.: *qrqy* (III 19); *qrqhm* (III 19-20).
Pael: *trqhm* (III 6); *'rqhm* (III 6); *ḥbzthm* (II B 7).
Haphel: *thšbhm* (III 6); *thskrhm* (III 2); *yhwnnh* (II B 16); on the infin.: *hmtty* (III 11, 15; II B [8]).

(3) Classes of Verbs Represented

(a) Strong Verbs:
gzr (I A 7); *ygzr* (I A 40bis); *tgzr* (I B 43); *ygzrn* (I A 40; I B [41]); *šqrt* (I B [21], [33], [36], 38; II B [17]; III 9, 14, 19, 20, 27); *šqrtm* (I B 23; II B 9, 14; III 4, 7, 16, 23); *yšqr* (I A 14, 15, 24; II A [3]); *yšqrn* (I A [16]); *ymlk* (I A 25; I B [3]); *ymlkn* (I B 22); *yqtl* (II B 9bis; III 18); *yqtln* (III 11); *yqtlnh* (I B 27); *qtlw* (impv. III 21); *ktbt* (I C 2); *ktbn* (I C [1]); *yšbr* (I A 38); *tšbr* (I A 38); *tštq* (I B 8); *tšlmn* (I B [24]); *śgb* (I B 32bis); *prq* (I B 34); *yqrq* (I B 45; III 4, 19bis); *qrq* (ptc. III 4); *qrqy, qrqhm* (ptc. with suffix, III 19); *yzqn* (II B 8); *ygbr* (II B 19); *yršmn* (II C 3); *yhskr* (III 3); *yhskrn* (III 3); *thskrhm* (III 2); *hskr* (infin. III 2); *yskr* (aphel III 3); *tmšl* (III 9).

(b) Pe Nun Verbs:
ysk (I A [25],26); *tsk* (I B 38; III 5, 7); *ypq* (I A 28); *tnt'* (I B 29?); *ysr* (I C 17); *yṣrw* (I C 15); *yṣrn* (I B 8); *yś'* (III 15, 16, 26); *tś'* (I B 39; III 14); *yś'n* (II C [13]); *yb'* (II B 8); *nkh* (infin. III 12, 13); *tkh* (III 13); *tkwh* (III 13); *yqm* (III 12ter, 22); *tqm* (III 11); *ytnšy* (II A [14]).

(c) Pe Laryngalis Verbs:
'bdw (II B 2); *y'bd* (I C [20]); *t'bd* (I B [26]; III 22); *''bd* (III 3); *y'bdw* (I C 5); *tt'bd* (I C [7]); *yhrgn* (I A 24; II A [3]); *'hpk* (I C 19); *t'št* (II B 5); *ḥbzw* (III 24); *ḥbzthm* (II B 7); *y'brnh* (III 17); *t'šqny* (III 20).

(d) Pe Yodh Verbs:
mhynqn (I A [21]); *yhynqn* (I A 22bis, 23bis); *yqd* (I A 37); *tqd* (I A 35bis, 37); *tqp* (I B 29); *yqpy* (I B 29); *thb* (I B 38); *yrt* (I C 24); *yšb* (III 17); *'šb* (II B [7]); *yšbn* (I1I 6); *šbw* (III 7); *yhwnnh* (II B 16); *yhwnh* (II B 16); *yd'* (II C 8 ?).

(e) Pe Aleph Verbs:
y'kl (I A 27, [30]; II A [9]); *t'kl* (I A 27); *'kl* (I A 30); *'mrn* (I C 1);

y'mr (I C 18; II B [7]; II C [1], 4, 7, [8]); *t'mr* (= ti'mar I A 36?; I B 24, 26; II B 5, [8]; III 5, 7, 18, 21); *t'mr* (= tu'mar I A 33); *'bdt* (I B 36; II B 7); *'h'bd* (II C 4); *'hbd* (II C 5); *y'th* (I B 28bis, 32, [45] ; II B 13; III 11, 12bis, 20); *t'th* (I B 31; III 11); *t'twn* (I B [32]); *t'zl* (I B 39); *y'sr* (III 18); *'srh* (impv. with suff. III 18); *'gr* (II C 8).

(f) Ayin Laryngalis Verbs:
śhdn (I A 12); *yštḥṭ* (I A [32]); *ykhl* (I B 25, [34]); *tkhl* (I B [39]); *'khl* (I B [24], 33; II B 6); *yzḥl* (II C 6); *yb'h* (III 2, 11); *rḥm* (ptc. III 8); *yšḥdn* (III 28).

(g) Ayin Waw Verbs:
y'r (1 A 39bis); *y'wdn* (II B 4); *ymt* (II C 10); *ymwt* (III 16); *hmtt* (III 11, 15, 16); *hmtty* (II B [8]; III 11, 15); *ld* (II C 6, 9); *hldt* (II C 2); *'hld* (I C 18); *'hk* (III 6); *yhkn* (I A 24; II A [3]; III 5); *hšb* (III 20); *'hšb* (III 20); *hšbw* (III 24); *thšbhm* (III 6); *šbt* (III 25); *thrm* (III 5, 6).

(h) Ayin Yodh Verbs:
śm (I A 7); *śmw* (I B 6); *'śm* (I C 19); *yśmw* (I C 23); *yrb* (III 17, [26bis], 26).

(i) Ayin Ayin Verbs:
ymll (I B [26]; III [1], 2); *y'l* (I B 35); *'ll* (I A 6); *t'rr* (I A [40]); *y'rrn* (I A 41); *ysbn*<*y*> (I B 28); *ysb* (I B 34); *y'zz* (I B 44); *y'z* (II B 20).

(j) Lamedh Laryngalis Verbs:
yqḥ (I B 27); *ylqḥ* (I B 35bis); *tqḥ* (I A [42]; III 2); *yqḥn* (I A 42); *yšlḥ* (I B 25, [26], 27; III 8); *tšlḥ* (I B 37; III 17, 21); *'šlḥ* (I B 24; II B 6; III 8); *yšlḥn* (I A 30); *mšlḥ* (I B 34); *yšm'* (I B 21, [21]; II B [2], 3); *tšm'* (II B 4); *'šm'* (II B [5]); *yšm'n* (I B [21], [22]; II B 2, 3bis); *tšm'n* (I B [24]); *ytšm'* (I A 29); *ytšm'n* (I B 9); *yzr'* (I A 36); *yśb'* (I A 22bis, 23bis; II A [1], 1, [2bis]); *pqḥw* (I A 13); *ymšḥn* (I A 21); *ptḥh* (III 8).

(k) Tertiae Infirmae Verbs:
hwt (III 24); *hwy* (III 22); *thwy* (I A 25, 32; II A [4], 6); *yhwh* (II A 4); *yhww* (I A [31]; *ḥzyh* (I A 13); *ytḥzh* (I A 28bis); *yb'h* (II B 8; III 2, 11); *tb'h* (I B 39; II B 17); *thry* (I A 21); *ytnšy* (II A 4); *y'th* (I B 28bis, 32, [45]; II B 13; III 11, 12bis, 20); *t'th* (I B 31; III 11); *t'twn* (I B [32]); *šlw* (III 5); *rqh* (infin. III 6, 18); *trqh* (III 18, 19); *rqw*

(impv. III 6); *trqhm* (III 6); *'rqhm* (III 6); *nkh* (III 12, 13); *tkh* (III 13); *tkwh* (III 13); *tršh* (III 9); *tpnw* (III 7); *tśryh* (III 18); *znyh* (I A [41]).

(l) Lamedh Aleph Verbs:
ymḥ' (I A 42); *yś'* (III 15, 16, 26); *tś'* (I B 39; III 14); *yś'n* (II C [13]); *'rb'* (I B 30).

(m) Special Verb:
ysq (slq, I A 27; I B [3]; III 14, 15bis, 16); *ysqn* (I A 5; I C 4).

IV. Adverbs and Particles

(1) *'yk*: I A 35, 38, 39, [39], [40], [41].
(2) *'ykh*: I A 37.
(3) *'yt* (sign of accusative): I B 32; II B [8]; II C 5bis, 14; *'yty*: III 11; *'y<t>h*: III 13.
(4) *'l* (negative): I A 21, 22bis, 23bis, 24, 28, 29, 33, 36; I B 8; I C 24; II A [1bis], [2], 2, [3]; III 7, 18, [20].
(5) *'n*: II C 3.
(6) *hn* (emphatic): I B 36; III 4, 9, 14, 20.
(7) *kh*: I C 1, [1].
(8) *kym*: III 1 (see note).
(9) *kn*: I A 35, 37, 38, 39, 40, 41, 42; I B 43; I C 21.
(10) *k't* (temporal): III 24.
(11) *l-* (prefixed negative): I A 28bis; I B 21, [21bis], [22], [24bis], 5, [25], 31, [32bis], 34, 36, 38bis, [39], 39, 41; I C [7], 17; II B [2], 2, 3ter, 6bis, 16?, 17; II C 8?; III 4, 5ter, 6, 9ter, 14, 17, 18bis, 19, 20, 21, 22?.
(12) *l-* (sign of accusative): I C 4(?).
(13) *šm* (local): III 6.

V. Prepositions

(1) *'l* ('el): II B [13]; III 1ter, 19; *'ly*: I B [29]; III 8, 20; *'lwh*: III [8].
(2) *b-*: I A 5, 24, 26bis, 29bis, 30bis, 35, 37bis; I B 3, 12, 22, [23], 25ter, [27], [28], 28, 30, 31bis, 32, 33, 34, 36, 38, 41?; I C 4, 17, 20; II A [3], 7; II B 2, [2], 5bis, 6bis, [8], [9], 12, [14], 16, 18; II C 10, 13; III 2, 3, 4, 5, 6, 7bis, 9bis,

10, 13bis, 14bis, 16, 17, 19, 20, 21, 23, 27; *by*: III 9; *bk*: I B 25; II B [6]; *bh*: I C [22]; *bhn*: I B 36.

(3) *bn-* (bên-): *bnyhm*: III 18bis, 19.

(4) *k-*: I A 25; II A [4].

(5) *l-*: I A 13, [14], [15], [24], 25, 32bis; I B [7], 13, 21, 23bis, 26, 32bis, 33, [34], 34, [36], 40ter, [40], 42; I C 2, 3, [3], [6], [20], [23]; II A 3bis, [4]; II B [5], 7bis, [8], 9, 12, 18; II C 2, 4, 7; III 2, 3bis, 4, 7, 8bis, 11bis, 14, 15bis, 16bis, 23ter, 24, 25quater; *ly*: I B 29, 38; III 3, 6, 8, 9bis, 20; *lk*: I B 39; II B 19?; *lh*: III 18, [20]; *lhm*: III 3, 5bis, 7bis, 21.

(6) *mn*: I A 20, 30; I B 8, [9], 9, [10bis], 27bis; I C 15, 16, 18; II B 14; II C 2, 6, 7, 9, 16bis; III 2, 11, 12; *mny*: III 4, 6, 7; *mk*: III 22; *mnk*: II B 20; *mnhm*: I B 41; *m-*: I B 7?, 30.

(7) *'d*: I B 9bis, 10bis; I C [8]; II B 19?; III [24], 25.

(8) *'l* ('al): I A 26, 28, 42; I B 44, [45], 45; I C [7]; II B [7], 11; III 1ter, 5, 14bis, 15ter, 16bis, 17, 22bis, 26; *'ly*: I B 26; III 1, 22; *'lh* I A 32; *'lyh*: III 9; compounded: *l'ly*: III 2; *m'l*: I B 30.

(9) *'m*: I A 1, 2, 3bis, 4, 5quater, 6bis, [13]; I B 1, 2bis, 3ter, 4bis, 5bis, 11, [29]; III [26]; *'my*: I B 33; *'mk*: I B 43.

(10) *qdm* : I A [7], 8bis, [8], 9ter, [9], 10, [10], 11ter, [11], 12.

(11) *tḥt*: I C [5].

VI. Conjunctions

(1) *'w*: I B 26, 27, 35, 45; I C 19; III 1sexies, 4bis, 5, 8ter, 9, 10quinquies, 13ter, 17, 18, 22bis.

(2) *hn*: I A 14, [15], [16], 24; I B [23], [25], 28, 31, [32], 36, 37, 38, 43; II A [3]; II B 4, 5, [7], 16, 17; III 4bis, 6bis, 9bis, 11, 12, 13, 14bis, 15, 16, 17, 18, 19, 20bis, [22], [26], 27.

(3) *w-*: *passim*.

(4) *zy*: I B 41; I C [6]; compounded with prepositions: *kzy*: III 24; *mzy*: I A 25.

(5) *ky*: III 22.

(6) *'d*: III 6.

(7) *p-*: II B 4, 6.

D. SYNTAX

1. Pronouns

(1) Personal

(a) *Independent forms:*

(i) As subject: The personal pronoun may either precede or follow the verb; often it scarcely supplies any emphasis. Thus *'nh 'gr 'gr*, "I shall engage (you) indeed" (II C 8); *mh ktbt 'nh mt''l lzkrn,* "what I, Mati'el, have written (is to act) as a reminder" (I C 2). Similarly: *'d 'hk 'nh w'rqhm* (III 6); *'t t'th* (III 11); *w'l tšqny 't* (III 20); *w'tm lt'twn* (I B 31); *w't ltkhl ltś'* (I B 39); *wyzḥl h' mn ld* (II C 6); *ymt h' wbrh* (II C 10); *h' hwt* (III 24).

A special function of the independent form is that of subject of a nominal sentence: *whn ḥd 'ḥy h'*, "if it is one of my brothers" (III 13); *ky lṭb h' mk*, "for he is not better than you" (III 22). Similarly: *wnbšh h'* (I A 37); *whn qryh h'* (III 12); *zy 'dn ḥyn hm* (I B [41-42]); *w'dy 'lhn hm* (I B 6); *gbr 'dn 'nh* (II B [5]).

(ii) As present tense copula: *kl zy rḥm h' ly,* "anyone who is a friend of mine" (III 8); *gbr 'dn h' 'nh,* "I am an ally" (I B 24).

(iii) As the remote demonstrative: See below (I A [33]; I B [34]; I C 22).

(b) *Suffixal forms*: There are many instances of the pronominal suffix on nouns, expressing a genitival relationship, and on prepositions (see Morphology I 1 b; II 1). What is striking here is the lack of the prospective or the resumptive suffix that is found so frequently in later Aramaic. The only forms that call for some comment are the suffixes on verbal forms. These are mainly of two sorts:

(i) Object suffixes: *lhmtty,* "to kill me" (II B [8]; III 11, 15); *'l t'šqny,* "you shall not try to hinder me" (III 20); *yqpy,* "those surrounding me" (I B 29). Similarly: *ysbn<y>* (I B 28); *'srh* (III 18); *yhwnnh* (II B 16); *y'brnh* (III 17); *yqtlnh* (I B 27); *tšryh* (III 18); *tkwh,* "strike it" (3d sg. fem., III 13); *lḥbzthm* (II B 7); *thskrhm* (III 2); *trqhm* (III 6); *'rqhm* (III 6).

(ii) Genitival suffixes: *ḥlph,* "his successor" (if the form is participial, III 22 [see note]); *qrqy,* "my fugitive" (III 19); *qrqhm* (III 19).

(2) Demonstrative

The demonstrative pron. is either used absolutely or in a form of apposition modifying a noun in the emphatic state.

(a) *Absolute usage: ltmšl by bz' wltršh ly 'lyh,* "you must not (try to) dominate me in this (respect) or assert your authority over me concerning it," the pronoun refers to "road" in the preceding clause (III 9).

(b) *Attributive usage:* The pron. functions as an adj., agreeing in gender and number with the noun in the emph. state which precedes. Thus, *'yk zy ygzr 'gl' znh,* "just as this calf is cut in two" (I A 40). Similarly: *spr' znh* (I A [6]; I B [8], [23], 28, 33; II B [9], [18]; II C [14]; III [4], 14, 17, [23]); *bnṣb' znh* (I C 17); *gnb' znh* (I A 36); *š'wt' z'* (I A 35, 37, [42]); *nbš' z'* (I A [36]?); *byr' h'* (I B [34]); *'š' h'* (I C 22); *qryt' h'* (I A [33]); *'dy' 'ln* (I A 7bis; I B [7], [8], [11], 24, 38; II B [14]; III 7, 9, 19, 20, 27); *spry' 'ln* (II C [2], 9); *tšbr qšt' wḥsy' 'ln,* "(just as this) bow and these arrows are broken" (I A 38); this expression is not elegant, for the sentence begins with the fem. sg. verb, with which *qšt'* agrees, but then follows another subject in the pl., with the dem. adj. added as a sort of afterthought.

(3) Determinative-Relative

The pron. *zy* is found in these texts most frequently as a relative, either alone (as a simple or general relative) or in combination with other words.

(a) *Simple Relative:* The pron. in this case is preceded by an antecedent to which the *zy*-clause acts as an appositive. In the clause itself the pronoun may have different functions:

(i) *zy* as subject of a verbal clause: *'m bnwh zy ysqn b'šrh,* "with his sons who will come after him" (I A 5; cf. I C 3); *kl mh mlk zy ysq wymlk,* "any king who will come up and rule" (I B 2; cf. III 28). Similarly: *zy ymlkn* (I B 22); *zy ysb* (I B 34); *zy y'l wylqḥ* (I B 35); *zy y'wrn* (II B 4); *zy y'z mnk* (II B 20); *kl gbr zy yb'h rwḥ 'pwh* (III 2); *zy yšb 'l khs'y* (III 17).

(ii) *zy* as subject of a nominal clause: *'dy' zy bspr' znh,* "the treaty which is in this inscription" (I B [23], 28, 33; II B [9], 18; II C 13; III 4, 14, 17, 23); *spr' zy bnṣb' znh,* "the inscription which is on this stele" (I C 17). Similarly: *wkl zy bh* (I C 22); *kl zy rḥm h' ly* (III 8); *zy bydy* (III 5, 10, 13); *kl mh zy špr wkl mh zy ṡ ṭb* (III 29).

(iii) *zy* as object of a verbal clause: *'dy' 'ln zy gzr br g'yh,* "this treaty which Bar-Ga'yah concluded" (I A 7). Similarly: *'dy 'lhn hm zy śmw 'lhn* (I B 6); *zy 'bdw* (II B [2]).

(iv) *zy* used with adverbial force: *bywm zy y'bd kn,* "on any day on which he will do so" (I C 20). Similarly: *bywm zy ...* (I B 31); *bkl mh zy ymwt* (III 16).

(b) *General Relative:* The pron. in this case functions doubly, in the main clause and in the relative clause itself. Thus *wy'mr lzy lyd'*, "and should he say to someone who does not understand" (II C 8); *hn hšb zy ly 'hšb zy lh,* "if he has restored mine, I shall return his" (III 20). In this last instance the form *zy ly* functions almost like the later common poss. pron.; but possibly it retains here its basic meaning, "that which is to me ...."

(c) *Combinatory Usage:* The pron. *zy* is also found with various preps. or advs., composing with them what appears to be a separate conjunction. Thus *'n zy,* "where": *bty 'lhy 'n zy y[r]šmn,* "the bethels, where they are written" (II C 3). *'yk(h) zy,* "just as ": *'yk zy tšbr qšt' whṣy' 'ln,* "just as (this) bow and these arrows are broken" (I A 38). Similarly: I A 35, 37, 39, [39], [40], [41]. *kzy,* "when": *wkzy ḥbzw 'lhn byt 'by,* "and when the gods struck my father's house" (III 24). *mzy,* "as long as": *mzy ymlk 'šr,* "as long as Asshur rules" (I A 25).

In two instances the simple *zy* has a nuance that may have developed from some combined usage: *zy 'dn ḥyn hm,* "because it is a living pact" (I B 41 [but the reading and interpretation are not certain]); *zy kl lḥyh ltt'bd 'l byt mt''l,* "that no evil may be done against the house of Mati'el" (I C 6).

(d) *Determinative Usage:* In three instances the pron. *zy* seems to function in the manner of the determinative pron. that is so common in later Aramaic, expressing a genitival relationship and being a substitute for the construct chain. Thus *wmlkn zy sḥrty,* "and as for kings of my vicinity" (III 19); *wkl mlky' zy sḥrty,* "now as for all the kings of my vicinity" (III 7); *hdd zy ḥlb*, "Hadad of Aleppo" (I A [11]; but see Fakh 1, 13bis, 17, 23; cf. Degen, *AG*, 89 [§68]). Possibly one should also include II A 12 (*zy byt*).

(4) Indefinite

(a) *'ḥrn,* "another." This pron. occurs only as the object of the prep. *l-* (III 24).

(b) *kl*, "all." The form is either construct or suffixal.

(i) Construct: *kl 'lhy 'dy',* "all the gods of the treaty" (I B 23; II B 9, 18; II C 13; III 4, 14, 16, 23); *kl 'lhy rḥbh* (I A 10); *kl 'lhy ktk* (I A 12); *kl mlky 'rpd* (II B [3]; II C 15); *kl mlky'* (I B 22; III 7); *kl zy ysb* (I B 34; cf. I C 22; III 8); *kl 'ly 'rm* (I A 6); *kl 'll byt mlk* (I A 6); *kl 'lhy'* (I B 8); *kl b'l ḥṣy'* (I B 29); *kl nbš* (I B [40]); *kl lḥyh* (I C [6]); *bkl rbrby* ... (II A 7); *kl rbwh* (II C 15); *kl gbr zy* (III 1); *lkl ḥṣpy* (III 8); possibly II B 12.

A special instance of the construct use is found with *mh*, when the combined *kl mh* forms an indefinite pron. "anyone at all": I A 26bis, 30; I B 2, 26, 29; III 16, 28, [29], 29.

(ii) Suffixal form: One clear instance is found in I A 5, *'m 'rm klh*, "with all Aram," lit., "with Aram, all of it." The same form is restored in I B 4. Cf. "The Syntax of כלא ,כל in the Aramaic Texts from Egypt and in Biblical Aramaic," *Bib* 38 (1957) 170-84, esp. 183-84.

(c) *mn:* Actually this pron. means "who?" and is an interrogative. But in these texts it is found only as a general relative or an indefinite pronoun. The former is found in I C 16: *wmn lyṣr,* "whoever will not observe." Cf. *wmn y'mr* (II C 1); *mn yś'* (III 26), where it functions as a subject in the relative clause. In II B 9 (*yqtl mn yqtl,* "let him kill whomever he would kill") it is the object. More frequently it occurs as an indefinite pron., often combined with *ḥd.* It precedes the noun it modifies, which may be either pl. or a collective sg. Thus, *mn ḥd mlk,* "some king" (I B 30); *mn ḥd byt 'by,* "anyone of my father's household" (III 9); *mn ḥd bny,* "anyone of my sons" (II B [7]; III 10). Similarly: *mn ḥd 'ḥy* (III 9); *mn ḥd ngdy* (III 10); *mn ḥd pqdy* (III 10); *mn ḥd 'my'* (III 10); *mn ḥd śn'y* (III 10).

(d) *mh:* "What?" This pron. occurs in its interrogative function in I B 26 (*mh t['bd],* "what are you going to do?"). Otherwise it is used as an indefinite pron. either combined with *kl* and preceding a sg. noun (see b above) or preceding *zy* (III 16, 29, [29]) or as a general relative (I C 1; III 3).

(5) Numeral

Only two numbers occur in these texts, *ḥd*, "one," and *šb',* "seven." Aside from the instances of *mn ḥd,* mentioned above, the cst. *ḥd* occurs frequently, functioning either as the subject or object of a verb. Thus, as subject: *ḥd mlkn* (I B 26, 28); *ḥd śn'y* (I B 26); *ḥd pqdy* (III 4, [13]); *ḥd 'ḥy* (III 4, 13); *ḥd srsy* (III 4); *ḥd 'bdy* (III 13); *ḥd 'm'* (III 13). As object of a verb: *ḥd 'ḥwh* (III 17). As object of a preposition: *'l ḥd mlky 'rpd* (III 1); *'l ḥd srsy* (I B 45). The absolute masc. *ḥd* occurs only in III 22, as the subject of a verb (*wyqm ḥd dmy,* "someone will avenge my blood"). Its fem. counterpart is used similarly in I B 8 (*w'l tštq ḥdh mn mly spr'*). The suffixal form *ḥdhm* functions as the subject of a verb (I B 45) and as the object of a prep. (III 19).

The numeral *šb'*, found only in this masc. form, precedes in these texts fem. nouns, either sg. or pl.: *šb' ssyh*, "seven mares" (I A 22), acting as the subject of a pl. verb. Similarly: *šb' šwrh* (I A [22]; II A [1]); *šb' bkth* (I A 24; II A [3]); but *šb' ś'n yhynqn* (I A 23; II A 1); *šb' 'zn* (II A [2]); *šb' mhynqn* (I A [21]). As an adverbial construction, one finds *šb' šnn,* "for seven years" (I A 27ter; II A [5], [6]).

II. Nouns

(1) Apposition: The juxtaposition of a noun with either another noun or a pronoun. Thus: *mh ktbt 'nh mt''l lzkrn lbry*, "what I, Mati'el, have written (is to act) as a reminder for my son" (I C 2); *'m mt''l br 'trsmk*, "with Mati'el, son of 'Attarsamak" (I A 1, 3, 14; I B 13); *'dy br g'yh mlk ktk*, "the treaty of Bar-Ga'yah, the king of KTK" (I A 1, [15]). See further *mlk* (I A 1, 3, [13], [14]; I B [1], 7). If the words are not dittographical, then *mlkt ḥl* (I A 25) also belongs here.

(2) Nomina Recta: This usage consists of the juxtaposition of two nouns, the first of which (*nomen regens*) is sometimes modified in form to express its state of relationship to the second (*nomen rectum*), which in almost all cases in these texts expresses a genitival relation: *mlky 'rpd*, "the kings of Arpad" (I B [41]; II B [3]; II C 15; III 1, 3, 16, 27); *mn ḥd byt 'by,* "any one of my father's household" (III 10, *'by* is the *nomen rectum*); *lkl 'lhy 'dy'*, "to all the gods of the treaty" (I B 23, 33; II B [9], [18]; II C [13]; III 4, [14], 17, 23). The *nomen rectum* can be a name or a common noun, which is either suffixal, emphatic, or absolute (e.g., I B 6, 24; III 16). Similarly: *'by* (II B 8; III [24], [25], 25); *'dm* (I A 10); *'ḥy* (III 4, 9, 13, [21]); *'ḥwh* (III 17); *'lhn* (I B 6); *'lhy'* (I B [8]; II C 3, 7, [10]); *'nš* (III 16); *'pwh* (III 2); *'ryh* (II A 9); *'rm* (I A 6); *'rnb* (I A 33); *'rpd* (I A [1], 3, 4bis, [12], [14bis]; I B [1], 4, [5], [6]); *byr'* (I B [34bis]); *byty* (I B 40, 44); *bry* (I C 3; III 1, 12bis, 15, [26]); *brk* (III 12, 15); *brh* (I C 8; II C 14; III 25); *bny* (II B [7], 13; III 10, 21); *brd* (I A [26]); *btn* (I A 32); *br g'yh* (I A 1, 2, [2], 13, [15]; I B 1, [2], [7]); *gbr* (III 1); *gš* (I A 16; I B 3, 11; II B 10); *dbhh* (I A 31); *ḥbrw* (I A [4]); *ḥwh* (I A 31); *ḥl* (I A 25bis; II A [4]); *ḥpsy* (III 8); *ḥsy'* (I B 29); *ḥrn* (II B 12); *knr* (I A 29); *ktk* (I A 1, 3, 4, [12], [15]; I B 4bis, 5); *l'wyn* (? I B 30); *lḥyh* (I C [6]); *lḥm* (I A 24; II A [3]); *mlk* (I A 6); *mlkn* (I B 26, 28); *mlky'* (I B 22; III 7); *mlky* (I C [6]); *mrq* (I A 29); *mt''l* (I A 2, 3, [38], 41, [42]; I B 1, 2; I C [7]); *ngdy* (III 10); *nmrh* (I A 31; II A [9]); *spr'* (I B 8; I C 17); *srsy*

(I B 45; III 5); *'bdy* (III 13); *'dn* (I B 24; II B [5]); *'lb* (11 C 10); *'m'* (III 5, 13); *'my'* (III 10); *'my* (III 21); *'ml* (I A 26); *'qh* (I A 33); *'qry* (III 12, [21]); *'qrk* (III 15); *'qrh* (I A [2], 41); *'qrb* (I A 31); *'trsmk* (I A 1, 3, 14; I B [1], [14]); *pqdy* (III 4, [10], 13); *ṣby* (I A 33); *ṣdh* (I A 33); *ṣy* (I A [32]); *ṣll* (I B 3; II B 10); *ṣ'qh* (I A [29]); *rbwh* (I A 39, [41]; II C 15); *rḥbh* (I A 10); *śn'y* (I B 26; II B 14; III 10, 11; *š'wt'* (I A 39, [42]); *š'l* (I A 33); *šrn* (I A 33); *tḥth* (I A 6).

(3) Construct Chain as Nomen Rectum: This is in reality a special form of the preceding noun function, a compounded construct chain in which one or more nouns in the construct state depend on the preceding construct: *'m kl 'll byt mlk*, "with everyone entering the royal palace" (I A 6: three constructs); *'w mn ḥd byt 'by*, "or anyone of my father's household" (III 9); *'dy b'ly ktk*, "the treaty of the lords of KTK" (I A 4; cf. I B [5]). Similarly: *kl 'lhy rḥbh* (I A 10); *kl 'lhy ktk w'lhy 'rpd* (I A 12); *'dy 'lhy 'rpd w'dy 'lhy ktk* (I B 5); *lkl 'lhy 'dy'* (I B 23; II B [9], [18]; II C [13]; III 4, 14, 17, 23); *šybt byt 'by* (III 24); *kl b'l ḥsy'* (I B [29]); *dm br bry* (III 12); *lbb br brk* (III 15); *'dy bny br g'yh* (I A 2ter; I B 1, [1]); *mn ḥd mlk l'wyn* (? I B 30); *kl* (or *ḥd*) *mlky 'rpd* (II B [3]; II C 15; III 1, [3]); *lbb mlky 'rpd* (III 16); *ṭby mlk br g'yh* (I B 6); *lkl nbš byty* (I B 40); *kl 'ly 'rm* (I A 6); *'m 'qr kl mh mlk* (I B 2).

(4) Noun Subject in a Nominal Sentence: Thus, *ptḥh ly 'rḥ'*, "the road shall be open to me" (III 9); *wtl'ym wkpryh wb'lyh wgblh l'by*, "and Tal'ayim and its villages, its lords, and its territory belonged to my father" (III 23). Similarly: *ṭby* (I B 6); *nbš'* (I A [36]); *nṣb'* (I A [6]); *'dn* (I B 41); *'dy* (I A 1bis, 2, 3, [3], 4bis; I B 1bis, [4], 4, 5, 6); *qryh* (III 12).

(5) Noun Predicate in a Nominal Sentence: Thus, *gbr 'dn h' 'nh,* "I am an ally" (I B 24; cf. II B [5]); *wb'mh hml mrq whmyt ṣ'qh wyllh,* "but among its people let there rather be the din of affliction and the noise of crying and lamentation" (I A 29). Similarly: *'dy'* (I A 7); *śhdn* (I A 12); *nbšh* (I A 37); *ṭb* (III 3, 22, 29); *rḥm* (III 8); *špr* (III 29).

(6) Noun Subject of a Verb, Which Normally Precedes: According to E. Y. Kutscher ("Aramaic," 362) the verb normally precedes the subject; he counted 45 instances of verb-subject in Old Aramaic, over against only 15 instances of subject-verb.

In these inscriptions the verb precedes the subject in the following cases: *wyšlḥn 'lhn mn kl mh 'kl b'rpd,* "and may (the) gods send every sort of devourer against Arpad" (I A 30); *zy śmw 'lhn,* "which (the) gods have concluded" (I B 6; I A 24). Similarly: *'ḥwh* (I A 28-29, 32); *'lhn* (I C 15, 21; II B 2; III 24bis); *'nrt* (I A 38); *'rbh* (I A 27); *'rpd* (I A 32, 35); *br g'yh* (I A 7); *br* (III 16,[26]); *bry* (I B 25; II B [6], 8; III [17], [26]); *brh* (II C 11); *bnth* (I A [35]); *bny* (I A [16]); *bnwh* (I B [21]; II B 2b); *gbr* (I A 39); *gbrt* (I A [42]); *hdd* (I A [25], 36, 38); *ḥylk* (I B [28]); *ḥṣy'* (I A 38); *ḥṣr* (I A 28); *yrq* (I A 28); *mlky* (I B 41); *mlkth* (I A 25; II A [4]); *mt''l* (I A 14, [24], [37], [39], 40; I B 21; II B [2]); *nbšk* (I B 39); *nšy* (I A 41ter, [42]); *'gl'* (I A 40); *'mh* (I B [21]; II B 3); *'qr* (I A 15); *'qry* (I B 25; II B [6]; III 26); *pm* (I A [30], 31ter; II A 9ter); *qbrh* (II A [4]); *ql* (I A 29); *qryt'* (I A [33]); *qšt'* (I A 38); *rbwh* (I A 40; II B 3); *š'wt'* (I A 35, 37); *šršh* (I C [24]); *twy* (I A 28); *twl'h* (I A 27); *tl'ym* (III 25). On I A 34-35 there is a series of names of towns that follows a single verb.

In the following instances the subject precedes the verb: *'šmh* (II A [4]); *br* (III 12); *brk* (III 2-3, 11); *ss* (I A 31); *ssyh* (I A 22); *'zn* (II A 2); *'qr* (III 3); *'qrk* (I B [32]; III 3, 12); *qml* (I A 31); *ś'n* (I A 23; II A [2]); *šwrh* (I A 23; II A [1]). In one instance the noun subject of a following verb is preceded by the prefixed negative: *wl'š yhwnnh*, "and let no one oppress him" (II B 16).

(7) Noun as Direct Object of Verbs

(a) *With the Perfect*: *wkzy ḥbzw 'lhn byt 'by*, "and when (the) gods struck my father's house" (III 24); *hšbw 'lhn šybt byt 'by*, "(the) gods have brought about the return of my father's house" (III 24). See also I A 7.

(b) *With the Imperfect*: In three instances the direct object precedes the verb: *wpgr 'rb' m'l pgr*, "and I shall pile corpse upon corpse" (I B 30); *w'dy' 'ln kl 'lhy' yṣrn*, "all the gods will guard this treaty" (I B 7); see I B [25]. Otherwise it either follows the verb immediately or the verb and the subject: *wšb' ssyh yhynqn 'l*, "should seven mares suckle a colt" (I A 22; see II A [1]); *wyzr' bhn hdd mlḥ wšḥlyn*, "and may Hadad sow in them salt and watercress" (I A 36); *w'l yrt šršh 'šm*, "and may his scion not inherit a name" (I C 25). Similarly: *'bny* (I A [26]); *'mr* (I A 23; II A [2]); *'š'* (I C 21); *byth* (I C 22); *br* (II C 14); *brh* (II C 14); *dm* (III 12bis, [12]); *dmy* (III 11, [22]); *gdh* (II A 2); *ṭbt'* (I C [4], 19); *yd* (I B 25, [25], [27]); *ydh* (I B 27); *ktk* (II C 5); *lḥm* (I B 38, 39; III 5, 7); *lhmy* (I B 38); *lšn* (III 21); *lšnk* (III 17); *mwddwh* (III 14); *ml'ky* (III 8); *ml'kh* (III 8); *mlh* (I B [41]); *mly* (I C 17); *mly'* (III 2); *mlk* (III 28); *mlkh* (II C 5); *mrmt* (III 22); *mt''l* (II C 14); *nbšhm* (III 5, 6); *spry'* (II C [4]); *'gl* (I A 23; II A [1]); *'dy'* (I

B 24); *'lym* (I A 22); *'mhm* (II C 16); *'qrh* (II C 15; III 13); *qšt* (I A [38], 39); *r'šy* (II B [8]; III 11); *rwḥ* (III 2); *ś't* (I A 21); *śgbwh* (III 13); *šdyhn* (I A [21]); *tḥtyth* (I C 23).

(c) *With the Imperative*: *qtlw 'ḥk 'w 'srh*, "kill your brother or imprison him" (III 18); *qtlw mr'km*, "kill your lord" (III 21). Similarly: *spry'* (II C 9); *'ynykm* (I A 13).

(d) *With the Infinitive*: The direct object of the infin. always follows the verb (contrast the Biblical Aramaic usage, cf. BLA §85c).[1] Thus, *lmšlḥ yd bmy byr'*, "to raise a hand against the water of the well" (I B 34). Similarly: *'šmhm* (II B 7); *byty* (I B [32]); *br* (III 15); *bry* (III 11); *spry'* (II C 2, [6]); *'dy* (I A 13); *'qry* (I B [32]; III 11, 16). See III 4 f.

(8) Nouns as Predicates in Verbal Sentences: Thus, *wthwy 'rpd tl*, "and may Arpad become a mound" (I A 32); *yhwh 'lh qq btn,* "may they become towards it the throat of a serpent" (I A 32); *whwy ḥlph*, "and be his successor" (III 22).

(9) Noun Object of Prepositions: Thus, *kl mh lḥyh b'rq wbšmyn,*"every sort of evil on earth and in heaven" (I A 26); *wyqḥ mn 'rqy 'w mn mqny,*"and he will take some of my land or some of my possessions" (I B 27). Similarly: I A 1, 2, 3, 4, 5ter, [5bis], [6], 8quater, [8ter], 9quater, [9bis], l0bis, [10]; 11ter, [11ter], 12ter, [13], [14], 15, [15], 24, 25ter, 26bis, 28, 29bis, 30ter, 32, [32], 35, 37, [37], 42; I B 1, 2bis, 3ter, [3], 4, [4], 5bis, [7bis], 8, 9ter, [9bis], [10], l0ter, 11, l2bis, 13, 21, 22, [23], [25bis], 26, 27bis, [28], 28, 30, [30], 31bis, 32, 33bis, 34, 36, 38, 40bis, 42, 45; I C 2, 3, [3], [4], 5, [6], 7, [8bis], [9], 15, 16, 17, 18, 20bis, [24]; II A [3], 3, [4ter]; II B [2bis], 5, [5bis], 6bis, [6bis], [7], [8], [9], 11, 12, 13bis, 14, [14], [18]; II C 2, 7, 9, 10, 13, 16, 17; III 1quinquies, 2ter, 3ter, 4, 5bis, 6, 7bis, [7], 8, 9, 10, 11, 12, 13bis, 14quater, 15ter, 16, [16], 17bis, 19, 20, 21ter, [21], 22, [22], 23bis, 24, [24], 25quater, [25], 26ter, [26], 27.

(10) Noun Used as an Adverb: *wšb' šnn y'kl 'rbh,* "for seven years may the locust devour (Arpad)" (I A 27); *wyhkn ḥlb,* "and should they go to Aleppo" (III 5). Similarly: I A 27, [27]; II A 5, 6.

1 See J. Carmignac, "Un aramaïsme biblique et qumrânienne: L'infinitif placé après son complément d'objet," *RevQ* 5 (1964-66) 503-20.

(11) Noun in Casus Pendens Construction: This usage, which can also be called a nominative absolute, is clear in two cases: *wkl mlky' zy sḥrty 'w kl zy rḥm h' ly,* "and as for all the kings of my vicinity or anyone who is a friend of mine" (III 7); *wmlkn zy sḥrty,* "and as for kings of my vicinity" (III 19). Possibly also I B 34 (*wbyr' h' kl zy ysb*).

(12) Nouns Dependent on zy as Substitute for the Construct Chain: There are three instances of this usage. Two occur in the *casus pendens* construction (§11 above); the other is *ḥlb* (I A [10]).

(13) Nouns Used in Attribution: These nouns may also be called adjectives; they follow the noun they modify and agree in gender, number, and state. Thus, *wymll mln lḥyt l'ly*, "and should he utter evil words against me" (III 2); *zy 'dn ḥyn hm*, "because it is a living pact" (I B 41). See also *rb* (I B 7); *rbt* (I A [35]).

III. Verbs

(1) Uses of the Perfect

(a) *In main clauses:*

(i) To express the historical past: *šbt tl'ym,* "Tal'ayim returned" (III 25); *hšbw 'lhn šybt by[t 'by]*, "(the) gods brought about the return of my father's house" (III 24). Similarly: *hwt l'ḥrn* (III [24]); *nṣb' 'm spr' znh śm* (I A 7); *kh 'mrn wkh ktbn* (I C 1).

(ii) To express the future perfect in the apodosis of a condition: *šqrt b'dy'*, "you will have been unfaithful to the treaty" (I B 38, [27], [36]; III [9], 19, 20, 27); *šqrtm* (II B 14; III 7); *šqrt lkl 'lhy 'dy'*, "you will have been unfaithful to all the gods of the treaty" (I B 23; II B 9; III 4, 16, 23); *šqrt* (I B [33]; II B [17]; III 14).

(b) *In subordinate clauses:*

(i) Relative, expressing past time: *zy gzr br g'yh,* "which Bar-Ga'yah has concluded" (I A 7). Similarly: *zy śmw 'lhn* (I B 6); *zy 'bdw 'lhn* (II B 2); *mh ktbt 'nh mt''l lzkrn lbry* (I C 2).

(ii) Temporal, expressing past time: *kzy ḥbzw 'lhn byt 'by,* "when the gods struck my father's house" (III 24).

(iii) Conditional, expressing the future perfect, with the imperfect in the main clause: *hn hšb zy ly 'hšb zy lh,* "if he has restored mine, I shall return his" (III 20).

(2) Uses of the Imperfect

(a) *In main clauses:*

(i) To express the future in a direct utterance or quotation: *'hld mn mlwh*, "I shall efface some of its words" (I C 18). Similarly: *'hpk ṭbt' w'śm llḥyt* (I C 19); *mh t'bd* (I B 26); *'šm' lbr g'yh* (II B [5]); *'šb 'l krs' 'by* (II B [7]); *'h'bd spry'* (II C 4); *'hbd 'yt ktk* (II C 5); *'nh 'gr 'gr* (II C 8); *wpgr 'rb' m'l pgr* (I B 30); *''bd lhm* (III 3).

(ii) To express future stipulations in the treaty: *rqh trqhm wthšbhm ly,* "you must placate them and return them to me" (III 6). The nuance of "must" is derived from the treaty-context much more than from the verb-form itself, which does not differ from the preceding class of uses. Similarly: *tb'h* (I B 39); *ygbr* (? II B 19); *lygzrn mlh* (I B 41); *lykhl lprq* (I B [34]); *ltkhl ltś'* (I B 39); *w'khl* (I B 33); *pl'khl l'šlḥ* (II B 6); *ltqḥ mly' mn ydh* (III 2); *yqm ḥd dmy* (III 22); *yś'n kl 'lhy 'dy'* (II C [13]); *'qrk yskr l'qry* (III 3); *thskrhm* (III 2); *yhskr* (III 3); *yhskrn* (III 3); *y'zz qlbt byty* (I B 44); *yšḥdn* (? III 28).

(iii) To express the present: *wyb' wyzqn,* "for he (i.e., my father) is babbling and is growing old" (II B 8).

(iii) To express the jussive: *yqtl mn yqtl,* "let him kill whomever he would kill" (II B 8); see also I B [9], *ytšm'n.*

(iv) To express prohibitions (either negative commands or negative jussives): *'l tpnw b'šrh,* "do not return to his region" (III 7); *'l tštq ḥdh mn mly spr' znh,* "let not one of the words of this inscription be silent" (I B 8). Similarly: *'l tšryh* (III 18); *'l t'šqny* (III 20); *'l t'mr* (I A 36); *ltmšl by* (III 9); *lthrm nbšhm* (III 5); *ltršh ly 'lyh* (III 9); *ltšlḥ lšn bbyty* (III 21); *wl'š yhwnnh* (II B 16).

(v) To express wishes: *thwy 'rpd tl,* "may Arpad become a mound" (I A 32); *'l thry,* "may she not conceive" (I A 21); *yzr' bhn hdd mlḥ wšḥlyn,* "may Hadad sow in them salt and weeds" (I A 36). Similarly: *yśb'* (I A 22bis, 23bis; II A [1], 1, [2bis]); *yhrgn* (I A 24; II A [3]); *thwy* (I A 25; II A [4], 6); *ysk* (I A [25], 26); *ysq* (I A [27]); *ypq* (I A 28); *ytšm'* (I A 29); *yšlḥn* (I A 30); *yštḥṭ* (I A [32]); *t'mr* (I A 33); *yhww* (I A [31]); *yṣrn* (I B 8); *y'bdw* (I C [5]); *yṣrw* (I C 15); *yhpkw* (I C 21); *yśmw* (I C 23); *yrt* (I C 24); *ytnšy* (II A [4]); *yhwh* (II A 4); *ymt* (II C [10]); *y'kl* (I A 27, [30]; II A [9]); *t'kl* (I A 27).

To these wishes one should probably relate the use of the future apodosis in conditional sentences, which express the treaty stipulations, or in comparative sentences. Thus, with *kn* correlative to *'yk zy*: *kn tqd 'rpd,* "so may Arpad be burned"; or more simply, "so shall Arpad be burned." *kn yqd mt''l,* "so may Mati'el be burned" (I A 37). Similarly: *yšbr* (I A 38); *y'r* (I A 39); *ygzr* (I A 40); *ygzrn* (I A 40); *y'rrn* (I A

41); *yqḥn* (I A 42); *tgzr* (I B 43).

In conditions: *'nh l'khl l'šlḥ yd bk,* "I shall not be able to raise a hand against you" (I B 24); *lykhl bry lyšlḥ yd bbrk* (I B 25); *y'th ḥylk,* "your army must come" (I B 28). Similarly: *wtqp yqpy wtnt' ly* (I B 29); *ltsk lhm lḥm* (III 5); *lt'mr lhm* (III 5); *'t t'th wtqm dmy ... wbrk y'th yqm dm bry ... wbr brk t'th yqm dm br bry w'qrk y'th yqm dm 'qry* (III 11-12); *nkh tkwh bḥrb* (III 13); *nkh tkh 'y<t>h* (III 13); *ltšlḥ lšnk bnyhm wt'mr lh* (III 17-18); *lyqtl wly'sr* (III 18); *'hšb* (III 20).

(vi) Finite Complement: The impf. is used instead of an infin. as a complement to the verb *khl*, appearing in the same form as the main verb itself; it is simply juxtaposed without any coordinating conjunction. Thus, *pl'khl l'šlḥ yd bk,* "then I shall not be able to raise a hand against you" (lit., I shall not be able, I shall not send a hand, II B 6); cf. I B [24]; *lykhl bry lyšlḥ yd bbrk* (I B 25); *lykhl ltś' lḥm* (I B 39). Contrast I B 34.

In this connection, when note is taken of the asyndetic coordination of similar verbs, one should recall that this phenomenon turns up in another context, where the introductory verb is scarcely modal. Thus, *wbrk y'th yqm dm bry mn śn'wh wbr brk y'th yqm dm br bry w'qrk y'th yqm dm 'qry,* "your son must come (and) avenge the blood of my son from his enemies; your grandson must come (and) avenge the blood of my grandson; your offspring must come (and) avenge the blood of my offspring" (III 11-12).

(b) *In subordinate clauses:*

(i) Temporal: *'d 'hk 'nh w'rqhm,* "until I come and placate them" (III 6); *mzy ymlk 'šr,* "as long as Asshur rules" (I A 25). Perhaps the expression in III 8 should be included here: *w'šlḥ ml'ky ... 'w yšlḥ ml'kh?*

(ii) Comparative: *'yk zy tqd š'wt' z' b'š,* "just as this wax is burned by fire" (I A 35, 37). Similarly: *tšbr* (I A 38); *y'r* (I A 39); *ygzr* (I A 40); *t'rr* (I A [40]); *tqḥ* (I A [42]); *ymḥ'* (I A 42).

(iii) Simple Relative: *kl gbr zy yb'h rwḥ 'pwh,* "any man who rants" (III 2); *bkl mh ymwt br 'nš,* "in whatever way a man shall die" (III 16). Similarly: *bry zy yšb 'l khs'y* (III 17); *zy ysqn b'šrh* (I A 5; I C 4); *zy ysq wymlk b'šrh* (I B [3]); *zy ymlkn b'rpd* (I B 22); *kl zy ysb* (I B 34); *zy y'l wylqḥ* (I B 35); *bywm zy y'bd kn* (I C 20); *zy y'wrn* (II B 4); *zy y'z mnk* (II B 20); *'n zy yršmn* (II C 3).

(iv) Compound Relative: *yqtl mn yqtl,* "let him kill whomever he would kill" (II B 9). Similarly: *mn lyṣr mly spr' ... wy'mr* (I C 17); *... wymll 'ly* to *wymll mln* (III 2); *mn yś'* (? III 26); *mn y'mr lhldt* (II C [1]).

(v) Conditional (protasis): *whn yšqr mt''l ... lbr g'yh,* "and if Mati'el ... should be unfaithful to ... Bar-Ga'yah" (I A 14; cf. I A 15, 24, [16]; II A 3); *whn tšm'n wtšlmn 'dy 'ln wt'mr,* "and if you obey and fulfill this treaty and say . . . ." (I B 24). Similarly: *whn mlh ymll 'ly ḥd mlkn ... wt'mr* (I B 26); *wyqtlnh wyšlḥ ydh wyqḥmn 'rqy* (I B 27); *whn y'th ḥd mlkn wysbn<y>* (I B 28); *lt'th ... lt'twn ... ly'th* (I B 31-32); *tšlḥ* (I B 37); *whn lthb lḥmy ... wltsk* (I B 38); *phn tšm'* (II B 4); *hn t'mr bnbšk wt'št blbbk* (II B 5); *whn y'mr mn ḥd bny ... wyb'h* (II B 7-8); *hn yhwnnh* (II B 16); *hn tb'h*(II B 17); *whn yqrq mny qrq ḥd ... wyhkn ḥlb* (III 4-5); *whn lyšbn b'rqk* (III 6); *whn thrm nbšhm mny wtsk lhm lḥm wt'mr* (III 6-7); *whn ... yb'h* (III 9-11); *hn 'yty yqtln* (III 11); *whn ysq 'l lbbk wtś' 'l śptyk ... wysq ... wyś' ... 'w hn ysq ... wyś' ... whn ysq 'l lbb mlky 'rpd* (III 14-16); *whn yrb bry ... 'w y'brnh ... whn rqh trqh bnyhm* (III 17-19); *whn t'bd mrmt* (III 22); *whn yrb bry ...* (III 26).

The conditional nuance of the impf. is sometimes not introduced by the conj. *hn*, but occurs with the conj. *w-*. Thus, *wyhynqn 'lym wšb' mhynqn ymšḥn šdyhn,* "and should seven nurses anoint their breasts and nurse a young boy" (I A 21-22); *wšb' ssyh yhynqn 'l,* "and should seven mares suckle a colt" (I A 22; cf. *yhynqn*, I A 23bis; II A [1bis, 2]). Similarly: *yhkn* (I A 24; II A [3]); *wlyšm' mt''l* (I B 21; II B [2]; cf. *lyšm'n,* I B [21-22]; II B 2b, 3bis); *wyqrq ḥdhm wy'th* (I B 45); *wyzḥl h' mn ld ... wy'mr* (II C 6-8).

(vi) Consecutive: *wlythḥzh yrq, wlythḥzh 'ḥwh,* "so that no green may be seen, that its vegetation may not be seen" (I A 28).

(3) Use of the Imperative

The imperative expresses a command: *pqḥw 'ynykm lḥzyh 'dy br g'yh,* "open your eyes (O gods), to gaze upon the treaty of Bar-Ga'yah" (I A 13). Similarly: *ld* (II C 9); *rqw* (III 6); *šbw* (III 7); *'srh* (III 18); *qtl* (III 18); *qtlw* (III 21); *hwy* (III 22).

(4) Use of the Infinitive

(a) *Complementary:* The infin. is used as a complement to modal verbs: *lykhl lprq wlmšlḥ yd bmy byr'*, "he will not be able to destroy (it) or raise a hand against the water of (that) well" (I B 34). Similarly *lhldt* (II C 2).

(b) *Epexegetical:* This infin. explains the function of a preceding expression: *wyb'h r'šy lhmtty wlhmtt bry,* "seeks my head to kill me and to kill my son" (III 11). Similarly: *lhmtty*(II B [8]; III 15); *lhmtt* (III

15, 16).

(c) *Final: pqḥw 'ynykm lḥzyh 'dy br g'yh,* "open your eyes (O gods), to gaze upon the treaty of Bar-Ga'yah" (I A 13 [in this case the infin. may be epexegetical). Similarly: *lśgb* (I B 32bis); *l'bdt* (I B 36); *lḥbzthm* (II B 7).

(d) *Intensive:* This use of the infin. is under Canaanite influence and corresponds to the Hebrew infin. absol. It precedes the verb, is of the same root as the main verb that it modifies, but not necessarily in the same conjugation. Thus, *hskr thskrhm,* "you must hand them over" (III 2). Similarly: *mwt* (? I B 30); *'gr 'gr* (II C 8); *nkh tkwh* (III 12); *nkh tkh* (III 13); *rqh trqhm* (III 6, 18).

(e) *Object of a Preposition: wyzḥl h' mn ld spry' mn bty 'lhy'*, "and should that man be frightened from effacing the inscriptions from the bethels" (II C 6).

(f) *Position of the Infinitive:* In eleven cases the direct object follows the infinitive (I A 13; I B 32bis, 34, 36; II B 7; II C 2, 6; III 11, 15, 16); possibly it preceded in I B 33-34.

(5) Uses of the Participle

(a) *Predicative:* In a nominal sentence the ptc. serves as the predicate. Thus, *ptḥh ly 'rḥ',* "the road shall be open to me" (III 8). Similarly: *lzy lyd'*, "to someone who does not understand" (II C 8).

(b) *Substantive:* The verbal adj. is used as a noun. Thus, *tqp yqpy,* "you must surround those who surround me" (I B 29); *mhynqn,* "nurses" (I A [21]). Similarly: *'ll* (I A 6); *qrq* (III 4); *qrqy* (III 19); *qrqhm* (III 19); *ḥlph* (III 22); *znyh,* "a harlot" (I A 41).

IV. Adverbs

Under this heading are included those words that are not declined in any way and are simply juxtaposed to other words, which for the most part are verbs. The adverbs express modifications of time, place, manner, relation, or negation.

(1) Time:

Only one instance of a temporal adv. is found in these texts: *wk't hšbw 'lhn šybt byt 'by,* "now however the gods have brought about the return of my father's house" (III 24). The adv. *k't* is actually compound (= prep. *k-* + noun *'t,* "time"); it should be considered also from the standpoint of compounds (see below, § 6).

(2) Place:
A local adv. is found in III 6, *rqw šm ʿd ʾhk*, "placate (them) there until I come." The interrogative adv. of place, *ʾn*, "where," is found in II C 3, in composition with *zy*, to form an indefinite pronominal expression.

(3) Manner:
The majority of the adverbial expressions in these texts denote manner. Thus, *kh ʾmrn wkh ktbn,* "thus we have spoken and thus we have written" (I C 1); *kn tgzr ʾplʾ* (I B 43); *bywm zy yʿb[d] kn,* "on the day he will do so" (I C 21). The adv. *kn* often appears correlative to *ʾyk zy*, "just as . . . so ": *ʾyk zy tqd šʿwtʾ zʾ bʾš kn tqd ʾrpd,* "just as this wax is burned by fire, so may Arpad be burned" (I A 35). Similarly: I A 37, 38, 39, 40, 41, 42. Another adv. of manner is *hn*, which is always combined with the prefixed negative adv. *l-* in the expression, *whn lhn,* "and if not so." Thus, *whn lhn šqrtm lkl ʾlhy ʿdyʾ*, "and if (you do) not (do) so, (then) you (will) have been unfaithful to all the gods of the treaty" (III 4). Similarly: I B 36; III 9, 14, 20. The expression is elliptical. Two other adverbial expressions probably belong here: *kym* (III 1), which intensifies the following noun construction, *kl gbr zy*; and *lmgn,* "with impunity" (II C 4), if I have rightly understood this word.

(4) Relation:
It is not easy to say just where one should classify the sign of the accusative: should it be booked here or with the prepositions? The clear example of it in these texts is the form *ʾyt,* both with and without suffixes. It is used only sporadically, and it is not easy to say just what force was attributed to it. It occurs before names and definite common nouns used as direct objects of verbs; it also occurs with pronominal objects. Thus, *ʾhʾbd ʾyt ktk wʾyt mlkh,* "I shall destroy KTK and its king" (II C 5); *ʾyt Mtʿʾl wbrh* (II C 14, the verb is unfortunately lost); *wybʿh bry ʾyt rʾšy* (II B [8]); *lśgb ʾyt ʿqry* (I B 32). There is one instance of *l-* that is possibly so used: *lṭbtʾ yʿbdw tḥt šmšʾ*, "may they make good relations under the sun" (I C 4).
Two instances of the suffixal form of *ʾyt* occur: *ʾyty* (III 11) and *ʾy<t>h* (III 13).

(5) Negation:
(a) The most common form of the negative adv. is the prefixed *l-*. Not only is it prefixed to the adv. *hn*, "so" (see §3 above), but also to an adj., *lṭb hʾ mk,* "he is not better than you" (III 22; cf. *lydʿ* [II C 8]), and most frequently to verbs (usually the impf.): *wlythḥzh yrq,* "so that no

green may be seen" (I A 28 [the nuance is consecutive, not a negative wish, which usually is introduced by *'l*]). Similarly: *wlyšm' mt''l,* "and should Mati'el not obey" (I B 21); I B [21], [22], [24bis], 25, [25], 31, [32bis], 34, 38bis, 39, [39], 41; I C [7], 17; II B [2], 2b, 3ter, 6bis, 17; III 5ter, 6, 9bis, 17, 18bis, 19, 21. There is one peculiar use, where this adv. is prefixed to a noun: *wl'š yhwnnh,* "and let no one oppress him" (II B 16), but the text is not certain there.

(b) The negative *'l* is used with the impf. either to express a negative wish or a negative stipulation (jussive or prohibition).

(i) Wish: *w'l yśb',* "and may it not be sated" (I A 22). Similarly I A 22, 23, [23]; II A [1bis], [2], 2; *w' yhrgn* (I A 24; II A [3]); *w'l t'mr* (I A 33, 36); *w'l thry* (I A 21); *w'l ypq ḥṣr* (I A 28); *w'l yrt* (I C 24).

(ii) Stipulation: *w'l tštq ḥdh mn mly spr',* "let not one of the words of this inscription be silent" (I B 8). Similarly: *w'l ytšm' ql knr* (I A 29); *w'l tpnw* (III 7); *w'l tšryh* (III 18); *w'l t'šqny* (III 20).

(6) Adverbs in Composition: Here are listed the forms found joined with other words: *'yk* or *'ykh,* used with *zy* (I A 35, 37, 38, 39, [39], [40], [41]); *'n,* used with *zy* (II C 3); *k't* (III 24).

V. Prepositions

Being a word expressive of relationship, the preposition functions in these texts most frequently to introduce a phrase that is an adverbial modifier of the sentence as a whole or of the verb. Thus, *yšlḥ ml'kh 'ly,* "he will send his messenger to me" (III 8); *yzr' bhn hdd mlḥ,* "may Hadad sow in them salt" (I A 36); *thwy mlkth kmlkt ḥl,* "may his kingdom become like a kingdom of sand" (II A [4]); *šqrtm lkl 'lhy 'dy',* "you will have been unfaithful to all the gods of the treaty" (I B 23). Examples of such a relationship could be multiplied indefinitely. Much more important, however, are the following usages:

(1) Relating an Infinitive to a Verb: This relation may either express purpose or explanation. Thus, expressing

(i) Purpose: *pqḥw 'ynykm lḥzyh 'dy br g'yh,* "open your eyes, to gaze upon the treaty of Bar-Ga'yah" (I A 13). Similarly: *lśgb* (I B 32bis); *lḥbzthm wl'bdt* (II B 7); *[l]'bdt* (? I B 36).

(ii) Explanation: The so-called epexegetical infin.: *wyb'h r'šy lhmtty wlhmtt bry,* "and seeks my head to kill me and to kill my son" (III 11). Similarly: *lhmtt* (III 15, 16).

(iii) Complement: The complementary infin. is likewise

so introduced: *lykhl lprq wlmšlḥ yd,* "he will not be able to destroy (it) or raise a hand against (it)" (I B 34); cf. II C 2. In one instance the prep. *mn* also introduces an infin.: *wyzḥl h' mn ld spry',* "and that man shall be frightened from effacing the inscriptions" (II C 6).

(2) Introducting a Predicative Phrase in a Nominal Sentence: Thus *mh ktbt 'nh mt''l lzkrn lbry,* "what I, Mati'el, have written is (to act) as a reminder for my son" (I C 2); *'dy' zy bspr' znh,* "the treaty which is in this inscription" (I B [23], 28, 33; I C 17, [22]; II B [9], 18; II C 13; III 4, 14, 17). Similarly: III 3, 5, 10, 13, 20, [20], 23bis.

(3) Modifying a Noun: Thus *'dy br g'yh 'm mt''l,* "the treaty of Bar-Ga'yah with Mati'el" (I A 1). Similarly: I A 2, 3bis, 4, 5ter, 6, [13]; I B 1, 2bis, 3ter, 4bis, 5, 11; possibly also II B 12.

VI. Conjunctions:

These words are used to express various inter-word and inter-clause relationships. The following types of such relationship occur in these texts:

(1) Simple Relative Clause: The clause acts as an appositive to a noun antecedent. Thus, *yhpkw 'lhn 'š' h' wbyth wkl zy bh,* "may (the) gods upset that man and his house and all that is in it" (I C 21-22); *w'dy 'lhn hm zy śmw 'lhn,* "and this is the treaty of gods which gods have set up" (I B 6). See further the instances listed in Syntax, I 3 a.

(2) General Relative Clause: The pronoun-conjunction has a double function. Thus *mh ṭb b'yny ''bd 'lhm,* "what is good in my sight I shall do to them" (III 3). See further the instances listed in Syntax, I 3 b and I 4 d.

(3) Temporal Clause: Thus, *wkzy ḥbzw 'lhn byt 'by h' hwt l'ḥrn,* "when (the) gods struck my father's house, it (Tal'ayim) came to belong to another" (III 24); *thwy mlkth kmlkt ḥl, mlkt ḥl, mzy ymlk 'šr,* "and may his kingdom become a kingdom of sand, a kingdom of sand, as long as Asshur reigns" (I A 25); *rqw šm 'd 'hk w'rqhm,* "placate (them) there until I come and placate them" (III 6). Cf. II B 19.

(4) Causal Clause: Thus, *whwy ḥlph ky lṭb h' mk,* "and be his successor, for he is not better than you" (III 22).

(5) Direct Quotation: This type of clause is introduced without a conjunction; its nature as an utterance is indicated merely by a preceding verb of saying. Thus, *whn tšmʻn wtšlmn ʻdy' 'ln wt'mr gbr 'dn h' 'nh l'khl l'šlḥ yd bk,* "but if you obey and fulfill this treaty and say, ʻI am an ally,' (then) I shall not be able to raise a hand against you" (I B 24); *t'mr bnbšk yqtl mn yqtl, šqrtm lkl 'lhy ʻdy' zy bspr' znh,* "and (if) you say in your soul, ʻLet him kill whomever he would kill,' (then) you will have been unfaithful to all the gods of the treaty which is in this inscription" (II B 8-9). Similarly: I B 26; I C 18, 19; II B 5-6, 7; II C 4-5, 8, 9; III 5, 7, 18, 21-22.

(6) Adversative Clause: On one occasion the conj. *p-* occurs with apparently this nuance: *phn tšmʻ nḥt m[...,* "but if you obey, (may) tranquility ... " (II B 4).

(7) Conditional Clause: This type of clause is introduced either by *hn* or by *w-* and occurs in the following forms:

(a) *Elliptical conditions:* In this category belongs the clause, *whn lhn,* "and if not so." Thus, *whn lhn šqrtm lkl 'lhy ʻdy' zy bspr' znh,* "and if (you do) not (do) so, you will have been unfaithful to all the gods of the treaty which is in this inscription" (III 3-4). In each instance (see I B 36; III 9, 14, 20) the perfect in the apodosis has a future perfect nuance.

(b) *Future conditions:* By and large, these clauses express the stipulations of the treaties. Thus, *whn yšqr mtʻ'l br ʻtrsmk mlk 'rpd lbr g'yh mlk ktk,* "and if Matiʻel, the son of ʻAttarsamak, the king of Arpad, should be unfaithful to Bar-Ga'yah, the king of KTK, ... " (the apodosis is lost, I A 14-15); *whn y'th ḥd mlkn wysbn<y> y'th ḥylk 'ly ʻm kl bʻl ḥṣy',* "if one of (the) kings comes and surrounds <me>, your army must come to me with every archer" (I B 28). Similarly: I A [16], 24; I B [23], [25], [32], 38; II A [3]; II B 4, 5, [7], 16, 17; III 4, 6bis, 11, 14, 15, 16, 17, 18, 19, [22], [26]. Only in III 20 does one find a future perfect nuance expressed in the protasis: *hn hšb zy ly 'hšb zy lh,* "if he has restored mine, I shall return [his]." In two instances the protasis is a nominal clause: *whn qryh h' nkh tkwh bḥrb,* "and if it is a city, you must strike it with a sword" (III 12); *whn ḥd 'ḥy h' ... nkh tkh 'y<t>h,* "if it is one of my brothers ... , you must strike him" (III 13). The context is broken in the following instances: I B 31, 37, 43; III 27.

The sole problematical sentence in this regard is found in III 9-11. It begins with *whn,* which is followed by a long list of coordinated subjects, before the verb is introduced to which *w-* is prefixed. It has been suggested that this is *waw* of the apodosis, but this is not possible, since *wyb'h* is actually the verb in the protasis. Probably one has to reckon with anacoluthon here. The construction may be influenced by the conditional use of the conj. *w-* found elsewhere in these texts (see below, 8 d iii). The only instance of a conj. introducing the apodosis in these inscriptions is apparently *p-* in II B 6: *whn t'mr bnbšk wt'št blbbk gbr 'dn 'nh w'šm' lbr g'yh wbnwh w'qrh pl'khl l'šlḥ yd bk,* "and if you say in your soul and think in your mind, 'I am an ally and I shall obey Bar-Ga'yah and his sons and his offspring,' then I shall not be able to raise a hand against you."

(8) Coordination

The conjunctions *'w* and *w-* are used frequently throughout these texts as a means of coordination.

(a) *Coordination of Nouns: ḥd 'ḥy h' 'w ḥd 'bdy 'w ḥd pqdy 'w ḥd 'm' zy bydy*, "it is one of my brothers or one of my slaves or one of my officials or one of the people who are under my control" (III 13); *'dy br g'yh mlk ktk 'm mt''l br 'trsmk mlk 'rpd w'dy bny br g'yh 'm bny mt''l w'dy bny bny br g'yh w'qrh 'm 'qr mt''l br 'trsmk mlk 'rpd w'dy ktk 'm 'dy 'rpd w'dy b'ly ktk 'm b'ly 'rpd w'dy ḥb[r ...,* "the treaty of Bar-Ga'yah, king of KTK, with Mati'el, the son of 'Attarsamak, the king of Arpad; and the treaty of the sons of Bar-Ga'yah with the sons of Mati'el; and the treaty of the grandsons of Bar-Ga'yah and his offspring with the offspring of Mati'el, the son of 'Attarsamak, the king of Arpad; and the treaty of KTK with the treaty of Arpad; and the treaty of the lords of KTK with the treaty of the lords of Arpad; and the treaty of the union of ... " (I A 1-4). The nouns so coordinated are often subjects of verbs, objects of verbs, objects of prepositions, and even occasionally *nomina recta* in construct chains (*kl 'lhy rḥbh w'dm,* I A 10; *lrbq ṣy wṣby wš'l w'rnb wšrn wṣdh,* I A 33), and names (*wqdm mrdk wzrpnt,* I A 8). See further I A 6, 7; 8ter, [8], 9bis, [9], 10, 11, [11], 12bis, 31, [33], 34octies, [34], 35ter, 36bis, 37, 38bis; I B 7, [9], 11, 12; I C [8bis], 22; II B 2, 6bis, [6bis], 13; II C 11, 14, 15; III 11, 13bis, 14, 21, 23ter, [23], 26bis. In one instance the nouns are introduced by coordinated signs of the accusative (*'yt ktk w'yt mlkh,* II C 5).

(b) *Coordination of Verbs:* Verbs are coordinated within the same clause by the use of either *'w* or *w-*. Thus, *qtl 'ḥk 'w 'srh,* "kill your brother or imprison him" (III 18); *wyqrq ḥdhm wy'th,* "and one of them shall flee and come" (I B 45). Similarly: I A [21]; I B [3], 35, 38; I C

19; II B 7bis, 8; III 6, 8, 11, 17.

(c) *Coordination of Phrases:* This coordination is of two sorts, the coordination of a construct chain and the coordination of prepositional phrases.

(i) Coordinated Construct Chain: *mn ḥd 'ḥy 'w mn ḥd byt 'by,* "anyone of my brothers or anyone of my father's household" (III 9); *pm ḥwh wpm ʿqrb wpm dbhh wpm nmrh wss wqml ...,* "the mouth of a snake and the mouth of a scorpion and the mouth of a bear and the mouth of a panther, and a moth and a louse, and ... " (I A 31). For *'w,* see further I B 26, III 4bis, 5, 8, 10quinquies. For *w-*: I A [12], 26, 29, 30, 39, 41bis; I B 1bis, [4], 4, 5, [6], 29; I C 22; II A 9bis; II B 10bis; II C 15bis, 16; III 9, 21bis, [21], 29.

(ii) Coordinated Prepositional Phrases: *'w ʿl bny 'w ʿl ʿqry,* "or against my sons or against my offspring" (III 22); *qdm 'šwr wmlš wqdm mrdk wzrpnt wqdm nb' wtšmt wqdm 'r wnśk wqdm nrgl wlṣ wqdm šmš wnr wqdm sn wnkl wqdm nkr wkd'h wqdm kl 'lhy ...,* "in the presence of Asshur and Mullesh, and in the presence of Marduk and Zarpanit, and in the presence of Nabu and Tashmet, and in the presence of 'Ir and Nusk, and in the presence of Nergal and Laṣ, and in the presence of Shamash and Nur, and in the presence of Sin and Nikkal, and in the presence of Nikkar and Kadi'ah, and in the presence of all the gods of ... " (I A 7-10). Similarly for *'w:* I B 27, 45; III 1sexies, 8, 22; for *w-:* I A 5ter, 6, [9], 10, [10], [11ter, [11], 12, [24], 25, 26, 29, 30; I B 2, 3ter, 5, 10, [10], 34, 40bis, [40]; I C [3], 16; II A 3, [4]; II B [2]; II C 16; III 11, 23, 25ter.

One usage in particular must be mentioned here: *mn ʿrqw wʿd y'dy wbz mn lbnn wʿd ybrdw wmn dmśq wʿd ʿrw wm..w wmn bqʿt wʿd ktk,* "from ʿArqu to Ya'di and BZ, from Lebanon to Yabrud, from Damascus to ʿAru and M..W, and from the Valley to KTK" (I B 9-10).

(d) *Coordination of Clauses:* Only one instance of this coordination can be cited with the conj. *'w: 'w hn* following upon an introductory *whn* (III 14-15). The majority of instances introduced by *w-* are either the continuation of main clauses (such as I A 6, 7, 26, 27, 28) or the continuation of subordinate clauses (especially conditions, such as II B 8; III 14, 15). Special note, however, should be made of the following instances:

(i) Introduction of the conditional clause by *whn: whn yšqr mtʿ'l br ʿtrsmk mlk 'rpd lbr g'yh mlk ktk whn yšqr ʿqr mtʿ'l lʿqr br g'yh ...,* "Now if Matiʿel, the son of ʿAttarsamak, the king of Arpad, should be unfaithful to Bar-Ga'yah, the king of KTK, and if the offspring of Mati'el should be unfaithful to the offspring of Bar-Ga'yah ..." (I A 14-15). Similarly: I A [16], 24; I B [23], [24], [25], 28, 31, [32], 36, 37, 38, 43; II A [3]; II B [4], 7; III 3, 4, 6bis, 7, [9], 12, 13, 14bis, 16, 17, [18], 19, 20, [22], 25, 27.

(ii) Introduction of comparative clauses by *w'yk zy:* I A 38, 39, [39], [40], [41].

(iii) At times the simple *w-* seems to have conditional force. Thus, *wlyšm' mt''l,* "and should Mati'el not obey" (I B 21); *wt'mr gbr 'dn h' 'nh,* "and should you say, 'I am an ally'" (I B 14). See further I B [22]; III 19, 20. A more developed use of this instance is found in the curses: *wšb' ssyh yhynqn 'l w'l yśb' wšb' šwrh yhynqn 'gl w'l yśb',* "should seven mares suckle a colt, may it not be sated; and should seven cows give suck to a calf, may it not be sated" (I A 22-23). (The verbs are simply coordinated: "And seven mares shall suckle a colt and it shall not be sated," etc.) See further I A 21, 24; II A [1]-3.

GLOSSARY

References in square brackets [ ] indicate that some part of the word concerned has been restored. Since the degree of certainty or probability for the restoration varies considerably, one should consult the passage before discounting the instance so marked. Angular brackets < > indicate editorial additions to the text.

אב ("father"): אבי, II B 8; III 10, 23, [24], [25], 25

אבד ("destroy"): אבדת (pael infin.), I B 36; II B 7; אהאבד (haphel impf.), II C 4; אהבד, II C 5

אבן ("stone"): אבני, I A [26]

אגר ("reward"): peal infin. and impf., II C 8, 8

או ("or"): I B 26, 27, 35, 45; I C 19; III 1sexies, 4bis, 5, 8ter, 9, 10quinquies, 13ter, 15, 17, 18, 22bis

אזל ("go"): תאזל, I B 39

אח ("brother"): אחך, III 18; אחי ("my brothers"), III 4, 9, 13, [21]; אחוה ("his brothers"), III 17

אחו ("vegetation "): אחוה (3 sg. fem. suff.), I A 29, 32

אחרן ("another"): III 24

אית (sign of the accusative): I B 32; II B [8]; II C 5bis, 14; איתי, III [11]; אי<ת>ה, III <13>

איך ("just as," used with זי): I A 35, 38, 39, [39], [40], [41]

איכה ("just as," used with זי): I A 37

אכל ("eat"): יאכל, I A 27, [30]; II A [9]; תאכל, I A 27; אכל (act. ptc.), I A 30

אל (= ’al, "not"): I A 21, 22bis, 23, [23], 24, 28, 29, 33, 36; I B 8; I C 24; II A [1bis], [2], 2, [3]; III 7, [18], [20]

אל (= ’el, "to"): II B [13]; III 1ter, 19; אלי, I B [29]; III 8, 20; אלוה, III [8]

אלה ("god"): אלהן, I A 30; I B 6bis, 31; I C 15, 21; II B 2; III 24bis; אלהי, I A 10, [12bis]; I B 5, [5], 23, 33; II B [9], [18]; II C [13]; III 4, 14, 17, 23; אלהיא, I B [8]; II C 3, 7, [10]

אלן ("these"): I A 7bis, 38; I B [7], [8], [11], 24, 38; II B [14]; II C [2], 9; III 7, 9, 19, 20, 27

אמר ("say"): אמרן, I C 1; יאמר, I C 18; II B [7]; II C [1], [4], 7, [8]; תאמר (2d sg. masc. impf. peal), I A 36; I B 24, 26; II B 5, [8]; III 5, 7, 18, 21; תאמר (3d sg. fem. impf. yuqtal), I A 33

אמר ("lamb"): I A 23; II A [2]
אן ("where"): II C 3
אנה ("I"): I B [24]; I C [2]; II B [5]; II C 8; III 6
אנש ("man, human being"): III 16.
אסר ("bind, imprison"): יאסר, III 18; אסרה (impv. + 3d sg. masc. suff.), III 18
אף ("nostril, face"): אפוה, III 2; אפיה, I A 42
אפלא (?): I B 43
ארבה ("locust"): I A 27
ארח ("road"): ארחא, III 9
אריה ("lion"): II A 9
ארנב ("hare "): I A 33
ארק ("land"): I A [11], 26; ארקי, I B 27; ארקך, III 6; ארקה, I A 28; II A 8
אש (= ʼīš, "man"): II B 16; אשא, I C 21
אש (= ʼēš, "fire"): I A 35, [37], 37
אשם ("name"): I C 25; אשמה II A [4]; אשמהם, II B 7
אשר ("place "): אשרי, I C [4]; אשרה, I A [5]; I B 3; III 7; אשרכם, III 5
אשרת ("sanctuary"): אשרתהם, I B 11
את ("you," sg. masc.): I B [39]; III 11, 20
אתי ("come"): יאתה, I B 28bis, 32,45; II B 13; III 11, 12bis, 20; תאתה, I B 31; III 11; תאתון, I B [32]
אתם ("you," pl. masc.): I B [31]

ב ("in, on, among," expressing place or time): I A 5,26bis, 29bis, 30bis, 36; I B 3, 12, 22, [23], 28, 30, 31, 33, 36, 41; I C 4, 17, 20, [22]; II A 7; II B 2, [2], 5bis, [8], [9], 12, 16, 18; II C 13; III 2, 3, 4, 5, 6, 7, 9bis, 10, 13, 14, 16, 17, 21, 23; ("by, with," expressing manner, instrument): I A 24, 35, 37, [37]; I B 31, 32; II A [3]; II C 10; III 13,14; ("toward, against"): I B 25ter, [27], [28], 34, 38; II B [6ter], [14]; III 7, 9, 19, 20, 27
בין ("between"): בניהם, III 18bis, 19
ביר ("well"): I B [34]; בירא: I B 34, [34]
בית ("house, household"): I A 6; I B 3, [11]; I C [6], 7; II A 12; II B 10bis; III 9, 24, [24], [25]; ביתי, I B [32], 40, 44; III 21; ביתך, I B 40; ביתה, I C 16, 22; III [24]; ביתכם, I B 21; בתי (cst. pl.), II C 2, 7, 9; בתיכם, II C 16
בכתה ("hen"): I A 24; II A [3]
בעי ("seek"): יבעה, II B 8; III 11; תבעה I B 39; II B 17; בעה, (?) I B 35
בעי ("rant"): יבעה, III 2
בעל ("lord"): בעל (cst), I B [29]; בעלי, I A 4bis; I B 4, [5]; בעליה, III 23, 26

בר ("son"): בר (cst.), I A 1, 3, 14; I B 13; I C [3], [8]; II C 14; III 1, 12, [12], 15bis, 16, 25, [26]; בר (in a name): I A 1, 2bis, 7, 13, [14], [15]; I B 1, [2], [7]; II A 3; II B [5]; III [25]; ברי I B 25, 27, 45; I C 3bis; II B [6], 8, 13; III 1bis, 3, 11, 12bis, 15, [17], [26bis]; ברך, I B [25], 41; II B [6]; III 1, 2, 11, 12, 15; ברה, I A 25; I C [8], 8; II A [4]; II C 1, 14bis; III 25bis; בני (cst. pl.): I A 2quater, [16]; I B 1bis, [1], [2], 3; II B 13; III 21ter, [21]; בני (1 sg. suff. on pl.); II B [7], 13; III 10, 21, 22; בנוה, I A 5; I B [21]; II B 2b, 6

ברד ("hail"): I A [26]

ברה ("daughter"): בנתה, I A [35]

בתן ("serpent"): I A 32

גבל ("territory"): III 23

גבר ("surpass"): יגבר, II B 19

גבר ("man"): גבר (abs.), III 1; גבר (cst.), I A 39; I B 24; II B [5]

גברת ("woman"): I A [42]

גדה ("kid"): II A 2

גזר ("cut, conclude"): I A 7; יגזר, I A 40bis; תגזר, I B 43; יגזרן, I A 40; I B [41]

גנב (?): I A 36

דבהה ("bear"): I A 31

דם ("blood"): דם (cst.), III 12bis, [12]; דמי, III 11, [22]

הא (= hū', "he"): I B 24; III 8, 13, 22; (used as a demonstrative), I C 22; II C 6, [10]

הא (= hī', "she, it"): I A 37; III 12, [24]; I B [34], 42bis? (used as a demonstrative) I A [33]; I B [34]

הוי ("be"): הות, III [24]; יהוה, II A 4; תהוי, I A 25, 32; II A [4], 6; יהוו, I A [31]; הוי (impv. sg. peal), III 22

הוך ("go"): אהך, III 6; יהכן, I A 24; II A [3]; III 5

הם ("they"): I B 6, [42]

המיה ("noise"): I A [29]

המל ("din"): I A 29

הן ("so," adv.): I B 36; III 4, 9, 14, 20

הן ("if," conj.): I A 14, [15], [16], 24; I B [23], [25], 28, 31, [32], 36, 37, 38, 43; II A [3]; II B 4, 5, [7], 16, 17; III 4bis, 6bis, 9bis, 11, 12, 13, 14bis, 15, 16, 17, 18, 19, 20bis, [22], [26], 27

הפך ("upset"): אהפך, I C 19; יהפכו I C 21

הרג ("kill"): I A 24; II A [3]

הרי ("conceive"): תהרי, I A 21

-ו ("and"): I A [1], 2, [2], 3, 4bis, 5ter, 6ter, 7bis, 8quinquies, [8bis], 9quinquies, [9bis], 10ter, [10], 11quater, [11bis], 12ter, [12], 14, [15], [16], 21bis, [21], 22ter, [22], 23ter, 24ter, [24], 25, 26ter, 27ter, 28ter, 29ter, 30ter, 31sexies, 32, [32], 33septies, [33], 34octies, [34], 35ter, 36quater, 37, 38ter, 39bis, [39], 40, [40], 41bis, [41], 42, [42]; I B 1bis, 2, [3], 3ter, [4], 4, 5bis, [6], 7ter, 8, 9bis, [9bis], 10ter, [10bis], 11, 12, 21, [21bis], [22], [23], [24], 24, 25bis, [25], 26, [26], 27ter, 28bis, 29ter, 30bis, 31bis, [32], 33bis, 34bis, [35], 35, 36, 37, 38bis, [39], 39bis, 40bis, [40], 41, 43, 45bis; I C [1], [3], [8bis], 16bis, 18, 19, 22bis, 23, 24; II A [1ter], 1, 2, [2bis], [3ter], 3, [4bis], 4, [5], [6], 8bis, 9bis, [9]; II B 2, [2bis], 2b, 3bis, [4], 5, [5], 6bis, [6bis], 7ter, 8ter, [8], 10ter, 11, 12, 13, 16, 17; II C [1], 3, 4, 5, 6, 7, 8, 10, 11, 14bis, 15ter, 16bis; III 1, 2bis, 3ter, 4, 5ter, 6quater, 7quater, 8, 9bis, [9], 10, 11quater, 12ter, 13ter, 14quater, 15bis, 16bis, 17, 18ter, [18], 19quater, 20bis, [20], 21quinquies, [21], 22bis, [22], 23quater, [23], 24bis, 25quinquies, 26ter, [26], 27, 28, 29

זא ("this," fem. sg.): I A 35, [36], 37, [42]; III 9
זחל ("be frightened"): יזחל, II C 6
זי ("who, which," rel. pron.): I A 5, 7; I B 2, 6, 22, [23], 28, 31, 33, 34, 35bis; I C 3, 17, 20, 22; II A 12; II B [2], 4, [9], 18, 20; II C 3, 8, 13; III 2, 4, 5, 8, 10, 13, 14, 16, 17bis, 20, [20], 23, 28, [29], 29; (used with איך or איכה, "just as"): I A 35, 37, 38, 39, [39], [40], [41]; זי ("of"): I A [10]; III 7, [19]; זי ("because, that"), I B 41; I C [6]; see also כזי, מזי
זכרן ("reminder "): I C 2
זנה ("this," masc. sg.): I A [6], 36, 40; I B [8], [23], 28, 33, [37]; I C 17; II B [9], [18]; II C [14]; III [4], 14, 17, [23]
זני ("fornicate, be a harlot"): זניה, I A [41]
זקן ("be old"): יזקן, II B 8
זרע ("sow"): יזרע, I A 36

חבז (pael, "destroy"): חבזו, III 24; חבזתהם, II B 7
חבר ("union"): I A [4]?
חד ("one"): חד (abs.), III 22; חד (cst.), I B 26bis, 28, 30, 45; II B [7]; III 1, [3], 4ter, 5, 9bis, 10quinquies, 13ter, [13], 17; חדה (abs. fem.), I B 8; חדהם, I B 45; III 19
חוה ("snake"): I A 31
חזי ("see"): יתחזה (ithpeel), I A 28, [28]; חזיה (pael infin.), I A 13
חי ("living, alive"): I B [41]

חיל ("army"): חילך I B [28], 31; חילכם, I B 32
חל ("sand "): I A 25bis; II A [4]
חלף ("successor"): חלפה (with 3d sg. masc. suffix), III 22
חפץ ("business"): חפצי, III 8
חץ ("arrow"): חציא, I A 38; I B 29
חצר ("grass"): I A 28
חרב ("sword"): III 13, 14
חרן ("wrath"): II B 12

טב (= ṭūb, "happiness"): טבי (cst. pl.), I B 6
טב (= ṭāb, "good"): III 3, 22, [29]
טבת ("good [treaty] relations"): טבתא, I C [4], 19; II B 2
טלל (?): I B 42

יד ("hand"): יד (abs.) I B [25], 25, [27], 34; II B [6]; יד (cst.), II B 14; III 11; ידה ("his hand"), I B 27; III 2; ידי ("my hands"), III 2, 5, 10, 13
ידע ("know"): ידע (ptc.), II C 8
יהב ("give"): תהב, I B 38
יום ("day"): יום (abs.), I A 12; I B 31; I C 20; יום (cst.), II B 12; יומה ("his day"), I C 15; יומיהם, II C 17
יללה ("lamentation"): I A 30
יני ("oppress"): יהונה (impf. haphel), II B 16; יהוננה (energic impf. haphel with suff.), II B 16
ינק ("suck"): יהינקן (impf. haphel), I A 22bis, 23bis; II A [1bis], [2bis]; מהינקן ("nurses," fem. pl. haphel ptc.), I A [21]
יקד ("burn"): יקד (impf. peal), I A 37; תקד, I A 35bis, 37
יקף ("surround"?): תקף, I B 29; יקפי, I B 29
ירק ("green"): I A 28
ירת ("inherit"): I C 24
ישב ("sit, dwell"): ישב (impf. peal), III 17; אשב, II B [7]; ישבן, III [6]; שבו (impv. pl.), III 7
ישמן ("desolation"): I A 32

כ- ("like, as"): I A 25; II A [4]. See also כזי, כעת
כה ("thus"): I C 1, [1]
כהל ("be able"): יכהל, I B 25, [34]; תכהל, I B [39]; אכהל, I B [24], 33; II B 6
כהסא ("throne," variant of כרסא): כהסאי, III 17
כזי ("when"): III 24
כי ("for"): III 22
כים ("indeed"?): III 1

כל ("all"): כל (cst.), I A 6bis, 10, 12; I B [8], 22, 23, 29, 34, [40]; I C 6, 22; II A 7; II B [3], 9, 12, 18; II C 13, 15bis; III 1, 4, 7, 8bis, 14, 16, 23; כל מה, I A 26bis, 30; I B 2, [26], 29; III 16, 28, [29], 29; כלה (3d sg. fem. suff.), I A 5; I B [4]
כן ("so"): I A 35, 37, 38, 39, 40, 41, 42; I B 43; I C 21
כנר ("lyre"): I A 29
כעת ("now"): III 24
כפר ("village"): כפריה, III 23, 26
כרסא ("throne"): II B [7]
כתב ("write"): כתבת (1 sg. pf. peal), I C 2; כתבן, I C [1]

ל- ("to, for"): I A 13, [14], [15], [24], 25, 32bis; I B [7], 13, 21, 23bis, 26, 32bis, [33], [34], 34, [36], 40ter, [40], 42; I C 2, 3, [3], [6], [20], [23]; II A 3bis, [4]; II B [5], 7, [8], 9, 12, 18; II C 2, 4, 7; III 2, 3bis, 4, 7, 8bis, 11bis, 14,15bis, 16bis, 23ter, 24, 25quater; לי, I B 29, 37, 38; III 3, 6, 8, 9bis, 20; לך, I B 39; II B 19; לה, III 18, [20]; להם, III 3, [5], 5, 7bis, 21
ל- (sign of accusative ?): I C 4
ל- ("not," prefixed neg. adv.): I A 28bis; I B 21, [21bis], [22], [24bis], 25, [25], 31, [32bis], 34, 38bis, 39, [39], 41; I C [7], 17; II B [2], 2b, 3ter, 6bis, 16, 17; II C 8; III 5ter, 6, 9bis, 17, 18bis, 19, 21, 22; להן ("not so"): I B 36; III 4, 9, 14, 20
לבב ("heart"): לבב (cst.), III 15bis, [16]; לבבך, II B [5]; III 14
להן: see ל- ("not") above
לוד ("efface"): לד (peal impv.): II C 9; לד (infin.), II C 6; אהלד (1 sg. impf. haphel), I C 18; הלדת (haphel infin.), II C 2
לחי ("evil"): לחיה (fem. sg. abs.), I A 26; I C [6]; לחית (fem. pl. abs.), I C 20; III 2
לחם ("bread, food"): I A 24; I B 38, 39; II A [3]; III 5, 7; לחמי, I B 38
לחץ ("oppression"): II C 10
לילה ("night"): I A 12
לקח ("take"): ילקח, I B 35bis; יקח, I B 27; תקח, I A [42]; III 2; יקחן, I A 42
לשן ("tongue"): III 21; לשנך, III 17

מגן ("with impunity"?): II C [4]
מה ("what"): I B 26; I C 1; III 3; כל מה, I A 26bis, 30; I B 2, 26, 29; III 16, 28, [29], 29
מודד ("friend"): מודדוה, III 14
מות ("die"): ימת, II C [10]; ימות, III 16; מות (infin. ?), I B 30; המתת (haphel infin.), III 11, 15, 16; המתתי (with suffix), II B [8]; III 11, 15

מזי ("as long as"): I A 25
מחא ("strike"): ימחא, I A 42
מין ("water"): מי, I B 33, 34
מלאך ("messenger, ambassador"): מלאכי, III 8; מלאכה, III 8
מלה ("word"): I B [25], [41]; מלי (cst. pl.), I B 8; I C 17; מלן, III 2; מליא III 2; מלוה, I C 18
מלח ("salt"): I A 36
מלך ("rule, reign"): ימלך, I A 25; I B [3]; ימלכן, I B 22
מלך (= malk, "king"): I A 6; I B 2, 7, 26; III 28; מלך (cst. sg.), I A 1bis, 3, [13], [14], [15] ; I B [1], 30; מלכא, I B [35]; מלכה (3d sg. fem. suff.), II C 5; מלכן, I B 26, 28; III [19]; מלכי (cst. pl.), I A [5]; I B 41; II B [3]; II C 15; III 1, [3], 16, [27]; מלכיא, I B 22; III 7
מלך (= mulk, "kingdom"): I B 6; מלכי, I C [6]
מלכו ("kingdom"): מלכת (cst. sg.), I A 25bis; II A [4]; מלכתה (3d sg. masc. suff.), I A 25; II A [4]
מלל ("speak"): ימלל, I B [26]; III [1], 2
מן (= man, "whoever"): I C 16; II B 9; II C [1]; III 26; מן חד ("any one"), I B 30; II B [7]; III 9bis, 10quinquies
מן (= min, "from"): I A 20?, 30; I B 8, [9], 9, [10bis], 27bis; I C 15, 16, 18; II B 14; II C 2, 6, 7, 9, 16bis; III 2, 11, 12; מני, III 4, 6, 7; מנך, II B 20; מך (= m<n>k?), III 22; מנהם, I B 41; -מ (before laryngeal), I B 7, 30. See also מזי, מעל
מעין ("spring"): מעינן, I A 12
מעל ("above, upon"): I B 30
מצלה ("abyss"): I A [11]
מקנה ("possession"): מקני, I B 27
מרא ("lord"): מראכם, III 21
מרמה ("treachery"): מרמת III 22
מרק ("affliction"): I A 29
משח ("anoint"): ימשחן, I A [21]
משל ("dominate"): תמשל, III 9

נבע ("babble"): יבע, II B 8
נבש ("soul"): I B 40; נבשא, I A [36]; נבשי, I B 40; נבשך, I B 39, 42; II B 5, [8] ; נבשה, I A 37; נבשהם, III 5, 6
נגד ("officer"): נגדי, III 10
נחת ("tranquility"): II B 4
נכי ("strike") : תכה, III 13; תכוה, III 13; נכה (peal infin.), III 12, 13
נמרה ("panther"): I A 31; II A [9]
נסך ("pour out"): יסך, I A [25], 26; תסך, I B 38; III [5], 7
נפק ("come forth"): יפק, I A 28
נצב ("stele"): נצבא I A [6]; I C 17

נצר ("guard, protect"): יצר, I C 17; יצרן, I B 8; יצרו, I C 15
נקם ("avenge"): יקם, III 12ter, 22; תקם, III 11
נשא ("lift, take, bring"): ישא, III 15, 16, 26; תשא, I B 39; III 14; ישאן, II C [13]; שא., I B [38]
נשי ("forget"): יתנשי, II A [4]
נשן ("women"): נשי (cst. pl.), I A 41ter, [42]
נתע ("draw"?): תנתע, I B 29

סבב ("surround"): יסב, I B 34; יסבנ<י>, I B 28
סחרה ("vicinity"): סחרתי, III 7, [19]
סכר ("hand over"): יסכר (aphel impf.), III 3; יהסכר (haphel impf.), III 3; יהסכרן, III 3; תהסכרהם, III 2; הסכר (haphel infin.), III 2
סלק ("go up, ascend"): יסק, I A [27]; I B [3]; III 14, 15bis, 16; יסקן, I A 5; I C 4
סס ("moth'): I A 31
ססיה ("mare"): I A 22
ספר ("inscription"): ספרא, I A [6]; I B 8, [23], 28, 33; I C 17; II B [9], [18]; II C 13; III 4, 14, 17, 23; ספריא, II C 2, [4], [6], [9]
סרס ("courtier, eunuch"): סרסי, I B 45; III 5

עבד ("do, make"): עבדו, II B 2; יעבד, I C [20]; תעבד, I B [26]; III [22]; אעבד, III 3; יעבדו, I C [5]; תתעבד, I C [7]
עבד ("slave"): עבדי, III 13
עבר ("pass on, by"): יעברנה (aphel impf.), III 17
עגל ("calf"): I A 23; II A [1]; עגלא, I A 40
עד ("up to, until," prep.): I B 9bis, 10; I C [8]; III [24], 25
עד ("until," conj.): II B 19?; III 6
עדן ("treaty"): עדן, I B 24, 41; II B [5]; עדי I A 1bis, 2, 3, [3], 4ter, 13; I B 1bis, [4bis], 4bis, 5bis, 6; עדיא, I A 7bis; I B [7], 7, 11, 23, 24, [28], 33, 38; II B 2, [9], [14], [18]; II C [13]; III 4, 7, 9, [14], 17, 19, 20, 23, 27
עוד ("bear witness, testify"), II B 4
עור ("be blind"): יער (ophal impf.), I A 39bis
עזה ("she-goat"): עזן, II A [2]
עזז ("be strong"): יעז, II B 20; יעזז (pael impf.), I B 44
עין ("eye"): עיני, III 3; עיניכם I A 13
על ("upon, against, concerning"): I A 26, 28, 42; I B 44, [45], 45; I C [7]; II B [7], 11; III 1ter, 5, 14bis, 15ter, 16bis, 17, 22bis, [26]; עלי, I B 26; III [1], 2, 22; עליה, III [9]; עלה, I A 32. See also מעל
על ("colt"): I A 22; II A [1]
עלב ("torment"): II C 10
עלי ("upper"): I A 6

עלי ("upper part"): עליתה, I C [24]
עלים ("young boy"): I A 22
עלל ("enter"): יעל, I B 35; עלל (act. ptc.), I A 6
עלם ("eternity"): I C [9]; III 24,25; עלמן, I B [7]
עם (= ʻam, "people"): עמא, III 5, 13; עמה, I A 29, 30; I B 5, 11, [21]; II B [2],3; עמהם, II C 16; עמיא, III 10; עמי, III 21
עם (= ʻim, "with"): I A 1, 2, 3bis, 4, 5ter, [5], 6, [6], [13]; I B 1, 2bis, 3ter, 4bis, 5bis, 11, [29]; III [26]; עמי, I B 33; עמך, I B 43.
עמל ("trouble"): I A 26
עקה ("magpie"): I A 33
עקר ("offspring"): I A 3, 15, [15]; I B 2bis; III 3; עקרי, I B 25, [32]; II B [6]; III 1, 3, 11, 12, 16, [21], [22], 26; עקרך, I B [25], [32]; II B [6]; III 1, 3, 12, 15, [26]; עקרה, I A [2], 25, 41; II A [4]; II B 6; II C 15; III 13, 25
עקרב ("scorpion"): 1 A 31
ערר ("strip naked"): תערר, I A [40]; יעררן, I A 41
עשק ("oppress, wrong"): תעשקני, III 20
עשת ("think"): תעשת, II B 5
עת: See כעת

פ- ("and, but"): II B 4, 6
פגר ("corpse"): I B 30bis; II B 11bis
פם ("mouth"): I A [30], 31ter; II A 9ter
פני ("turn, return"): תפנו, III 7
פקד ("official"): פקדי (1 sg. suffix on pl.), III 4, [10], 13
פקח ("open [the eyes]"): פקחו, I A 13
פרק ("destroy"): פרק (peal infin.), I B 34
פתח ("open"): פתחה (fem. sg. pass. ptc.), III 8

צבי ("gazelle"): I A 33
צדה ("owl"): I A 33
צי ("desert animal"): I A [32]
צעקה ("crying"): I A [29]; II A [8]

קבר ("grave"): קברה, II A [4]
קדם ("before, in the presence of"): I A [7], 8bis, [8], 9ter, [9], 10, [10], 11ter, [11], 12
קל ("voice"): I A 29
קלבת(?): I B 44
קמל ("louse"): I A 31
קק ("throat"): I A 32
קריה ("town, city"): III 12; קרית, I B 36; קריתא, I A [33]

קרק ("flee"): יקרק, I B 45; III 4, 19bis; קרק (ptc., "fugitive"): III 4; קרקי, III 19; קרקהם, III 19
קשת ("bow"): I A [38], 39; קשתא, I A 38
קתל ("kill"): קתלו (impv. pl.), III 21; יקתל, II B [8], 9; III 18; יקתלן, III 11; יקתלנה, I B 27

ראש ("head"): ראשי, II B [8]; III 11
רב ("great"): רב, I B 7; רבת, I A [35]; רבוה ("his nobles"): I A 39, 40, [41]; II B 3; II C 15; רברבי, II A 7
רבא ("multiply"): ארבא, I B 30
רבק ("house, lodging"): רבק (possibly cst. sg. noun), I A [32]
רוח ("breath"): III 2
רום ("raise, lift up"): תהרם, III 5, 6
רחם ("friend"): III 8
ריב ("quarrel"): III 17, 26, [26bis]
רקי ("please"): רקה (peal infin.), III 6, 18; pael: "placate": תרקה (2d sg. masc. impf.), III 18, 19; תרקהם, III 6; ארקהם, III 6; רקו (impv.), III 6;
רשי ("assert authority"): תרשה, III 9
רשם ("write"): ירשמן, II C [3]

שאה (= ś'h, "ewe"): שאת, I A 21; שאן, I A 23; II A [2] (or = š'h)
שבע ("be sated"): ישבע, I A 22, [22], 23, [23]; II A [1], 1, [2bis]
שגב ("strengthen"): I B 32bis
שהד ("witness"): שהדן, I A 12
שים ("place, set up"): שם, I A 7; שמו, I B 6; אשם, I C 19; ישמו, I C 23
שנא ("enemy"): שנאי I B 26; II B 14; III 10, 11; שנאוה, III 12
שפה ("lip"): שפתיך, III 14; שפתוה, III 15, 16

שאה (see š'h above)
שבע (= šb', "seven"): I A 21, 22, [22], 23, 24, 27ter; II A [1], 1, [2], [3], [5], [6]
שבר ("break, shatter"): ישבר, I A 38; תשבר, I A 38
שד ("breast"): שדיהן, I A [21]
שוב ("return"): שבת, III 25; השב, III 20; השבו, III 24; אהשב, III 20; תהשבהם, III 6
שוט ("search"): I A 24; II A [3]
שורה ("cow"): I A 23; II A [I]
שחד ("bribe"): ישחדן, III 28
שחט ("destroy"): ישתחט, I A [32]
שחלין ("watercress, weeds"): I A 36
שיבה ("return"): III 24

שית ("thorns"): II A 5
שלי ("stay quietly"): שלו, III 5
שלח ("send"): ישלח, I B 25, [26], 27; III 8; תשלח, I B 37; III 17, 21; אשלח, I B [24]; II B 6; III 8; ישלחן, I A 30; משלח, I B 34
שלם ("peace"): III 8
שלם ("fulfill"): תשלמן (aphel impf.), I B [24]
שם ("there"): III 6
שמין ("heaven"): I A [11], 26; I B 7
שמע ("hear, obey"): ישמע, I B 21, [21]; II B [2], 3; תשמע, II B 4; אשמע, II B [5]; ישמען, I B [21], [22]; II B 2b; 3, [3]; תשמען, I B [24]; יתשמע, I A 29; יתשמען, I B [9]
שמר (?): II B 15
שמש ("sun"): שמשא, I C 5
שנה ("year"): שנן, I A 27bis, [27]; II A 5, 6
שעוה ("wax"): שעותא, I A 35, 37, 39, [42]
שעל ("fox"): I A 33
שפר ("beautiful"): III 29
שקר ("be unfaithful to"): שקרת (pael pf.), I B [27], [33], [36], 38; II B [17]; III [9], 14, 19, 20, 27; שקרתם, I B 23; II B 9, 14; III 4, 7, 16, [23]; ישקר, I A 14, 15, 24; II A [3]; ישקרן, I A [16]
שרב ("noble"): III 13
שרי ("loose, let go free"): תשריה, III 18
שרן ("wildcat"): I A 33
שרש ("scion"): שרשה, I C [24]
שתק ("be silent"): תשתק, I B 8

תוי (?): I A 28
תולעה ("worm"): I A 27
תחת ("under"): I C [5]; תחתכם ("your place"), III [7]
תחתי ("lower"): תחתה, I A 6
תחתי ("lower part"): תחתיתה, I C 23
תל ("mound, tell"): I A 32

NAMES

1. Persons and Gods

אל ('El): I A 11
אנרת ('Inurta): I A 38
אר ('Ir): I A [8]
אשר (Asshur): I A [7], 25(?)

בר גאיה (Bar-Ga'yah): I A 1, 2, [2], [7], 13, [14], [15]; I B 1, [2], [7]; II A 3; II B [5]; III [25]

גש (Gush): I A 16; I B 3, 11; II B 10

הדד (Hadad): I A [10], [25], 36, 38

זרפנת (Zarpanit): I A 8

כדאה (Kadi'ah?): I A 10

לץ (Laṣ): I A 9

מלש (Mullesh): I A 8
מצר (Miṣr): I A 5
מרדך (Marduk): I A 8
מתעאל (Matl'el): I A 1, 2, 3, [13], 14, 15, [24], 37, [37], [38], [39], 40, 41, [42]; I B 1, 2, 13, 21; I C [2], [7]; II B [2]; II C 14

נבא (Nabu'): I A 8
נכל (Nikkal): I A [9]
נכר (Nikkar): I A 10
נר (Nur): I A 9
נרגל (Nergal): I A 9
נשך (Nusk): I A [8]

סבת (Sibitti): I A 11
סן (Sin): I A [9]

עלין ('Elyan): I A 11
עתרסמך ('Attarsamak): I A 1, 3, 14; I B [1], [14]

צלל (ṢLL): I B 3; II B 10

שמש (Shamash): I A 9

תשמת (Tashmet): I A [8]

2. Places

אדם (Adam?): I A 35; in I A 10 [אדמ]

ארם (Aram): I A 5, 6; I B [3]
ארנה (Arneh): I A [34]
ארפד (Arpad): I A [1], 3, 4bis, [12], [14bis], 26, 29, 30, 32, 35; I B [1], 4, [5], [6], 22, [30], [41]; II B [2], [3]; II C 15; III 1, 3, 16, 27
אשר (Asshur): I A 25(?)

בז (BZ): I B 9
בינן (BYNN): I A 34
ביתאל (Bethel): I A 34
בקעת (the Valley): I B 10

דמשק (Damascus): I B [10]

חבורו (Ḥaburu): I A 4
חזז (Hazaz): I A 35
חלב (Aleppo): I A [10]; III 5

יאדי (Ya'di): I B [9]
יברדו (Yabrud): I B [9]

כתך (KTK): I A 1, 3, 4, [12], [15]; I B 4bis, 5, 10; II C 5

לאוין(?): I B 30
לבכה(?): I B 35
לבנן (Lebanon): I B 9

מבלה (MBLH): I A 34
מדרא (MDR'): I A 34
מזה (MZH): I A 34
מצר (Muṣr): I B 12
מרבה (MRBH): I A 34; I B 12

ערו ('RW): I B 10
ערקו ('Arqu): I B 9

רחבה (Raḥbah): I A 10

שרן (Sharun): I A 34

תואם (Tu'im): I A 34
תלאים (Tal'ayim): III [23], 25, 26

Reviews of the First Edition of This Book

Albright, W. F., *BASOR* 186 (1967) 54.
Ben-Hayyim, Z., *Lešonenu* 35 (1971) 243-53.
Beuken, W., *Bijdragen* 29 (1968) 431.
Brock, S. P., *Journal of Theological Studies* 19 (1968) 713-14.
Caquot, A., *RHR* 175 (1969) 211.
Coppens, J., *Ephemerides theologicae lovanienses* 44 (1968) 244.
Delcor, M., *BO* 25 (1968) 379-80.
Driver, G. R., *Booklist* (1970) 66-67.
Eissfeldt, O., *OLZ* 65 (1970) 366.
Greenfield, J. C., *JBL* 87 (1968) 240-41.
Grelot, P., *RB* 75 (1968) 280-86.
Hartman, L. F., *CBQ* 30 (1968) 256-60.
Herranz, M., *EstBíb* 28 (1969) 367-68.
Klíma, O., *ArOr* 40 (1972) 180.
Richter, W., *BZ* 13 (1969) 291.
Rowley, H. H., *Expository Times* 89 (1968-69) 182.
Soggin, J. A., *ZAW* 80 (1968) 126-27.
------. *Protestantismo* 25 (1970) 106-7.
Vesco, J.-L., *Revue Thomiste* 68 (1968) 299.
Zobel, H.-J., *Theologische Literaturzeitung* 94 (1969) 259-60.

INDEXES

I
INDEX OF BIBLICAL REFERENCES

Proverbs

Qoheleth

Isaiah

II
INDEX OF MODERN AUTHORS

III
INDEX OF OTHER NORTHWEST SEMITIC TEXTS

IV
INDEX OF SUBJECTS

PLATES

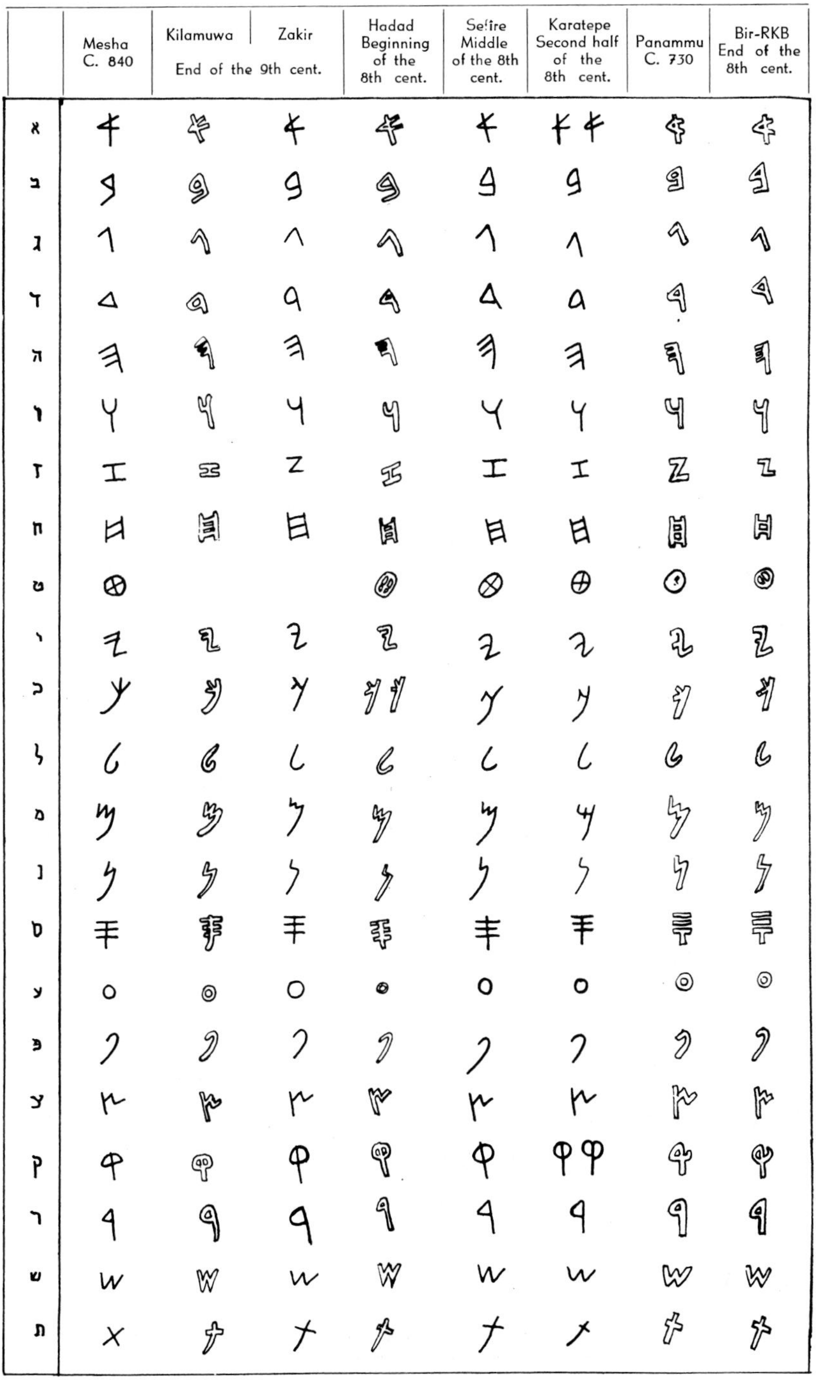

	Mesha C. 840	Kilamuwa	Zakir	Hadad Beginning of the 8th cent.	Sefîre Middle of the 8th cent.	Karatepe Second half of the 8th cent.	Panammu C. 730	Bir-RKB End of the 8th cent.
		End of the 9th cent.						
א								
ב								
ג								
ד								
ה								
ו								
ז								
ח								
ט								
י								
כ								
ל								
מ								
נ								
ס								
ע								
פ								
צ								
ק								
ר								
ש								
ת								

PLATE I: Comparative Table of the Scripts of the Main Northwest Semitic Inscriptions of the 9th-8th Centuries B.C.

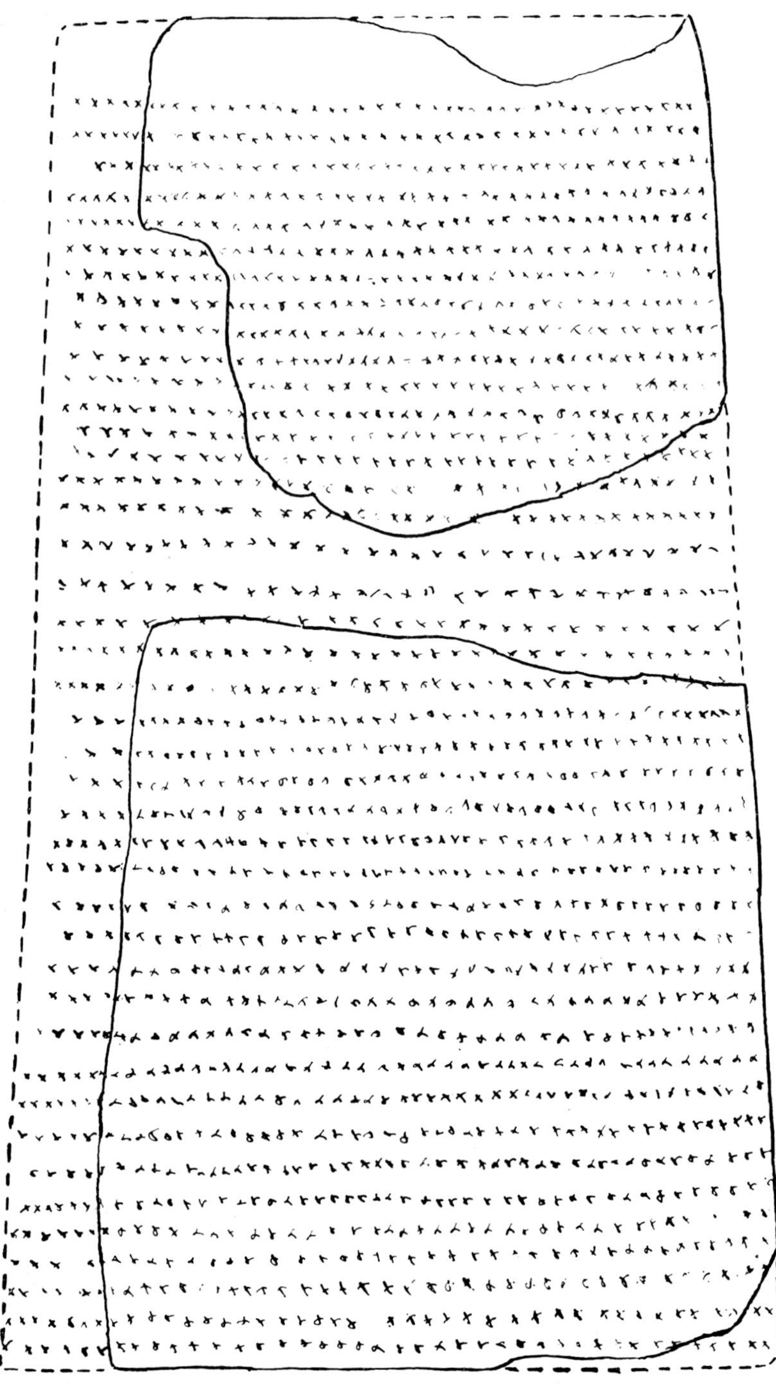

PLATE II: Stele I — Diagram Showing the Relative Position of the Fragments

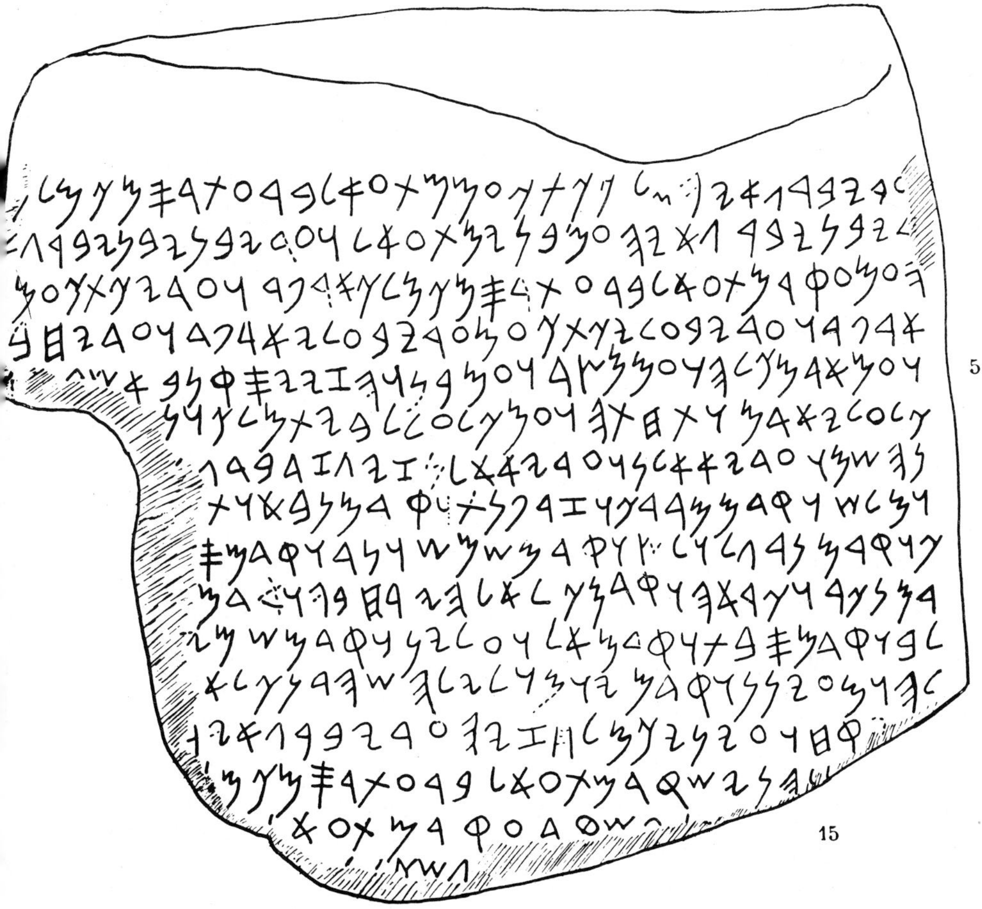

PLATE III: Stele I — Face A, Upper Portion

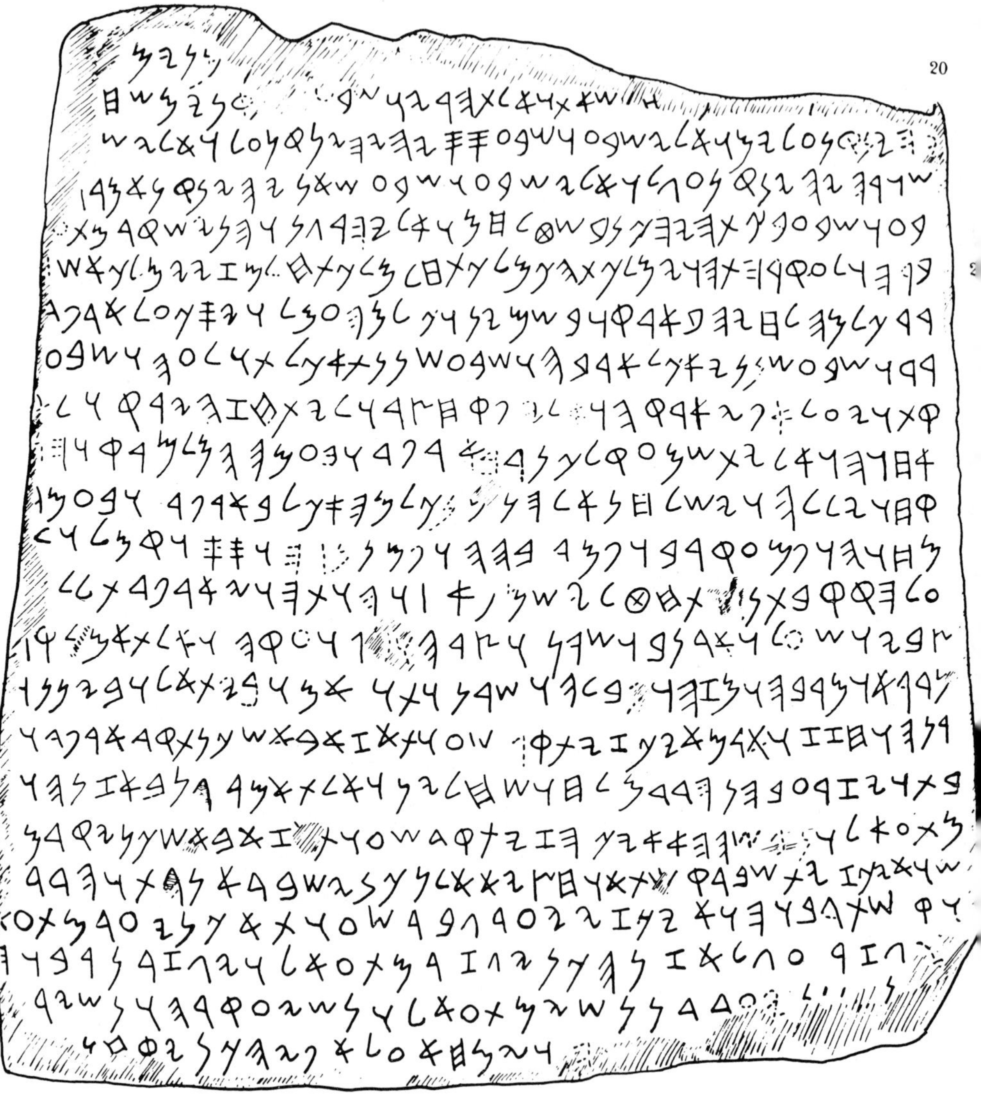

PLATE IV: Stele I — Face A, Lower Portion

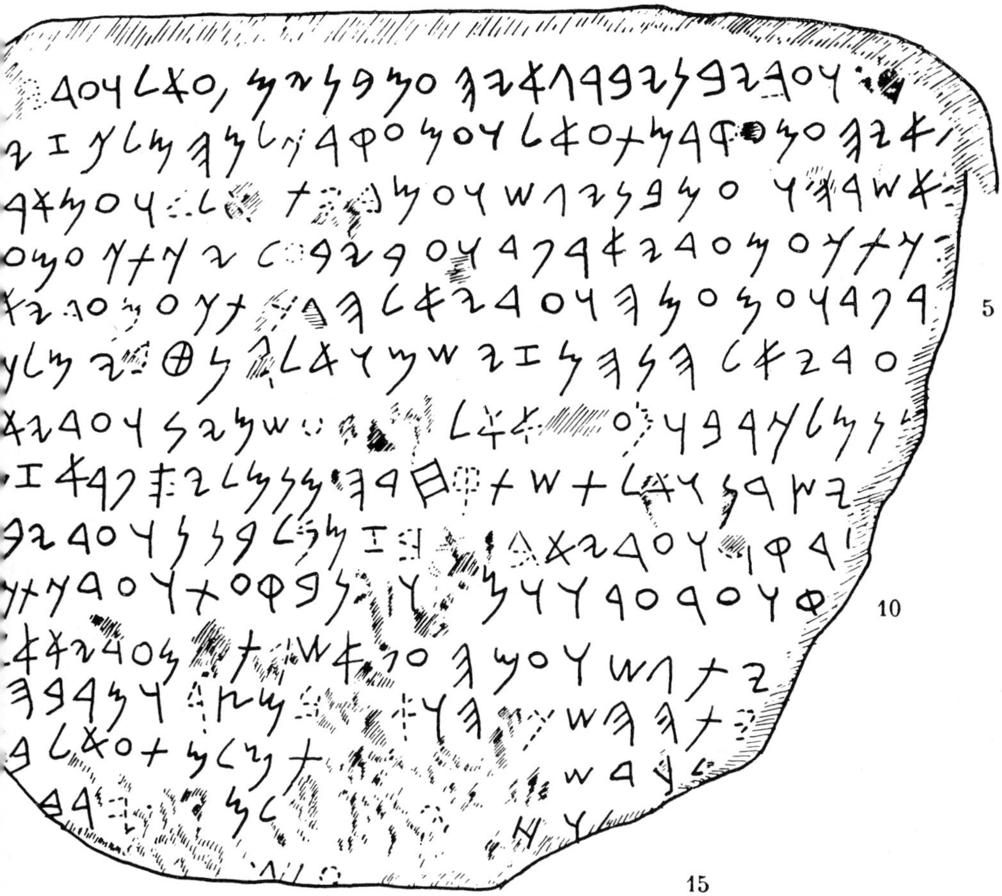

PLATE V: Stele I — Face B, Upper Portion

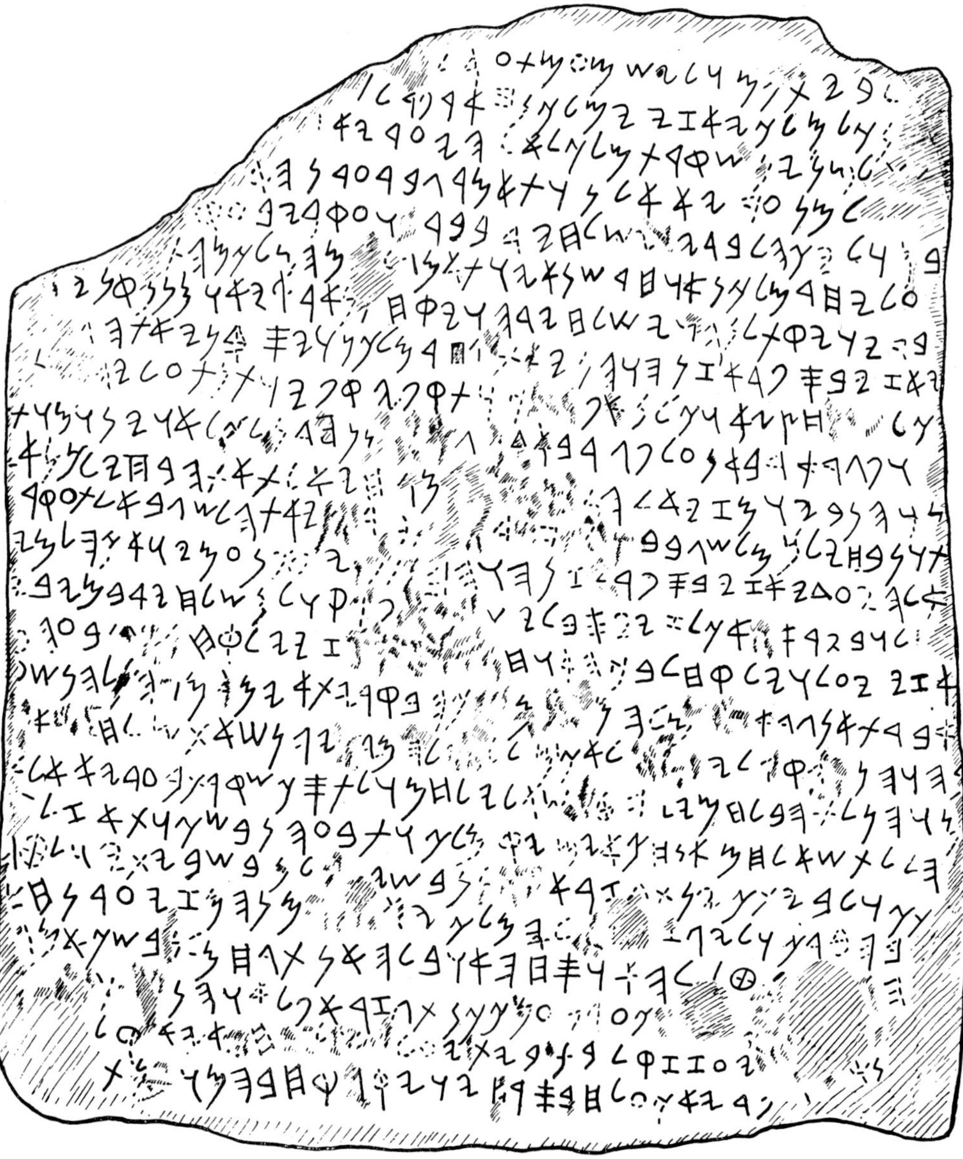

PLATE VI: Stele I — Face B, Lower Portion

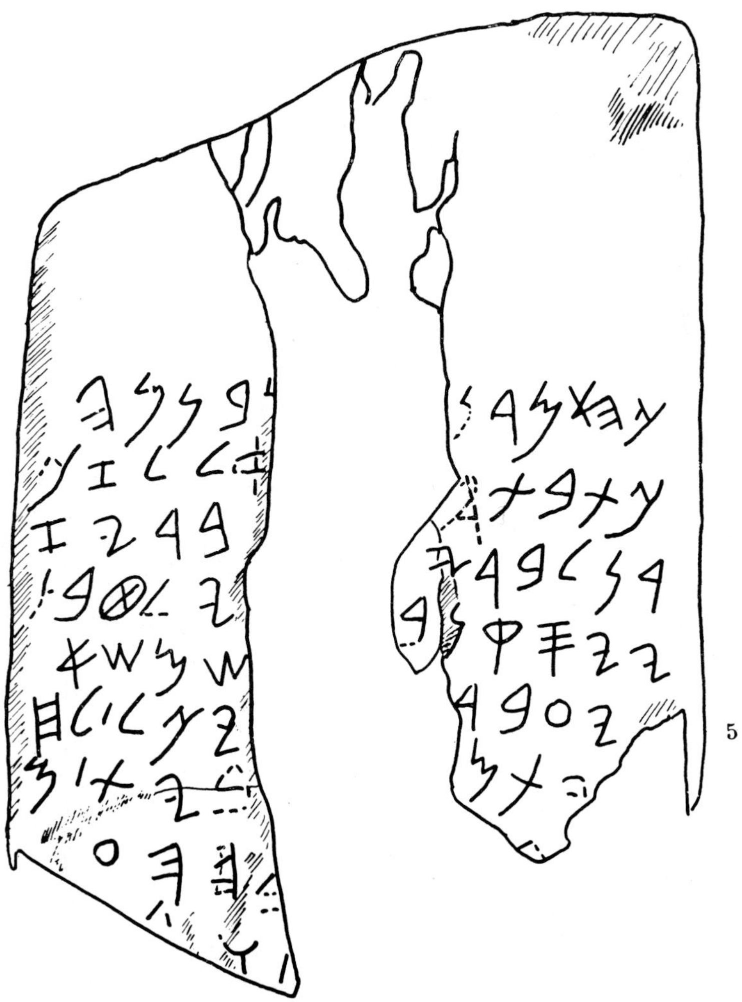

Plate VII: Stele I — Face C, Upper Portion

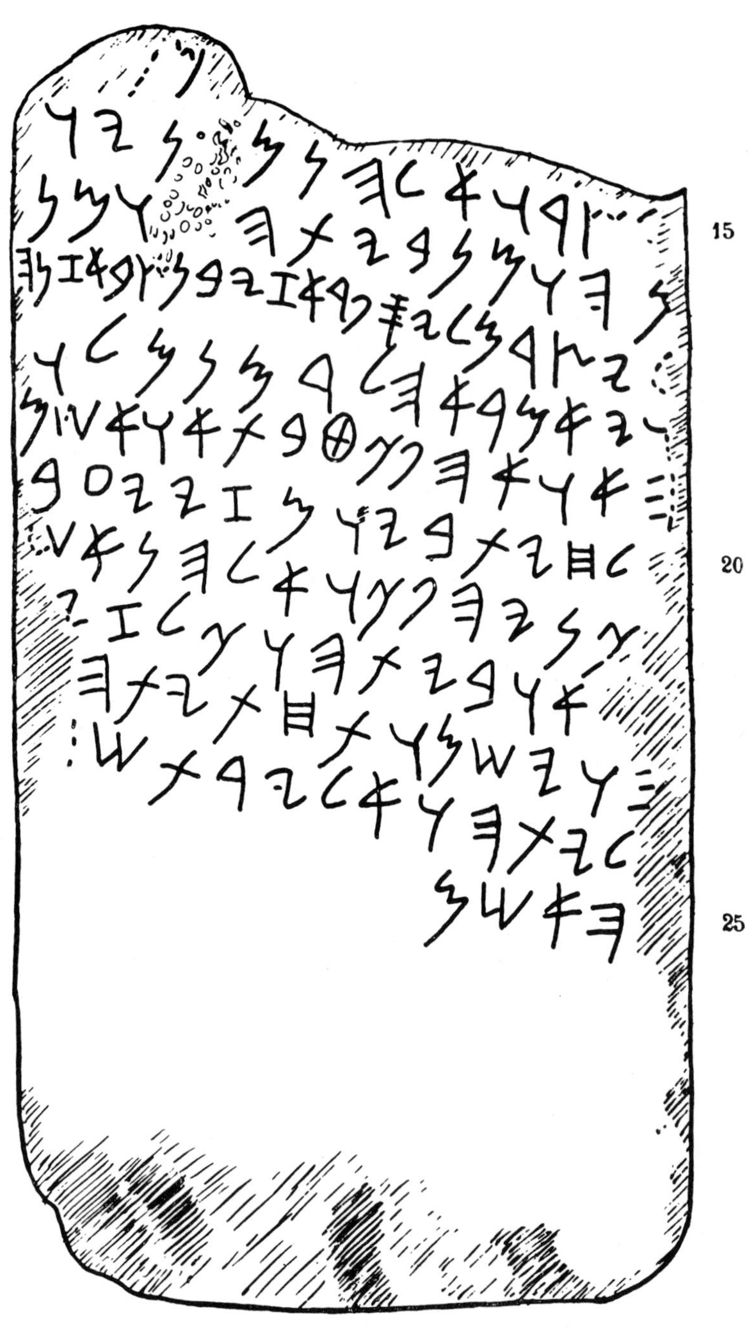

PLATE VIII: Stele I — Face C, Lower Portion

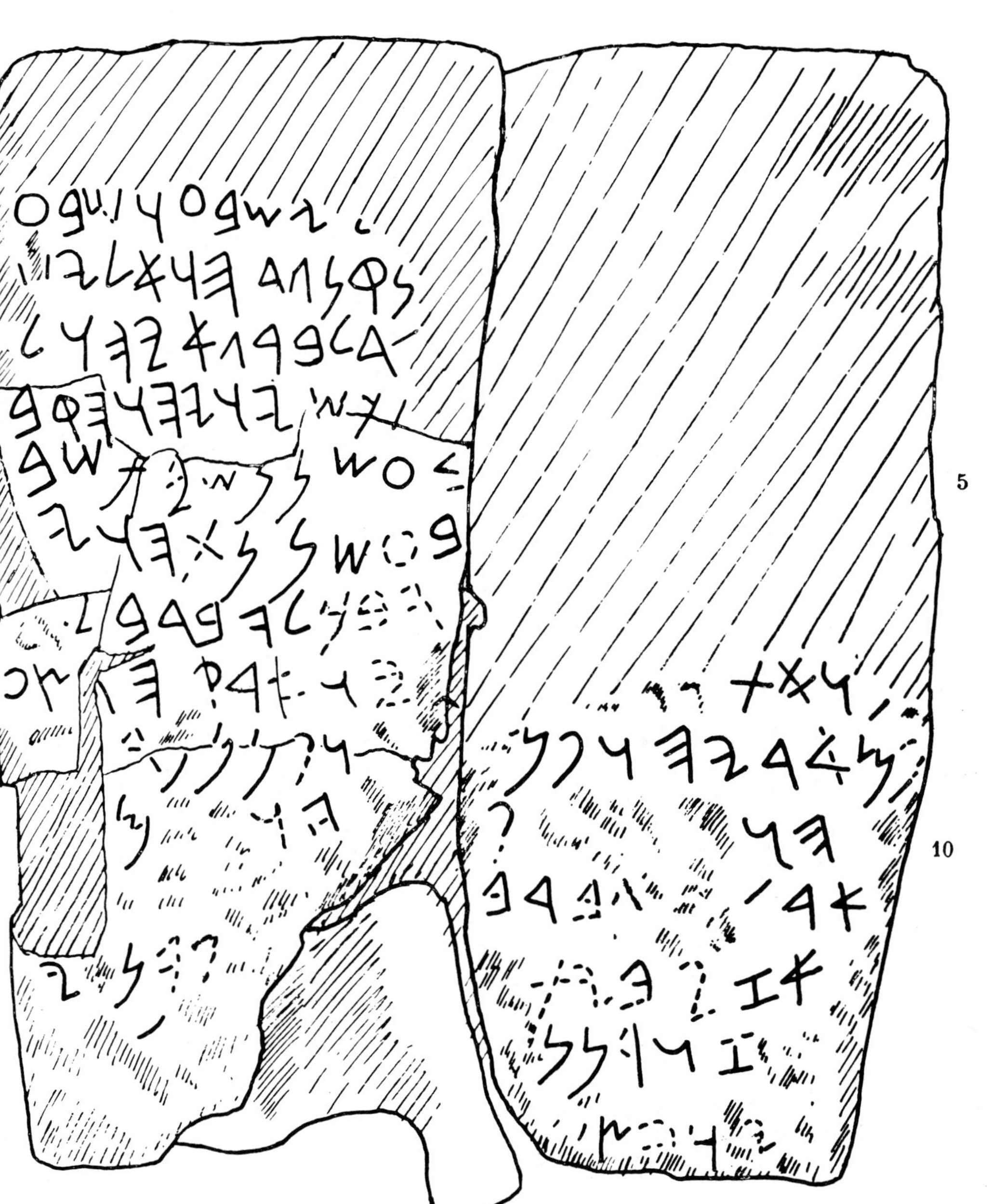

Plate IX: Stele II — Face A

Plate X: Stele II — Face B

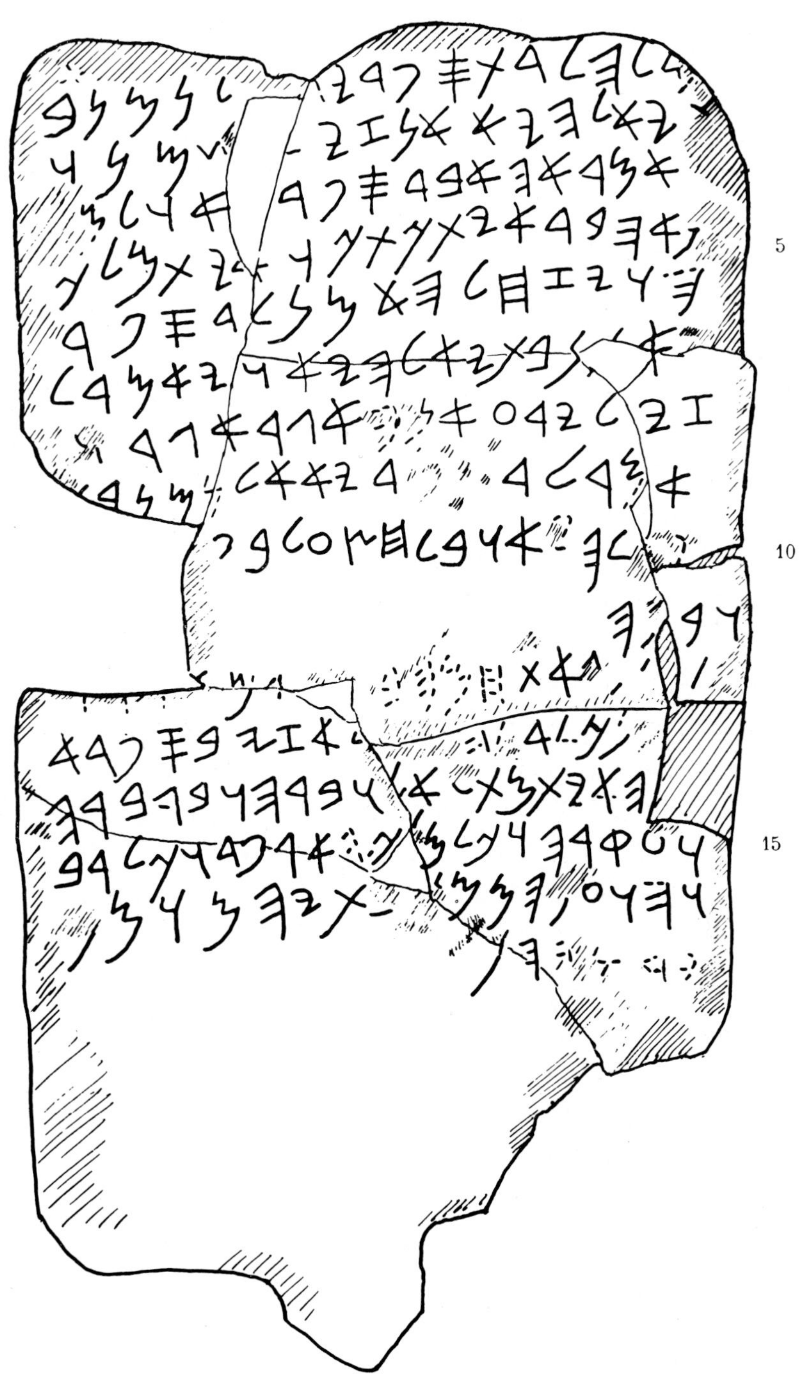

Plate XI: Stele II — Face C

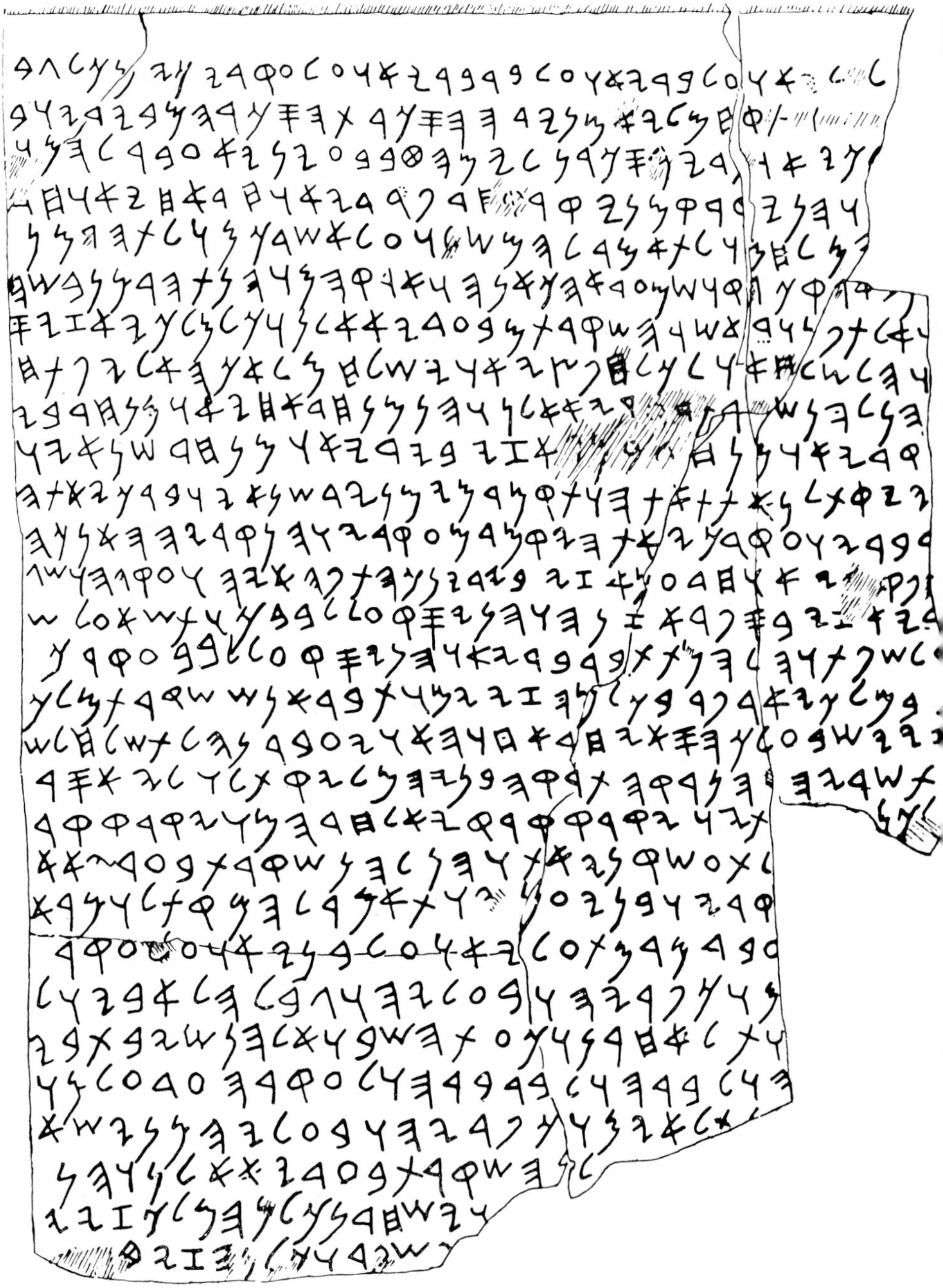

Plate XII: Stele III — Left Side

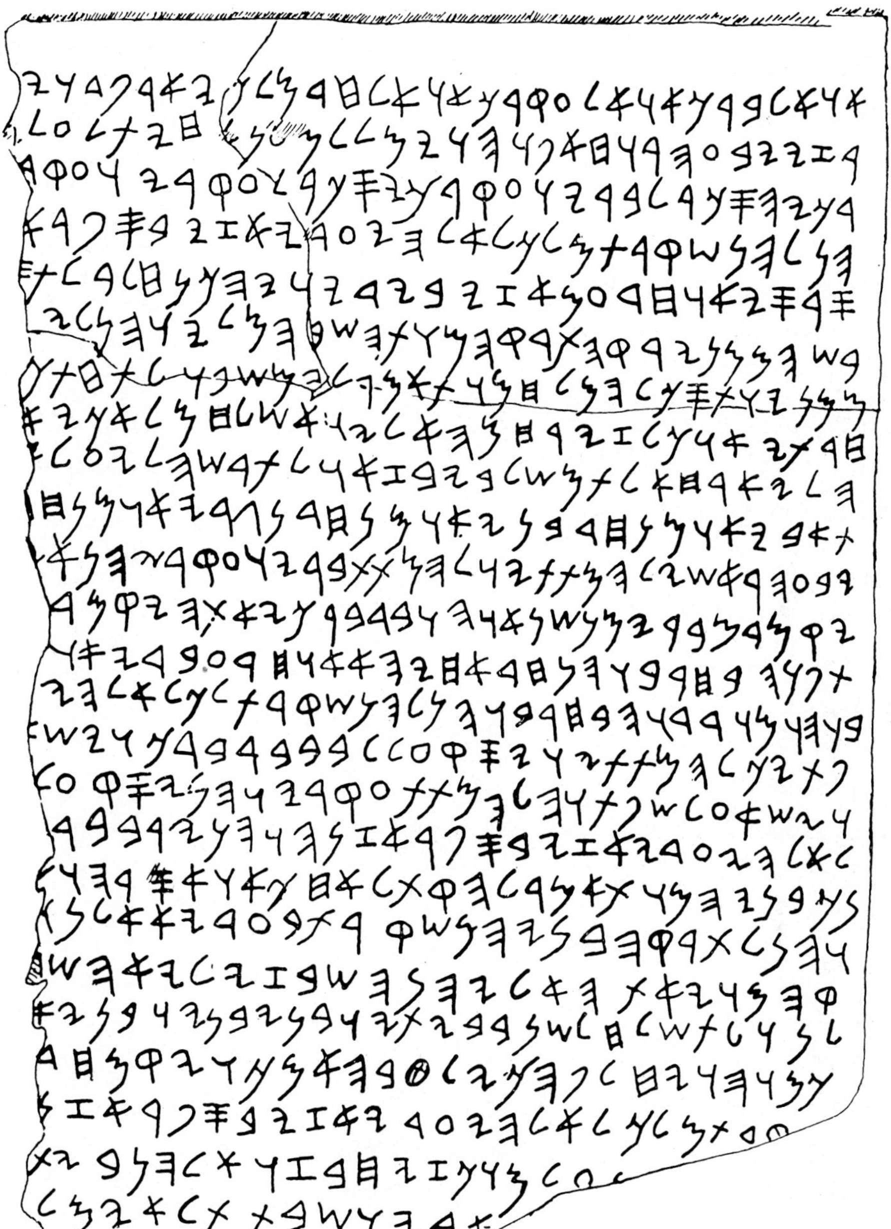

Plate XIII: Stele III — Right Side

PLATE XIV: Stele I A (a-b) — Photographic Reproduction

PLATE XV: Stele I B (b) — Photographic Reproduction

PLATE XVI: Stele II B — Photographic Reproduction

PLATE XVII: Stele III — Photographic Reproduction

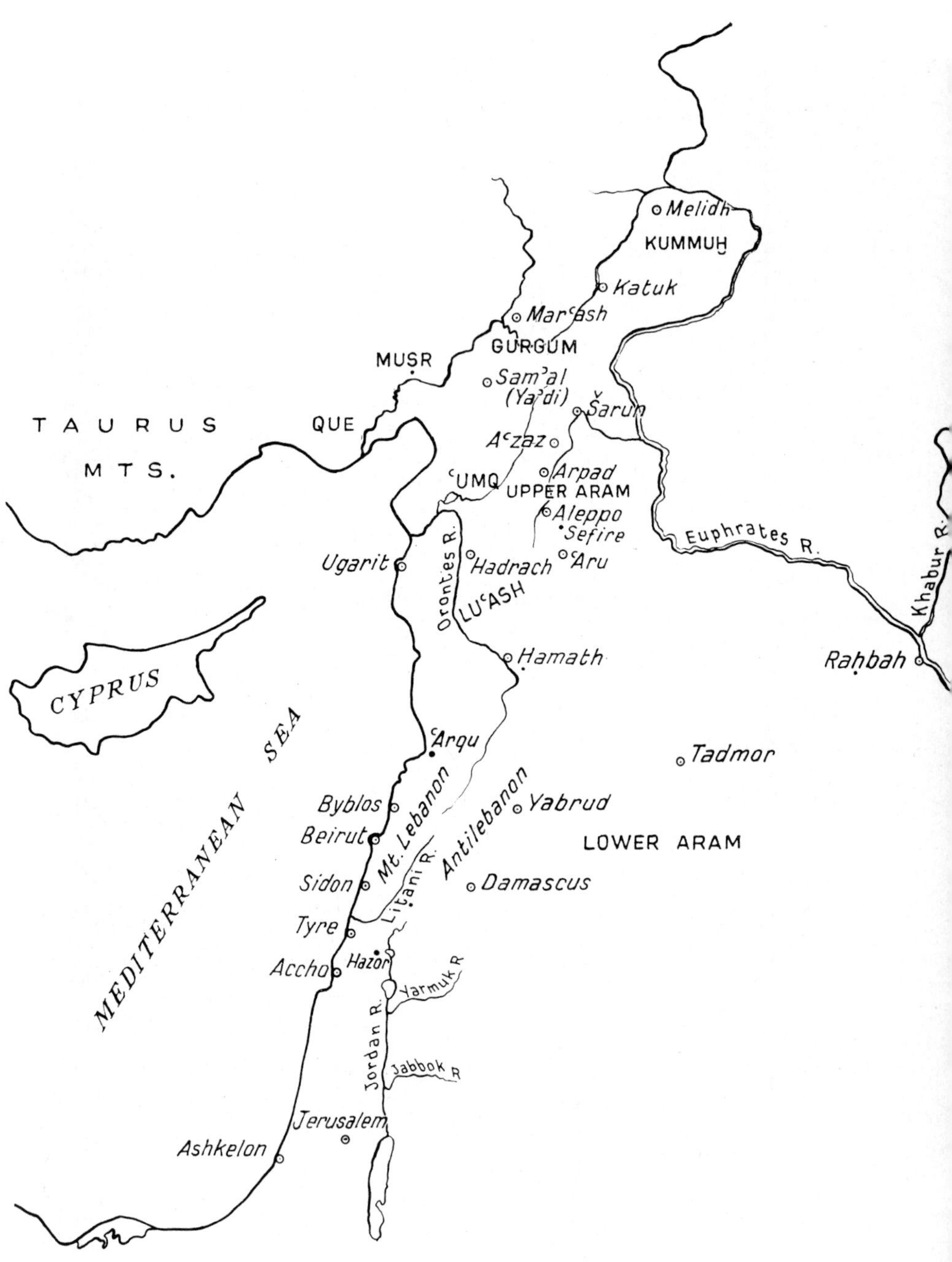

PLATE XVIII: Map of the Ancient Near East with reference to the Sefîre Inscriptions